CREATIVE DIFFERENCES
Profiles of Hollywood Dissidents

by

Barbara Zheutlin and David Talbot

SOUTH END PRESS
BOSTON

Library of Congress Card Number: 78-63627
ISBN 0-89608-043-9 paper
ISBN 0-89608-044-7 cloth
cover design by Kevin O'Callaghan
Printed at Maple Vail, U.S.A.
Design, typesetting, and paste up were done by the collective at
**South End Press, Box 68, Astor Station
Boston, MA 02123**

SPECIAL THANKS

To the sixteen people in this book who shared their lives with us.

To the more than sixty other individuals we interviewed while researching this project.

To Bob Gottlieb for his political insight, wild enthusiasm, and unfailing support. To Claudia Fonda-Bonardi for her critical appreciation of the wonders and ironies of popular culture. To Bruce Dancis for his deep interest in "the red decade and the silver screen" and his evaluation of the historical section.

To Jim Richardson, Debby Rosenfelt, Larry Ceplair, Janis Helbert and Al Berger for helping to make our studies a social experience. To Cathy, Cindy, and Dave for living with us through it all (we made it!). To Marcy, Harry, and Robin for what cannot be printed. To Wendy, Jono, Clint, Dick, Eric, Irene, Karina, Lorna, Marge, Mary Jo, Richard, Sarah, and many others for the good times that kept us human. And to our large and loving families.

To the Film Fund for expanding the range of cultural possibilities.

To South End Press, a publishing group which understands the value and power of books.

Photo Credits

TABLE OF CONTENTS

"Contradictions are our hope!"

Bertolt Brecht

Introduction

A Hollywood writer turns in a TV script about work-related disease which places the blame squarely on corporate negligence. His producer feels it is too controversial, and the writer is relieved of his duties. They have experienced what is known in the entertainment industry as "creative differences." A director goes way over budget in the process of shooting a motion picture. He too is fired. The reason: "creative differences." An actress refuses to play a scene in the nude, a cameraman insists upon photographing a dramatic feature in a documentary style, a set designer fails to laugh at a studio executive's jokes. They are all given their walking papers. "Creative differences" once again.

The term "creative differences" has been used in countless studio press releases to explain why certain individuals were removed from the payroll. It can refer to any one of a wide variety of political, economic, artistic, and personal conflicts which commonly arise between Hollywood employers and employees. Some of these conflicts are relatively inconsequential; they affect no one except the individuals who are directly involved. But other "creative differences" which surface in Hollywood are of a far more significant nature. They can shape the films and TV shows which are viewed throughout the world, and change the industry itself.

This book examines the lives of sixteen people who work, or have worked, at various levels of the entertainment industry. Among their number are office workers, technicians, writers, directors, actresses, an agent, and an executive. All of them have substantial creative differences with the industry which employs them. They are critical of Hollywood for presenting flat and stereotypical depictions of people, particularly women and minorities, and for distorting stories with important social themes or altogether avoiding them. They are also critical of ways in which the industry is operated: they deplore the emphasis on profit-making, the industry's unforgiveably high unemployment rate, the extremely competitive nature of Hollywood work, discrimination in hiring and promotion, and the lack of control which most entertainment workers have over what they do.

Although these people see many fundamental flaws in the entertainment industry and its products, they believe Hollywood has enormous creative and social potential. And there are occasions, they maintain, when the industry comes close to realizing its potential. This is why most of them came to Hollywood—to participate in the production of these rare, enlightened moments—and this is why most of them remain here. We too believe that Hollywood is capable of flashes of insight, and this is partly why we undertook the writing of this book— to understand how and why these flashes occur. To understand those who try to make them occur. To understand what is, and is not, possible within the commercial framework of the entertainment industry.

Hollywood is controlled by large-scale private interests, and there is a strong tendency for its films and TV shows to reinforce conventional social values. Those who own and operate the major studios have an obvious stake in preserving the status quo. Yet it is not the media moguls themselves who perform the creative work in Hollywood. It is not they who manufacture the cultural products which bring Hollywood its profits. For this, the industry must rely upon a vast legion of creative employees. These employees, though they are generally anxious to please those who pay them, cannot always be trusted to follow the ideological line of their bosses. That is, they cannot always be counted on to sing the praises of rugged individualism, acquisitiveness, male dominance, and strong-willed authority. Some of these employees, like those in the book, have social outlooks which clash in various ways with those of their employers. Some of these employees are led by their artistic instincts to draw upon real-life stories, issues, and conflicts which disturb the status quo. As a result, there are at least a few films and TV shows in Hollywood's annual output which sparkle whith social criticism.

The Hollywood production and distribution system is riddled with delightful contradictions. Case in point: Francis Coppola's *Godfather II*. This film, like its predecessor, was financed and released by Paramount Pictures, a subsidiary of Gulf and Western, a multinational corporation with interests in everything from candy to coal mines. In recent years, G & W has become a leading symbol of U.S. imperial power, particularly in the Dominican Republic, where it owns a sprawling sugar cane operation, a major tourist complex, a local film company and manages an "industrial free zone" (a place for foreign companies to operate free of export duties, income taxes, strikes, and minimum wage laws). G & W's penetration of the island's culture and economy was accomplished with the help of former Dominican president Joaquin Balaguer, who was installed in office after the 1965 U.S. military invasion. Balaguer consolidated his power, and that of Gulf and Western, by dismantling the country's trade union movement and disrupting the opposition political parties.

Despite the fact that *Godfather II* was bankrolled by a large conglomerate, it may be interpreted, on one level, as a critique of corporate power. The film draws explicit parallels between Mafia operations and "legitimate" business activity. In one memorable scene, representatives of U.S. multinationals and organized crime gather together in a boardroom to slice up a cake in the shape of Cuba. Appropriately enough, Coppola shot this and the rest of the film's Cuban sequences in the Dominican Republic. Like the Dominican Republic of today, pre-Castro Cuba was the prize possession of U.S. business interests. And like the Dominican Republic, this possession was guarded by a local authoritarian regime. Why did Gulf and Western board chairman Charles Bluhdorn allow Coppola to make a film which contained material like this? The filmmaker was asked this question by a journalist in 1975. "Because he didn't think that it jeopardized anything, I guess," replied Coppola. "...I would guess that he really saw it all as an adventure story." Regardless of what Bluhdorn saw in *Godfather II*," however, there was much more going on in the film than gangland violence. *Godfather II* embodies a critique of the very system which financed it.

Another case from the G & W/Paramount file: Bluhdorn, an Austrian immigrant who worked his way up from a $15-a-week job in a cotton brokerage to the chairmanship of one of the nation's largest conglomerates, is a zealous defender of the U.S. capitalist system. He takes every available opportunity to applaud its accomplishments and upbraid its critics. "Those people who complain about our system," declared Bluhdorn in a 1976 speech, "apparently don't understand what it means to own a piece of America. To appreciate that they would have to go to Russia where they cannot own a piece of anything...I have never said that free enterprise is the perfect way of life, but here on this earth it comes about as close as you can get to what mankind has been aspiring throughout the centuries."

And yet it was Charles Bluhdorn's Paramount Pictures which distributed Bernardo Bertolucci's Marxist epic, *1900*, in the United States. Bluhdorn must have been involved in Paramount's decision to handle the film, for by all accounts he plays a dominant role in the studio's operations.* Paramount did insist that Bertolucci cut the film from five hours and ten minutes to four hours and five minutes, but the shorter version retained the passionate anti-capitalism of the original. American film critics, by and large, were shocked by *1900's* forceful and blunt political perspective when it was finally released here in late 1977.

The deep irony in all of this—that is, in *1900's* being distributed by a major U.S. conglomerate—was not lost on Bertolucci. "This movie is a monument to the contradictions of the system in which we live,"remarked the filmmaker in a 1977 interview,"—the same system in which every director works, using capital which, if not American, is Italian. (And I don't see the difference; I don't find Italian money any cleaner than American money.) It seems absurd, the contradiction between the capital which supports the movies and the idealistic themes of many talented directors, but this contradiction has always existed. I tried to enter into it and make it explode and, judging from the reactions, I have succeeded."

This is not to say that progressive filmmakers who function within the Hollywood system enjoy vast amounts of creative freedom. Generally they do not. For every Coppola and Bertolucci there are a hundred socially concerned film artists who cannot attract any studio financing for their screen projects. They are told politics do not sell, messages and entertainment do not mix, audiences cannot think and laugh at the same time. This cultural policy means that oppositional ideas are usually consigned to the fringes of public consciousness. When progressive filmmakers do succeed in getting studio support, they are put under great pressure to conform

---

*Perhaps Bluhdorn felt that *1900* would make as much money as Bertolucci's previous film *Last Tango in Paris*. In their avid desire for profits, Hollywood's corporate overseers sometimes release pictures which they find politically objectionable.

to certain dramatic conventions. These Hollywood conventions—such as focusing on one dynamic person, defining social conflict in personal, moral terms, and resolving problems in a simplistic, final manner—can shape the political meaning of a film in ways which the filmmaker did not intend.

Nonetheless, we believe there are significant opportunities for socially concerned filmmakers in Hollywood—enough to make their involvement in the industry worthwhile. Hollywood is a massive and powerful cultural machine. Its movies are seen by 20 million Americans each week; during an average minute of prime time, more than 40 million households in the country are tuned in to its TV programs. Millions more around the globe absorb its images and ideas. It would be unrealistic to advise all concientious filmmakers to repudiate Hollywood. There is no retreating from a cultural system as vast and encompassing as this. As Hans Enzensberger has written, "It might be a better idea to enter the dangerous game, to take and calculate our risks."*

This is precisely what the people in this book have done. They have entered the entertainment industry and tried to use its awesome power for their own humane purposes. In the process, they have been subjected to a variety of pressures and enticements. They have been blacklisted, promoted, celebrated, overworked, underpaid, and ignored. It has taken all their inner strength not to bend completely to the industry's will. Earlier we said that this book is about what is possible in Hollywood. It is also about the experience of working in a commercial environment which is determined to rob you of your spirit and integrity.

Hollywood is not the only industry where progressive people are charmed and coerced into sacrificing their ideals. This process occurs everywhere people work—in schools, hospitals, factories, government agencies, newspapers, and research institutes. But the seductive powers of the entertainment industry are particularly strong. After all, Hollywood is

---

*Hans Magnus Enzensberger, "The Industrialization of the Mind" from *The Consciousness Industry* (The Seabury Press, 1974)

where dreams come true, where fortunes are made (and lost) overnight, where people become larger than life. It is extremely difficult to put things in their larger perspective in a work arena where fantasies abound.

There is no way of making yourself absolutely invulnerable to the promises and threats of a commercial environment—especially one like Hollywood. But there is a way of reminding yourself of what truly matters in life, and of responding to the industry's pressures with challenges of your own—and that is by joining with other like-minded people to form a progressive movement. Hollywood is in dire need of such a movement—one that would bring together the various types of entertainment workers represented in this book. This movement must seek to change the industry's structure, products, and work conditions. In order to be as effective as possible, it should be linked with two outside networks of people whose work has direct impact on Hollywood: independent film and video makers, and media reformers. A media coalition such as this could not transform the country's political and economic structure. As somebody remarks later in this book, "Real democracy won't come about as a result of the Movie of the Week." But it could form an important part of a nationwide movement which *is* capable of changing the country.

This grand vision—of Hollywood employees, independent media producers, and media activists working together for social change—was sent aloft by the Socialist Media Group, a political organization which flourished on the fringes of Hollywood between 1974 and 1977. We were active members of the SMG; this book was inspired and guided by its ideas and activities. The group no longer exists, but the vision still lingers. In fact, it is more compelling than ever.

I.
BEFORE THE BLACKLIST
Preface
Albert Maltz
Abraham Polonsky

Preface

Any study of Hollywood dissidents, in order to be complete, must begin in the years before the blacklist, when the left was a significant force in the movie industry (and in other sectors of U.S. society). During the 1930s and 40s, leftists played an active role in the various entertainment guilds and unions—particularly in the Screen Writers Guild, which was led during its first year by the noted Hollywood radical, John Howard Lawson. Leftists were also integrally involved in the numerous organizations which arose in Hollywood to fight the worldwide spread of fascism, to elect progressive candidates, and to protect civil liberties. These organizations included the 5,000—member Hollywood Anti-Nazi League, which gained widespread public attention in 1937 when it forced Vittorio Mussolini, son of the Italian dictator, to cut short his visit to the film capital and again the following year when it succeeded in closing the studio gates to Nazi filmmaker Leni Riefenstahl; the Motion Picture Artists Committee, which was formed by film industry figures such as Dashiell Hammett, Gale Sondergaard, Lillian Hellman, Dorothy Parker, and Donald Ogden Stewart to support Loyalist Spain and China's war of resistance against Japan; the Motion Picture Democratic Committee, which helped put New Deal liberal Culbert Olson in the California governor's chair in 1938; the Hollywood Writers Mobilization, a 3,500-member organization formed during World War II to provide the government with anti-Nazi propaganda and to encourage the production of socially enlightened features; and the Hollywood Arts, Sciences, and Professions Council, which campaigned for Progressive Party presidential candidate Henry Wallace in 1948 and fought against censorship and blacklisting in the media industries.

Around the various political groups which emerged in Hollywood during the thirties and forties a lively radical subculture developed: there were Marxist study groups, writers' clinics, schools, publications, radio shows, cabaret revues, parties, benefits, theatrical performances, and movie premieres. Today's socially concerned entertainment workers often feel cut off from one another and find it difficult to preserve their political identities; but there was a strong sense of community among Hollywood progressives in the years before the blacklist. "Imagine having 250 friends in this town," says Abraham Polonsky. "And I really mean friends. No leftist ever had the problem of not knowing where to go for an evening. You never had to go out by yourself. There were dinners, parties, meetings, causes..."

Much of the energy, initiative, and direction in this political subculture was supplied by members of the Hollywood Section of the Communist Party. Only about 300 people passed through the Hollywood Section in the pre-blacklist period, but the Party exerted a wider influence in the movie community than its membership figures indicate. The Party's efforts to build a radical movement in Hollywood were hindered by its undemocratic structure, its Soviet orientation, and its policy of secrecy. Yet despite these serious, deep-seated flaws, the CP gained a prominent position in the film capital's progressive circles in the years before the blacklist. Communist Party members were respected for their deep social commitment and their stirring visions of an egalitarian world.

Albert Maltz and Abraham Polonsky both belonged to the Communist Party. They were among those Party members who resisted the organization's authoritarian bent, its tendency to demand complete conformity. Maltz, in particular, was punished for exerting his intellectual independence. But both men stuck with the Party, far into the grim days of the Cold War, when membership was widely regarded as treasonous. They did so because they believed "that the Communist movement represented that force in the United States—and internationally—which was the best hope of humanity." To be part of it, they felt, was to be part of the main progressive momentum of their day.

To Maltz and Polonsky, the Party was not a set of rigid principles to be either scorned from a distance or followed with blind devotion. It was a living, changing entity composed of real people who made tragic mistakes as well as courageous and intelligent decisions. "In the real world of events," says Polonsky, "only those who have never committed themselves to anything can take satisfaction in never having been wrong. For the rest of us, it's catch-as-catch-can with history."

Maltz and Polonsky came to Hollywood with similar ideas about movies. Writing screenplays was a way to make a living, but what really mattered in life was the writing of serious fiction. Once they started working in the film industry, however, they applied themselves wholeheartedly to their assignments. Their movies reflect their deeply held views; their film stories are filled with references to the anti-fascist struggle, the plight of women and blacks, and the agonies of life under modern capitalism.

Most left wing filmmakers in the 1930s and 40s appreciated the social significance of Hollywood movies. But Polonsky took one step further. He came to regard film not only as a vehicle for social ideas, but also as an art form. Some of his screen work stretches the aesthetic boundaries of commercial film.

The following profiles of Maltz and Polonsky, which focus primarily on the years before the blacklist, should not be read as a definitive history of this period. These are the stories of two men only. But both men have lived rich, full, complicated lives. Throughout their stories are woven a number of intriguing dilemmas: the difficulty of balancing a political life and a writing career, the tension between intellectual independence and organizational involvement, the challenge of working in an intensely commercial enviroment, and the awesome problem of learning how to function in a politically repressive period. There are lessons to be learned from the ways these men confronted these dilemmas.

Albert Maltz

Albert Maltz began his writing career in the early 1930s as a socially concerned dramatist. Among the plays he wrote during this period were *Peace on Earth* (with George Sklar) and *Black Pit,* both of which were produced by the Theatre Union, a stage company established in 1933 to present "plays that reflect the lives and discuss the problems of the majority of Americans—the working people." It was not until he turned to short story writing, however, that Maltz began to fully display his talent as a creative writer. Many of the short stories which Maltz wrote in the 1930s were immediately reprinted in anthologies. One titled *The Happiest Man on Earth,* about a hungry and desperate fellow who grabs at the chance to haul nitroglycerin for a living, took first prize in the 1938 O. Henry Memorial Awards. (Second and third prizes that year went to Richard Wright and John Steinbeck.) *Man on a Road,* the story of a West Virginia miner stricken by a fatal lung disease, is one of the most powerful pieces of American short fiction to come out of this period. But neither his plays nor his short stories could provide Maltz with a living wage, and he supplemented his income in those years by teaching extension classes at New York University.

As the forties began, Maltz's economic situation deteriorated. A novel he published in 1940 did not catch on with the reading public. His short stories stopped selling as they had in the past. And students deserted his classes in growing numbers for factory jobs as the country tooled up for war. Two close friends of his—left wing playwrights Michael Blankfort and George Sklar—had just moved to Hollywood in search of employment, and with the bills piling up around him, Maltz decided that he would join them.

"I came out to Hollywood because I had a child who was practically owned by Bloomingdale's Department Store in New York," Maltz remarks. "I was in debt to the store, I think, over $800. That was an awful lot of money in the Depression."

Maltz had a definite plan in mind. He would work on motion pictures as long as it took to pay off his debts and get a little bit ahead. Then he would quit and write another novel. He had no desire to devote his life to screenwriting. It was not that he regarded movie work with contempt; he understood why you turned to it when you did. "The writer's life is a gambler's life," says Maltz. The simple fact was that literature interested him more than screenplays.

There were those in New York's left wing circles who sneered when celebrated social dramatists such as John Howard Lawson and Clifford Odets turned up in Hollywood. It was widely assumed that any "serious" writer who went to work in the film industry had sold his or her soul for a pile of gold. But Maltz did not feel that he had to sacrifice his political principles when he moved to the Coast. It was simply a matter of economic necessity. After all, left wing writers had to make a living too. "I remember that when I met John Howard Lawson for the first time, which was around 1934 or 35, I already knew some of his work as a playwright. I knew that he was a man of quality and sincerity. He had gone out and worked some years in film. I didn't know particularly what he had done, but I knew he'd been there. And then he came back and had a couple more plays put on by the Group Theatre. It was at that time that I met him. And I never had a sense, well, this man having been several years in Hollywood comes back tainted and no longer pure and that kind of nonsense."

As soon as he arrived in Hollywood, Maltz got an agent and began looking for work. A few days later, veteran movie director Frank Tuttle hired him to adapt a Graham Greene suspense story for the screen. Tuttle had made a name for himself in the silent era by directing popular melodramas about men who proved their manliness by rescuing damsels in distress, women who succumbed to the temptations of jazz life only to redeem themselves by the last reel, and true romances imperiled by scheming vamps and obstinate fathers. In the thirties, Tuttle turned out a series of forgettable farces and routine musical comedies (starring Bing Cosby more often than not). Tuttle was the type of Hollywood workhorse studios could count on to speedily make movies with all the pieces in place. He was also a man with a social conscience who worried enough about the rise of fascism in the 1930s to join the Communist Party, the most vigilant opponent of Hitler and native Nazis he could find in Hollywood at the time. He handed over 4 percent of the $3,000 a week salary he made from his screen concoctions to the Party. Not every Holly-wood director knew and admired Maltz's class-conscious fiction, but Tuttle did and he put Maltz to work.*

Maltz labored on the screenplay throughout the summer of 1941 in Tuttle's pool house. Tuttle liked to sit beside the pool in his swim trunks while he worked, but Maltz reported for duty each morning in the suit he had worn on the train from New York—a heavy green tweed which he had bought for winter wear back East. Tuttle urged him to wear some-thing lighter, but Maltz could not yet afford a new California outfit.

Maltz found it very difficult to translate the Greene story into cinematic terms; there were just too many twists and turns in the plot which did not make sense to him. But Tuttle was an old hand at making the improbable play on screen, and he convinced his writer that the story problems could be solved. "It was a learning process for me," Maltz says, "because Tuttle had been a silent film director and he had an attitude which you'll find among a good many old-timers in the business: There's nothing you can't crack. There's no problem you can't solve in a piece of film material if you go at it hard enough and long enough."

What Maltz finally produced bore much resemblance to Greene's original story, although the setting was changed from England-on-the-brink-of-war to California-on-the-brink-of-war. The script, like the story, was not exactly

---

*Tuttle later came to regret his political associations. In May 1951, after being blacklisted by the film industry, he went before the House Un-American Activities Committee as a cooperative witness. Among those he identified as Communists was his former screen-writer, Albert Maltz. Tuttle explained his decision to give names in this way: "I believe that there is a traditional dislike among Americans for informers, and I am an informer, and I have thought about this constantly. I believe all decent people who share this dislike for informers, if they think about this carefully, will agree with me that at this particular moment it is absolutely vital. In a case like this, with ruthless aggression abroad in the world, the aggres-sors, I believe, are as ruthless with their own people as they are with those they consider their enemies; and I feel that today it is absolutely necessary for Americans to be equally ruthless."

socially profound, but it did manage to work international political intrigue into the action: Philip Raven is a professional killer, a cold-blooded man who "feels fine" after gunning down his victims. He is hired by Alvin Brewster, a wizened and tyrannical chemical manufacturer, to eliminate a company employee who is blackmailing Brewster. When Raven learns he has been paid in stolen bills by Brewster's agent and is marked for arrest, he sets out with single-minded fury to find the industrialist and wreak his revenge.

During the hunt, Raven hooks up with Ellen Graham, a nightclub singer who has her own reasons for tracking Brewster. She has been recruited as an undercover agent by a U.S. Senator who is investigating the chemical magnate's dealings with fascist Japan. She tries to convince Raven that he should give up the idea of killing Brewster and turn his personal vendetta into a political investigation. "I want you to make him spill the story," urges the singer. "Who's behind him—names—everything. I want a signed confession. That's much more important than killing him. It's important to your country!"

Ellen's patriotic pleading fails to move the hard-boiled Raven, who insists that he will "take care" of the man who double-crossed him "my way." Ellen herself, however, has touched a soft spot in Raven's heart. And in the screenplay's violent finale, when the professional gunman bursts into Brewster's executive suite, he forces a confession from the traitorous businessman before he exacts his own punishment. Raven, in turn, is shot down in a blaze of police gunfire. As he lies dying, he asks Ellen, "Did I...do all right for you?" She nods yes, tears welling up in her eyes, and Raven expires.

The script had something to say about those who traded with foreign fascists for profit, but this statement was certainly not an integral part of the melodrama. "I don't think I thought of it particularly as a film with social perspective," reflects Maltz. "I think whatever small grains of social relevance there were, like the businessman who sells poison gas to Japan, were probably put in not for any political reason, but because we were seeking motivation for a story. And in that ambience at that time it was a perfectly acceptable motivation that someone would do a thing like that. I certainly didn't think of it, and never have thought of it, as a political something-or-other."

But compared to the movie assignments his friends were being burdened with at the time, Maltz's script was remarkably relevant. At least it took note of the burgeoning world crisis. (George Sklar, with whom Maltz was staying until he found a place of his own, was stuck with the most foolish and unlikely story material Columbia Pictures owned—plots the studio had bought, stored away, and forgotten about for years; treatments which other hired hands had failed to properly assemble. "I found myself working on frivolous little things called *Angel Cake*," recalls Sklar, "things which were loaded with gimmicks and cute comic ideas, and musicals and so forth—while I was dying to work on the stuff that was pertinent and had some relation to the war.") By Hollywood standards, Maltz had fared well—he had drawn a mildly provocative assignment as his first screen job.

This Gun For Hire, featuring Alan Ladd as the professional trigger-man and Veronica Lake as the nightclub performer-turned-Congressional investigator, opened in May 1942 to positive reviews and large responsive audiences. "...Melodrama, straight and vicious—that's what this picture is," wrote Bosley Crowther in the *New York Times*. "But it is a good cut above the average, both in its writing and in its tensile quality."

Maltz's screenwriting career got underway just as the film industry entered a dramatic new era. Three weeks after Maltz completed his work on *This Gun For Hire*, the Japanese bombed Pearl Harbor and Hollywood went to war. Movies with war themes were rushed into production. Big name directors volunteered to film front line action. Movie businessmen organized a War Activities Committee to shoot and show patriotic shorts. At the first Oscar ceremony following the outbreak of war, Academy president Walter Wanger, speaking on behalf of the assembled Hollywood luminaries, dedicated the industry to an all-out war effort: "There is no one in this room who does not realize the potentialities of the film, who does not realize the importance today of psychological warfare and the part that film can take in the front lines of enlightened entertainment and morale."

The left in Hollywood also devoted itself wholeheartedly to victory. A fight to the death with fascism, a monumental conflict between the forces of slavery and freedom—this was how the Communist Party saw the war. And motion pictures had a vital role to play in the struggle, according to the Party's cultural spokespeople. "Films are about as important as bullets, as necessary as tanks," wrote David Platt, the *Daily Worker's* movie critic, one week after Pearl Harbor. "The war against fascism—the first just war for America since Thomas Edison invented the Kinetoscope a half century ago—will be won with the aid of this superb instrument for uniting the nation, for stirring the people."

Film industry Communists played a crucial part in organizing the Hollywood Writers Mobilization, a 3500-member force which provided the government with documentary film scripts, radio plays, Army and Navy camp sketches, War Bond and Blood Bank speeches, war agency brochures, posters, slogans, and songs. The Mobilization also urged its screenwriters to compose meaningful war features. "We have a duty in this war," declared the organization in its weekly newsletter. "It is a simple straight-forward assignment. We must do all we can to make the American people realize the enormity, the magnitude of this conflict. We have to grab Old Man Apathy by the scruff of the neck and hurl him out the door. That's our job. And (it) represents the greatest writing assignment in history."

But as the first year of war came and went, Maltz found himself unable to fulfill this historic assignment. Not one of the pictures on which he was put to work during this period had the vaguest relation to the war. For the better part of 1942, Maltz was stationed at Paramount, a studio extremely reluctant to convert from light comedies and musicals to war dramas.* Maltz was less than an expert at song and dance extravaganzas, so the studio assigned him to a variety of odd

---

*In order to get the *This Gun For Hire* writing assignment, Maltz had to sign a minimum one-year contract with Paramount. After it expired in mid-1943, he never signed another year-round studio contract.

jobs. "They gave me something called *The Man on Half Moon Street*. Never saw the film. But it remains a laugh whenever I think of it. This was about some guy who was really about—I don't know—110 or 120 years old, but looked 21. Because he drank radium. He lit up at night. Honest to God, this was the material. And he had a girl that he was pursuing, you see, and they never explained what would happen when he would light up at night."

Maltz's big break came in March 1943, when Paramount loaned him to Warner Brothers. Warners—home of the relevant melodrama, friend of the New Deal. Warners drew praise from progressive circles in the 1930s for dramatizing social controversy in pictures like *The Public Enemy, I Am a Fugitive from a Chain Gang, Wild Boys of the Road, They Won't Forget, Black Legion,* and *The Life of Emile Zola*. The *New York Times* commended the studio "for combining good citizenship with good picture-making." The Communist press called Warners the only studio in Hollywood with "a consistent record for outstanding achievement...They have produced over a score of distinguished New Deal films dealing with such topics as lynching, chain gang slavery, Jim Crow, juvenile delinquency, unemployment, tenant farming, medical science, racketeering, democracy, and the menace of fascism."

The brothers Warner had made their feelings known about Nazism long before the U.S. declared war. In 1939, the studio released *Confessions of a Nazi Spy*, a blunt warning against fascist subversion at home which rankled both the German-American Bund and the isolationist bloc in Congress. In June of the following year, studio president Harry Warner called together his 6000 employees to address them on the dangers of creeping Hitlerism. "Think of it! That right in our very studio, here in my own car, I have found literature sowing the seeds of intolerance and advocating the overthrow of American democracy," he announced to his assembled work force. "Think of it! Somebody knew who placed that literature in these cars, and we allow them to do it. It is just impossible, folks, it is impossible for the American government to stop it. They couldn't hire enough people...Why if they took the entire FBI and brought them just to this one studio, they couldn't protect you. You have got to join together for yourselves.

"...I would rather see my children in the earth, buried," stated Warner solemnly, "than to live under any such system as the one I am trying to prevent them from living under. I want you to know that my father and mother lived under such a system, and that's why we were brought here."

After Pearl Harbor, Warner publicly declared, "I don't want Warner Brothers to be known as the studio that made the best musical comedies during the war." In the months before Maltz arrived, the studio put a number of powerful and effective war pictures into the field, including *Action in the North Atlantic*, *Casablanca*, *Air Force*, *Watch on the Rhine*, and the controversial *Mission to Moscow*. Maltz knew his transfer was appropriate. If any studio in Hollywood was suitable for a writer with Maltz's literary and political record, it was Warners.

Maltz was originally brought to the Burbank studio to work on a movie which would have pitted Humphrey Bogart and Ida Lupino against a raging forest fire, but when spiraling cost projections forced the studio to abandon this project, Maltz was picked up by producer Jerry Wald to revise a naval thriller titled *Destination Tokyo*. Wald felt that the first draft of *Destination Tokyo*, which had been written by director Delmer Daves, lacked social and dramatic impact. Like other Wald movies, *Destination Tokyo* was inspired by a newspaper item. Wald liked his pictures to carry the timely punch of a headline story and he trusted Maltz to add this missing element. Wald was familiar with Maltz's passionately concerned literary work; he had tried unsuccessfully to convince Warners to buy the writer's award-winning story, "The Happiest Man on Earth." He knew the kind of touches Maltz's hand would bring to the material.

"He wanted some more immediacy to the statement," Maltz says. "We were in wartime. And he wanted it to be not just a drama of the submarine, but he wanted—if you will—anti-fascist content. I don't think he ever said that to me in those words because he didn't talk that lingo. He was a non-political man, Jerry Wald, purely a film guy really, a mixture of aesthetics and commercialism that was very interesting. But he also had an attunement to the time."

Maltz did not alter the fundamental direction of the screenplay, which chronicled the voyage of the *Copperfin*, a U.S. submarine bound for the dangerous waters of Tokyo Bay. But he did add a few moments of social commentary. The *Copperfin* first runs into trouble in the movie when it is spotted by a Japanese fighterplane and subjected to an aerial assault. One bomb crashes through the submarine deck but fails to explode. A brave young sailor volunteers to slip through an aperture and defuse it before it can go off. At this juncture in the script, Maltz inserted a bit of dialogue which was inspired by a public controversy from the pre-war period. The submarine skipper (played by Cary Grant) shows the bomb's detonator cap to his crew and remarks bitterly, "Appeasement has come home to roost, men. This cap has 'Made in the U.S.A.' stamped on it."

During the late thirties, leftists and pacifists vehemently protested the shipment of scrap metal to Japan. Japanese factories converted the scrap into bombs which were used against the Chinese populace. Up to late 1940, U.S. companies supplied Japan with more than 90% of its scrap iron and steel. Maltz had not forgotten. "It is true," he says, "that weapons that came back, and shells that came back on Pearl Harbor came from scrap iron that we had sent. Now this was a straight political comment, but this was something that delighted Jerry Wald. And Cary Grant was delighted to say it. And audiences accepted it, and it gave the film some intellectual content."

Maltz is quick to declare that he never *forced* messages into his scripts. The old charge that he, among others, tried to subvert innocent American audiences still lingers in his mind. "I never tried to put in things for political reasons," he says. "When I had the captain say 'Made in the U.S.A.' about this piece of Japanese weaponry, why all the papers were talking about it. It was a natural thing for a man to say at that moment, a natural bitter thing. Because the newspapers were full of it. But I never considered that I was going to try and use films to express my political attitudes. Certainly they *reflected* attitudes that I had, and these were manifested in the way my characters spoke and what they thought about and so forth. This has to be borne in mind in reference to any film, or any piece of writing: The minds of the people who have worked on it are reflected by what they say or what they don't say."

Maltz vigourously opposed fascism on political, moral, and intellectual grounds. To him, the Axis powers did not just represent a military threat to U.S. security—they were a dangerous ideological force which had to be crushed at all costs. As vice president of the League of American Writers, he had helped rescue refugee intellectuals from Europe. He had delivered speeches against Franco. In the 1930s he co-founded a magazine called *Equality* to counteract the anti-Semitic sermonizing of Father Coughlin. It is not surprising, then, that one of the additional characters Maltz created for *Destination Tokyo* was a committed anti-fascist sailor nicknamed "Tin Can." Maltz has Tin Can (Dane Clark) explain why he hates Nazism in a passionate speech to his shipmates:

> I had an uncle lived in the old country, see? A high class guy. You know what he was? A teacher of philosophy. And to be that in *Greece,* the very home of philosophy, you've got to be A-1 smart! That was my uncle! So they killed him! Those Nazis. Why? Because he had brains—Everybody in the world's gotta be their slaves...an' them that won't—like my uncle—they kill! You know something? My old man was no good—a boozer—he died in bed with the D.T.s. But my uncle, a man with charity in his heart, who used to send my ma what to eat with when we were kids—*him* they stood up against a wall. That sticks in here with me. (He points to his head) The difference between them and us is that with us even a no-good gets a chance to die in bed. So I don't forget my uncle. I read that an American flyer gets killed an' I think of my uncle. I read where a Russian guerrilla gets hanged an' I think of my uncle...I eat with it and I sleep with it.

Overall, Tin Can's speech sounds like a wail for a dead relative, but certain political ideas are suggested—the war is being fought for intellectual freedom and the right of even the lowliest among us to live and die peacefully. Tin Can feels compassion for the Soviet fighter as well as the American. It's not much, but this speech and the Captain's comment on appeasement represented nearly everything *Destination Tokyo* had to offer in the way of topical remarks. Neither scene would have been there if Maltz had not been hired to put a little bite into the script.

Critics for the major dailies and magazines generally found *Destination Tokyo* exciting and action-packed, but did not take note of the socially conscious moments. The reviews in the Communist papers, however, picked these scenes out for special praise. "...There are several important statements of the meaning of the war—not isolated speeches, but statements growing out of the character and action," wrote Virginia Warner in the *People's World. Daily Worker* critic David Platt thought he detected "the hand of Maltz...in many places in the film." The "courageous" anti-appeasement scene, stated Platt, "aims a two-ton bomb straight at the heart of the American fifth column."

Destination Tokyo ranked among the top box office hits of 1943. Producer Wald appreciated Maltz's assistance on the picture, and he pressed the writer to continue working for him. Wald wanted to follow *Destination Tokyo* with a movie based on the life of Marine hero Al Schmid, who had been blinded in a fierce battle on Guadalcanal after killing 200 Japanese soldiers. In spring 1944, Maltz agreed to turn the Schmid story into a screenplay.

Maltz succeeded in writing a war movie which was as forceful and honest as Hollywood made them. The story begins on the eve of Pearl Harbor. Al Schmid is a spirited but naive young foundry worker who knows more about hunting and sports than he does about the world he lives in. When war breaks out, he joins the Marines, just to experience the thrill of combat. Schmid returns from overseas a hero, but his eyesight has been destroyed. His understanding of why he fought is scant, yet now he faces a lifetime in the dark. The dramatic crux of the scenario is Schmid's struggle to adjust to civilian life as a blind veteran.

The most extensive piece of social commentary in the script comes when a group of hospitalized GI's, including Schmid, launch into a heated discussion about the future that awaits them in post-war America. Jobs are their big concern. "Now that I'm going home I'm scared," says one. "I wasn't half as scared on Guadalcanal as I am now. If a man came along—anybody—and told me I'd have a decent job for the rest of my life, I'd get down on my knees and wash his feet!"

"Sure, everybody's working now," says another young Marine, "but back in peace time the only job I had was to take things to the hock shop so my folks could eat."

"How about the GI Bill of Rights?" chimes an optimist. "I'm going to law school on that."

But the others aren't convinced. "It all boils down to economics," says one bitterly. "That's what runs this world—so the GI Bill will send some guys to school...so maybe there'll even be prosperity for two years after the war while we catch up on things, making diaper pins and autos. The things that poor civilians did without. But after two years what happens? Answer me that!"

"A bonus march," Schmid declares.

"Nossir," shoots back a corporal who has great faith in American democracy. "I'll tell you what happens. We're part of the people—that's what happens. You think because we done the front line fighting we can take a ride on the country for the rest of our lives? Nossir! There's no free candy for anyone in this world. I know what I fought for—for me, for the right to live in the U.S.A. When I get back into civilian life, if I don't like the way things're goin'...okay...it's my country, I'll stand up on my two legs an' holler. And if there's enough of us hollerin', we'll go places.

"Don't tell me we can't make (this country) work in peace like it does in war," continues the corporal. "Don't tell me we can't pull together. Don't you see it, you guys. Can't you see it."

The Marines seem persuaded, with the exception of Schmid, who snaps, "You askin' me—I don't see a thing," and stalks out of the hospital room.

Maltz knew these young soldiers well. They were the luckless drifters and weary workers from his stories of the thirties. "Bear this in mind:" he says, "the background for the psychology of the men in that scene would have been the fact that this is 1943 and up to 1941 there still were 10 million unemployed. So that all of these were children of the Depression.... For many of them joining the Marines could've been an idea of getting three squares. Because these would've been young guys out of the steel towns, coal towns, you know, mill towns of all sorts. And therefore that was in their psychology, you see. That concern about jobs—will we have jobs?—was the concern of the Depression-minded fellows."

The hospital scene gave Maltz a chance to use some of the tough language that filled his fiction. But, according to Maltz, the scene was not his idea. Wald suggested it: "At a certain point in the film, Jerry Wald said to me, 'You know, you don't have enough content in this.' He said, 'These guys ought to be talking about what life is going to be like afterwards.' I felt that what Wald was suggesting was just too...really propagandis-tic. It wasn't right, it was going to stick out. It wasn't right for what the picture should be. But he said, 'No, no,—we've got to have some content in it.' And so I said, 'Well alright, I'll write it.' The whole idea for the scene was his idea. I said, 'I'll write it and then we'll see how it is.' And it remained in. Now there was an example where I'm sure anybody in the know who saw the film would have said, 'Well, there's Maltz shoving in some propaganda.' But it was Jerry Wald in this instance...At his insistence I tried it, and it seemed alright so I said, 'Well, it's not so bad,' and it stayed in."

One of the Marines who shared Al Schmid's foxhole on Guadalcanal and withstood the Japanese assault was a young Jewish waiter from Brooklyn named Lee Diamond. Maltz made Diamond a character in his screenplay and endowed him with a special awareness about the war. The script's introduc-tory notes describe Diamond "as typical of the generation of native born Jewish American youth stemming from foreign born parents. He was brought up with the awareness that his father had good reason for leaving Tsarist Russia...and consequently he knows the goodness of being an American. He has reflected about the meaning of democracy more deeply than Al (Schmid)...because he takes it less for granted."

On board the train which is taking Schmid back home to Philidelphia, Diamond tries to revive his blind friend's sagging spirits. "Believe me, you ain't been a sucker," Diamond tells Schmid. "There ain't one guy who got killed or disabled in this war who's a sucker. It's a stinking war but it has to be won." Schmid only sinks deeper into self-pity and gloom, however, and Diamond grows exasperated with him. "Listen, other guys have problems too," says Diamond.

"What problems have you got?" Schmid demands. 'You're

in one piece ain't you? Your wife don't have to turn over inside when she sees you. When you go for a job, there's nobody gonna say 'We got no use for ex-heroes like you.'"

Diamond's response is filled with emotion: "That's what you think...there's some who won't hire me because my name's Diamond instead of Jones—because I celebrate Passover instead of Easter...You an' me—we need the same kind of world—we need a country to live in where nobody gets booted around for *any* reason."

Diamond's comment on anti-semitism, stresses Maltz, was in keeping with his character and it made sense in terms of the social period. It was not contrived for political effect, states the writer. "Discrimination against Jews was a part of reality," he says. "More of a reality then than now. This has been a changing thing in our society. It was very much more of a reality when I was a child than it is today. And it was a reality then that a man like Diamond would've thought of in the year 1942." Maltz makes a strong distinction between controversial dialogue which grows logically out of a screenplay's dramatic course, and controversy which is shoved arbitrarily into a script. The social commentary in his movies, asserts Maltz, made dramatic sense.

Maltz heard executive producer Jack Warner's reaction to his movie immediately after it was previewed. "After the movie was over, I went downstairs to the urinal, and there, standing by my side, was Jack Warner, head of the studio, who had also been to the preview. And he said to me, 'Fine film,' and so on. And he said, 'I particularly like that scene between Diamond and Schmid on the train.' "

Two years later, in May 1947, during an executive session of the House Un-American Activities Committee, Warner was asked by Chairman J. Parnell Thomas if Maltz managed to slip much propaganda into the Marine movie. "There is one little thing," testified Warner, "where the fellow on the train said 'My name is (not) Jones, so I can't get a job.' It was this kid named Diamond, a Jewish boy, in the Marines, a hero at Guadalcanal." He had his suspicions about that piece of dialogue, said the studio chief, but he could not be certain. "Some of these lines have innuendos and double meanings, and things like that," Warner explained to the Committee, "and you have to take eight or ten Harvard law courses to find out what they mean."

"The very thing in the movie that he had applauded me for doing was the thing that came to his mind at that moment as an example of communist propaganda!" exclaims Maltz. "That always has *fascinated* me, that he would choose *that*..."

If the studio had its doubts about the movie's political overtones at the time it was made, producer Jerry Wald did not let on. Wald, in fact, made an effort to sell the movie to the public on the basis of its controversial moments. "Ninety percent of the story is concerned with Schmid's return to civilian life," Wald told the New York newspaper *PM* on the eve of the movie's release. "We talk about it realistically, the kind of thing a lot of people are afraid to put on the screen. We even have a few things to say about race prejudice—no hedging...the audience can take it...it's good for 'em. Our fighting men don't want to come back to civilians who don't know what they've been experiencing—they don't want to come back, like the ads say, to everything the way it was. A lotta people say, 'Sh,sh—can't talk about the bonus or selling apples.' Well I don't wanna duck the problems."

Warner Brothers titled the film *Pride of the Marines* and released it in late August 1945, just after the war ended. John Garfield starred as the blind Marine hero. The movie impressed most of the critics as a sensitive and serious treatment of an urgent problem—the rehabilitation of disabled GIs. "There is nothing mawkish about it," wrote Bosley Crowther. "The story is told in a straight, colloquial style, clean and crisp in its dialogue and real in its pictorial imagery." *Time* found it "exciting—because the screen is so unaccustomed to plain talk—to see and hear the angry discussion of postwar prospects which Scripter Albert Maltz has written for the hospitalized marines." *Time* also praised the movie's statement on anti-semitism. "But *Pride of the Marines*," concluded the magazine's film critic, "is more than a rostrum for liberal polemics. It is a good hard-hitting movie."

Maltz himself did not go to war; a few weeks before his induction date, the government passed a regulation which excluded men his age (35) from military service. But Maltz felt that his wartime movies performed a national duty:"On both

Destination Tokyo and *Pride of the Marines,* I did feel consciously that both of these films could have an effect on morale, and also promote some understanding of what the war was about. This was always a constant problem, to get people to really understand it, rank and file people."

Maltz's cinematic perception of the war meshed with prevailing public attitudes. The period supported his democratic sentiments. "This was a period of more harmony among different political attitudes—left and center, let's say—in the United States than there had been in the thirties or was to be later after mid-1946. Because everybody was anti-fascist, except let's say the extreme right wing. So that if you had a left wing writer working for a not particularly political producer or director, and writing an anti-fascist film about the war, that was okay with the producer and okay with the studio and okay with the audience. It was a particular harmony resulting from a special period of history."

The Communist press found much of Hollywood's wartime output worthy of applause. David Platt declared that the industry was entering an era of enlightenment: "The ostrich age is over as far as the silver screen is concerned...Never before in the history of the screen has there been such a fast succession of pictures with a purpose." "There's a deep ferment throughout the film industry, affecting everyone, including executive producers and even the stockholders of powerful studios financially dependent on Wall St."

Before the war, few voices outside the Party had taken up the chant for socially significant movies. But after Pearl Harbor, many inside and outside the industry called upon Hollywood to help interpret the underlying issues of the war. "In the furnace of these times our world is being reshaped day by day," stated a *New York Times* movie reviewer, "democracy is being rediscovered and given a new value in the agony and effort of soldier and civilian; it has left none of us untouched ...let us have dramas and characters that will be commensurate in stature (with the conflict), that will illuminate the motives and issues on which free men stand today. That is the most and the least that Hollywood can do." According to a poll taken by the *Film Daily* in fall 1943, sixty-two percent of the nation's film commentators agreed that the screen should deal with controversial social and political issues.

New Deal officials spoke out during the war about the public responsibilities of film. Nelson Poynter, of the Office of War Information's motion picture bureau, encouraged Hollywood to downplay the blood and thunder and illuminate the war's "intangible factors." Vice President Henry Wallace told a film industry gathering that it was possible to make movies which not only entertained the public but also "fulfill(ed)...the preambles of the Constitution."

In October 1943, more than 1200 people came together during a three day Writers Congress at UCLA to discuss the social obligations of mass media during and after wartime. Those who attended the motion picture seminar heard Darryl Zanuck urge scenarists to write movies which dealt realistically with "the causes of wars and panics, with social upheavals and depression, with starvation and want and injustice and barbarism under whatever guise." Dress the screenplay "in the glittering robes of entertainment and you will find a ready market," promised Zanuck.

There was still strong opposition in the film industry to relevant picture-making. Sam Goldwyn declared that the soldiers "don't want war pictures...they want escape pictures." A poll taken by the *Motion Picture Herald* in spring of 1943 found that the vast majority of theater operators felt Hollywood was producing too many "war pictures and themes of stress and strife."

But the war called escapist movies more into question than ever before. At a time when the government was trying to toughen up the public's spirit, there was something vaguely unpatriotic about pure illusion. As Lowell Mellett, chief of the OWI's film bureau, stated: "The habit of sitting three or four or even more hours, with one's mind afloat in a fictional world, hardly equips the American population for the serious job of dealing with real life. That way lies degeneration rather than growth." Harry Warner's response to those in the film industry who advocated more escapism was stern and bluntly worded: "Any arbitrary exclusion of war films, either to satisfy a small appeaser element or for personal reasons without regard to the general public interest, is equivalent to sabotage." It was the screen's duty, Warner told fellow film executives, to explain each "why and wherefore" of the current world struggle to the American people. "If it has been our good fortune to be among the pilots of an industry capable of presenting information and understanding in the most palpable form yet devised, then let us steer a proper course. Were we to do anything else at such a moment, when so many are making so many great sacrifices, there would be little justification for our existence."

A producer who appreciated the theatrical value of a little social controversy; a studio committed to serving the war effort; and a general spirit of public service throughout much of the industry—these were the factors going in Albert Maltz's favor until V-Day. It was an encouraging combination of circumstances for a left wing screenwriter. But it was not enough to make him change his mind about movie-writing as a primary pursuit.

"I was absolutely delighted to have material of that quality," says Maltz of his two Jerry Wald assignments. "But I wouldn't have done those films if I hadn't needed the money. Because I could write books or stories that would enter the same field if I chose. The point is I had a goal; my goal was not to be a screenwriter, though I was not invalidating that as a profession. My goal was to write fiction. That's all. At the same time, it didn't mean that when I got a piece of screen work to do, I didn't do it as best I could and as earnestly as I could, and that I didn't take pride in what I did. Suppose you have someone who wants to be a painter, but has to earn a living, so he can only paint weekends and nights. And in the meantime he's a spraypainter on automobiles, or he's a housepainter. It doesn't mean that he doesn't do house-painting as well as he can and take pride in that."

Maltz tried to devote as much time as possible to his own writing. Screenwriting remained an economic necessity but he made time between movie assignments for his novels. During the war, he spent about five months a year on fiction, seven on film. Occasionally, Maltz even found it possible to do his own work on studio time: "I began working on a novel while I was still on my first screenplay at Warner Brothers. I remember at the time you had a certain quota; you were supposed to hand in about twenty pages of script every week at the studio. And I worked very hard and could get my quota done before lunch...Many of the writers would spend time chatting, reading the *Hollywood Reporter*, making phone calls, going out for coffee, and so on. But I kept my door closed and nobody came and visited me, and the minute I got into the studio I was at work and I worked intensively until about one o'clock. By that time I had finished my stint. Then I had lunch and took a little walk by myself. And then I went right to work on my novel until quitting time. At Warner Brothers you couldn't leave until five or five-thirty, that was a stern rule."

*****

Maltz's fiction hammered home social points. His stories were bound up with the labor struggles of the day. On a car trip through the coal fields of West Virginia in 1934, Maltz picked up a hitchhiker who told him about a local mine tragedy. Hundreds of miners were slowly dying from silica dust they had inhaled while drilling a water-power tunnel for a Union Carbide subsidiary. The company had not even bothered to equip the miners with masks. Maltz relayed the information to newsmen in New York and then turned the man's account into a powerful short story. The publicity resulted in a 1936 Congressional investigation.

Maltz went to the auto towns of Michigan during the great sit-down strikes of 1937 to research his first novel, *The Underground Stream*. He met the Reuther brothers, he sat in on union meetings, he gathered information about the Black Legion—a band of vigilantes dedicated to destroying the union by any means necessary—and he was tear-gassed by company police outside the GM plant in Flint. Maltz found the "richness of reality" much more compelling than anything he could have dreamed up.

Maltz's work drew mixed reactions from the established literary reviews. Critics admired the writer's fierce compassion for the poor and exploited. "Albert Maltz's favorite subject is pain—the appearance of pain, the conditions of pain," wrote Alfred Kazin. "Yet it is because he writes out of a hot lacerating fury that never rises to a scream that (his) stories are so burningly effective." Unfortunately, stated some reviewers, Maltz felt compelled to take a political stand on suffering. He was told that one could not be both a partisan and a first class artist. "Maltz, as I think, should detach himself from political and social movements (and) function as artist, dramatist and story teller," opined a *New York Times* book critic. "(He should) open men's eyes and warm their understanding, leaving it to others in their respective fields to tackle immediate problems." The *Saturday Review of Literature* found *The Underground Stream*, which examined the world of industrial conflict through the eyes of a Communist labor organizer, particularly disturbing: "Mr. Maltz has never denied his party bias, but it explains in part why *The Underground Stream* fails so completely. His earlier short stories were less concerned with ways out of depression than with depression itself; his present, first novel is frankly communist..."

Maltz does not apologize for the political perspective in his fiction. "It's an enormously complex problem. You take a painter like Giotto. He was, I'm sure, a devout Christian, and he was expressing the orthodox Christian world view. And if you walk into his chapel in Padua, as I have, it's overwhelmingly beautiful. But at the same time he's expressing an orthodox Christian point of view...Or take Graham Greene, for example, who became a Catholic. Reviewers might say, 'Well, this novel about Mexico would have been truer if he hadn't intruded his Catholic philosophy about Mexico.' It could be that in a given book a Catholic philosophy would distort the truth, or certain aspects of character. But it also could be that it might unearth truth. The same is true of political beliefs. And the reviewers who criticize a writer for his beliefs *themselves* have an attitude. They have a political attitude—even if their attitude is to say that a writer should *not* have ideas. He should just render people and life. As though a writer can have an empty head!...The fact is there was a war of attitudes going on, which some critics were more concerned about than others."

Political activities absorbed a generous amount of Maltz's time in the 1930s and 40s. His literary heroes were the "citizen writers" of history: Zola, Gorky, Thoreau, Whitman. Those who plunged into the turbulent affairs of their day. "...Vast numbers of the literary men and women of the past have been guerrilla fighters for unpopular causes," Maltz told a conference of writers in 1947.

...The list of the great in literature is heavy with names of those who in their time were objects of censorship, who were social radicals, who were the subject matter of police reports and the object matter for slander, ridicule, misrepresentation and, always, bad advice...Yet, it is to the eternal credit of many that they scorned the police reports with defiant courage, they accepted the slander with stubborn dignity, and they rejected the bad advice. Indeed, if only the literary and political Bourbons of each period had written their own histories of literature, it would reveal to us today that the writers of each generation have suffered to an astonishing degree from a series of related distempers, contaminations, and corruptions; among these corruptions would be listed: the possession of ideas that were unusual and unaccepted or, even worse, unpopular with the powers that be—even radical; the corruption of leaving the writing desk to talk and walk in the marketplace with other citizens, particularly members of political parties in opposition to the status quo; the corruption of having convictions and a measure of courage about them. And all of these contaminations and corruptions are the very reason we honor them today—the reason why they not only lived as they did, but wrote as they did.

Maltz now feels that the amount of time he put into writing literature and the amount of time he devoted to public affairs were terribly out of balance. He is convinced that he would have made a greater social impact if he had spent more time at his writing desk: "As I look back on my life in the thirties and forties, I was much more active than I wish I had been...And I say that only for this reason. I used to be called on to make speeches about the Spanish Civil War, or on behalf of the Theatre Union. And I would get in the subway and travel an hour to Brooklyn and speak to fifty people and travel an hour back. Well, I think I could've used my time better. Now not that that was *wrong* to do. And why did I do it? I did it because there's always the fact that if you are concerned about humankind—issues like civil liberties and fascism—you feel its urgency. And you respond to it. Now if you are able to make public speeches, as I am—certain people are not—you're called upon: 'Please, we need speakers, do this, do that.' So you respond out of your own sense of the urgency. Jesus, when it's a question of saving the Scottsboro boys or Angelo Herndon, I spoke. And you write leaflets and you do all of the other things. You join organizations of this and that. But they are enormously time consuming, and the question is could you spend time any better in the long run. Well I think I could have. By writing! By having more time for writing.

"I remember periods at certain times in the thirties when I might have only fifteen hours a week for writing; the rest of the time I was doing other things. All very valuable—but not writing. And I would go away for four months in the summer, and then get in some writing. Well, I think that was the wrong choice. And I regret it. I regret it because I would've written more than I have written—that's all, simple. And you never know what will happen with a book. It can fall like a stone in a well. But it can also reach a great many more people than you can reach with your own voice. Certainly my short stories have reached a great many more people than I've ever spoken to, because they've been reprinted a great deal."

While Maltz laments the inordinate amount of time he devoted to organizational duties, he does not regret having been part of the left wing movement. His memory of that involvement is still a warm glow inside him. "I felt that I had attached myself to a movement that was going to bring about human brotherhood, and an end to all discrimination in the world. I want to say this: If you read classic Marxist literature—and don't know anything about what has happened in the Soviet Union and other socialist countries—I think you read the noblest body of literature that has ever been penned by man. Because it speaks of moving the world into brotherhood, of moving it into true democracy, of ending all exploitation in every area—wage exploitation, exploitation of colonies by imperial powers, of women by men, of colored people by white people. There is no area of exploitation that it doesn't say: 'We will abolish it. We will arrive at true equality.' Now that's a marvelous dream! And a *moral* dream, in my code. And I do not feel embarrassed today that I adhered to it. And I felt that my greatest dignity as a human being was that I did adhere to it.

"Now it was very important to me to try and be a good writer; but I would say in those years if I had to choose between losing my identity as part of that movement and stopping writing, I would have chosen to stop writing. Because I did feel that my integrity as a human being came from being part of the movement—and after all you are a human being before you are a writer or a lawyer or any other goddamn thing. You know, what are you in your human clay? What's in your heart and soul? What do you live for? That vision was to me a most nourishing one. And I felt proud to be associated with what I thought was going to move the world into human brotherhood."

Maltz joined the Communist Party in the mid-thirties. He had not been exposed to radical politics as a boy. His father, a Jewish immigrant from Lithuania, had fared well in the new country, working his way up from grocer boy to building contractor. His mother, whose eyesight was badly damaged by trachoma, discouraged him from reading books and newspapers. "Because reading was a strain for her," says Maltz, "she thought reading was a strain for everyone. She was not a woman with any education. And she kept saying to me, 'Save your eyes until you go to college.' " It was during his college years that Maltz began to examine the world politically. "When I was in my junior year at Columbia, in '29, the Crash occurred. Friends of mine started to leave school within a few months; their parents could no longer keep them in college. So everybody began to think at that time. And it was while I was up at the Yale School of Drama, in those two years there, that I started to read other things and move toward the left."

The Communist Party remained a central part of Maltz's life up to 1950. "I have heard people," he says, "for instance I heard (Dalton) Trumbo give a long interview on KCET.* And he was asked what he felt about the period when he'd been in the Communist Party, what it was like. Well, he said, it was like belonging to the PTA. Well, that's bullshit! And he should have been ashamed of himself for saying a thing like that. Because if it was like being a member of the PTA, why was he a member? The fact is that in the thirties the Communist Party of the United States did magnificent things—also may have

---

*A public television station in Los Angeles

done some stupid things. But it did some magnificent things. It was the organization that saved the Scottsboro boys from death, and Angelo Herndon from death. And it had members beaten to death in the South for trying to unite black and white sharecroppers. And it was the one that organized the unemployed. And it was the organization that was foremost in the fight against fascism. And the building of the CIO was impossible without the Communist Party. So to turn back on that now...this is a different period, we've learned a great deal. I've learned a great deal. But you can't deny those past achievements."

What doomed the Party, says Maltz in retrospect, was "its slavish refusal to think for itself or to take any political position not advocated by the Soviet Union." He has come to believe that the USSR, despite its "extremely significant accomplishments in the fields of public education, health care, science, and technology," represents a serious distortion of the socialist dream. "The concept of socialism," Maltz says, "involves the extension of human freedom, not the institution of thought control and government tyranny."

But back in the 1930s and 40s, he acknowledges with regret, his belief in the great Soviet experiment was unshakeable: "Some knew. Way back during the Moscow Trials in the thirties they said, 'Hell, these are phonies.' But I didn't believe it, along with many others. There were a great many people like me who said, 'Why it would be impossible for people who fought so bravely and honestly against Czarism to betray their own comrades, and to frame their own comrades.' It was inconceivable! It would never occur to me to frame a friend by my side, and I know it would not occur to him to do it to me. I mean you couldn't *conceive* that these presumably pure in heart people would do what was done."

Like most Communists, Maltz kept his membership in the Party a secret. A later generation of leftists would charge that this policy was dishonest and blame it for undermining the effort to build a popular following for socialism; it fortified the public impression that the Party was a subversive outfit which had something to hide. But Maltz contends that Communists had very little choice in the matter. You could not declare yourself a Communist, he says, without risking your job and, in some situations, your physical safety. He compares the Communists' predicament with that of the Abolitionists in the South. The country's political environment, states the writer, made public disclosure a dangerous proposition—even during the relatively enlightened years of the New Deal.

Hollywood, adds Maltz, was even less tolerant than other communities: "Hollywood was much worse because it was a company town. You could be a novelist and announce your Party membership as Richard Wright did after *Native Son* became a Book-of-the-Month Club choice. He had a press conference, and he said, 'I am a Communist, and a card-carrying Communist.' And they would still publish his novels, because the publishing fraternity was more liberal. It was an individual thing; an individual house could publish him. But we had companies here in Hollywood which played ball with the gangsters Bioff and Browne* and paid them off and so on. Announce it in Hollywood? Not a chance. You'd never work again."

In 1941, Hollywood Communists broke tradition by issuing a leaflet in the Party's own name. The leaflet, which was put out by the trade union section of the Hollywood CP, attacked the widespread practice of red baiting in the International Alliance of Theatrical Stage Employees. "We felt that it was necessary to begin speaking in the Party's name," recalls a former Hollywood organizer for the CP. "Particularly on the question of red baiting. Anybody who said anything in the IA was being called a Communist." But the cultural section of the Party (screenwriters, directors, actors) reacted negatively when it learned about the leaflet. "The cultural section pratically hit the ceiling over it," says the ex-Party organizer, "because this meant that we were revealing that there actually

---

*Chicago hoodlums Willie Bioff and George E. Browne ran the International Alliance of Theatrical Stage Employees from 1934 to 1941, when they were convicted of extorting a total of $1.2 million from the motion picture industry. In return for the money, Bioff and Browne promised studio executives immunity from labor troubles. Their big AFL union represented Hollywood's 12,000 craft workers.

were Communists in the studios, you see. They were just furious at us...this was the kind of concern there was." The Hollywood CP thereupon resumed its practice of camouflaging itself.

The level of political activity in Maltz's life dropped significantly during the writer's first years in Hollywood. On occasion he delivered speeches: he participated in the opening ceremonies of a Communist-sponsored school called the People's Educational Center, which offered course titles ranging from "Political Economy" to "Body-Building and Dance." (The school's fall 1945 catalogue announced a course titled "It's a good picture but..." which promised to bring stars like Bette Davis, Burgess Meredith, and Danny Kaye face to face with progressive fans to discuss the social content of Hollywood features.) He volunteered to write the English commentary for *Moscow Strikes Back*, a Soviet war documentary which graphically depicted the Nazi drive on the Russian capital. "This was the town of Istra...this was a high school...a kindergarten..," explains Maltz's grim narration as the camera moves over stacks of corpses and the charred remains of buildings. (The film was given a special documentary award by the Academy of Motion Picture Arts and Sciences in 1942.)

But in general Maltz put much less time into political service between 1941-45 than he had in New York. At one point he excused himself from Party meetings long enough to write a novel about moral resistance within Nazi Germany called *The Cross and the Arrow*.

Nevertheless, Maltz continued to identify strongly with the Party. In 1946, he found himself dead center in a political maelstrom which would have driven a less committed Party member out of the Communist movement. The storm, which tossed and turned the Party's intellectual community for several months, was precipitated by an article Maltz published in the left wing magazine, *New Masses*, called "What Shall We Ask of Writers?" For years, Communist writers had been guided by the militant slogan "Art Is A Weapon." Broadly interpreted, it meant that no literary work was value free; literature either reflected or attacked society's dominant beliefs. To the new breed of proletarian writers which emerged from the "art for art's sake" environment of the 20s, the slogan once seemed a profound and exhilarating insight. But by the 1940's, the maxim had become, in Maltz's mind, a literary "straightjacket." The left's narrow interpretation of the slogan, stated Maltz in his article, constricted socially conscious writers: "(It has come) to mean that *unless* art is a weapon like a leaflet, it is worthless or escapist or vicious."

Left wing literary critics, continued Maltz, had a habit of judging a work of fiction in terms of its political line rather than its overall artistic effect. "If a work, however, thin or inept as a piece of literary fabric, expresses ideas that seem to fit the correct political tactics of the time, it is a foregone conclusion that it will be reviewed warmly, if not enthusiastically. But if the work, no matter how rich in human insight, character portrayal, and imagination, seems to imply "wrong" political conclusions, then it will be indicted, severely mauled or beheaded—as the case may be."

Maltz went on to defend the literary work of writers who were considered by the Party to have fallen from political grace: "An artist can be a great artist without being...a progressive thinker on all matters." Though James T. Farrell and Richard Wright had abandoned the CP, they were still capable of writing superb novels. "Writers must be judged by their work, and *not* by the committees they join," Maltz declared.

Maltz's article, in effect, called for sweeping revisions in the Party's cultural canons. The fact that his fiction was so ardently admired in left wing circles lent power and credibility to his argument. (One Party critic ranked Maltz with such literary greats as Steinbeck, Dreiser, and Hemingway.) But the article was badly timed; it appeared the same month the Party expelled its former leader, Earl Browder, for tampering with classic Marxist principles. Gripped by a fundamentalist fervor, the Party was in no mood to consider revising its time-honored line on culture.

Immediately following its publication, the Maltz essay was dissected by a host of Party literati in the pages of the *New Masses* and the *Daily Worker*. There were some valid intellectual concerns. Was Maltz, for instance, cleaving the writer into two separate halves—citizen and artist? But the critics were more intent on branding Maltz's ideas as politically dangerous than on advancing Marxist aesthetics. Novelist Howard Fast accused Maltz of promoting the "liquidation" of "all creative writing which bases itself on progressive currents in America." *New Masses* editor Joseph North declared that Maltz, if heeded, would "destroy the fruitful tree of Marxism."

The most vitriolic remarks flowed from the pen of *Daily Worker* columnist Mike Gold. "Albert Maltz seems to have let the luxury and phony atmosphere of Hollywood at last poison him," wrote Gold. "It has to be constantly resisted, or a writer loses his soul. Albert's soul was strong when it touched Mother Earth—the American working class. Now he is embracing abstractions that will lead him nowhere."

Few Hollywood Communists sided publicly with Maltz. Most were anxious to show the Party that their souls remained untainted by the tinsel and glamour. At a special meeting held at the home of a Hollywood Communist, one speaker after another rose to denounce the Maltz position. "I remember three people who got up and defended him," says a screenwriter who attended the session. "But in general, the writers who disagreed with the Party felt it was easier to give in—that was the whole kind of feeling about it. You didn't want to split it (the Party), you know."

Under intense pressure, Maltz finally reversed himself. In an article published eight weeks after the original one, Maltz wrote: "I consider now that my article—by what I have come to agree was a one-sided, non-dialectical treatment of complex issues—could not, as I had hoped, contribute to the development of left wing criticism and creative writing. I believe also that my critics were entirely correct in insisting that certain fundamental ideas in my article would, if pursued to their conclusion, result in the dissolution of the left wing cultural movement." He was guilty, Maltz stated, of exaggerating the inadequacies of left wing criticism. He had also erred in his judgement of James T. Farrell's writing abilities: in truth, Farrell had lost his gift after converting to Trotskyism. "I know of the manner in which a poisoned ideology and an increasingly sick soul can sap the talent and wreck the living fibre of a man's work," wrote Maltz.

The Party welcomed Maltz back into the fold at a mass meeting in Los Angeles' Embassy Auditorium. The evening, titled "Art—Weapon for the People," was hosted by screenwriter John Howard Lawson and featured speeches by *Daily Worker* literary editor Samuel Sillen, Dalton Trumbo, and Maltz himself. "If the term 'weapon' seems crude, remember the struggle is grim," Sillen told the assembly. Applause swept the auditorium when the critic proclaimed that Lawson, Trumbo, and Maltz represented "the advance consciousness of the artist."

Press reports on the Maltz controversy began appearing even before it had run its course: this was how the Party regimented its artists, remarked news accounts; Maltz had shamelessly sacrificed his intellectual integrity by giving in to the pressure. "Maltz's (retraction) casts pathetic light on the Communist psychology of confession," wrote Arthur Schlesinger Jr. in *Life*. History books tell and retell the story; it has become a classic symbol of party intolerance.

Why did Maltz switch his position? For a "combination of emotional and intellectual" reasons, he says. "After reading some of the things that others said about the first article, I felt that by God there *were* things that I didn't put right or omitted or I might have done differently. And I am not someone who has considered himself all-wise, and anything I've ever said I've got to stay with—I think that's a stupid position...But what intervened between the first article and the second article, more important than anything said, were my emotions in the face of these attacks...At that point in my life, I felt that the Communist movement represented that force in the United States—and internationally—which was the best hope of humanity...I felt that I was, let's say, a better human being for joining hand-in-hand with those people in our country and internationally who were willing to make sacrifices for humanity, for its welfare...I didn't want to be *separated* from this Movement and all that I held dear. By accident, this article of mine came at a particular time of crisis in the American Communist movement. It was when it changed from the Browder policy it had been following back into a policy of saying 'Yes, there is a class struggle in the United States.' And at a meeting, I think, of the central committee of the

Communist Party, seeking to find examples of Browderism, a spokesman in the Party council said 'This article is.' So it took upon itself a freight of importance that it really didn't have. And that put me on the spot; if I had stood by that article, I would have been expelled.

"You know," he continues, "there was this terrible word, 'renegade.' It was a word for someone who turned against something good. And see, there was this fact, and this is very important—a great many of the people who left the Communist movement over those years were not just, say, seekers after truth who couldn't stand what they had found within it. Now such a man, I believe, was (Arthur) Koestler—when he left it, I believe he *was* seeking after truth. But a lot of them turned up, within a fairly short period of time, as arch-reactionaries. People like Benjamin Gitlow and Isaac Don Levine who became, you know, the Hearst press columnists, the testifiers before HUAC, the FBI informers....One had seen so many people who left the Communist movement and turned up as hatchet men for reaction. So many 'renegades.' That's why it was a word one didn't want to be associated with."

*****

Several months after the U.S. detonated atomic bombs over Hiroshima and Nagasaki, Warner Brothers asked Maltz and screenwriter Ring Lardner Jr. to work on a story about nuclear espionage.* The specter of "the Bomb" had begun to haunt the United States' post-war dreams. Maltz was supplied with story materials and technical advice by the Office of Strategic Services (OSS); the movie was to dramatize the spy agency's successful efforts to smuggle nuclear physicists out of Europe during the war. Maltz was not particularly excited by the way the project turned out, and his memory of the job is vague. Though Fritz Lang directed it, the picture comes across as a fairly hum-drum diversion. One of the few noteworthy

---

*The two screenwriters apparently went about their business independently of one another, for Maltz does not recall working directly with Lardner on the project.

aspects of the film is its attitude toward nuclear weapons.

In an opening scene, university physicist Alvah Jesper (Gary Cooper) is asked by the OSS to help them learn how far the Nazis have progressed on atomic energy research. Jesper finally agrees to do it, but only after he delivers a speech bitterly condemning the militarization of science: "For the first time thousands of Allied scientists are working together—to make what? A bomb! But who was willing to finance science *before* the war—to wipe out tuberculosis? When are we going to be given a billion dollars to wipe out cancer? I tell you we could do it in a year."

Later, in the final days of the war, Jesper and a squad of commandos are dropped inside Germany to destroy the Nazis' last atomic plant. To their dismay, they find it has been dismantled and moved to some place on the globe "where the Nazis have a foothold—like Spain or Argentina." "Our secret!" exclaims one commando with harsh irony. "Our ultra, hush-hush absolutely exclusive, super-protected top secret. Peace? There's no peace! It's year one of the Atomic Age and God have mercy on us all!" But Jesper qualifies this gloomy forecast. "No, no," says the scientist. "God have mercy on us only if we're fools. God have mercy on us if we ever thought we could really keep science a secret—or ever wanted to. God have mercy on us if we think we can wage other wars without destroying ourselves. And God have mercy on us if we haven't the sense to keep the world at peace."

Jesper's remarks echoed those of real-life Manhattan Project scientists such as Niels Bohr and Edward U. Condon, who declared it was folly to think the U.S. could maintain a postwar atomic monopoly. By 1946, that kind of statement could get a scientist in trouble with Congresssional investigators. If Jesper had been more than just a figment of Maltz's and Lardner's imaginations, he might have been threatened with a HUAC subpoena. As it happened, Jesper's words of wisdom never reached American movie audiences. The film's entire last reel was inexplicably lopped off by Warner Brothers over Fritz Lang's objections. He assumed the footage was removed, Lang later stated, because not enough time had elapsed since the bombings of Hiroshima and Nagasaki.

Cloak and Dagger, as Warners titled the picture, appeared in truncated form in October 1946. It got no livelier a reception from critics than any other run-of-the-mill spy thriller. Only the Catholic publication, *The Commonweal*, noticed anything exceptional in the film: "I am glad," commented their reviewer, "...that *Cloak and Dagger* makes the point that a destruction-bent society is by no means ready for experiments in atomic energy."

Maltz received one more major Hollywood credit in the postwar period. In March 1947 he was hired by producer Mark Hellinger to rewrite *The Naked City*, a grimy New York murder story. A young model who came to the big city with big dreams is found brutally murdered in her apartment. Homicide cops from the Chelsea station poke about New York's squalid corners to find out who is responsible.

This essentially was the tale, but Maltz gave it some interesting shading; the movie emphasizes the painstaking and methodical character of police work. As a young detective diligently pounds the pavements in search of clues, the film narration comments wryly: "You go home, you go to bed, you get up—you start all over. 'Mister, ever see a man who looks like this?' "

Environment plays a major role in the picture. How did their daughter get mixed up in such a wild side of the city, wonder the murder victim's heartbroken parents. "It was my fault," decides the father, a poor gardener. "When she was fifteen she was working already—in a five and ten cent store. Depression. Oh, it was hard."

The city itself dominates the story. The movie opens up with a montage of Manhattan at night—a silent building in which a scrubwoman sighs, "Sometimes I think this world is made up of nothing but dirty feet;" the city room of a metropolitan daily during the graveyard shift; a factory where we are asked by the soundtrack, "Do the machines in a factory ever need rest?" Model Jean Dexter loses her life in the dead of night, but the rest of the city continues to go about its business. The point of view is tough, urban, and impersonal. By the next day's evening edition, Dexter has become nothing more than titillating news copy. Over shots of subway commuters riveted to their newspapers, the narration remarks: "The day's work is over now. People are on their way home. They're tired, they're hot, they're hungry...but they're on their way home. In the paper there's a new murder story—full layout with pictures. It helps to while away the time if you live in Jackson Heights." Even in its closing lines, the movie constantly reminds us of the enormity and impassivity of the city: "There are 8 million stories in the Naked City. This has been one of them."

The Naked City won critical acclaim for its hard-bitten style and it's on-the-spot New York camerawork. "(It) may at times remind you of yellow journalism," declared one reviewer, "but it is also a fascinating portrayal of life in the big city—when its glamor has been stripped away." The film inspired a wave of "authentic" crime pictures and, ultimately, a television series. It is one of the few pictures Maltz worked on that he still enjoys watching.

Maltz says he wrote one "real propaganda movie" in the postwar years, a fifteen minute plea for racial and religious tolerance called *The House I Live In.* The production, which took its title from a song originally made popular by Paul Robeson, was launched during a dinner party by director Mervyn Leroy and his guests—Maltz, singer Frank Sinatra, and producer Frank Ross. In those days Sinatra had a reputation for being a vehement opponent of prejudice. He lectured against it on the high school circuit; he changed song lyrics if he felt they were offensive to blacks; once while he was with the Dorsey band, he punched someone on the jaw for making an anti-Semitic remark. At Leroy's dinner party, the young singer suggested it would be a good idea to make a film about discrimination and he offered to play the leading role. Ross promptly agreed to produce the film. Leroy promised to direct, and Maltz said that he would write the script. The next morning, Ross came up with the basic idea for the film, and Maltz proceeded to develop it.

The movie was brief and to the point. Sinatra steps outside a recording studio for a breath of fresh air and spots a group of kids chasing a small boy because he's "got a different religion." Taking charge, the singer convinces them that discrimination is all wrong: "Don't you get what I'm telling you? Religion doesn't make any real difference, except to a Nazi or a dope...My father came from Italy. But I'm an American, and should I hate your father, Tommy, because he came from Ireland or France or Russia? Wouldn't I be a fathead?" Sinatra caps off his lecture by singing the tender and democratic title tune: "What's America to me?..It's the house I live in, a plot of earth, a street/ the grocer and the butcher and the people that I meet/ The children in the playground, the faces that I see/ All races and religions—that's America to me!"

The House I Live In was composed by the left wing songwriters Earl Robinson and Lewis Allan. Robinson, creator of songs like "Joe Hill," "Ballad for Americans," and "Lonesome Train," had pioneered in the crossbreeding of politics and folk music. Allan was the composer of a haunting Billie Holiday song about a Southern lynching ("Strange Fruit"), and a scenarist at Columbia Pictures, where he dreamed of making relevant musicals. (Allan, whose real name is Abel Meeropol, and his wife Anne later adopted the sons of Julius and Ethel Rosenberg.)

To some, bobbysox idol Sinatra must have seemed a peculiar choice to sing and dramatize a "people's song" like *The House I Live In*. But Robinson thought Frankie worked out just fine. "He isn't a folk singer of course," the songwriter told the *Daily People's World*, "—the best way to describe him is that he sings for folks—he sings the way the average guy wishes he could sing, not with vocal tricks, but natural, with a warm expression of how people feel."

RKO released the short in fall 1945; profits went to various worthy causes. It was awarded a special Oscar by the Motion Picture Academy. "It then played in high schools and elementary schools all over the United States for years and years," Maltz says. "I used to meet kids who had seen it. It played to millions." Why did the studio back the nonprofit pitch for equality? "That was the temper of the times," replies the writer.

*****

In the months that immediately followed World War II, Communists and non-Communists generally continued to co-exist quite nicely in Hollywood. The card-carrying rubbed elbows with the uncommitted at the Actors Lab and in film classes at the People's Educational Center. Communist scenarists went on playing an active role in the leadership of the Screen Writers Guild. In October 1945, the Hollywood Writers Mobilization and UCLA began jointly publishing the *Hollywood Quarterly*, the film capital's first scholarly journal on mass media. The *Quarterly*, which campaigned against the commercialization of film, radio, and television, was edited by the prominent Hollywood Communist, John Howard Lawson, and several UCLA professors. Contributors ranged from CP screenwriters to artistically inclined film technicians to university psychologists. This period afforded the Communist movement in Hollywood its highest status ever.

Maltz's screenwriting career was also at its peak; three box office hits had made him a hot Hollywood property. His experience in the industry had been very gratifying: 'First, almost exclusively, I had very interesting material to work with. Secondly, I had good people to work with. And third, everything I did was immediately produced. Three marvelous ingredients."

But by 1948, nothing with Maltz's name on it could get filmed in Hollywood; and all traces of the organized left in the movie community were being thoroughly wiped out. The screenwriter's record of wartime successes did not shield him; the Party's patriotic performance during the war was disregarded. The political current turned against the Hollywood left with a vengeance.

Throughout the war, anti-communists had kept a steady watch over Hollywood. California State Senator Jack B. Tenney sounded a loud alarm in fall 1943 when he learned that the Hollywood Writers Mobilization was going to hold a Writers Congress on the UCLA campus. Tenney, chairman of the state's Fact-Finding Committee on Un-American Activities, labeled the conference "Communist inspired" and demanded that university officials cancel it. In February 1944, anti-communist film figures—including Sam Wood, Walt Disney, Victor Fleming, James K. McGuiness, Rupert Hughes, and Morrie Ryskind—banded together to form the Motion Picture Alliance for the Preservation of American Ideals. The group vowed to protect the screen from those "totalitarian minded" people who sought to use it as "an instrument for the dissemination of un-American ideas and beliefs." But the momentum was not yet on the anti-communists' side. Tenney could not stop the Writers Congress from taking place as scheduled at UCLA; nor could he prevent Franklin D. Roosevelt from sending the conference his presidential greetings. The Motion Picture Alliance failed to win the industry's endorsement. *Variety* challenged the Alliance to prove that Hollywood was indeed rife with subversives. Thirty-eight talent, labor, and producer groups issued a joint statement which repudiated the Alliance's "unwarranted, unprincipled, and vicious attacks" on the film industry.

The years 1946-47 were pivotal ones for anti-communism in America. As the U.S.-Soviet wartime pact fell apart, the government grew increasingly intolerant of the domestic left. In September 1946, FBI director J. Edgar Hoover delivered a widely publicized address on "the growing menace of Communism in the United States." Soon afterwards, newly designated HUAC chairman, J. Parnell Thomas, announced that his Committee would "expose and ferret out" all Communists who occupied positions of influence in American life. In May 1947, President Truman gave the campaign against communism his executive approval by instituting a loyalty program for all federal employees.

The hunt for Hollywood Reds took on a political significance it never had before. *Hollywood Reporter* publisher, Billy Wilkerson, began using his front page column on a regular basis to excoriate movieland communism. Wilkerson's primary target was the Screen Writers Guild, which he correctly identified as the stronghold of the left in Hollywood. He caricatured left screenwriters as Soviet operatives who were told what to write and how to vote on guild issues. He published the names of scenarists whom he considered troublemakers and asked if they held Communist Party cards No. 46805, No. 25113, and No. 46802. He suggested the blacklist as a practical means of eliminating Communist influence in Hollywood.

In late 1946, John Howard Lawson was forced off the editorial board of the *Hollywood Quarterly*. "I was called into the office of (UCLA provost) Clarence Dykstra," remembered Lawson in a 1973 interview, "...and with great regret and with apologies, he told me that he had been told that he had to either drop the *Hollywood Quarterly*, to sever all relations between it and the University, or else I had to resign as one of the editors. 'Well,' I said, 'I don't want to hurt the magazine, so I'll resign.' "

In March 1947, Motion Picture Association president, Eric Johnston, went before two different congressional committees to denounce communists and assure the federal legislators that Hollywood was on guard against subversion. Later, after returning to Los Angeles, Johnston urged screenwriters to fall into line. "I want to see it become a joke to be a Communist in America," he told a special Screen Writers Guild meeting. "I want it to be fashionable to radiate conviction and pride in our democratic capitalism."

The pressure mounted steadily. In May 1947, a HUAC subcommitte headed by Chairman Thomas arrived in Hollywood to conduct a preliminary investigation of the film industry. "Scores of screenwriters who are Communists have infiltrated into various studios," the Committee later reported, "and it has been through this medium that most of the Communist propaganda has been injected into the movies." The FDR Administration, added the HUAC report, was responsible for encouraging Hollywood to produce Communist propaganda films during the war. A few days after releasing its preliminary report, HUAC announced it would hold a major public hearing in the fall.

The Hollywood left battled passionately to save itself: there were "counter attack" forums to protest "the plot against free expression;" there were letter writing campaigns against anti-communist movies; a boycott of the *Hollywood Reporter* was attempted. Film industry communists strove mightily to preserve their old wartime coalition with New Deal liberals. In the summer of 1947, the Hollywood chapter of the Progressive citizens of America, the organizational base of presidential aspirant Henry Wallace, held a five-day conference on "thought control" at the Beverly Hills Hotel. The conference, which included Communists as well as liberal Wallace-ites among its speakers, resolved that "it is immaterial whether we agree with the views or politics of those being prosecuted (by HUAC)—no progressive citizen is safe. Their defense is our own first line of defense."

Maltz was among those at the conference who denounced HUAC's harassment of writers and intellectuals. "What a loathsome spectacle in our national life," he exclaimed, "when individuals who are the political scum of our nation are seated in Congress, and when they are given the power to intimidate decent citizens!" Two months later, the Committee summoned the men who were to be its chief exhibits in its case against Hollywood. Among those served with bright pink subpoenas was Albert Maltz. "When the subpoena came in September, I was completely surprised," says Maltz. "As soon as we got the subpoenas, we knew it was serious. Because no such thing had happened before."

Maltz represented exactly what the Committee most despised; here was a man who moved with ease between the Communist subculture and the commercial setting of Hollywood. He had produced vehement works of fiction about social suffering and class conflict and he had written exciting Hollywood spectacles about love and war. The fact that HUAC investigators had failed to turn up any conclusive examples of communist propaganda in his scripts made no difference. It was the very idea that an ardent leftist like Maltz could make it in the popular field which unnerved the Committee. "They were trying to drive into ratholes everybody whose politics they didn't like," Maltz says.

What Maltz's scripts *were* laced with were Rooseveltian visions; they advocated democratic rights, economic security, religious freedom, world peace. During the war these dreams had stirred the nation. But HUAC was intent on branding New Deal thought subversive. "HUAC was made up of highly conscious political people of the right," comments Maltz. "And their general attitude, I would say, would be semi-fascist, and if there were a fascist government in the United States, fully fascist. Because bear in mind, here you had an outfit that had considered Roosevelt a fellow traveler of the Communist Party—this was the mentality that you were dealing with. They said it, I'm not inventing it. This was said by Parnell Thomas, who was chairman of the Committee."

HUAC opened its hearings on Communist infiltration of Hollywood with great fanfare on October 20, 1947. Maltz and the other "unfriendly" witnesses called to testify in Washington had made a bold decision. They would challenge the Committee's very right to exist by refusing to answer any questions put to them about their political beliefs and associations. "Although none of us had asked for a subpoena," says Maltz, "when we were hit with it we had to respond. The question was, well, *how* were we going to respond. And the suggestion arose—I don't know from where—that we had a chance, if we wanted to take a stand on the First Amendment, of destroying this Committee. Now the only way you could destroy this Committee legally was by challenging its right to haul individuals before it and ask them questions about their politics or their political associations. Because then the Committee would hold persons who did that in contempt, and you'd have to go to court. But you'd get the Committee into court with you. Now with the Committee in the courts, it was the analysis of our lawyers...that if we took the proper Constitutional position we'd lose in the lower court without any question because the jury would be made out of government workers; we'd lose probably in the appellate court as then constituted; but in the Supreme court, as then constituted, we would win—by a 5-4 or 6-3 majority. With that, not only HUAC but every other such committee which operated by hauling people before it and exposing them—not for crimes but for opinions or associations—all of them would be out of business. And it is my belief—strong belief—that there would've been no McCarthyite period at all if we had won our case."

One by one, each member of the Hollywood Ten positioned himself before the newsreel cameras and exchanged fire with the Committee. By happenstance, Maltz was the only one who managed to deliver a preliminary statement without being abruptly cut off. "The American people are going to have to choose between the Bill of Rights and the Thomas Committee," he warned. "They cannot have both. One or the other must be abolished in the immediate future." The Committee's questions came in quick succession: "Are you a member of the Screen Writers Guild? ...Are you now or have you ever been a member of the Communist Party?" "Next you are going to ask me what religious group I belong to," Maltz shot back. Their questions violated his Constitutional rights, he advised the Committeemen. "Typical Communist line," retorted Chairman Thomas, and the witness was dismissed.

Their plan to jam the Committee's gears required the Ten to be defiant and uncooperative during their interrogation. But why did they continue to conceal their political views outside the Committee chambers? "Now what would have been the effect on the public at large," Maltz says, "if someone had gotten up on the stand and said, 'I won't answer the questions;' and then in the hall outside he would say, 'I am a member of the Communist Party' or 'I am not a member of the Communist Party, but this Committee doesn't have the right to ask me.' The Committee then would subpoena you right back in, which they could do, and say, 'Did you say in the hall so-and-so?'—'Yes, I did say that in the hall.'—'Alright, now we ask you: Are you a member of the Communist Party?'—And again, 'I refuse to answer the question because you have no right to ask it.' I think, or we thought, the public would say, 'What the hell kind of games are they playing? What kind of nonsense is this? If they say it in the hall to reporters, why can't they say it to Congress?' This was our judgement on it. I still think it was right. It would have been utterly confusing."

As Maltz and the others had anticipated, Congress quickly cited them for contempt and turned them over to federal authorities for prosecution. The New York financiers and corporate executives who were the ruling powers behind the film industry took this as their cue. Soon after contempt citations were voted, the studios issued a decree which banished the defiant ten from Hollywood: 'We will forthwith discharge or suspend without compensation those in our employ, and we will not re-employ any of the ten until such time as he is acquitted, or has purged himself of contempt, and declared under oath that he is not a Communist." Here was a twist the Ten had not foreseen; they had taken industry spokesman Eric Johnston at his word when he vowed on the eve of the hearings: "There'll never be a blacklist. We're not going totalitarian to please this committee."

"We knew that we might go to jail," Maltz remarks. "That was the gamble we were taking, but we thought that we were going to win at that time. What we *didn't* know was that we were going to be blacklisted. And what we certainly didn't know was that five of our number, who were contract writers, would have this holy of holies in capitalist society—a contract—torn up by the studios who said, 'Screw you—sue us.'...That was a blow we had not expected. For the industry to turn on us...All of a sudden we were out."

The final blow landed in the summer of 1949, as the Ten waited to hear whether the Supreme Court would review their contempt convictions. As expected, they had lost their case in both the District Court in Washington and the appellate court; all hope now rested on a favorable high court decision. But that summer, Justice Frank Murphy and Justice Wiley Rutledge—the two youngest and most liberal men on the bench—died within a few months of each other. The political make-up of the court changed and the Ten's appeal to be heard was turned down.

There was no holding back the Committee now. Nine months after the Ten were packed off to various federal prisons around the country, HUAC staged a Hollywood investigation more massive and malicious than its 1947 probe. Ninety industry figures were called to the witness dock this time; the names of 324 people were entered into the record as suspected Communists. More than half of those subpoenaed stood firm and fended off the Committee's questions by invoking the Fifth Amendment. But there were also many disheartening defections during the new round of hearings.

In April 1951, director Edward Dmytryk, one of the Ten, returned to Washington and told the Committee exactly what it wanted to hear. He named close friends as Communists; he denounced fellow members of the Ten for following the Party line; he labeled the CP "conspiratorial, subversive and even in certain cases treasonable." New developments like the Korean War, explained the director, had altered his political outlook. Maltz, who had served time with Dmytryk at the Mill Point Prison Camp in West Virginia, was stung by the betrayal. "The truth about Dmytryk is simple and ugly," Maltz wrote in an angry open letter which was published in the *Hollywood Reporter*. "He believed in certain principles, no doubt very sincerely, until the consequences of those beliefs became painful. He has not now made a peace with his conscience, he has made it with his pocket book and his career."

The following year, Michael Blankfort, one of Maltz's dearest friends, also went before the Committee and renounced his past. Blankfort and Maltz had known each other since the early thirties, when they were both rising stars in New York's left wing cultural circles. Maltz dedicated his first novel, in part, to the other writer. Not long after Blankfort made a successful transition to screenwriting, Maltz joined him in Hollywood. In his testimony before the Committee, Blankfort declared he had only written reviews for the *Daily Worker* and the *New Masses* in order to grab some free books and theater tickets. He was "shocked" when he learned that groups he once belonged to were riddled with Communists and he vowed that we would never again join "an organization that (has) been called subversive." As for the Hollywood Ten, whose First Amendment stand he had once defended, he now believed "they were wrong in taking the attitude they did." The Committee was only trying to do its duty by probing communism in Hollywood, he agreed.

By the time Blankfort concluded his testimony that day, his relationship with Maltz was over. Ever since then, Maltz has refused to speak to him. "He has tried many times to see me," says Maltz. "I have contempt for him. And you know, apropos of this—because it involves the whole question of the behavior of these people—I have a phrase that is very important to me, and that is: To understand all is not to forgive all."

*****

Maltz was blacklisted by the film industry from 1947 to 1964. During those seventeen years, two of his movies were produced but neither of them carried his name. He declines to reveal the title of one picture "because someone else put his name on it and I can't speak about it." All he will say is that it was produced by an independent company and was "enormously successful." The second picture was *The Robe*, a Bible-era epic based on the best-selling novel by Lloyd C. Douglas. Filmed in stupefying CinemaScope, the movie proved to be a major moneymaker for 20th Century-Fox. But the studio did not see fit to acknowledge Maltz's participation in the project.

Maltz wrote the original version of the script before the blacklist, but production was delayed for several years. In

1951, producer Frank Ross journeyed to Cuernavaca, where Maltz had moved after leaving prison, to make a special request of the screenwriter: "Ross, who is a very nice man, came down to Mexico and said that 20th was ready to go ahead with *The Robe*, but only if I would take my name off it. And he hoped I wouldn't stand in his way, getting this thing made, which had meant so much to him. And it had. He had worked very hard." Maltz agreed to give up his credit and when the picture appeared it carried the name of screenwriter Philip Dunne, who had written a revised version of the script. Dunne, who did not learn about Maltz's involvement until years later, had been told the screenplay was a crazy-quilt made from the pieces of many different scripts.

The blacklist was an astonishingly extensive system. On March 14, 1949, 20th Century-Fox announced it had purchased the screen rights to a forthcoming Maltz novel called *The Journey of Simon McKeever*. Walter Huston was going to play the lead; Jules Dassin was slated to direct. Two weeks later, the studio suddenly terminated the project. Not only were scripts with Maltz's name to be banned in Hollywood; his books were also forbidden material. Even Maltz's ability to publish fiction was impaired by the blacklist. In 1953, the State Department removed books by Maltz and more than forty other authors from its overseas libraries. Many public libraries around the country promptly followed the government's lead. The following year, Maltz submitted a new novel to seventeen different U.S. publishing houses and received rejections from every one—the first set of rejections in his publishing career. The author received sixteen foreign contracts for the same novel. During the rest of the fifties, Maltz could only find publishers for his fiction outside of his own country.

No blacklisted Hollywood writer thrived in the underground, Maltz declares. "I might explain something about the blacklist. There's a general myth that writers just went right on writing under other names and everything was hunky-dory. That's *completely* erroneous. When the new rounds of Hollywood hearings occurred, starting in '51 and then '52 and '53, the major studios had *nobody* writing for them who was on the blacklist. They clamped down absolutely tight. They had an exchange of lists—although they denied it because that would have been a conspiracy. And since there was a central payroll place, nobody could be hired and nobody got work. But there were certain independents from whom people could get some work. And there might be certain producers who might hire somebody, but they would also have a script being prepared by somebody outside. So there was *some* work for *some* of the people, but for most it was terrible going. For instance, there were two friends of mine who wrote some of the most brilliant Abbott and Costello movies. One has been a salesman ever since. The other one was a maitre d' in a hotel, and then he came back and drove a taxi. His wife opened a shop. Then he was able to catch on and do a little TV work under other names, he had about five different names. The two men who wrote *The Defiant Ones* also had to make new lives for themselves. Ned Young worked for years as a bartender in the Windsor restaurant downtown. Hal Smith ran a commercial fishing boat out of San Pedro for years. This is what happened to the great majority of people. It just isn't so that they went merrily on writing. It isn't so at all."

*****

Maltz is often cited nowadays as one of the few blacklist victims who made a successful come-back in the film industry. But actually his movie career since his return from Mexico in 1962 has been filled with frustrations. Most of what he has written for the screen in recent years has not been produced. His only post-blacklist screenplay credit to date is the Clint Eastwood-Shirley MacLaine Western, *Two Mules for Sister Sara* (1970), which Maltz says, "was badly directed and came off indifferently." He was so disappointed with the way Universal produced another of his movies, *The Beguiled* (1971), that he took his name off it. In 1975, he wrote a television film about the blacklist called *Witchhunt*, but NBC canceled the project after CBS' "Fear on Trial," the story of blacklisted radio personality John Henry Faulk, flopped in the ratings.

However, Maltz continues to write both fiction and film. In recent years he has published his second volume of short stories, *Afternoon in the Jungle*, and has continued work on a long novel. Currently he has a screenplay on the market, *The Lovers*, based on the life of Modigliani, and another almost completed. Once again there are plans to turn his novel, *The Journey of Simon McKeever*, into a dramatic feature.

Nowadays he declines most invitations to make speeches and all suggestions that he become active in organizations. He wants all of his working time to go to writing. But he still strongly believes in the social visions for which he once actively fought. "Individuals retire sooner or later from social controversy and combat," Maltz stated at a 1974 ACLU banquet which honored the Hollywood Ten. "Nevertheless, there is no necessary mortality for the principles and goals they cherished." The issues which were at the heart of the Hollywood Ten conflict are just as pressing now as they were then, Maltz told the gathering. "The case of the Hollywood Ten can now be seen as one of many thousands of social struggles that began at least as early as the arrest of newspaper editors in the 1790s for alleged violation of the Alien and Sedition Laws. All societies are always in flux, changing economically, politically, culturally. And in all modern societies that I know anything about there has been, there is, and there will be, a constant struggle between those forces and interests that try to suppress the liberties of individuals and those that try to defend and expand them."

Through tributes, memoirs, movies, and time, the good names of the Hollywood Ten and HUAC's other show business enemies have finally been restored. Once mercilessly excoriated, they now are honored for having stood up for what they believed while so many others sat by. The blacklist is no more; but its imprint on Hollywood, even at this late date, has not altogether faded. It is there in the conspicuous absence of an industry-wide community of leftists; it is visible in the quiescent policies of the guilds and unions. And it is apparent in the gap between Maltz's generation of Hollywood leftists and the latest generation.

Maltz is surprised when we tell him that there are many young socially concerned film workers in Hollywood today: "It interests me very much that you say there are left wing people here who want to accomplish something—I haven't known any of them. I'm sure it would be refreshing to meet some of them." Political activism in the entertainment industry skipped a long beat because of the blacklist. As a result of the interruption, old blacklistees know little about those who are continuing their fight. And Hollywood's young leftists have only a vague understanding of their legacy.

"If there had been a continuing movement..." muses the writer. "If, for instance, the Communist Party had remained one that was of interest to younger people, then there would have been continuity. People would have been given literature about earlier periods. I know that when I first came around the left in the thirties, I'd never heard of Mother Jones, for instance. Or certainly not of Big Bill Haywood. But I read their books and found them very instructive. And so it could be. But...anyway...the striving for human brotherhood will never cease."

Abraham Polonsky

Of all the Marxists who came to Hollywood before the blacklist, it has been said, Abraham Polonsky was the most successful in giving full expression to his political views. The scripts for his three postwar pictures—*Body and Soul, Force of Evil, I Can Get It for You Wholesale*—examine the agony of the capitalist myth of success. They show characters who have so completely given themselves to money and ambition that they become contemptible to those closest to them and ultimately to themselves. Polonsky's postwar film work won immediate acclaim in Europe, not only for its powerful social perspective but its distinctive cinematic style. *Force of Evil*, which Polonsky directed as well as coauthored, was singled out by British and French critics as a major screen achievement—one of the leading examples of what became known as *film noir*. Much later, after years of relative obscurity, the film was elevated to the same status in the United States. By then, Polonsky was blacklisted.

Once, as a grim joke, it was pointed out to Polonsky by a film historian that he was the only blacklistee who was "justifiably" banished from Hollywood. In a sense, this is an accurate observation. It was the House Un-American Activities Committee's express purpose to remove those film artists from the motion picture industry who were responsible for making pictures which were radically critical of "the American way of life" (translate to read "the prevailing social order"). And indeed there is embedded within Polonsky's movies a profound critique of the private enterprise system—a critique which goes far deeper than the social uneasiness in Hollywood's so-called "message pictures."

As far as he was concerned, says Polonsky, it was never a question of inserting bits of social commentary into his scripts to give them social meaning. "Someone once asked me, 'How do you take up the question of content?' I *never* take up the question of content. I don't ask myself, 'Now what are the social issues I have to realize here?' There's a Marxian world view behind my films, not because I plan it that way. That's what I am."

This was not the case with all left wing screenwriters in the 1930s and 40s. Some acted with more self-conscious determination. "It's true," he says, "there were people out here at that time who became members of the left wing or even members of the Communist Party. They had acted but not as yet acted out the philosophical consequences of self-change. They were radicalized but not radicals. They may have to say, 'Wait! I ought to get a little more content in.' There was a lot of that going on out here. Because if social consciousness is abstract, if their social consciousness is a determination on their part to be effective social citizens—and not yet their idea of the nature of things, then they will have to keep reminding themselves of what their style, their subjects, their sentences really mean."

By the time Polonsky came to Hollywood in the mid-forties, however, his political beliefs were part of his personal identity. He had lived his life "having things happen to me, trying to make things happen, enjoying it if I could, and trying to when I couldn't, fascinated by the rush of things and frightened by the fragility of belief. A Marxist of sorts, a writer one way or another, and committed to social change, that is, the liberation of what is suppressed by custom, cruelty, and bad literary habits."

Years of living had prepared him for what would turn out to be a highly creative—and abbreviated—tenure in postwar Hollywood.

It was during his undergraduate years at City College of New York in the first stage of the Depression that Polonsky became ambiguously involved with the Communist Party. It was all part of a natural progression. Polonsky had been raised in a socialist Jewish milieu. Political consciousness grew in him as part of his growing awareness of life. Some of his earliest and most vivid childhood memories are of political events. He recalls the roundup of left wing dissidents ordered by Attorney General A. Mitchell Palmer in 1919. "Remember, D'Artagnan is upstairs, the soldiers raid below. They leave all doors and windows open. The whole place is abandoned to the world. I saw a Palmer raid. They raided an Italian anarchist's house. The federal detectives went right in, blew the whole thing open, arrested some people and went right out. I remember a girl coming home—she didn't know where her parents were."

He recalls being taken to parades by his father, a pharmacist and a socialist who had emigrated from Russia. "We would go to the funerals of the socialist dead. All these people marching down the street. This isn't an official parade on Fifth Avenue. How could we go there? He's dead and he's a socialist." In his father's library were books by Marx and others who wrote of the historical mission of the proletariat—books in Russian, German, Yiddish, English. His father spoke seven languages. "I'm not *reading* these books as a child," says Polonsky. "What I'm doing is getting it by a process of osmosis and dust. I used to dust the books. I loved the illustrations. Especially, *Pathogenic Micro-organisms*. My favorite."

There were others in Polonsky's family circle who shared his father's views. His father's sister attended medical school in the United States and returned to Russia after the revolution in order to help out there. "So you see," says Polonsky, "socialism is not a strange idea (in my particular environment). The same is true for a lot of New York Jews. Socialism is a philosophical bias that educated people have one way or another about this complicated problem called history and life...I mean, the attitude was, what civilized person is not a socialist?"

Because of his childhood experiences, says Polonsky, it did not seem extraordinary to him when he came in contact with Communist Party activities in college. Communists turned out to be "the very same people you knew before—only now they're Communists...So it wasn't a mystery to me. I wasn't a college student who found 'a brand new world.' Karl Marx? I'd heard of Karl Marx, Jesus Christ, and my other relatives in the Bronx Zoo at the same time."

City College in the 1930s was a center of political and cultural ferment. During Polonsky's undergraduate years, there were continual battles between the student body and the college administration over issues such as free speech, ROTC training, and faculty firings. Frederick B. Robinson, the college's reactionary president, regularly suspended student activists for challenging his ban against on-campus political activity. One of the principal targets of Robinson's repressive measures was the Social Problems Club, a radical organization whose members included Joseph Starobin, Adam Lapin and other future editors of the Communist Party press. Student discontent over the Robinson administration's policies culminated in a campus-wide strike in winter 1933.

All this activity earned City College a reputation for being a "hotbed" of radicalism. A New York City judge commented from his bench that "this institution is supported by over-burdened taxpayers to largely inculcate into the majority of its students the doctrines of communism..." "The student body was poor and smart," says Polonsky. "They were without jobs, caught in the depths of the Depression, going to City College because it was *free*. Everybody wanted to go there. There was nowhere else to go. The student body *is* radicalized, in the sense that they'll try anything because there's nothing else for them to do. They actually only want to get ahead. Their major ambition was at that time—to get a job in the civil service! That meant security. Preferably as a teacher."

Polonsky was part of an intellectual set at City College which included Paul Goodman and Leonard Boudin. All three belonged to the campus literary society, Clionia, and revived its literary magazine, *Lavender*. "I was more interested in aesthetics than politics, but radical disbelief was in all of us."

Polonsky and his literary associates were bright, well-read, and thought very highly of themselves. They were aware of the left wing cultural movement which was developing in New York at that time. They knew the work being done by "proletarian writers." At the same time, Polonsky and his friends considered these works to be considerably below the aesthetic standards they had set for themselves. They fully believed that they were capable of achieving literary careers; it was only a matter of time. Meanwhile, they filled in with "intellectual fever, intellectual snobbery, radical self-esteem and the deep respect for Professor Morris Raphael Cohen, and his hard thinking questioning of easy, overall solutions."

Polonsky's attitude toward movies at this point in his life was typical of most left wing intelletuals. The only "serious" films, in his opinion, were those from Russia. He loved Hollywood movies, says Polonsky. "But my general impression of Hollywood is the same I have of Tin Pan Alley—it's music, but is it art?...Art is *Fine* Art." As a socialist, Polonsky says, he knew that popular culture was *sociologically* significant. "But I didn't think it meant anything (artistically). It's in fact dying as it is born. Whereas the stuff we're finding in and out of college seems much more important." Their analytical efforts were reserved for "serious" art. "We are then saying things like, 'That's a socially aware picture.' Those words are used. But no one would be so trivial as to take them seriously. Because the most socially aware film is nowhere near the level of literature. True stories of how real people live save us from despair. Art, no matter how tragic, liberates all those hopes that make us human. By fine art we, of course, meant a commitment to ultimates in meaning and expression. Later I discovered that talent and self-esteem were survival factors in all compromised situations such as politics and the popular art forms. Nevertheless, in the end it didn't matter. Just as the philosopher could see the universe in a grain of sand, the critic might find an artist in a lump of Kitsch. Or at least he could pretend to. Anyway, very high hopes of the artist for himself should be a private concern.

"Fundamentally," Polonsky declares, "I thought all Hollywood films were lies. I can see that some are more useful than others, as is the case with politicians. When I listen to Franklin Roosevelt, whom I think highly of, I know I don't agree with him. I mean all the way. But just the same, I'm glad he's around."

The Marxists in Polonsky's post-collegiate circle prided themselves on their intellects and their independent spirit. Though some were members of the Communist Party, they did not feel bound automatically to accept its political and cultural formulations. Like nearly all political organizations, the CP bureaucracy was largely composed of unimaginative functionaries * and, says Polonsky, there was "a constant tendency" on their part to "mold members in." Nonetheless,

---

*The more restricted a person is intellectually," says Polonsky, "—the more conventional a Marxist of the period he is—the higher he will probably be in the Party and the more power he will have. Although it must be said that the Party at all levels is full of people

he declares, there was a certain degree of intellectual autonomy in the lower echelons of the Party, a certain independent
life which flourished in spite of the organization's bureaucratic will. The particular Marxist discussion groups which he
belonged to during his undergraduate years at City College
and afterwards, were, according to Polonsky, "full of wild
individualists." In the course of these groups' debates about
proletarian culture, the relation between intellectuals and the
working class, and current artistic developments, the Party's
cultural ideologues would be quoted. "But," says Polonsky,
"the more talented the discussions, the less relevance they
had."

While Polonsky strove to maintain a healthy critical
distance from the Party, he never doubted it stood at the
center of the movement for social change. "The heart of the
left wing movement is the Communist Party," he says. "It ties
it all together. And even when you disagree with it, you know
it forms the spine. Because it can deliver the forces when
action is required. No other party can deliver the forces. It is
the only radical party that can show up with some people
someplace when you need it. Or many if it's really necessary.
Because they have the people who work...There's an enormous amount of dedication on the part of certain people,
certain groups and so on. This has a tremendous effect, an
effect way out of line with the numbers involved—as in all
historical movements."

After graduating from City College, Polonsky enrolled in
Columbia Law School. "I enjoyed the philosophy of law," he
remarks. But not, as he later found out, the practice of it.
Polonsky paid his way through law school by teaching night

------

with flexible minds. And so real maverick thinkers can sometimes
squeeze into important positions. Because the same thing happens
within the Communist Party that happens in any party which has
size—there's a strong center, and there's a left and right. And then
there are always certain individuals who have great confidence in
themselves as human beings—because they have talent or whatever
else it is—and it enables them to operate with ease. Why can he or
she do that? For personality reasons. The cult of the personality is
universal." (he laughs)

classes in English literature and composition at City College. His primary ambition was still to become a serious writer of fiction. But, in the meantime, there were practical matters, like earning a living.

Upon his graduation from Columbia, the young man went to work for a New York law firm at an extremely modest salary. Among the firm's largest clients was the leading trade assocation of textile dyers and printers. Polonsky was given the unenviable task of defending the association against all minor lawsuits. It was tedious work, and seemed to stretch on forever.

A change appeared in the form of Gertrude Berg, the well-known radio performer. Berg, who was owner, writer, and star of a popular serial called "The Goldbergs," came around one day seeking advice about one of her episodes, which featured a courtroom scene. She and her problem were quickly ushered into the office of young Polonsky, the newest and least important lawyer in the firm. "She comes in,' recalls Polonsky. "She doesn't know anything about me and my literary background, or hopes. To her I'm just some lawyer sitting there. I'm very busy and irritated and I say, 'Well, what do you want to know?' And she tells me. And I call in a secretary and dictate the scene. I'm just unloading this thing. I don't think I'd ever heard of her show at that time...But this is a miracle which has just taken place before her eyes. She takes it home, and they must have used it, because I get a check in the mail for $25, which is more than I make in weeks at the law firm. Just for a few minutes work.

"A law case on a soap opera doesn't stop after just one show. It goes on forever. The next day she still had the problem. She started coming around quite often. And I used to dictate these things, and help her plot out the story a bit. On occasion I met with her at her house; we got along very well. Then the law case was over and that was it."

In 1937, Berg was signed to write a screenplay for a child movie star. She was nervous about coming to Hollywood, so the law firm asked Polonsky to accompany her. "I was supposed to help her in case there were any problems. It was not considered a writing assignment. I got travel expenses for myself and my wife and $75 a week. It was an enormous sum."

This was how Polonsky's first trip to the movie capital came about.

Soon after arriving in Hollywood, Polonsky called up old friends from City College who promptly introduced him to the left wing movie community. The film industry itself still held no particular attraction for Polonsky. But the political community which had grown up around this peculiar industry was, Polonsky says, spirited and intriguing. His most vivid memories of his stay in Hollywood are of mass rallies in support of Loyalist Spain addressed by Ernest Hemingway and Andre Malraux, and a political fundraising party where comedian Ben Blue performed a striptease a la Gypsy Rose Lee.

By the time he returned to New York, Polonsky had come to the decision that he no longer wanted to work as a lawyer. Berg had asked him to become a regular contributor to the radio program she was launching, and Polonsky felt that the income from these writing assignments plus the small sum of money he was making as a teacher at City College would be enough for him and his wife. In between his two jobs, Polonsky went to work on a novel which was so ambitious that neither he nor his publisher could understand it. ("But that means it's good," he quips.)* During this period, Polonsky also continued to be deeply involved in the radical movement in New York. He joined an advanced Marxist study group which amiably called itself "The Super Marxists." The group was made up of left wing professors who taught at City College, New York University, and Columbia—some of whom were later blacklisted during the 1941 Rapp-Coudert hearings on "subversive activities" in the New York City schools (a precursor to the anti-Communist inquisitions of the postwar period.)

---

*The potential publisher for this novel went out of business. According to Polonsky, the book is about "middle class people living in isolation, making fools of themselves intellectually...radicalism... the effect of the Spanish Civil War on people's minds...and the possibility of socialism in an utopian state...All the people who've read it say it's the best book I ever wrote. But then all unpublished books are the best you ever wrote."

These were critical times. Spain had fallen to Franco's army, while the Western democracies stood idly by, and European fascism was growing at an ominous speed. At home there was an urgent campaign to build progressive reforms into the failing capitalist system, and to mobilize the American spirit against the world-wide threat of fascism. Playing a key role in this struggle was the dedicated membership of the Communist Party. The Party's hopes for success rested on the burgeoning strength of organized labor—in particular, the newly founded Congress of Industrial Organizations (CIO). The CIO's drive to organize the country's basic industries was accomplished with the active support of the Communist Party and its sympathizers.

In 1939, Polonsky and his wife moved to Briarcliff, a small town in Westchester County. By then Polonsky was making $300 a week from radio writing. He commuted regularly to the city to fulfill his responsibilities at City College. (Teaching, says Polonsky, is both a "useful" and "enjoyable" relationship to have with people.) Polonsky did not remove himself from politics when he settled in Briarcliff. His new home, says Polonsky, was located near a "red belt" where many Communists lived at the time, and there was constant political activity. As soon as he got there, he was contacted by a local Party leader, who asked him to get involved in the autoworkers' organizing effort which was underway at a nearby GM plant. You never feel useless, Polonsky remarks, when you are part of a major political movement. There is always something impossible to be done.

Within a short time, Polonsky became educational director of the CIO in Westchester County. He helped put together classes for union members, wrote leaflets and pamphlets, edited the local CIO newspaper, and delivered speeches. He went to CIO conventions and got involved in the organization's internal disputes. He walked picket lines and had the usual run-ins. "I was having a good time," says Polonsky. "But it was also good trade union experience."

While Polonsky was living in Briarcliff, Hitler's armies invaded the Soviet Union, putting "a cheerful end to a cheerless Nazi-Soviet nonaggression pact." News of the invasion was greeted with a vast sigh of relief by Party members in the United States. The signing of the Pact in August 1939—and the subsequent CPUSA policy shift*—had created a profound moral crisis within the Party. "I think it damaged the spirit of the Party forever," remarks Polonsky. "It was not the Pact itself; what damaged it were the theoretical reasons given for the Pact, not its tactical necessity. They destroyed the *virtue* of being a Marxist, that is, the dream of socialism as a moral truth."

The German invasion of Russia confirmed what Polonsky and other U.S. Communists had known all along: that all-out war with the Nazis was inevitable. That was clearly "the bias of history," he says, ever since fascism had entrenched itself in Europe. "The ferocity of that war," remarks Polonsky, "cannot be overcome by any diplomatic maneuvers or temporary solutions to the problem. The weather of that war is too enormous." Four months after the invasion, the Japanese attacked Pearl Harbor and the United States went to war.

Polonsky tried, "like all my radical friends," to enlist in the armed services, but was turned down because of his poor eyesight. "The thing you really must understand," he says, "is that this is a war that everybody (on the left) wants into. Just like the Spanish Civil War...The fight against fascism is a generalized solution to being a radical." Polonsky was not to be denied the opportunity to take part in the war. He joined the Office of Strategic Services (OSS). According to Polonsky, the clandestine intelligence agency investigated his background, but it was not at all disturbed; in fact, they thought his background would be an asset, since many of those in the European underground were also left wing.

Just before he was to begin training in Washington, Polonsky received a telephone call from Paramount Pictures. Someone in the studio's story department had read and admired a piece of popular fiction which Polonsky had

---

*The Communist Party in the United States went from emphasizing the horrors of Nazism and preparing the U.S. people for war against Germany to a pacifist stance which highlighted the dangers of British imperialism and U.S. militarism. "The Yanks are not coming," became the Party slogan of this period.

published in *American Magazine*,* and the studio wanted to hire him as a screenwriter. Polonsky still had nothing more than a mild curiosity about movie-making. Besides he was about to go to war. But right around this time, it was announced that such labor contracts, like other jobs, would be protected after the war. So that he (and his growing family) would have a job after the war, Polonsky decided to sign with Paramount. While he was shipped off to Europe to engage in operations which he characterizes as "the so-called destruction of enemy morale," his family went on to Los Angeles, to await his return.

*****

Polonsky returned from Europe in the summer of 1945. He was in Los Angeles when, by President Truman's order, atomic bombs were dropped on Hiroshima and Nagasaki. The OSS wanted to send him on to China, says Polonsky, "to (help) prevent the coming of socialism" in that country. "Luckily for me," he remarks, "the war was over," and because he was a civilian volunteer the OSS could not hold him. "I would have resigned."

After leaving the service, Polonsky reported for duty at Paramount. This had to be one of life's amusing ironies, he told himself: for someone with his political and artistic prejudices to wind up working in the absurd environment of a major motion picture studio. During one of his first days on the job, Polonsky bumped into John McNulty of the *New Yorker*, an acquaintance who had also taken a "permanent" temporary position with the movies. "What are you doing here, Polonsky? This is no place for you." McNulty then led him onto a movie set and pointed out a love scene in progress. Alan Ladd was standing on a box, kissing an actress who was somewhat taller than he, while the cameraman filmed them from the shoulders up. "*That's* movies!" said McNulty. "Go back home to New York." "I found it enchanting. But what I had in mind was to make some money and go back east."

---

*A war story called *The Enemy Sea* which Polonsky had written in four weeks at the beginning of the war. It was later published in book form by Little, Brown and Company.

"It's not contempt," remarks Polonsky. "You see, people always think you either have contempt for the movies or you love them. The movies are something Americans see all the time for enjoyment. But that doesn't mean you should work in them. After all, I'm an artist—what am I doing in the movies? Or I'm a radical, or a revolutionist, or something like that. But am I a screenwriter? Yet here I am about to write screenplays." And, he adds, "I got up on the box."

The Communist Party regarded the movie industry as an important arena to be active in because of the immense power it had to shape public attitudes. But the reasons leftists generally came to Hollywood, says Polonsky, were the same ones which brought everybody else. "They come to get a job," he remarks, "like all the rest. An organizer may be sent out here because the Party knows how socially important it is, and the people who come out here for the jobs know how socially important it is. But they don't come out here because it's socially important. That's just what they *say* when you ask them what they're doing here. What they mean is 'Paramount called me up,' or 'I needed a job,' or 'I wanted to work in the movies because it's glamorous and exciting and you meet all these pretty people.' "

Polonsky's initial experiences as a writer confirmed the usual reports about the Hollywood creative process. Paramount first assigned him to write an original screenplay about the liberation of Paris, an event which Polonsky saw the tail end of as an OSS operative. Studio officials were actually quite pleased with the way he had written the story, says Polonsky. But they decided that the public was not interested in war movies at that particular moment.

Paramount raised his salary, however, and put him to work on another movie—a spy melodrama set in pre-war Germany which was to feature Marlene Dietrich. Dietrich was to play a beautiful gypsy who gets involved in a daring British intelligence operation. The film was produced and released in 1947 under the title of *Golden Earrings*. Polonsky was surprised to discover, when the picture appeared, that hardly any of his material (as written) was left in it. He had carefully researched gypsy life under the Nazis. Gypsies, Polonsky points out, were among the first victims of the holocaust. But this was glossed over in the final version, he says, with "all the usual junk."

After this, he was assigned to write a screen adaptation of Dan Wickenden's *The Wayfarers*, a novel steeped in the social psychology of the Depression. Polonsky found the project to his liking. In his screenplay, are the same dramatic conflicts which he explored, with more subtlety and skill, in his later films. The mood of the script is also in keeping with that of his later work. The screen play is suffused with the same heavy, dark sadness which characterizes *Body and Soul* and *Force of Evil*. The mood is set in the first scene, where a drowning man gives up his last breath, as an offscreen voice remarks: "When you drown they say you suddenly see your whole past and your whole future in a single glance. Every mistake is terribly clear and you wish with all your heart for one more chance...Just one more chance out of all the thousands you spent like water."

The project had the strong support of Harry Tugend, one of the studio's leading producers. It was given further impetus when Polonsky lined up Edward G. Robinson to play the chief protagonist. "That was no problem in those days," remarks the writer. "I just called up two friends in the Communist Party, and on the third call I reached Robinson. He said, 'Sure, I'd love to read it.' He read it and said, 'I'd love to do it.' He invited me over to his house, showed me his art collection, and everything was set." Paramount scheduled the movie for production. But at the last minute, the studio's New York office cancelled it as "too depressing." "By then, says Polonsky, "I understood the movies."

After this string of disasters, Polonsky contemplated leaving Hollywood and returning to a more sensible line of work. The high salary he was drawing was nice, but he figured he could make almost as much as a popular fiction writer. After all, he had received $15,000 for *The Enemy Sea*. The constraints of Hollywood screenwriting seemed insufferable. "I would never remain in a profession," he states, "in which I believed for a moment that I could never do what I longed to do."

If Hollywood was a frustrating place to work, it was a fascinating place to live. It had a vigorous social and political life. He had become involved in local Party activities as soon as they settled there, "a nice, homey feeling." Polonsky was a member of "the international fraternity of Communists," and wherever he traveled—Paris, London, New York, Los Angeles—there were people who shared his innermost dreams about the world. Those within this international community, says Polonsky, enjoyed a spiritual solidarity.

During his first year in the film industry there were many signs of the horrors to come. The left became deeply embroiled in the bitterly fought Conference of Studio Unions strike, which dragged on over a long period of time and finally exhausted much of the progressive bloc's strength.* Broad-based coalitions such as the Hollywood Writers Mobilization which had been forged during the war began to come apart. If you were politically astute, says Polonsky, you knew the anti-communist onslaught was being mounted as early as 1943 or 44. "It started in the unions and it started in politics. I met it in the OSS. It was there in the struggle that went on within the OSS over whether we should give arms to the Communists in the Resistance. So it was no secret to me."

Despite the uncertain future he saw ahead for the left, Polonsky took an active political role in Hollywood. There is a point to getting involved in social struggle, Polonsky realizes, even when history is against you. There was still a variety of ways to participate in radical politics in Hollywood. While he was at Paramount, Polonsky helped form a Communist Party unit at the studio which consisted of two writers, an actor, and two of "the most literary backlot workers I've ever met." He also wrote for a dramatic radio series called "Reunion U.S.A.," which explored the problems confronting returning war veterans. The series, which was broadcast over the ABC radio network, portrayed returning soldiers as "ordinary people faced with problems which, if not exactly 'ordinary,' were rapidly becoming statistically probable"—rather than as the wildly abnormal characters who were then popular in com-

---

*The strike grew out of a jurisdictional dispute between the militant CSU and the International Alliance of Theatrical Stage Employees (IATSE), a rival craft union with a history of crooked leadership. (See previous chapter)

mercial drama. The show tried to shift the spotlight from the psychological damage caused by war to the common stresses and strains of postwar society.

Polonsky also became involved with the Hollywood Writers Mobilization, as that organization turned its attention to postwar problems such as the erosion of civil liberties and the threat of atomic war. He stayed abreast of current developments in atomic science and diplomacy and was sometimes called upon to give talks on the subject. In June 1946, Bernard Baruch, the United States delegate to the U.N. Atomic Energy Commission, unveiled the U.S. plan for nuclear arms control. Polonsky was invited to appear at a local meeting of the Federation of Atomic Scientists and present his political views on the Baruch proposal. Polonsky criticized the plan as simply another way of maintaining the United States' nuclear superiority. He declared that neither the Soviet Union nor any other powerful nation which might arise in the future would accept such an arrangement. Some honest and realistic plan had to be developed, he stated, to bring this situation under international control. By way of punctuating his remarks, Polonsky held up a teacup from Hiroshima which had been rendered partly transparent by the burning heat of the bomb. The cup had been given to him by a friend who was one of the first naval officers to land in the city after its destruction. "As I held up this cup," recalls Polonsky, "an atomic fact went through that whole room. That was a group, (perhaps the only group), within the entire Federation of Atomic Scientists which voted to oppose the Baruch plan."

Later that year, Polonsky joined the editorial board of the *Hollywood Quarterly*. He took the place of John Howard Lawson, who had been forced to resign by the University of California regents.* There was in the early issues of the *Quarterly* an ongoing effort to develop a sophisticated brand of radical film criticism, a type of criticism more attuned to film aesthetics than the Communist Party press, and more attuned to social content than the apolitical film journals. Polonsky's reviews

---

*See previous chapter.

of *The Best Years of Our Lives, Odd Man Out,* and *Monsieur Verdoux* are good examples of this new school of criticism. In his review of *Best Years,* Polonsky explored the ways in which the content of a Hollywood picture is shaped by its dramatic form. He notes that writing for the movies was "writing under censorship" and that "the censorship forces stereotypes of motive and environment on the creators." The task of the film artist, declared Polonsky, was "to press enough concrete experience into the mold to make imagination live."*

Life in Hollywood's left wing community before its disintegration was hectic and stimulating, recalls Polonsky. There was always too much to do and never enough time. The left was engaged in film union activities, in local and state politics, in national and international debates, and, of course, in constant internal disputes over theoretical issues. There were meetings, parties, benefits, rallies. "No leftist ever had the problem of not knowing where to go for an evening," remarks Polonsky. What was the effect of all this on an individual's life? "Well," he says, "it made your life interesting instead of dull. Instead of being devoted *merely* to adultery, drinking, and getting ahead, you were devoted to politics— which is much more varied than those obsessions. That didn't prevent people from indulging in the other three. But the main subject was politics."

At the center of this political whirl was the Communist Party. Coming out of the war, the Party was at the peak of its prestige and strength. "Everybody wants to be part of it," says Polonsky. "If you can't join, or don't want to, you want to be associated with it. Its ambience was struggle, passion, ideas, a heady mixture in a company town. Intellectual prestige. Because it is the Communist Party. And the Communist Party in the United States—no matter what anyone tells you looking back—at that time, is a fascinating organization, secretive and public, haunted by history and victory in war. And it's an honor, dubious indeed, but an honor nonetheless to be in it and to be thought well of by people in it...So I would say that just like to be in the Movement was something in college during the 1960s, to be in the Party was something, not

---

Hollywood Quarterly, April 1947.

everywhere, but somewhere. In a bohemian society like Hollywood, with actors, directors, speculators investing money in dreams and jokes and personality, (the Communists) are about the most solid people around who are different. They're interested in history, they talk about important subjects, they seem to know about things other people don't know or care about, they involve themselves in strange labor struggles— the lettuce workers' strike or the plight of the Spanish refugees. They get invited to the Russian consulate, or something crazy, you know. So it's no curse to belong. If it were, no one would join. It's great to belong. The curse is coming."

Those film artists and technicians who belonged to the Party were not an entirely different breed. They were subject to the same influences and pressures which operated upon the rest of the Hollywood work force. "Like everybody else," Polonsky says, "they wanted to be successful. And in that sense you wouldn't be able to distinguish them from the others. This is a highly competitive industry." Hollywood's caste system was not completely ignored in Party circles. "The writer who wrote a shooting script, and was known as someone who could, was a much more important person than the writer who was endlessly re-written." But all this was tempered by the fact that they knew better. And sometimes they acted better. They conformed to the industry's expectations—but they went against them. They were ambitious and obsessed with money—but they were high-minded and selfless. "They were," says Polonsky with characteristic irony, "poisoned by their radicalism. So, no matter how much they're like the others, they're different. They have a tendency to help each other more. They have a tendency to do socially conscious movies if they can. They cannot be members of the Communist Party without doing what they're supposed to do as a Communist Party member. They not only have to participate in union activities, they have to walk picket lines, they have to fight race discrimination. If they're not involved, they're going to be kicked out. And the last thing in the world they want is to be kicked out. The most exclusive club in town is the Communist Party, because it takes a little courage, a little morality, some social responsibilty, and a touch of madness to belong."

Communist screenwriters often complained, says Polonsky, about the endless organizational work required of them. Some felt, even then, that too much of their time was going into political activity and their writing was suffering as a result. Says Polonsky, "There *was* too much politicking going on. That's the nature of bureaucracy. People tend to call meetings. They ask you to come. If you're effective, you find out that you are invited to every meeting in town. Going to meetings is a kind of radical madness, yet basic to action. There are people who have a great sense of duty, and they give themselves too much—and there are people who are always evaders, who prefer the symbolism of action. You've got to catch them. And the Communist Party is *right* to catch them. Because the Party was, theoretically, a disciplined organization, where everybody gets together, where the goals are decided upon, where work is divided. And if you don't do your job, the Party should try to find out why.

Polonsky believes there is no reason why film artists should *not* be asked to walk picket lines once in a while like everybody else. But he also believes that a political organization must be attuned to the unique abilities of its various members, and draw on them in different ways. "One of the faults of the Party," he says, "was that it tried to turn everybody into the same kind of communist. It is a terrible error, which you pay for. You turn out neither communists nor artists."

He personally never felt any dramatic conflict between his art and his politics, declares Polonsky. "Now it is true that quiet and solitude is good for everybody," he remarks. "And it can't hurt a writer either. You want to think of your sentences too. But writers manage. Everybody is doing something else until they become famous. After that they're too busy to do anything else. But when you're young and full of energy and excitement, it isn't that there's too much life. There's always not enough. When there's too much life, there's something wrong with you. You're getting old or you're getting bored. Or you're getting famous.

"My personal message to anyone who wants a message from me is that politics won't interfere with your life. It will create your life. And it will create your artistic life too."

It was not until Polonsky moved from Paramount to Enterprise Productions in fall 1946 that he found the room to practice the art of filmmaking. Creative possibilities which he had once thought nonexistent in Hollywood (because they did not exist for him) began to open up after he made this transition. Enterprise had been organized in February 1946 by Charles Einfeld, former vice president of Warner Brothers, and David Loew, former vice president and board director of Loew's Inc. It was one of the grander independent film companies launched in the postwar period. Soon after coming into being, the company took possession of the old California Studios, put over $700,000 into refurbishing the facility, and announced that it would produce six motion pictures in its first year of operation.

Among the first projects planned by Enterprise was a film about Barney Ross, the former boxing champ and Marine hero who became addicted to drugs and subsequently turned himself in to the authorities. The film was to serve as a vehicle for John Garfield, the tough and tender screen star whose style was formed in the social theater of the 1930s. Originally, a left wing writer from New York named Arnold Manoff was lined up to write the screenplay. But the Ross story was a controversial one and Manoff had a great deal of trouble coming up with a script which was both truthful and capable of passing the movie censor's strict examination. In the end, he gave up and took another job at Paramount.

Manoff arrived at the studio just as Polonsky was preparing to write it—and all of Hollywood—off as a dead end. But Manoff, who was a friend, told Polonsky about Enterprise. Perhaps, Manoff suggested, Polonsky would have more luck in solving the dramatic problems of the Garfield film than he did. Polonsky took his friend's advice. A meeting with Garfield and Bob Roberts, the actor's business manager and producer, was arranged.

"I went over to Enterprise, which was just a couple of blocks away from Paramount," recalls Polonsky, "and the three of us discussed movie code problems. They said, 'What do you think we should do?' And I said, 'Make up another story.' They said, 'What story?' And I said, 'I'll tell you one.' They were very enthusiastic. They called Einfeld. They held a big meeting. Enterprise was the kind of place where you held a meeting and everybody came. I told the story again. But by this time I had thought about it. I was thinking about myself and Paramount and the air was full of passion, frustration, and the bitterness of hope. As Roberts tells me, they asked, 'What do we do now?' And I said, 'Find yourself a screenwriter,' and walked back to Paramount." By the time he reached Paramount, says Polonsky, Enterprise had arranged to borrow him for $2,000 a week—$1,000 of which went to Paramount, and $1,000 to the writer himself. "Suddenly I was a $2,000-a-week writer. This had nothing to do with anything *but* accident. If you understand that, you understand the nature of this town."

The film story which Polonsky dreamed up, and completed in late November 1946, was called *Body and Soul*. As critics have noted, the boxing picture shares some of the dramatic conventions of Clifford Odets' 1937 play, *Golden Boy* (which in turn was highly reminiscent of boxing movies like *Kid Galahad*): the hungry young man from the Lower East Side who is desperate for money and recognition, the concerned parent who'd rather he fight for a cause than for cash, the opportunistic manager and the crooked promoter who take control of his life. (It adds the unusual presence of a black champion he unintentionally betrays in his bid for glory; the final decision to risk all to recapture his self-esteem at any cost; and flashback, not as explanation or illustration, but as narrative inevitability, present and past as one.)

But *Body and Soul* lacks the silly contrivance and sentimentality which spoiled *Golden Boy*. Polonsky draws the young boxer's drive to the top in much starker terms than Odets does. The choice for Charlie Davis (Garfield) is not between a career as a classical violinist and prizefighting, but between the terrible oblivion of poverty and the violence (and glory) of the boxing ring. His ambition does not have the same dreamy quality as Joe Bonaparte's in *Golden Boy*. It is raw desire, fueled by the terror and self-contempt which come from a lifetime without money. For awhile, in deference to his mother, Charlie holds his ruthless ambition in check. But when he is forced to watch her submit to the intrusive questions of a social worker, he explodes. "Get me that fight from Quinn !" he screams to his friend. "I want money. Money!"—"I forbid!" cries his mother with equal hysteria. "Better you go buy a gun and shoot yourself!" Charlie: "You need *money* to buy a gun!" In this quick and feverish exchange is packed the desperation of an era.

While the first part of Polonsky's script is about the sources of Charlie's ambition, the latter part is concerned with its effects. In the process of getting ahead in the boxing world, he gives up pieces of himself—to the avaricious people who begin to take an interest in his career. "You know what they're making of Charlie," complains Shorty, his neighborhood friend, "—a money-machine, like oil wells, like gold mines. They're cutting him up a million ways." When Charlie reminds the gangster Roberts, that "you're only buying into my contract—not me," Roberts coolly replies: "Sure, Charlie. It's a free country. Everything's for sale." Later Roberts pressures Charlie into agreeing to "throw" a title fight, and cautions him that "businessmen keep their agreements."

The boxing milieu which Polonsky creates is a world where people are owned by other people—but almost everyone denies it; where human beings are turned into "money-machines"—but are only vaguely aware of it; where people must live up to contracts which they did not freely enter into. Economic forces dominate people and make their wishes small and irrelevant. "Don't try," Roberts tells Charlie, after the boxer asserts that he is capable of winning the fight which he is supposed to "throw." "The books are all balanced," says the gangster, "the accountants have made their reports. It's a business. You've got to be business-like, Charlie. Look at the numbers. People use words, but they mean numbers. Everything is addition and subtraction. The rest is conversation." In Polonsky's hands, the vicious fight racket becomes a metaphor for capitalist society in general. This symbolic connection is hinted at in *Golden Boy*, but in *Body and Soul* it is made much more explicit.

"The film," says Polonsky, "is not so much about how mean *prizefighting* is; it's about how mean *life* is. Prizefighting distills it."

Polonsky's screenplay closes on an ambiguous note. At the last moment, Charlie decides to break his "businessman's agreement" with Roberts. Instead of taking a dive, he throws himself furiously into the fight and succeeds in knocking out his opponent. "What makes you think you can get away with this?" says Roberts, as the champion is escorted from the ring. The boxer's response is just the right blend of defiance and resignation: "What are you going to do, kill me? Everybody dies." Charlie has at last won back his self-esteem. He has finally taken a stand against the forces which have brought death and decay to his life. For this moment, he is free, but his fate is left in doubt.

The director of *Body and Soul*, Robert Rossen,* wanted to end the picture in a much more grim and final manner. According to Polonsky, Rossen felt that Charlie should be gunned down as he exited the boxing arena and left sprawling in the street next to an overturned garbage can. Polonsky took strong issue with this. He argued that Rossen's ending was much too morbid a way to conclude a picture which was full of "humanity and feelings" and the spirit of the 1930s. "I knew that (*Body and Soul*) was, in essence, a romance of the streets," says Polonsky. Both endings were filmed, but in the end, Polonsky's version prevailed. Charlie's fate was left an open question. "Bob Rossen was fundamentally an anarchist by disposition," comments Polonsky. "He was also fundamentally mean, in many respects of the word. He also thought that death was truer than life, as an ending. But we who are radicals know the opposite is true."**

There were other disagreements between Rossen and Polonsky during the making of the film. The director tried repeatedly to change lines, but Polonsky was on the set every

---

Body and Soul was Rossen's second directing assignment. According to Polonsky, he was chosen by the producer, Bob Roberts, because of his experience as a movie writer, his previous directing credit, and his left wing politics. It was felt, says Polonsky, that he would bring the right attitude to the film. Rossen was (at one time) a member of the Communist Party, as were other key people involved in the making of *Body and Soul*—a fact later brought out by anti-Communist witchhunters, who excoriated the movie as a classic example of left wing collaboration in Hollywood. Later, when the pressure grew intense, Rossen turned against his former friends and associates and became an informer.
**cf: Robert Parrish, *Growing Up in Hollywood*. Won Academy Award editing *Body and Soul*.

day and he made sure that his script remained intact. "My relationship to *Body and Soul* was constant," says Polonsky, "in all stages of production."

Body and Soul was released in fall 1947 through United Artists and became an immediate critical and box office success. It was the first—and only— Enterprise picture to reap substantial profits. Garfield gave a dynamic performance in a role which was perfectly tailored for him. He was supported by an excellent cast which included Anne Revere as his weary and distraught mother; Canada Lee as a proud, unbending black boxer; and Lloyd Gough as the sinister Roberts. The stark photography of James Wong Howe properly accentuated the mood of the story. It was an exceptional coming together of film talents; and the result was a movie which was bleak and brutal, but full of the vitality of human aspirations.

Spirits soared at Enterprise after the success of *Body and Soul*. Garfield and producer Bob Roberts were so pleased with the outcome of the film that they asked Polonsky to direct, as well as write, the star's next Enterprise picture. Garfield, according to one of his biographers, was convinced that he and Roberts "had discovered the director-writer of the age in Abraham Polonsky." * This was an outstanding opportunity, Polonsky realized—to direct John Garfield in a million-dollar Hollywood feature. After all, he had never directed before, "not even in summer camp." But, says Polonsky, his manner was full of self-confidence and he seemed to have a gift for getting his way, so they assumed he would be a "natural." "After I'm around awhile, I sound like I understand everything. Not true, but it generates confidence in others, which mixed with their terror of failure creates an artistic ambience. It's the divine cult of personality."

----

*Larry Swindell, *Body and Soul: The Story of John Garfield* (Wm Morrow and Co., 1975). Polonsky wrote the introduction to another book about Garfield: *The Films of John Garfield* by Howard Gelman (The Citadel Press, 1975). It is full of interesting insights into the offscreen and onscreen character of the film star, and his tragic death at the age of thirty-nine while being relentlessly stalked by HUAC.

By this time, Polonsky had come to appreciate film as a serious art form. He was now watching movies with a critical eye, and closely observing the techniques of various Hollywood directors. "I realize," he says, "that even conventional films made by certain gifted directors really contain interesting aesthetic changes, though their stories are absolutely insane. I mean anybody who knows anything about art knows these stories are crazy. These are crazy stories about crazy people. They're crazy the way dreams are crazy. They're about American life, but life distorted by social madness—which is very much like reality, but innocently so rather than deliberately so as in black humor."

It did not occur to him, says Polonsky, when he got the chance to create a John Garfield film that he should only make an acceptable melodrama. It was a rare occasion to explore the nature of the film medium. "I believed that they would only let me do one, before they found me out, so I might as well enjoy myself. I treated it like I was a member of Clionia (his college literary society) and a Marxist. I was going to make an aesthetic experiment with a Marxist meaning. And I did." He had once written that the goal of the Hollywood filmmaker should be to "press enough concrete experience into the mold to make imagination live." But on this film, Polonsky would attempt to change the mold itself a little.

Polonsky was told to come up with a melodrama—"about gangsters or something"—which would be suitable for Garfield. He suggested adapting *Tucker's People*, a wonderful novel about the New York numbers racket by a Pulitzer Prize winner, Ira Wolfert. "It's ostensibly a melodrama," says Polonsky, "but it's really an autopsy on capitalism." His employers weren't excited about the book "but by then," comments the filmmaker," anything I said was alright—I had the Midas touch that year." Polonsky and Wolfert worked together to produce a screenplay, altering the novel in the process. It was completed in spring 1948 and went before the cameras soon afterwards. The title of the picture was changed to *Force of Evil*.

Polonsky's choice of *Tucker's People* as film material and his interpretation of the novel reflected the darkening political/cultural climate of the period. The air was clouded with fear, betrayal, and guilt. Polonsky was, of course, acutely aware of the ominous forces at work in the country. "I'm not innocent of the obvious," he says. "I see and feel what's going on, like any dog or child."

Force of Evil is a much gloomier film than Body and Soul. As critic Richard Corliss has pointed out, "The corruption (Force of Evil) defines is immediately established as the norm, and not as a contagious aberration personified by Roberts, the fight boss."* Joe Morse (Garfield), the principal figure in Force of Evil, is so deeply compromised a character that it is impossible to call him a "hero" in the conventional Hollywood sense. "Unlike the fighter of Body and Soul," William Pechter has written, "...Morse...is not so simply and understandably the product of social determinations. We first see him as a successful lawyer; he is not fighting to escape poverty, but to annex greater wealth. Nor is he unaware of the nature of his involvement, or without moral understanding. One is never certain that the fighter of Body and Soul is wholly aware of his moral predicament; but Joe Morse acknowledges full responsibility, without even pleading the excuse of weakness. By his own admission, he is 'strong enough to get a part of the corruption, but not strong enough to resist it.' "**

As the film begins, Morse is embroiled in a scheme with Ben Tucker, a New York crime magnate, to monopolize the numbers racket and turn it into a "legitimate business." (Again Polonsky draws the parallels between underworld activities and capitalism.) In the process of trying to legitimize crime, Morse destroys the life of his brother Leo, the owner of a small gambling operation; he destroys his relationship with Doris, Leo's young naive employee, before it can even develop; and finally, he destroys all hope for his own moral redemption. Leo and Doris are not simply innocent victims, however. They too are tainted characters. Leo proudly resists being absorbed by the Tucker monopoly, but he is nonetheless a petty crook.

*Richard Corliss, Talking Pictures: Screenwriters in the American Cinema (Overlook, 1974).
**"Abraham Polonsky and 'Force of Evil' " by William Pechter, Film Quarterly; Spring 1962.

Doris' moral stance is weakened by the fact that she is an inarticulate and confused character and even somewhat intrigued by Morse's evil behavior.

At the center of the film is the complex and destructive relationship between the two brothers. Leo, who has sacrificed in the past to put his younger brother through law school, berates him for misusing the professional training he never received. He assumes a moral superiority which both of them know to be false. Morse is driven by an intense need to pay back his older brother. This, in fact, is his one redeeming human quality. The way he does this, however, is by involving Leo, against his better instincts, in the corrupt—but profitable—Tucker operation. Morse convinces himself that he is doing his brother a great service, but Leo knows better and he is overcome by a profound sense of guilt. (Because he has allowed his brother to become an agent of corruption, and because he has allowed himself to be corrupted.) The relationship which Polonsky draws between these two men is a masterpiece of tangled emotions, miscommunication, and self-deception.

Every character in *Force of Evil* is shown to be—in varying degrees—poisoned by the general atmosphere of corruption. The law is depicted either as a distant and invisible force (as in the case of the district attorney), or as part of the criminal element (as in the case of the police). Where does moral authority reside in the picture? "It rests," says Polonsky, "in the group of characters as a whole...They are all trying to save this idea of themselves, their self-esteem, one way or the other. That's where the moral authority is—in the undestroyed element left in human nature which wants to look at itself and say, 'This is myself, I'm not terrible, I believe in myself, I have a good opinion of myself. I have a self that I can recognize, that's mine.'...This is in all of them. It doesn't come from any one character at all. It comes from the general social feeling that these people have together. Each one shows it one or another throughout the film.

"If you are a social creature living in any kind of society where social relations exist, whether it's primitive or extraordinarily complex, one of the things which is generated, along with the other things, is brotherhood among people.

Self-esteem. It's the nature of social life, or else no social life is possible."

The language of *Force of Evil* is remarkable for its odd and poetic beauty. Morse, particularly in his conversations with Doris, sounds like someone in the midst of a deeply troubled sleep. Polonsky says he was creating a "language of the unconscious."

The photographic images in the film were also conceived like debris from remembered dreams. There is a memorable shot midway through the film, after Morse has discovered that his moneymaking schemes have collapsed and he will never be able to return to his "fine office up in the clouds." The lawyer runs without direction down the dark, empty streets of the financial district. "He is a small shadow in the immensity of these blank buildings that lean over his head."* The closing passage of the film is equally eloquent. Morse descends flight after flight of stairs, in the shadows of early morning, to find the body of his brother, which has been dumped on the rocks along the river. His descent is so long and steep, and the sight of his dead brother so terribly final that it is evident Morse will never fully regain his humanity—despite his declared intention of turning himself in to the district attorney.

Force of Evil was not well received by U.S. critics when it was first released in December 1948 (with a few notable exceptions such as Bosley Crowther of the *New York Times*, who hailed the film as "a sizzling piece of work" and Polonsky as a new director with "imaginative and unquestioned crafts-manship.") They failed, for the most part, to detect the intricate psychological layers within the simple narrative and tended to be annoyed by the peculiar dialogue. The film was completed as Enterprise slid into bankruptcy, and was dis-tributed indifferently by MGM, so it never had a real chance to catch on with the public. It was prevented from fading into complete obscurity, however, by the British film periodicals *Sequence* and *Sight and Sound*, both of which recognized it as an innovative and artful motion picture. The film's power,

---

*From the screenplay.

commented *Sequence* (in the person of the then film critic, Lindsay Anderson), derived from "its combination of a terse, forceful realism in the presentation with a terse unrealistic poetry (in the dialogue and images)."* Later, in the 1960s, *Force of Evil* was rediscovered by U.S. film critics and proclaimed to be "one of the great films of the modern America cinema."**

The film industry did not rush to offer Polonsky another directing assignment after *Force of Evil*. His financial backers had allowed him complete artistic freedom on *Force of Evil* because they assumed he would turn out another box office smash like *Body and Soul*. Instead he had created a film classic. They were not eager to make the same mistake twice.

Hollywood, Polonsky points out, is not the best place in the world to be if you want to experiment with film style. The studio system of the 1930s and 40s, he says, was more virulently opposed to aesthetic innovation than it was to left wing social content. "If you came out for socialism in films, the producer might say, 'I think you're going too heavy on that. Change some of those lines.' But if you said, 'Shoot it in this different way,' he would throw you off the (studio) lot and have you run out of town on the grounds of professional incompetence."

Polonsky was one of the few Hollywood leftists of this period who approached filmmaking in a systematic fashion. He placed as much emphasis on developing a radical film style as he did on creating radical content. Polonsky says that he is not absolutely certain there is such a thing as a "Marxist film aesthetic." But he does know that his films in some way reflect a Marxian concept of history. ("The dialectical process as I understand it," says Polonsky, "means that we constantly have in motion, at all levels, uneven contraries which interact with each other, and this interaction creates the energy which is the nature of the world.") There is a sense in Polonsky's films that nothing is permanent, that there are no happy

---

*Sequence; Summer 1949.
**Andrew Sarris, *The American Cinema: Directors and Directions, 1929-1968* (E.P. Dutton and Co., 1968).

endings which solve everything for all time,* that out of resolutions grow new conflicts.

Is there a Marxist film aesthetic? If so, what is it? How can radical filmmakers extend the boundaries of film style? These kinds of questions were never debated within Communist Party circles while he was in Hollywood, declares Polonsky. The overriding question of the day was: How can progressive content (subject matter, dialogue, ideas, etc.) be introduced into movies. There were, among the screenwriters of this period, men like John Howard Lawson who had been ardent innovators in other creative fields. Lawson wrote three ground-breaking plays in the 1920s—*Processional, Roger Bloomer,* and *Loud Speaker*—before coming to Hollywood. But his screenplays followed the conventional lines of Hollywood melodrama. "As a movie writer," says Polonsky, "Lawson was more interested in accomplishing certain social objectives which were related to his political beliefs. And he knew that aesthetic innovation kills quicker than social commentary."

Film content became the dominant concern of the Hollywood left, says Polonsky, because it was assumed that stylistic experimentation was out of the question in the movie industry. Hollywood Communists, he adds, were also influenced by the philosophy of art which had become institutionalized in the Soviet Union during the 1930s. "Their attitudes (about film) reflected—to a certain extent—what was going on in the Soviet Union, which had destroyed the dynamic aesthetic movement of its late 1920s. So they thought of aesthetics in terms of social content. To them, the social content of a film *was* its aesthetic. If the Party line or progressive social ideas or progressive subjects were treated in a film—*that* was communist aesthetics."

After finishing *Force of Evil,* Polonsky decided to leave Hollywood and to write a novel which had been bothering him. He proposed to his family (which now included two small children) that they move to the south of France "like all the

---

*"Although," Polonsky inserts, "I believe in happy endings, because my life has had many happy endings."

famous writers do," and live off his movie earnings until his book was completed. This seemed agreeable to everyone so they took off for Paris, where Polonsky renewed his friendships with old comrades from the Resistance. From there, it was on to Cannes, where the family took a house and Polonsky set to work on his book.

The World Above, which was published in 1951 by Little, Brown and Company, was the first serious novel of Polonsky's to appear in print. In it Polonsky traces the personal, political, and intellectual growth of a brilliant Freudian psychiatrist named Dr. Carl Myers. The story follows Myers from the beginning of his promising career in the Depression, through his wartime service, to the final realization of his professional goals in the postwar years. Unlike his brother, who is an organizer for the CIO, Myers is not a socially committed man. He moves through the turbulent years of the 1930s and the '40s curiously untouched by what is going on around him. His emotional life too is led at a level of semi-consciousness; he finds himself unable or unwilling to form deep, lasting personal relationships. His single constant passion is his scientific work. Myers' probing intellect leads him to question some of the fundamental assumptions of the psychiatric profession, and ultimately to develop a new theory based on the idea that social influences are the main causes of mental illness. He succeeds in establishing a veterans hospital after the war which puts this new psychiatric theory into practice. When the hospital's innovative work becomes too threatening to the mental health establishment, Myers is brought before a Congressional committee and asked, in effect, to publicly renounce his therapeutic ideas. He refuses to do this, even though it means his career will be severely damaged. "If my scientific work," Myers tells the committee with deep conviction, "leads me to criticize, or even condemn, a society which creates the illness which it is my duty to treat, then I shall devote my life to exposing this society, condemning it and changing it." This act of defiance becomes Myers' first step toward his own psychological liberation.

The World Above is a restless and engaging book to read. Polonsky's exploration of the politics of psychotherapy gives the book a contemporary value; the questions he raises about society and mental illness have become increasingly pressing in recent years. Dr. Myers' insistence that psychiatric patients not be simply molded in order to fit back into an unhealthy society, but rather encouraged "to participate in the understanding and alteration of those societal influences which (have) damaged (them)" is echoed today by the radical therapy movements which were spawned in the early 1970s.

As the book neared completion, Polonsky and his family began to run low on funds. William Morris, the writer's Hollywood agency, was beckoning him with promises of lucrative film jobs, so at last they decided to return. The movie industry did not place much value on Polonsky's directing abilities, but he was still considered a "hot" screenwriter. Soon after arriving in Hollywood in the summer of 1950, he was signed by 20th Century-Fox to write a screenplay based on a treatment by Jerome Weidman. Weidman had originally been hired by the studio to write a screen adaptation of his 1937 novel, *I Can Get It For You Wholesale,* a venomous portrait of an ambitious Jewish garment manufacturer. But the Fox hierarchy decided the script was too anti-semitic ("which it was," says Polonsky), so they had Weidman write a completely new story about the garment industry using the same title. Polonsky was then brought in to turn it into a screenplay.

He completed the job in August; it went before the cameras under the direction of Michael Gordon, who, says Polonsky, followed his script to the letter. When the movie appeared in spring 1951, some critics compared it unfavorably with the book whose title it used. They charged that the virulent atmosphere of the garment industry, which had been evoked in the novel, was "deodorized" in the movie. (Polonsky says it was "deodorized" with carbolic acid instead of Jewish anti-semitism, anti-union and anti-radical hostility.)

The film version of *Wholesale* is not without some intriguing qualities, however. In the process of rewriting his novel, as a movie treatment, Weidman changed the principal character from a ruthless ex-shipping clerk named Harry Bogen to an ambitious ex-model named Harriet Boyd (played in the movie by Susan Hayward). Harriet's foil is Teddy Sherman (Dan Dailey), a good-looking, breezy salesman with whom she launches a dress business. In Polonsky's hands, Weidman's

conventional relationship between these two characters becomes a fascinating confusion of desires. Love, greed, and possession are mixed together in their unusual business part-
nership. Teddy loves Harriet because of her looks and style,
but he doesn't trust her business drive. Harriet admires Teddy
for his salesmanship and personality, but she doesn't trust him
as a lover and is wary of getting emotionally entangled.

In one memorable scene, Teddy becomes outraged when
he sees Harriet using her personal charms to win over a pro-
spective buyer—something Teddy does all the time with
female buyers. He tells her that it is one thing for him to
operate that way, but quite another for her to. Harriet, however, will hear none of it.

> Harriet: Let's you and me be very clear, (Mr.) Sherman.
> I'm exactly like you. Sex is part of my stock in
> trade, along with my talent, my brains, and the
> $5,000 I put into the business.
>
> Teddy: I don't like your idea of business.
>
> Harriet: And I don't like your man's world where the
> woman is supposed to keep her eyes closed, her
> brain half soaked with alcohol and not know that
> everything in pants, including the loving hus-
> band and father, is two-timing the woman he's
> supposed to love with every other woman that
> comes along. When he can. And when he can't,
> he's thinking of it. I'm not grateful for the vote,
> mixed bathing, community property and a black
> negligee on Mother's Day. I believe in the single
> standard, even if it's yours, and you know what
> that is.
>
> Teddy: You trying to reform me?
>
> Harriet: Heaven forbid, and spoil our business?
>
> Teddy: Then I want out. Find a new partner.
>
> Harriet: (leaning forward, her face close to his) I've got a
> partner, and it's you. The best (salesman) in the
> business, and you're going to help me get rich
> and get ahead and be free of men like you. The
> contract's sealed, signed, delivered. Unbreakable.
> And you won't get out. Never. So like it!

There is a feminist sensibility in the portrayal of this relationship, which was very rare for that period in Hollywood.

(Of course, says Polonsky, "the woman question" was something which the Party was aware of and discussed, even if they never resolved it.) Polonsky brings out the fact that love and marriage between men and women are often commodity relationships. Teddy declares his love to Harriet and says he wants to marry her, but Harriet says what he really means is that he wants to own her. Their relationship is polluted by the business ethic which guides their lives.

The movie takes an ambivalent attitude toward Harriet's consuming ambition to become a major dress designer and manufacturer. There is sympathy for her desire to become financially independent and free of men's domination. But there is a strong sense that she is giving up much of her humanity in the process of getting ahead. Polonsky concedes that he has contradictory feelings about those women and other oppressed members of society who fight their way to the top. "On the one hand," he says, "they are achieving something great for a repressed element of human and social life. Therefore, it's an act of liberation. On the other hand, it's an act of self-destruction. So that's the drama." Harriet resolves this dilemma, in the end, by lowering her career expectations and returning to her uneasy relationship with Teddy. This move was made necessary by the conventions of the Hollywood romance. But there is still a distinct feeling as the picture fades out that all is not resolved between the two, and she will never resign herself to a submissive role.

As Polonsky was working on *I Can Get It for You Wholesale*, the political mood in Hollywood and the rest of the country grew more forbidding than ever. In June 1950, war broke out in Korea. The following month, the FBI arrested Julius Rosenberg for stealing the "secret" of the atomic bomb. In August they came for his wife, Ethel. That same summer, the Hollywood Ten began serving their prison sentences. For some time, Polonsky had been thinking about making a movie out of *Mario and the Magician*, Thomas Mann's allegorical tale about Italian fascism. He decided that the right moment was now upon him.

Polonsky planned to move his family back to Europe after the completion of *Wholesale* and work on *Mario* there. Before leaving the country, Polonsky paid a visit to Mann at the German emigre's home in Pacific Palisades. Mann warned Polonsky that fascism was coming to the United States just as it had come to his own country. He would be wise, Mann told him, to stay abroad.

Polonsky did not agree with Mann's assessment of the political situation. Reaction was taking hold of the country, he believed, not fascism. The distinction was critical. Yet Polonsky must have been deeply relieved, all the same, to get out of the country and return to a pleasant home in Cannes. After re-settling in France, the financial backing which he had hoped to find failed to materialize, and Polonsky was forced to set the film project aside.

He turned his attention at that point to writing another novel. This one would ultimately be published in 1956 by Cameron Associates under the title of *A Season of Fear*. It is a tale about blacklisting and loyalty oaths in the Los Angeles water and power department. Polonsky vividly evokes the terrible atmosphere of panic and mass conformity which characterized the 1950s.

While he was at work on *A Season of Fear*, the second wave of Congressional hearings on Communist activities in Holly-wood got underway. Friends and political associates back in California began receiving their subpoenas to appear before the Committee—subpoenas which everyone knew meant the end of their film careers. Polonsky was faced with a major decision: should he remain in France and avoid a direct con-frontation with the repressive political machinery? He had, after all, been acclaimed as a gifted filmmaker by European critics and there was a possibility he could continue making pictures there. Or should he return home and go through the ritual of resistance and defeat? He would be subpoenaed, he would refuse to cooperate with his inquisitors, he would be immediately discharged from the ranks of popular film-makers.

Polonsky and his wife discussed the matter at length. He decided to go home. Polonsky explores this question of com-mitting oneself to futile battles in *A Season of Fear*. There is a water engineer in the book named Al Hamner who decides to take a one-man stand against the department's loyalty oath. "You're in a losing fight," his boss warns him. "Well, somebody has to be in the losing fight," Hamner replies, "or else nothing would ever happen." Hamner's (and Polonsky's) decision to fight back, despite the overwhelming odds, reflects his sense of history. Nothing changes, he believes, without losing struggles.

After returning to Hollywood, Polonsky was signed by 20th Century-Fox to write and direct a movie about government corruption—"it was perfect for me," he comments. But, he realized, it was only a matter of time before the Committee caught up with him. He was named as a Communist early in the spring 1951 hearings by three cooperative witnesses— screenwriter Richard Collins, agent Meta Reis Rosenberg, and actor Sterling Hayden (who had belonged to Polonsky's group at Paramount).* Soon afterwards, he received his subpoena to appear before HUAC.

Polonsky took the witness stand in Washington on April 25, 1951. He invoked the Fifth Amendment** when the Committee asked him to reveal his political affiliations and those of people he knew. Polonsky's wartime service in the OSS was of particular interest to the Committee. They pressed him to talk about his personal experiences in the spy agency and the political leanings of his former colleagues. This line of questioning was abruptly halted, however, when an unidentified man in the audience stood up, walked over to the Committee's table, and spoke quietly with them. Polonsky assumes this man was connected with the CIA, the postwar

---

*Hayden came to deeply regret his role as an informer. "...He was not just passive about it," Polonsky told *Look* Magazine in 1970. "He wrote a book (*Wanderer*) telling what an awful mistake he had made. He did better than beg the pardon of the people he had hurt. He changed."

**The left's strategy had changed as a result of the Hollywood Ten's defeat. Uncooperative witnesses no longer refused to answer the Committee's questions on the basis of the First Amendment because it had been demonstrated that this would only lead to costly legal battles and, ultimately, prison sentences.

incarnation of the OSS. Committee member Harold H. Velde (Rep.-Ill.), who believed Polonsky to be a master spy of some sort, called the filmmaker the most dangerous man in America. ("I *was* the most dangerous man in America," Polonsky later quipped, "but dangerous only to myself.")*

Following his appearance before the Committee, Polonsky went back to work on the 20th Century-Fox picture. Immediately, the Hollywood trade papers began demanding to know why he was still on the studio's payroll. Fox production chief Darryl F. Zanuck and producer Sol Siegel, says Polonsky, made an effort to keep him employed but the pressure soon became too intense. His contract was terminated; for the next seventeen years, he would be blacklisted.

Polonsky has stated that, like everybody else who was blacklisted, he was offered the opportunity to "compromise," to name a few names. Just enough to establish the fact that he had surrendered his will. Then he could go right back to his career as a film director-writer. "But," commented Polonsky in a 1970 interview with *Film Culture*, "compromise never occurred to me as a possible action. I never thought of doing that. It never even occurred to me as a possibility. I mean, I knew compromise existed as a possibility, because it had been offered to me, and I had seen it operate around me, but it never occurred to me. I mean, it just doesn't occur to me that that's a thing I should do. Now, of course, someone might ask, 'What would you do if you were hungry and starving?' Well, nobody was hungry and starving in that time because it wasn't that kind of situation."**

Film critics have bemoaned Polonsky's blacklisting as a major loss to the film world. In the estimation of Andrew Sarris, "Polonsky, along with (Charlie) Chaplin and (Joseph) Losey, (was) one of the great casualties of the anti-Communist hysteria of the fifties."*** Polonsky himself says that he might have gone on "to do something better" as a film director in the 1950s. But, he remarks, that is all just speculative

---

Look, June 16, 1970.
**Film Culture*, Fall/Winter 1970.
***Sarris, *American Cinema*.

"junk." "What really happened was the blacklist; what really happened was the fact that I never directed anything—until much later in life." Polonsky says he never paused to ruminate about "what might have been" had his Hollywood career been allowed to continue. "...That's the worst form of punishment that the enemy can inflict, I would guess. To make you think, 'My God, how good things would have been if I had only cooperated with the Committee! What a lifetime of punishment that must be!'"*

The blacklist, Polonsky had commented, was a terribly effective instrument of repression. "The only more effective tool," he once remarked, "is execution."** Polonsky once defined the blacklist as "a secret agreement to ignore someone's existence." But, he added, "we have our own existence."*** Polonsky continued to function as a political and creative being throughout the blacklist period. The life of the blacklisted writer, he has said, was not as "narrow and sterile as one might believe."****

After his banishment from Hollywood, Polonsky moved back to New York with his family. "New York was pretty good," he says, "because it's a cosmopolitan town full of foreigners and gangsters and bums, and the rich life of a city. And, therefore, there was room in it." There was a small avant-garde film movement taking shape in the city at that time, but he never became involved in it. Over the years, he has often asked himself why. After all, he had already demonstrated that he had a feeling for film. Why should he have allowed himself to be pushed out of the medium altogether? He had been denied the opportunity to make feature films, but why did he never try to make dramatic shorts or documentaries? As he points out, "Film is like language—you don't have to write novels, you can write poems, you can write essays, you can write short documents."

---

*Film Culture, Fall/Winter 1970.
**Look, June 16, 1970.
***Los Angeles Times, February 27, 1970.
****Film Culture; Fall/Winter,1970.'????

There are several reasons he did not go this experimental route, says Polonsky. First of all, he says, he did not yet think of himself as a member of "the film art forum." He had not decided to become a filmmaker the way some people decide to become painters. He had stumbled into film and had enjoyed a brief infatuation with it, but his primary identity was still that of a writer. Secondly, the prospect of making $10,000 experimental films after working on million-dollar Hollywood features was not, to be frank, enormously attractive to him. And finally he had no idea of how one would go about raising even moderate sums of money for filmmaking. "It simply would have taken more experience and knowledge than I had," he concludes. "So I went back to practicing the profession which I knew—which was fiction writing."

After completing *A Season of Fear*, Polonsky eventually began writing for movies and television under the table. During the blacklist years, he wrote or rewrote a number of film scripts, using various pseudonyms and "fronts." Like Maltz, he will not reveal the titles of the screenplays, because he does not want to compromise those people who put their names to them. In any case, he says, only one or two are of any merit. Blacklisted writers worked under conditions which were less than ideal.

One of the movies which Polonsky wrote while he was blacklisted has already been disclosed: *Odds Against Tomorrow*, which starred Harry Belafonte as a hard-pressed nightclub entertainer who is forced into committing a robbery with an embittered white racist. When the movie appeared in 1959, it carried the name of black novelist John O. Killens, who was a friend of Polonsky's and Belafonte's. But the director of the movie, Robert Wise, later revealed that Polonsky had actually written it. Polonsky says that he and Belafonte planned to do four pictures together after that one. Each one, he says, was going to cover some area of black history. But none of them ever got off the ground.

Polonsky speaks with some pride about the television work he did during the fifties. He and two other blacklist victims, Arnold Manoff and Walter Bernstein, succeeded in becoming the chief writers of the widely acclaimed "You Are There" series, which premiered on CBS-TV in 1953. The program, which was directed by newcomer Sidney Lumet, recreated famous historical events as if they were just happening and being reported as news. Polonsky says that he and the other writers picked "all the forbidden subjects," including the trial-of Socrates, the Spanish Inquisition, Galileo's conflict with the Church, and the heroes and traitors of the American Revolution. Each show, he says, was a thinly veiled assault on the reactionary trend in American politics. "...It was probably the only place," he comments, "where any guerrilla warfare was conducted against McCarthy in a public medium."*

Polonsky and his co-writers worked "undercover" with the tacit cooperation of a few others. Their experience as blacklisted TV writers later became the basis for Bernstein's 1976 movie, *The Front*. Looking back, says Polonsky, there was a delightful irony to the whole experience. The series was a big hit for CBS and won the network a great deal of critical esteem. It was distributed to high schools throughout the country. The sponsor of the program was one of the nation's largest insurance companies. "And who's writing it?" laughs Polonsky. "Three blacklistees."

Polonsky continued to be active in radical politics after his blacklisting. It was his unwavering belief that socialism was the most just and equitable way of organizing modern life. And the Communist Party, in his mind, was still the best vehicle for bringing about a socialist transformation of society. His involvement with the Party was never free from certain tensions. As he had in the past, Polonsky saw there were undeniable contradictions between socialism's utopian goals and the Party's undemocratic bent. He was too strongly commited to the free reign of the intellect not to be offended by the Party's handling of the Maltz affair in 1946.** Polonsky was one of the few members of the Hollywood Section who defended Maltz's controversial essay on the artistic integrity of the writer. ("I strongly agreed with his opinion," says Polonsky, "that no intellectual ever endangers the Party. All he or she does is to encourage the Party to think.") But despite

---

Film Culture, Fall/Winter 1970.
**See previous chapter.

his aversion to that which was dogmatic and dull witted in the CP, he remained a Communist. The Party, he says, was *the* organizational expression of the left. To be outside it was to be outside of the main historical momentum of his time. During the years he belonged to the Party, declares Polonsky, there was no real possibility of operating effectively as an independent Marxist.

So one worked within the Party to make its programs and activities better, more thoughtful, more effective, more in tune with the contemporary American situation. And when a senseless directive was passed down from above, you could, on occasion ignore it. "You tell them one thing," remarks Polonsky, "and you do another thing. That corruption is a form of morality, not to persist in an error. Because only fools persist in errors." And when the Party committed you to a course of action from which you could not veer, without being expelled, you resigned yourself to it and looked to the future. Political involvement always carries with it a certain amount of irony, confusion, and error. No political party ever plots a flawless course through history, says Polonsky. "To have charity and clarity, so to speak, and always be right is just a dream, that's not the way it is. What it is is that people are mean, though they are often generous; people are confused, though they are often clear; and people are always wrong, even though they are sometimes right. That's the way, and the Party goes that way too. Then you hope a socialist society is established, and it serves so profound a need that it survives no matter what errors it makes."

In summer 1956, the storm of debate over the CP's authoritarian character and its subservient relationship to the Soviet Union, which had long been brewing within the Party ranks, at last began to erupt. The crisis was precipitated—and exacerbated—by Khrushchev's startling report on the crimes of the Stalin era which was delivered at the 20th Soviet Communist Party Congress in February and made public in June. For a period, it seemed as if the upheaval within the Party might lead to its revitalization as a political force. Internal discussion of the Party's failings was more frank and free-wheeling than at any other time in its history. There was hope that American Communists would at last develop a political form which was more democratic and more relevant to the U.S. situation.

It was in the wake of Khrushchev's revelations and the subsequent upheaval inside the CPUSA that Polonsky was asked by the Party publication, *Masses and Mainstream*, to write a review of *The Mandarins*, Simone de Beauvoir's provocative novel about the political and intellectual dilemmas of the left in postwar France. Polonsky took the opportunity to set down his thoughts about the relationship between artists and the Party, intellectual freedom and social commitment. The tendency of political parties, Polonsky wrote, is to demand absolute allegiance from their members. But the role of the artist, he stated, must always be to challenge accepted notions and provoke people "into new areas of experiment and expression."

"...If people are offended," he wrote, "because their cherished illusions are shaken or their covering faiths outraged, well, that is the very point of literature, that is the very motion of truthful life, to be shaken up, to be disturbed, to be awakened, even from a dream of the American or Soviet Paradise. There is no idea, no theory, no way of life that cannot be reshaped, illuminated, and made more human by being subject to the imagination and criticism of the artist."*

Polonsky's article restated and expanded upon the issues which Maltz had raised in his essay, "What Shall We Ask of Writers?" ten years earlier. These were issues which had been suppressed within the Party ever since that time, because of the withering criticism and abuse to which Maltz was subjected. Polonsky had not forgotten the way Maltz was treated when he "rather gently" endorsed the notion of artistic freedom. He compared the Party's treatment of Maltz to the way dissident intellectuals were handled by HUAC. "...Just as the House Committee is not merely content to attack those it thinks wrong but demands recantation and personal abasement, so it

---

*"The Troubled Mandarins;" *Masses and Mainstream*, August 1956. Polonsky used the nom de plume, "Timon," because, he says, he did not want people to write him letters.

was with Maltz at the hands of his friends. Tyranny is always the same even if it wears the mask of socialism."

It was Marx and Engels, wrote Polonsky, who "preached that only through socialism could intellectual freedom and personal liberty come to its legitimate and universal birth." Socialism "as a political economy," he declared, was rapidly coming into existence in various places around the globe. But for the coming of socialism to truly signify the liberation of the human spirit, he wrote, the Communist parties of the world must directly confront the undemocratic tendencies within them. "If this present crisis among Marxists," he concluded, "should end merely in a shakeup which perpetuates the mentality, and fears of inflexible men who have created the situation, then socialism may indeed come to this world as other societies have come, bringing enough happiness and enough pain, but not the promise and the intellectual spirit which was its challenge to every political economy before it."

The publication of Polonsky's forthright piece in *Masses and Mainstream* gives some indication of how tolerant the Party was in this period—although he was forced to withdraw the piece twice before the editors finally agreed to publish it in its original form. By the following year, however, the thorough-going process of re-examination, of which his article had been a part, had ground to a halt. Those in the reform bloc of the Party simply did not have the strength or numbers to prevail. Many of those who shared their progressive views had fled the Party after the initial shock of the Khrushchev revelations; others, demoralized by long years of struggle and resignation, left in the middle of the battle. In the end, the forces of orthodoxy reasserted their control over the Party. From that point on, it was doomed to political irrelevance.

"Many people left the Communist Party because they disagreed with it, fewer left because it disagreed with them, but most found themselves without a Communist Party since it, like the Cheshire cat, slowly disappeared from view except in the anti-Communist press. It became lifeless. It became, in fact, a figment of the imagination, and has no viable life in America today. The Communist Party known during the New Deal, the war, and the early stages of the Cold War no longer is anything but a historical lesson which like all history once learned should be, in fact, forgotten forever. We can't destroy the past but we must invent our own future. If Marxism ever meant anything at all, this is what it meant most to the radical mind, the scientific bent, the moral passions of my time as I tried to understand and live it. Success and failure are not useful judgements in measuring a human life. This is the message of art to science and ethics. It is obviously the character of radical art itself. Just as the nature of science is the ultimate absorbing question in a scientific life, so the very nature of politics is the most puzzling question in a political life. What we can't avoid is what we must choose not to avoid. The significant thing about communism (as about Christianity, American democracy, and the Roman Empire, for example), is that it happened and is happening."

What, in Polonsky's mind, is the most important legacy which the Communist Party has handed down to younger generations of leftists? "That it's possible," he says. "That it's possible to have a radical socialist party, an organized radical movement. We are still living in an economic and constitutional crisis which only radical politics can solve. The Communist Party was part of the historical tradition of socialism. And it played a role in the perpetuation of that dream, in the articulation of it. In the real world of events, only those who have never committed themselves to anything can take satisfaction in never having been wrong. For the rest of us, it's catch-as-catch-can with history."

*****

The blacklist ended for Polonsky in 1968, when Universal executive Jennings Lang and producer Frank Rosenberg allowed him to put his name on the movie *Madigan*, a police drama which he had been hired to rewrite. But his return as a Hollywood filmmaker was not complete until 1970, when Polonsky wrote and directed *Tell Them Willie Boy is Here*, a stylized and meaningful Western which featured Robert Blake, Katherine Ross, and Robert Redford. *Willie Boy*, which was Polonsky's second directing assignment in 22 years, was generally well-received by film critics. The film, which revolved around a young Indian's fatal stand against the forces of law and order, was interpreted by some reviewers to be Polonsky's statement on the deepening conflict between blacks, students and Vietnamese and the iron-fisted Nixon Administration. The following year, Polonsky directed *Romance of a Horse Thief*, a "fairy tale" about Jews and Cossacks in 1904 Poland. The picture was distributed ineffectually by Allied Artists and received little attention. Polonsky has not directed another film since *Romance of a Horse Thief*.*

In the flurry of interviews with Polonsky which appeared around the time of *Willie Boy's* release, the filmmaker emphasized that he had many future projects in mind—foremost of which was the screen adaptation of *Mario and the Magician*, a story which still seemed highly compelling to him. But so far the opportunity to make these pictures has eluded him. As he grows older, he says, his chances of directing another picture become more and more slim. Directing a feature-length movie, he points out, is very strenuous work. "But if the opportunity came along to direct a picture that I was genuinely concerned with," he remarks, "I would certainly give it a try."

There is, naturally, a vast difference between the film milieu Polonsky works in today and that of the 1940s. The Hollywood writers who lived under the studio system of the 1930s and 40s, Polonsky observes, generally thought of themselves as exploited workers who had little or no control over the products of their labor. But young people who enter the movie industry today, he says, regard themselves as "filmmakers," that is, as some kind of cross between an artist and an entrepreneur. They fashion their film projects and then seek financial investors. "In the Old Hollywood," says Polonsky, "they didn't let you think for a moment that you were anything more than an employee."

---

*cf: "Polonsky Retrospective"; *National Film Theatre*, March 1978. Re: *Romance of a Horse Thief*: "His films have an underlying optimism and concern which led Tom Milne in his generous review of this movie to refer continually to Renoir. The film, which I saw in Paris some five years ago, has taken long to surface here. It is a complicated and beautiful film, an historical romance set in a Polish village—near the German border—in 1904, part fantasy, partly real. Like Polonsky's other films, it is personal, willful and quite simply, not to be missed."

Hollywood filmmakers' newly developed sense of self-importance is, from a political point of view, both a good and a bad thing. On the one hand, people who think of themselves as creators and promoters are less inclined to develop a militant collective consciousness. On the other hand, people with an artistic sensibility have greater creative expectations and are more easily frustrated by the industry's rigid codes.

One of the main factors militating against progressive change in Hollywood is the absence of community among film workers. Again, this has not always been the case. The structure of the industry in the 1930s and 40s brought film workers into close, ongoing contact with one another. The old studios, which had hundreds of employees on contract all year round, were, says Polonsky, "enforced" communities. "When this town was made up of the great film 'baronies,' as I call them, then each barony was a community—enforced by violence and greed, which are two of the best elements for forming a society that I know of. And so they were real communities... Every studio had a writers table where all the writers sat and ate together; writers hung out in the same building and exchanged ideas. So even if you're working on nonsense, you're working *together*."

Today, however, there are only the vague outlines of a movie community in Hollywood and no organized radical life on an industry-wide scale. There is no formal political context in which these people can come together on a regular basis. Until one develops, the power relations within the entertainment industry will remain largely the same. The present state of inertia and fragmentation which afflicts the American left, he says, will at some point give way to a new political momentum.

"Now, somewhere, someplace, given the nature of things, this will happen. It always happens; it has happened before and it will happen again. There is no instant solution. There is no general answer. I mean there is no secret formula. The formula, as always, is simply passion, indignation and necessity."

II.
AT THE TOP:
WHAT CAN ONE PERSON DO?

Preface
Haskell Wexler
Jane Fonda
Thom Mount

Preface

It is often assumed that progressive individuals who reach top creative and managerial positions in Hollywood can make whatever they please: all they must do is exert themselves and their dreams are turned into films which become everyone else's dreams.

The following people are among the most powerful and celebrated progressives in the film industry. Haskell Wexler, winner of two Academy Awards, is generally considered to be one of the best cinematographers in Hollywood. Jane Fonda is one of the few "bankable" female stars—that is, she is one of the few actresses in Hollywood whose name can attract financing for a major motion picture. Thom Mount is a top executive at Hollywood's busiest, most prosperous studio.

These three people have indeed been at least partially responsible for some of Hollywood's most socially enlightened features in recent years: *Bound for Glory, Julia, Coming Home, The China Syndrome, Which Way Is Up?* and *Blue Collar*. But as they themselves readily admit, there are distinct limits to what they as individuals can do in the movie industry.

Filmmaking, Wexler remarks, is a collective process. So he must accomodate himself to the creative visions of those with whom he works. Wexler also says that Hollywood, as a whole, is ideologically opposed to films which are profoundly critical of the status quo. Fonda is somewhat more optimistic about the social potential of Hollywood films. But she concedes that it is very difficult—even for someone with her individual power—to push socially provocative films through studio channels. Fonda also says that she is hindered in her efforts by the short supply of talented, left wing screenwriters. In order to maintain his high-ranking studio position, Mount must turn out "a balanced program" of movies—that is, everything from the socially objectionable to the merely diverting to the deeply enlightening. Mount also can go only so far in defending a filmmaker's creative autonomy without risking his job.

All three Hollywood figures agree that audience tastes further limit their creative options. They believe that U.S. moviegoers, in general, will not sit still for films that are politically and aesthetically complex. This assumption, which is debatable, has led these Hollywood progressives (and others) to make films which are more action oriented, more swiftly paced, more narrowly focused, more superficial than they probably need to be. Hollywood's progressive filmmakers would do well to reexamine their conceptions of the movie audience, which is likely ready for much more than they have been given.

There is something distinctly contradictory about progressive-minded individuals, who are committed to a democratic reordering of U.S. society, wielding large amounts of cultural power—even if their power is somewhat constrained by various industry-related factors. But as long as the entertainment industry is structured the way it is—with a small number of executives, agents, producers, and film artists firmly in control—it would be impractical and unwise to ask Wexler, Fonda, and Mount to give up their elite positions. They are, after all, among the few people in Hollywood's upper echelons who feel a strong sense of social responsibility. If people like them were to fade away, Hollywood's film output would become noticeably less pertinent and provocative.

What we must ask of influential progressives in the film industry is not that they yield their power, but that they become more socially accountable. As long as they operate as isolated individuals, they will tend to be more sensitive to commercial pressures than public wishes. They must find ways to stay systematically in touch with those for whom (and with whom) they produce culture. Fonda took an important step in this direction when she became involved in progressive organizations like the Campaign for Economic Democracy (CED). But, so far, CED has not made the democratic restructuring of Hollywood a fundamental part of its political strategy.

Progressive stars and executives should not give up their inordinate power—not while Hollywood is still controlled by a powerful elite. But they should help develop a movement whose aim, in part, is to redistribute cultural power among a wider range of film workers and consumers. They must, in other words, be courageous and committed enough to assist in the overhauling of a cultural system from which they derive personal benefits.

Haskell Wexler

Haskell Wexler's career as a cameraman dates back to the years following World War II when he worked on several labor films, including *Deadline for Action* (1946), a forty minute documentary financed by the left wing United Electrical, Radio and Machine Workers union (UE). *Deadline for Action,* which was written and directed by Carl Marzani, analyzed the postwar economic situation from a UE worker's point of view, focusing on the nationwide CIO strikes of 1945-46. Wexler also shot films for the United Packinghouse Workers of America and former vice president Henry Wallace's progressive movement as well as a documentary about Alabama cotton mill workers called *A Half Century with Cotton.* Wexler believed that film should serve an important social purpose. "I never made a separation," he says, "between film as a political tool and as a technique. When you express yourself you should try to express those things which are most important to you. And if you're lucky you can do that; if you're like most people in the world you say what you get paid to say. But the ideal is to do what you enjoy doing professionally and have it express what you believe."

Wexler became politically active during his youth in Chicago. "I was involved in a lot of radical things. I was a member of practically every organization on the Attorney General's list.* I was against Franco's Spain. At that time I was in high school. In fact, some of the information I got under the Freedom of Information Act showed that the FBI and the Dies Committee (HUAC) had spoken to my eighth grade teacher and my teachers in high school. I was a member of the American Students Union, in fact I was on the national committee of it. And this was all in the record." Young Wexler, who had shot his family's home movies as a boy, quickly became known within Chicago's left wing community as someone who knew how to use a camera. "If something was happening," he

---

*In 1947 Attorney General Tom Clark published a list of dissident organizations operating in the U.S. The list successfully undermined the political effectiveness of those groups which were cited.

remembers, "like a strike or a demonstration, somebody would say, "Oh well Haskell does movies, you know, and can take some pictures.' "

The left wing movement helped promote Wexler's development as a filmmaker and it benefited from his growing expertise. By the mid-fifties Wexler had established a reputation as one of the leading cameramen in Chicago. He worked steadily on television commercials and educational films. He photographed a documentary about urban renewal for Encyclopedia Britannica Films (*The Living City*) which won a 1954 Academy Award. In between his commercial assignments, the young cameraman continued to work on movies which reflected his social views.

As the Cold War intensified, however, political filmmaking became more and more problematic. In 1949, the CIO expelled UE and ten other progressive unions for refusing to endorse the government's Cold War policies. Unions such as UE had provided left wing documentary filmmakers with important economic support, but after the split UE became too weak to continue underwriting the production and distribution of films. In 1951, blacklisted Hollywood filmmakers Herbert Biberman, Paul Jarrico, and Michael Wilson set out to make *Salt of the Earth*, a feature-length dramatization of a New Mexico copper miners' strike. The project, which was undertaken in cooperation with the Mine, Mill and Smelter Workers Union (one of those purged from the CIO), ran into a series of nearly insurmountable difficulties. The film crew was harassed by local vigilantes while on location in Silver City, New Mexico; the leading actress, Mexican Rosaura Revueltas, was deported before shooting was completed; film laboratories throughout the country refused to process the footage. Wexler gave some crucial assistance to the beleaguered filmmakers. "I didn't really know them personally," he says, "but Biberman came to me in Chicago and he told me that they had this film that they made and no laboratory would develop it. And he wanted to know if I could do it. I knew a guy at Crescent Film Labs in Chicago. And he and I went in there for three nights from 6:30 at night until 6:30 in the morning and processed *Salt of the Earth*. I don't think we developed the whole film, but we did a good part of it. Just me and the other guy and the machines." When the feature was finally completed, only a handful of theater owners dared to screen it. Hollywood labor boss Roy Brewer ordered union projectionists not to run the film, and the American Legion threatened to picket theaters where it was scheduled to play.

In 1956 Wexler moved to Hollywood in order to work on dramatic features. He stopped shooting labor films after coming to the Coast and began to concentrate solely on developing his craft and building his career. The political context which had given his documentary work shape and direction no longer existed. "We were all cut off from our roots," remarks Wexler, "because the left wing movement had fallen apart. There were no groups, there was nothing, it was every man for himself...I always wanted to have films express my views, which change, you know. But in the fifties, when my views tended to be amorphous, when they were diffused and defused, I think I probably worked more on the technical end of filmmaking." While he was in Chicago, the government had taken away Wexler's passport (soon before he was to leave for England to shoot a series of historical films). The camera-man knew people in different lines of work who were blacklisted because of their political backgrounds (although they were generally led to believe that they were being fired because their work had slipped). Like many others who were subjected to political harassment during the Cold War period, Wexler grew very cautious. "I got scared. I mean I had the FBI following me. I had different things that scared me. I didn't suddenly say, 'Oh, I'm scared, I'm not going to be political any more.' But I did just start concentrating on being a pro-fessional."

Despite the credits he had accumulated in Chicago, Wexler was unable to break into the highly exclusive Holly-wood cinematographers union for a number of years. "The union here is not what unions are supposed to be," he says. "Unions are supposed to organize people, to get workers to come together. 'If you want to join the union, come join, get better working conditions, better wages and so forth.' That should be their attitude. But the unions here have become like a lot of businesses, closed and special. I'm very pro-union, but I'm against those unions which have forgotten their most important responsibility—which is to elevate the status and protect the status of the working person."

While waiting to be admitted into Hollywood's elite labor pool, Wexler worked on a string of low-budget assignments. *Stakeout on Dope Street*, a graphic little drama about the heroin trade (one of the first to deal forthrightly with the subject of narcotics), and *The Hoodlum Priest*, the story of a Jesuit priest who dedicated himself to the rehabilitation of delinquents and ex-convicts, won praise from some critics for their tough documentary-style treatment of controversial themes. *New York Times* critic A.H. Weiler noted the "sharp, authentic, pictorial look" of *Hoodlum Priest*; Wexler, he commented, photographed the "cheap saloons, alleys and slums" of St. Louis (where the drama was set) "in newsreel detail." "All I knew was reality, the documentary," Wexler later remarked about his work on *Stakeout on Dope Street*. "So my ignorance of the other way sort of helped."*

Other features Wexler worked on in that period, such as *Five Bold Women*, a slightly risqué Western about a group of female convicts on their way to the penitentiary, and *Angel Baby*, a steamy melodrama about the love between two evangelical preachers, made less of a critical impression. "The movie is maddeningly cynical," wrote the *McCall's* movie critic of *Angel Baby*, "playing for easy emotionalism, making no attempt at realism, using blatant background music to heighten cheap and often sordid situations designed for the evil minded. It is a revolting example of the worst Hollywood has to offer, and we urge you to stay away from it." Since he was barred from shooting union pictures, the range of films Wexler could work on was fairly limited. How discriminating was he at that point in his career, before he had firmly established himself in Hollywood? "Just slightly," he says with a smile.

In the early 1960s, Wexler's naturalistic camerawork on low-budget features began to attract the attention of Hollywood's top creative echelon. Director Elia Kazan tapped him to photograph *America, America* (1963); soon afterwards he was

---

Film Quarterly, Spring 1968.

hired to shoot another major Hollywood feature, *The Best Man* (1964), and with the support of the film's producer he finally broke into the organized ranks of Hollywood's cinematographers. Wexler developed a reputation as a hard working and imaginative craftsman who took an active interest in the film as a whole. "While most Hollywood cameramen concern themselves solely with the way a picture looks," commented a *New York Times* entertainment reporter in 1966, "Wexler commits the heresy of also being interested in what it has to say." "I actually worked on the script of *The Best Man*, somewhat," recalls the cameraman. "In fact, whenever I worked on a film, in order for me to see it photographically, I would always rewrite the script. For instance, I might say, 'Wouldn't this scene be better if it were played in a bus station?' and then I would change a couple lines. I think every person who works on a film—if they think of themselves as a filmmaker—should involve themselves deeply in the process of the film."

Following his debut in union pictures, Wexler proceeded to draw a series of major Hollywood assignments, including *The Loved One* (1965) and *Who's Afraid of Virginia Woolf?* (1966). His work on the latter film won the cameraman the 1967 Academy Award for best black and white photography. Wexler created a stir when he accepted his statuette by declaring, "I hope we can use our art for love and peace," a sentiment which—at that stage in the Vietnam War—carried political significance. "His seriousness and obvious sincerity startled the Academy Awards audience, long used to the standard thank yous to co-workers and producers," wrote a *Los Angeles Times* reporter. "I realized I might never get another chance at an audience of 60 or 70 million people," Wexler told the reporter. "It seemed too big an opportunity to miss. What was I supposed to do—thank my gaffer and Jack Warner?"

While Wexler was establishing a place for himself in the film industry in the early sixties, the spirit of protest and social struggle, which had long been dormant in the United States, began to be revived by the growing civil rights movement. As he observed what was going on in the country, the Hollywood cameraman—who had not shot a political film since his days in the Chicago left—felt the urge once again to document the making of history. In August 1963, Wexler took a leave of absence from the movie industry and set out to make a film about the March on Washington, which had been called by civil rights leaders to press for the passage of federal anti-discrimination laws. "I was interested in the civil rights movement," he later told *Film Quarterly*. "I had worked in the south a long time ago when there was no civil rights movement, and I had not done anything except follow the box score, so to speak. I thought the best way for me to reacquaint myself with what the young people were doing, what was going on, was to make this film."

Wexler and two assistants boarded a Greyhound bus which was taking thirty-seven black and white freedom marchers from San Francisco to the nation's capital and they spent the next three days and two nights filming the passengers as they sped toward their destination. *The Bus*, the 60-minute documentary which Wexler later assembled from this footage, is a modest but moving film which evokes the intense idealism and commitment of the period. In one sequence, an elderly black man recalls the time he was chased from Washington by a group of whites during a 1919 race riot. "This time, he remarks, "I won't be scared because there'll be 100,000 people with me." A cluster of clean-cut teenagers pass time aboard the bus by singing protest songs like "Down by the Riverside" and "Blowin' in the Wind" with the spirited feeling of the newly committed. At a rest stop along the highway, several black passengers talk about the harassment and physical abuse they have been subjected to during the freedom rides in the South. One reports that Southern police sometimes use electric cattle prods on civil rights marchers. "We *will* overcome though," declares another, breaking the grim mood with good-natured determination. Wexler's camera follows the passengers as they emerge from the bus in Washington and join thousands of others who are converging on the Lincoln Memorial. There is a tremendous outpouring of human energy: singing, chanting, marching in step. The film ends with a sweeping shot of the massive demonstration.

The Bus received positive reviews but Wexler could not convince any Hollywood distributors to pick it up and the film ultimately returned only a small fraction of the $60,000 he put into it. Wexler insisted that the manner in which *The Bus* had been photographed was "the only way" to make movies. "The problem," he added, "is that when you make them you may have to eat them..."* Soon after he finished shooting *The Bus*, Wexler was back in Hollywood working on high salaried commercial assignments.

As the sixties progressed, Wexler grew increasingly critical of Hollywood features. He told a *New York Times* reporter in 1966 that the "vast sums of money" invested in studio pictures "create awesome pressures on the director, the actors and the crew" and discourage innovation. "The ideal picture," he remarked, "should cost maybe $100,000 and should be made by people who are willing to try anything." After *Virginia Woolf*, he worked on two movies with director Norman Jewison, *In the Heat of the Night* (1967) and *The Thomas Crown Affair* (1968), both of which he publicly disparaged. *Heat of the Night*, which starred Sidney Poitier as a big city detective and Rod Steiger as a redneck sheriff who is forced to rely on the black man's services, "had a mediocre script" Wexler commented, "—a fake sociological script, with little understanding of today's South. I resent films that talk about subjects that I'm interested in and pretend to be on the good side but are superficial."** In a June 1968 article in *Boston After Dark*, Wexler criticized the shallowness of *Thomas Crown*, a slickly produced crime drama which employed a large amount of visual gimmickry. "A great deal of talent went into *Thomas Crown*," he remarked, "—the cast and crew are all vastly experienced professionals—but all that talent adds up to nothing. *Thomas Crown* is a hyped-up picture replete with vacuity...When you know it's about absolutely nothing, you try to infuse it with all the tricks in the book to confuse the audience into thinking something's there. *Thomas Crown* is a *great* commercial picture."

Wexler believed that Hollywood features simply did not reflect the fundamental social changes which were occurring in the United States in the sixties. Different cinematic forms

---

Film Quarterly, Spring 1968
**Film Quarterly,* Spring 1968.

were required, he felt, to depict what was really going on in the country. "I would like to find some wedding between features and cinema-verite," he declared in a Spring 1968 *Film Quarterly* interview. "I have very strong opinions about us and the world, and I don't know how in hell to put them all in one basket."

Early in 1968, Wexler was asked by a Paramount Pictures executive if he would like to direct a film adaptation of a novel which the studio had bought called *The Concrete Wilderness*. The novel, which was about a lonely boy and a magazine photographer who explore the hidden world of wildlife in New York City, did not particularly interest Wexler. But he jumped at the chance to direct. ("When you're the cameraman all you can do is make suggestions," he had stated the previous year to the *Los Angeles Times*, " and when they're accepted the director usually gets the credit.") "I told the studio, 'Yeah, I want to direct,' " recalls Wexler, " 'but do you mind if I change the script a little bit?' They said, 'No, do whatever you want.' So I proceeded to change the script. In fact, I just wrote a completely new one."

The new screenplay, which Wexler began filming in Chicago in summer 1968, was concerned not with nature but with the deepening conflicts in U.S. society. It had a fictional plot, but Wexler planned to build the story around the Democratic Convention, which was expected to be—and which turned out to be—a tumultuous political event. He titled the film *Medium Cool*.

The central character in *Medium Cool* is TV news cameraman John Cassellis, a man who is accustomed to viewing the world with cool professional detachment. As the social turmoil around him intensifies, Cassellis is strongly challenged to reevaluate his work, its influence on the public, the corruption of the media, and his personal responsibilities. "You are the exploiters," a black radical tells him during a tense confrontation. "You're the ones who distort and ridicule and emasculate us...You don't know the people. You don't show the people...Why don't you find out what really is? Why do you always got to wait till somebody gets killed, man? 'Cause somebody is gonna get killed!" The cameraman's illusions about being a neutral observer are further shaken when he learns that his television station has been letting the police and

FBI study his news footage. "What am I—a fink?" he explodes. "How can I go out and cover a story? It's a wonder more cameras haven't been smashed! I want to know *why* nobody told me what the hell's been goin' on, because you can bet your ass out there in the streets, *they* know." In the film's concluding scenes, the newsman is swept up in the storm outside the Democratic Convention—an event which he had set out to cover, but which turns out to be the indirect cause of his death.

It occurs to Cassellis, at a late stage in his disillusionment, that the media is guilty of a monstrous deception: he accuses it of "draining off" the public's emotions into scripted channels. The public's grief, rage, and bitterness over the assassinations of Robert Kennedy and Martin Luther King in spring 1968 are given ritualized expression, comments Cassellis, in a "nation-wide coast-to-coast network special called 'Mourn the Martyr.'" *Medium Cool* was a strong indictment of the way mass communications dilutes the meaning and impact of social experience. Wexler's attempt to integrate fiction and reality was rough and awkward, but the documentary footage of the Convention hall hysteria and police violence in Grant Park gave the film a political immediacy which no other Hollywood picture of the period carried.

Paramount maintained minimal supervision over Wexler during the making of the movie. "Since it was a negative pick-up—since I was paying for everything up front myself—they didn't bother with it much," he says. "They didn't have to write checks all the time. And they figured, 'Well, it's a low enough budget if he makes the film, and he shoots it in Chicago instead of New York.' And I told them I had a scene in it with a kid who trained pigeons and all that kind of thing. So it was very loose."

When the film was finally screened for the studio executives, they were taken aback. "They came out looking like somebody hit them on the head," says Wexler. "They literally didn't know what to think. They knew they were in the presence of a kind of film they hadn't seen before. It threatened them. They didn't know how to deal with the film, because most Hollywood films don't have anything practical to do with the real world—certainly not the immediate real world."

Gulf and Western, the conglomerate which owns Paramount, initially refused to release *Medium Cool*. It was rumored that Mayor Daley and other influential democratic politicians were greatly displeased with the film. *Time* reported that one member of Gulf and Western's board of directors threatened to resign if the film were ever released. "Gulf and Western's main objection to the movie was completely political," says Wexler. "But they decided not to launch a frontal attack on the film. Instead of saying they would not distribute the film because of its politics, they claimed there were legal problems."

Gulf and Western informed Wexler that his film could not be insured because he had failed to get signed releases from the people who appeared in the demonstration sequences. ("My contention," says Wexler, "was that these were people in a public place doing public things and I didn't need releases from them.") Attorneys for the conglomerate also told the filmmaker that if someone left a movie theatre after viewing *Medium Cool* and committed a crime, Gulf and Western executives could be held legally responsible. Recalls Wexler: "So I said, 'In other words, if someone goes in and sees *I Am Curious Yellow*, which was out at that time, and then goes out and sleeps with someone who is not his wife, then Barney Rosset can be put in jail for distributing the picture?' I mean it was just inconceivable. They said, 'No smartass talk. This is the law and we know the law.'"

Wexler finally hired ex-Supreme Court Justice Arthur Goldberg, who was in private practice in New York, to get his legal opinion about *Medium Cool*. I sat there with him while he saw the film," says Wexler. "And he said, 'Well, this is a very interesting movie—I've never seen one like it.' I said, 'Yes, but what about my legal problem. I have all this money tied up and everything. And he said, 'Well, it's my opinion that you don't have a legal problem. You were not invading (the demonstrators') privacy.' He gave me the whole legal background on it. And so we gave the opinion to Paramount. And that added force, plus the fact that some people in the corporation felt that enough time had passed since the convention and they could make some money, made them decide to release the film."

Medium Cool received a great deal of attention from film critics and entertainment reporters, but the audience turnout was disappointing. Nine months had passed since the film was completed, more than a year had gone by since the summer '68 Chicago demonstrations, and much of its immediacy had been lost. Despite the minimal amount of sex and nudity in the film, it was branded "X" by the Motion Picture Code and Ratings Administration. The rating, which Wexler calls "political," kept out a sizeable share of the youth audience. Wexler held a press conference to protest the X rating and went before the movie board to appeal their decision, but, says the filmmaker, Paramount failed to support him. "Ordinarily, a studio will fight against an X rating...But I was there alone." Wexler also faults the studio for not advertising the movie properly and for distributing it "in the worst way possible...They put it in theaters like the Oriental Theater in downtown Chicago which nobody goes to at all. They just dribbled it out." *Medium Cool*, concludes Wexler, was "effectively sabotaged" by the very corporation which financed the film.

His long, drawn-out conflict with Paramount over *Medium Cool* was an eye-opening experience for Wexler. "I was surprised," he says. "It was probably naive of me, but I figured that if you made an interesting film that was well reviewed and exciting, they would jump on it, they would publicize it, they would sell it. I was convinced that if you did something well enough they had to recognize it. And that just wasn't so. What *encouraged* me was that in the process of making the film, I learned a lot about young people, I learned a lot about the antiwar movement, I learned a lot about what was going on which I myself had lost some track of. And that was what was encouraging to me—there was a whole world out there that I could feel good about."

******

Wexler has not yet been given the opportunity to direct another commercial feature. In the 1970s he has divided his time between photographing Hollywood movies, making television commercials, and filming political documentaries. Since *Medium Cool*, he has relied fundamentally on his documentary film work to express his views. "Usually I'm more involved in what a documentary has to say," he remarks, "than in what a feature has to say." His list of documentary credits in recent years includes *Interviews with My Lai Veterans* (1970),

Brazil: A Report on Torture (1971), *An Interview with Salvador Allende, President of Chile* (1971), *Introduction to the Enemy* (1974), *Underground* (1976), and a 1976 campaign film he made for the left wing People's National Party of Jamaica.

Wexler is aware that he is serving a significant social purpose by recording modern history from a critical perspective. History is generally recorded by those in power, he points out. "I don't think we can rely on governments, no matter how benevolent, to be the sole chroniclers of history," commented the filmmaker in a winter 1975-76 *Sight and Sound* interview. But, says Wexler, he does not shoot documentaries solely for the public's enlightenment. His nonfiction films are learning experiences for him as well: they extract him from his Hollywood routine, they take him all over the world, they acquaint him with political struggles and leading actors in the global arena who most of us know only from a distance. They give him a sense of involvement in history.

"Just the other day," says Wexler, "I looked at the interview Saul Landau and I did with Allende—in the light of everything we've learned since the military coup. And boy it just about made me cry, because I realized that I was sitting right there with that man, who had tremendous compassion for the people. He was a medical doctor, you know, and he knew how much they suffered. And he was also in the Chilean Senate for years and he believed in democracy as we were brought up to believe in it. And that's what killed him! Because if he had done what Fidel probably told him to do—'Look, kick these generals out of the goddamn army and take so many people and line them up against a wall.' But he wasn't about to do it. In the interview, he talks about the importance of the law and the Constitution. And we asked about the CIA's involvement in the country. Well of course the U.S. government is doing some things monetarily, he says, but we haven't seen any real pressures. I mean, the beautiful naivete of this man! When I first heard about him, I said, 'Well here's someone I can truly...' I mean Chile was the first country where they voted a socialist government in. And he's going to try to maintain democracy, he's not going to step on people, and then—we know what happened. It really breaks you up. And so, at least to feel that in one way or another I was part of that historical moment is important to me."

Wexler's success as a Hollywood cinematogapher has provided him with the financial resources to make documentary films, but the possessions and personal obligations he has accumulated impose definite limits on the amount of time he can devote to non-commercial work. Wexler cannot afford to stay away too long from the Hollywood production line. "I'm subject to certain temptations and seductions," he says. "Like I have twelve cars. (he laughs) Simple example. I have two Arriflex BLs, each costing $52,000, plus a number of other expensive cameras. In other words I have the accoutrements of a wealthy person. I have advisors, I have accountants. I'm a big business; and the big business grabs you by the tail. Suppose I wanted to go to Angola to make a documentary—in fact, I *was* invited to go there with Saul Landau. So I think 'Well I have certain responsibilities, and if I go...' And a lot of the responsibilities relate to *having* things. Owning things. And the more things you have, and the more people become dependent on you, the more you have to do things you may not feel are important but which you have to do. First of all, you have to pay for things you own. Second, you have friends. Like I have a crew with whom I just finished 110 shooting days on a Hollywood picture. And these guys in the crew, if I work they work. If I don't work, they may or may not depending on the work situation. And then I have a family; my son's going to buy a house. I'm going to loan him the money—seventy-five grand... So what happens is that if you have things, you have to protect them, you have to insure them, you have to lock them up, you have to clean them, you have to maintain them. And if you have people who depend on you, because you're their father or their friend, you can't desert them."

Wexler has photographed several major Hollywood features in the 1970s including *One Flew Over the Cuckoo's Nest*, *Bound for Glory*, and *Coming Home*. He has turned down many more screenplays. Wexler says he would never work on a picture whose social viewpoint was fundamentally different from his own. "I don't think it has to do with politics per se. It's just that you invest so much of yourself when you work on a film, that you couldn't live with yourself if the film expressed views contrary to yours. If course they can't always coincide with your perspective as strongly as you want." No one can act in a steadfastly principled manner in a commercial environment like Hollywood, emphasizes Wexler. What you must do, he says, is carefully regulate how much you yield to the industry. "In this business, everything you do is a series of compromises. You figure out what compromises you're willing to make and when. I mean, to say you can be pure and continue to work is really utopian. It's just not possible. So you just have to figure out where to draw the line and how to draw the line... You have to function in this world and it's not a world totally of your own making. So you're going to have to work on some things which are not exactly what you want. And you'll do them. As long as you're aware of what you're doing, your integrity is protected to a certain extent. You say to yourself, "Well, this is the fourth time I've done this kind of job in the past year—I better start doing something else.' You have to have some threshold."

Perhaps Wexler's greatest concession to the market was Dove Films, a production outfit he co-founded after *Medium Cool* to make television commercials. Wexler and his partner built Dove into a very lucrative business. During his six years with the company, the cameraman shot commercials for a variety of well endowed clients including McDonald's, Volkswagen, Polaroid, and Plymouth. "I shot everything," he says. "I can still turn on the television and see all kinds of them." Wexler found that the best way of going about this work was in a detached frame of mind. "I'm sure that you've done this because you've both been students," he says, "but I always entered into them as if I were making sociological observations. I mean I would just listen to these people talk about things of absolutely no importance at all as if they were the most crucial things in the world; and then they would employ armchair Freudian techniques to influence people to do this and do that. And on the Kool-Aid commercials, the kids have to have excellent teeth because it has all this sugar in it. You know, hundreds of things like that."

But, admits Wexler, this way of approaching his work was "actually a kind of rationalizing. See, I would excuse to myself what I was doing by observing. And I observed a lot. I knew a lot about advertising and agency people and commercials. But I made them! I did them!" (he laughs) Why *did* Wexler film TV commercials, one of the more insidious forms of consciousness manipulation? "Well, to tell the truth, I liked getting all that money. (he laughs) I *really* liked it. But it just takes so much time. And you have to pay the price, you really have to pay the price."

There are few committed leftists in Hollywood with as much creative status as Haskell Wexler. He is generally regarded as one of the industry's top cinematographers. Yet Wexler does not feel that he wields a great deal of personal power. He has found that his ability to influence Hollywood's creative output is constrained by a number of factors. Wexler was relieved of his duties on a couple of major productions in recent years (*The Conversation, One Flew Over The Cuckoo's Nest*) after having artistic disagreements with the film directors. Milos Forman, director of *Cuckoo's Nest*, told entertainment publications that Wexler was replaced as cameraman midway through shooting because his lighting style was inhibiting the actors and changing the tone of the movie. Wexler strongly denied that his photographic approach had constrained the actors. "I set up two cameras to work instead of one because I wanted to try to get the impromptu things," he told the *Hollywood Reporter*. "I'm very acquainted with impromptu work. I'm working on documentaries all the time. That's my forte."

"Anybody in films," says Wexler, "has frustrations due to the fact that films are a cooperative art. I don't care who you are. I mean you'll always find people complaining that this son of a bitch wrecked that, or wishing that the film would be this way or that way. It's a danger of the medium. You're apt to be unhappy about certain things other people do."

What is his opinion of the way *Cuckoo's Nest* turned out? "I felt it could've been a better film. I think that it went for the cheap punch, but it worked. I mean there was a lot more in the script and in the actors and in the location—in the film that we shot—than what finally went on the screen. But maybe that's all that could be on the screen. Because I think people want the goods and bads, and they want things reduced to a more simplistic level than I like."

Wexler believes that at this stage in the evolution of American cinema, it is exceedingly difficult to integrate social commentary and entertainment in a sophisticated way. Movie audiences in this country, he says, are not accustomed to watching intricate treatments of social issues on the screen. They have been conditioned to look for easily identifiable heroes and villains and violent and simplistic dramatic resolutions. "The purpose of motion pictures is to provoke visceral responses," states the cinematographer. "They generally have very little aesthetic or intellectual content. I mean if you move somebody that means you move them by frightening them, by giving them goose bumps, by shocking them, even by disgusting them. The psychology behind watching movies is the same as that behind watching sports. People want to believe in something, they want a winner and a loser, they want my team and your team, and they want to simplify goods and bads. Our society has become so complex and so undefinable and so unresolvable. People experience many, many frustrations in their everyday lives which they can't easily cope with. So they look for the atom bomb in movies, they look for the shoot-em-up at the end. Bang, bang, all the bad guys are dead. And they look for the blitz—the blitz is a football term. Actually it's a World War II term that has to do with Nazi Germany's army. Blitzkrieg—lightening warfare. They look for the blitz. And this is part of what's in the air, in the collective unconscious."

Wexler says that he had high hopes for *Bound for Glory*, the story of hobo troubador Woody Guthrie. Guthrie's folk-singing career, which got underway in the Southwest Dust-bowl during the Great Depression, was marked by a passionate concern for the poor and downtrodden. And the people involved in the filming of his story were progressive individuals who wanted to show the real Woody. But, unfortunately, remarks Wexler, something went awry with the film. "I knew Woody. I was a Merchant sailor when he was shipping out so I spent quite a bit of time with him. My kids were brought up on his music. I really felt there was a chance of making a great film about a true American hero. So I tried to give my ideas about what I thought Woody represents to the film, to the script, to Hal (Ashby, the director). And everybody connected with the film, including the producers, wanted to make a film which represented Woody Guthrie. And Marjorie Guthrie (the folk-singer's widow) was on the set, Arlo (Woody's son) was there. Pete Seeger was there from time to time... But the film doesn't have any bite to it. I mean Woody Guthrie was blacklisted,

Woody Guthrie was called a Communist. Just eight years ago in Oklahoma they wanted to name a library after him and the American Legion blocked it because he was called a Communist. All the most controversial aspects of Woody Gutherie's life are not in the film."

Wexler says the reasons *Bound for Glory* fell short of his expectations are "a mystery" to him. "And it's not just this film either. There's something about the huge amount of money which is invested in Hollywood movies that does something to them. Those dollars, like some osmotic blood, seep into the project and it becomes more like everything else you see, more like the system. I really don't know. Because on that film and other films I've worked on you can say, 'He's a good person, he believes in this.' And then you go to the movie theater, and it's not that different from any other film you've seen...I don't know the explanation for it. I hate to condemn a film because it has a big budget or because it's a Hollywood film. It's just been my experience that it happens the way I describe it. It doesn't mean that you have to go out with your Super 8 camera with only $5 in your pocket. The reverse won't necessarily make you a good filmmaker or your film good. But I don't know how to overcome the other problem."

In Wexler's opinion, Hollywood has not yet produced "an honest working class film" or a "truly left wing political film." "When is the last time you saw an honest portrait of a factory worker in an American film?" he asks. After more than twenty years in the motion picture industry, Wexler has come to believe that it is impossible to make a powerful and fundamental cinematic critique of the system in Hollywood. "I just don't think it's possible to feed into the normal distribution channels a dramatic film which hits people in such a way as to make them want to do something right away," declares the cinematographer. "I mean if someone wanted to make a film which exposed the contemporary U.S. as a society which puts profit values above human values, a society which says to corporations, 'OK, you can send this cancer-causing gas into the air for the next seven years because we know it's going to cost a lot of money for you to stop it this year'...well, a movie like that is not possible, not possible. And they won't say that you can't do it because of the politics. They'll say it won't sell.

"In fact," he continues, "people won't even write such a film because they know in advance what sells and what doesn't. If you're a writer, you're not going to sit down and break your ass for months and months writing something that no one's going to put on television and no one's going to put in the theaters. You learn to practice self-censorship. Because the economic system says, 'If you want to make a buck, we will reward you with a buck if you write something about cops and robbers. If you write something about some crazy, dark, insane person who's like Robert De Niro or Al Pacino."

Although Wexler is deeply aware of the political limits of Hollywood features, he enjoys working on cultural products which will be viewed by the general public for years to come. He derives great pleasure from the knowledge that his work and ideas are preserved on celluloid. "I think the reason I like working on these films is that they give you a degree of immortality. I mean you look at an old movie on the TV and there's Lee Cobb or Gary Cooper. They're walking around and talking, and they've been dead for years! It's the same with filmmaking. If I do something I'm proud of, even if it's not magnificent, then something in the back of my mind says that when I'm dead what I've done is still living."

*****

Midway through the making of *Underground* (1976), a documentary about the Weather Underground which was produced by Wexler, Emile de Antonio, and Mary Lampson, the filmmakers were ordered to appear along with their negatives and tapes, before a federal grand jury in Los Angeles.* The film, which centered around an extensive interview with five fugitive leaders of the Weather organization, was an embarrassment to the Justice Department and the FBI, whose investigators had been unable to crack the clandestine political group. Wexler and the two other filmmakers declared that they would not cooperate with the grand jury, arguing that the subpoenas violated their First Amendment rights. Within two days, a group of concerned Hollywood personali-

---

*Wexler agrees with much of the Weather Underground's critique of the U.S. as an imperialistic power, but he is opposed to the tactics which the group employs to attack imperialism. Why did he agree to director de Antonio's request to shoot the film? His answer, which

ties (including Hal Ashby, Warren Beatty, Peter Bogdanovich, Jeff Bridges, Mel Brooks, William Friedkin, Elia Kazan, Shirley MacLaine, Terry Malick, Jack Nicholson, Arthur Penn, Frank Pierson, Rip Torn, Robert Towne, Jon Voight, and Robert Wise) was mobilized to support the filmmakers. They signed a statement in defense of "the right of people to make a film about any subject, and specifically the right of these people to make a film with and about the Weather Underground Organization." Ten days after the subpoenas were issued, they were withdrawn—in part because of the uproar they had created in movie industry circles.

The quick action taken by a segment of the industry to block the suppression of the film was an encouraging sign. Some observers thought it signaled a possible return to the passionate social commitment of the pre-blacklist days. "One unforeseen offshoot of (the) encounter may well be the reemergence of the intense sense of engagement that characterized Hollywood in the thirties and forties," wrote left wing journalist Peter Biskind in the *New York Times*. Wexler too was greatly heartened by the aid he received from his film colleagues. "I didn't expect that kind of support *at all*," he says. "It was a complete surprise to me—and a very pleasant surprise... After all, the Weather Underground is not the most popular type of organization in the liberal community... But (these Hollywood personalities) were perceptive enough to realize that this was a civil liberties issue. It had to do with *their* films. It had to do with the fact that if they made some film, the government could go in before they finished that film and say, 'Let's see the film—we want to see if there's anything censorable in it. We're not going to hurt you, we just want to look over your shoulder and examine your film and listen to your tapes.' It's really to those people's credit that they stood up against that kind of thing."

---

was somewhat surprising, is characteristically frank: "I think that adventure was probably high on the list of motivations. I mean I could think of more socially appropriate motivations (he laughs), but I really think that's closest to the truth. Second is that de Antonio is a very interesting, persuasive, exciting person and I talked to him and a lot of it was through that. And the third probably was curiousity, which is connected to the adventure thing."

But Wexler did not interpret the flurry of political activity around *Underground* as a significant new burgeoning of the left in Hollywood. It seems to Wexler that the community of socially committed people in the film industry is not particularly active or cohesive. Very few political causes win widespread attention and support in Hollywood, he asserts. "The Hollywood community has been fairly good on the farmworkers. It's the one exception that I can think of. (Oh, and of course the American Civil Liberties Union activities also get strong support.) I was at a Hollywood party a couple weeks ago and they raised $15,000 in this one guy's house for the farmworker' union. And while we were making *Bound for Glory*, we gave quite a lot of money and projectors and everything else to the farmworkers... You know, Hollywood—and actually the entire world, particularly because of television—tends to think of social issues in theatrical terms. And what could be more dramatic than a poor Mexican-American peasant leader trying to elevate the status of the workers in the fields. I mean that fits in with something that liberal views can support. Whereas things that are more complicated—like school busing—get a little too close to home."

As for himself, says the cinematographer, he is no longer politically active in the same way he was during his youth in Chicago. He still shoots political films, of course, but he is no longer deeply engaged in organizational politics. "We used to go door to door and sell the *Daily Worker*," he recalls.* "Or we would knock on doors and say, well I don't know what the hell we used to talk about, probably 'free the Scottsboro Boys' or 'free Tom Mooney'... Or we would get a group of people together and play symphony music or music from Republican Spain and talk about Marx and Lenin or the building of the CIO or discrimination against the Negroes...But today, what political activity did I do today? Well I called about fifteen

---

*For a period of time during his youth, Wexler belonged to the Communist Party.
**In March 1976, the State Department denied visas to five Cuban filmmakers who had been invited to participate in the fifth annual Los Angeles Film Exposition. The action, which came several months after Cuba's intervention in the Angolan war, was an outgrowth of the government's stiffening attitude toward Cuba.

people on the telephone, because the State Department barred these Cuban filmmakers from coming to Los Angeles.** So Bert Schneider was on the phone and I was on the phone and we called a lot of people and asked them to sign a public statement of protest and telegrams to Kissinger and so forth. And that's the extent of it you know. There are five or six of us in Hollywood who can call up people of some note and fortunately they respond."

Wexler briefly relived the experience of working with a political organization early in 1974, when he began planning *Introduction to the Enemy*, a documentary which was made under the auspices of a Los Angeles-based antiwar organization called the Indochina Peace Campaign (IPC). *Introduction to the Enemy* followed activists Tom Hayden and Jane Fonda, who were central figures in IPC, on a journey they made through North Vietnam in the spring of the same year. "When Jane and Tom and I started to talk about going to Vietnam," recalls Wexler, "I was able to meet a lot of the people who were hanging around IPC. Mostly very young people and very dedicated people, and hard working and attractive people. And it made me feel very good; it made me feel like the old days."

But, the cameraman quickly adds, he would find it very difficult to make an ongoing commitment to a political group. "If an interesting organization existed today, I don't know whether I'd fit in with them. I feel pretty much like a maverick. Of course I'm very much against dogmatic decisions, and maybe even group decisions, I don't know. I think that I may have grown away from some of those things that I started off with politically. So I'm not going to lament the fact that there are no groups that one can go into now, because I'd probably go into them and discover that I don't fit at all."

While Wexler does not feel inclined to affiliate with a political organization, he does feel deeply involved with "the Movement"—that hard-to-define community of political, social and cultural interests which has exerted a strong influence on his life and work since his adolescence. His own history is intertwined with that of the left. "I feel like my politics are connected to the length of time.." he declares. "I mean I saw Pete Seeger on stage with Arlo Guthrie the other night at the Santa Monica Civic Auditorium. And I really had a fantastically good feeling. To think that I knew Pete Seeger when he was a skinny kid! And I knew Woody standing right next to Pete just like that. I used to sit in union halls and watch them sing. It just made me feel like... I had a sense of a trajectory of time. And the audience was mostly a young audience. They weren't all old farts out there by any means... When I meet young people who are intelligent and dedicated and principled, that's marvelous for me to see. When you get older and you see young people that way, you feel, 'Well, when I kick the bucket, there are going to be a lot of young people around to carry the ball.' So that makes you feel good."

Postscript

In spring 1977, Wexler won his second Academy Award, this time for his dazzling camerawork in *Bound for Glory*. The Oscar ceremony that year was an intriguing affair; never before had the left made its presence so strongly felt. Jane Fonda, the leading symbol of Hollywood activism, served as one of the evening's hosts. Lillian Hellman, who had been expelled from the film industry in 1952 for refusing to "cut my conscience to fit this year's fashions," was welcomed back with a standing ovation. Barbara Kopple was awarded an Oscar for *Harlan County, U.S.A.*, the militant and inspiring documentary about Kentucky miners.

All the left wing filmmakers who occupied center stage that evening conducted themselves in a low-key and decorous fashion. There were no provocative remarks directed at the enormous TV audience. Ten years earlier, when Wexler picked up his first Oscar, he made a veiled reference to the Vietnam war. But as he accepted his gold statuette in 1977, the cinematographer simply acknowledged the contributions of his fellow workers. Wexler explains why he did not use the occasion to make an overtly political statement: "I did not know what I was going to say in advance, because I'm superstitious. I thought if I prepared a speech, I would surely lose. So on my way up to the stage, after my name was announced, I began quickly thinking of something to say. What I finally said, about the collective nature of filmmaking, is something I feel very strongly about. The making of the film, the social process of making the film, has always been very important to me. And in the absence of other overriding political issues, it seemed like it was even more important. I was thinking of the camaraderie, the cooperation, and the good feelings between all of us who worked on the film. And I felt that I should let my friends and co-workers know that they had helped me, rather than simply accept the award as a personal accolade.

"My remarks came out of the kind of times we're in. We are not confronted today with a burning political issue like the Vietnam war. If I could have thought of something to say in front of that audience that was of great significance, I certainly would have. Some message that would have provoked people to think about something they don't normally think about while watching TV. If I had had that in my power, I would have done it. But I didn't have it in my head. I didn't know what those words were. The times are different, that's the main thing."

After photographing *Coming Home* and *Days of Heaven* in 1977, Wexler made it known that he wanted to occupy the director's chair on his next Hollywood assignment. He was interested in several stories as potential features, but he found it difficult to find studio backing for them. In the meantime, he occupied himself with political documentaries and TV commercials. Why did he become involved again in the production of commercials? "It's just a way to shoot film. I don't like to sit at home. It's not that I need the money. It's simply a way to stay active. We don't do just any old commercials. We have some standards. But when you decide you're a whore, where you draw the line gets very difficult (he laughs)."

Among the documentaries Wexler filmed in 1977 were two films about former U.S. government officials—the man who blew the whistle on the disastrous swine flu vaccine program, and an ex-CIA agent who had been stationed in Angola. Wexler's partner on both these film projects was Saul Landau.

In early 1978, Wexler began work on a documentary about the nuclear arms race. For assistance, he called upon Focal Point Films, a group of young, socially conscious film-makers. Wexler admired the energy and commitment of the group. "You just have to walk into the Focal Point editing rooms (which were located until summer '78 on the second floor of a Santa Monica antique car showroom) to see that it's a unique kind of operation. It's completely different than walking into a studio or someplace like that. They think of films as living documents, as having some kind of relationship with what's out there. With the way people feel and think, with real problems and real issues. Because they operate on modest budgets, they can get closer to what's going on in the streets. They are not simply film freaks, people who love to shoot film for its own sake. They are film people and they are social human beings. I like that. And I like to be associated with that."

Jane Fonda

Jane Fonda believes that this is a very good time for progressive film workers to get involved in commercial feature production. After a brief withdrawal from Hollywood in the early 1970s, Fonda has renewed her acting career with increased vigor. In the past two years, she has starred in half a dozen motion pictures, including *Fun with Dick and Jane, Julia, Coming Home, Comes a Horseman Wild and Free,* and *The China Syndrome.* More screen projects built around the popular actress are being planned.

There is a sense of urgency in the way Fonda pursues her career nowadays. She has passed the symbolic 40-year mark and she senses that her days as a leading Hollywood actress may be numbered. "I will only be in a position of power in Hollywood—a position where I can do the kind of films that I want to do—for a while longer. Then it will be over, essentially. I can become a character actress, but I'm not going to have clout. So I want to use this period of time to do as much as possible. I want to milk it, I really do. Maybe with the women's movement and the new consciousness about women getting older, my years as (a bankable star) will be expanded. God knows there is still a lot for me to say. But whether or not it will be commercial, I don't know. That remains to be seen."

As long as she remains a top box office attraction, Fonda believes, there is a great deal she can accomplish in Hollywood. Commercial film production, she acknowledges, is controlled by large economic interests and is generally inclined to reinforce the status quo. Yet movies which are critical of the established order, and which show enlightened forms of human interaction, can and do get made in Hollywood, she declares. "It's amazing how riddled with contradictions our society is."

Fonda's associate, Bruce Gilbert, agrees with her optimistic assessment of what is possible in Hollywood: "I think that today it is wide open in terms of what kind of films can get made... We're making just what we've always wanted to."

*****

Fonda has not always been so enthusiastic about working in commercial features. There was a time when her Hollywood acting career seemed to be incompatible with her growing political commitment. After winning an Academy

Award for her performance in the 1971 movie *Klute,* Fonda was offered roles in several major pictures. But she turned them down because they seemed to reinforce negative sexual stereotypes. In 1972, she appeared in an unconventional movie called *Steelyard Blues,* but after that she temporarily disappeared from the Hollywood screen."... When I began to think about the consciousness of women in the broadest sense," Fonda told the *New York Times* in 1976, "I began to understand the role that movies play in making us feel a certain way about ourselves and placing us culturally into certain stereotypes. So I began to look very carefully at scripts I was being sent and I found there was hardly any script that didn't lie. Three or four years ago, I was at a place where the rage was so new that I could hardly function. A lot of people thought I was crazy, not working. But I made up my mind in 1972 that if it meant never working again, I would not work in the sort of things I used to do. I found it literally untenable to do something I couldn't believe in. Most people don't have a choice. I do."

Fonda began to reevaluate her perspective on Hollywood in discussions with other political activists. Tom Hayden, whom she met in spring 1972 and married the following year, helped her come to appreciate the power and significance of Hollywood features. "Tom was the first person on the left I had ever met who really took movies seriously. I mean he systematically went to movies and was very interested in them as a way of communicating. And I began to change the way I thought about my work."

Fonda continued to devote the bulk of her time during this period to political activities. She and Hayden co-founded the Indochina Peace Campaign (IPC) in the waning years of the war to counteract the Nixon Administration's efforts to keep the conflict hidden from the U.S. public. But at the end of the IPC workday, there were often discussions about Fonda's movie career and the social potential of Hollywood films. IPC activist Bruce Gilbert took a hopeful attitude toward the movie industry. Gilbert, who had an extensive background in antiwar activity, had been interested in filmmaking for some time. Independent documentary production did not appeal to him because it seemed to have little impact on the public. But much could be accomplished in Hollywood, he believed, if progressive filmmakers went about their business with sufficient determination and imagination. "My feeling," says Gilbert, "was that the sad state of Hollywood moviemaking was due more to a failure of will on the part of socially concerned filmmakers than to studio censorship. Because the studios clearly didn't know what the hell made a box office hit. It seemed to me that a studio would risk its money on just about anything as long as it had a clear story line and could appeal to the youth market."

In 1973, Fonda and Gilbert decided to form an independent production company called IPC films "to make the kind of movies which Hollywood should have been turning out but wasn't." Their first project, it was agreed, would be a dramatic feature about the impact of the Vietnam war on the American people. Fonda and Gilbert believed that after the war came to an end, there would be a bitter contest in the cultural arena over how this bloody chapter in U.S. history would be interpreted. They felt it was vitally important that at least one major Hollywood picture with a clear-cut antiwar perspective be produced and distributed during the postwar period.

Together they worked out the beginnings of a story: the setting was a small U.S. military base town during the height of the war. The principal characters were a Marine officer, his wife, and a parapalegic veteran. By focusing on these three people, the filmmakers hoped to bring home the terrible human costs of the war.

Turning this dramatic conception into a feature-length motion picture proved to be a long and arduous task. Five years passed before it finally appeared on the screen, under the title *Coming Home*. "Since the formation of our production company," says Fonda, "I've learned how hard it is to put movies together. It takes a tremendous amount of *chutzpah*, and lots of contacts. You really have to know who to go to, you have to have friends, you have to have influence. Even with all that, even though I'm Jane Fonda, even though I have things to say, it's still very difficult to find screenwriters who can combine the political and the emotional."

Gilbert agrees that the shortage of talented, socially conscious screenwriters in Hollywood is the main obstacle to making worthy movies. This shortage, says Gilbert, is due in part to the fact that "the overwhelming majority of people who went through the sixties automatically reject the idea of working in Hollywood. They don't see openings or possibilities so they're not here writing. The ones that are here often write too rhetorically, their material is not accessible. I have learned that movie characters have to express needs that are universal. A film can be as political as possible, but the characters have to connect with the audience."

Nancy Dowd, who had worked with Fonda on the FTA revue and the TV production of *A Doll's House*, was originally given the job of writing *Coming Home*.* Dowd later parted ways with Fonda and Gilbert and was replaced by screenwriter Waldo Salt (*Midnight Cowboy, Day of the Locust*). Eight weeks before film production was to begin, Salt suffered a heart attack and the writing assignment was quickly taken over by Robert C. Jones (who had been an editor on several of director Hal Ashby's previous movies).

Before the cameras started rolling, the script had to be approved by United Artists. UA executives experienced some last minute jitters about the project after reading the script. "A few days before production," recalls Gilbert, "the studio handed us four single-spaced pages of comments on the movie. They were nervous. They were about to commit several million dollars to a movie about Vietnam which had no action but a lot about the plight of crippled soldiers and everything else. There was discussion about whether the script was too political, whether the love story was strong enough, whether the parapalegic veteran was too self-pitying." But in the end the script was approved—without changes—by the studio.**

Once filming began, says Gilbert, UA executives "never came on the set and never asked to see dailies." United Artists, he points out, generally does not interfere with a film project

------

*Dowd made a name for herself in 1977 with *Slap Shot,* a hard-edged comedy about the brutal world of semi-pro ice hockey.
**The filmmakers themselves later changed much of the script during production.

once it approves the screenplay and the key creative personnel. "The fact that Jane was coming off of a commercial success (*Fun with Dick and Jane*)," Gilbert adds, "and that her upcoming film (*Julia*) was riding a certain momentum, and the fact that (director) Hal Ashby and (producer) Jerome Hellman were both respected by the studio—all of that also helped insulate the film from outside pressure."

The filmmakers, relatively free of commercial pressure, succeeded in creating a movie which was both politically and emotionally effective. *Coming Home* presents a critique of the traditional concepts of patriotism, loyalty, and manhood; it reintroduces the U.S. public to some of the forgotten casualties of the war; and it holds out the possibility that people can grow wiser and stronger in spite of being crippled by years of cruel propaganda and the brutalities of war. It does all this not by making explicit ideological statements, but largely by involving the audience in the dramatic complexities of a triangular love relationship. *Coming Home* seemed to vindicate Fonda and Gilbert's belief that if one could master the conventional dramatic techniques of Hollywood moviemaking, one could communicate progressive ideas to a mass audience.   *****

Jane Fonda's ability to function effectively in the arena of popular culture was greatly enhanced by the downfall of the Nixon Administration in 1974. In the early 1970s, Fonda's outspoken criticism of the war in Indochina and her advocacy of various left wing causes made her the target of government surveillance and harassment and severe media criticism. Federal agents dogged her steps; the CIA opened her overseas mail; her financial records were appropriated by the government without her knowledge; and her house was broken into. Legislators in several states (including Colorado, Michigan, Maryland, and South Carolina) introduced bills aimed at banning Fonda and her films. Some TV stations refused to broadcast her old movies. She was widely pilloried in the press as "anti-American," "a dupe," "a loudmouth," and "a spoiled rich girl."* There was talk of trying her for treason after her

---

*Some of the media's harsh treatment of Fonda was likely due to FBI

trip to Hanoi in 1972. "If it had been the fifties, I probably would have been electrocuted," says Fonda. "There was a concerted effort to go after me, to boycott my films, to blacklist me."

It was clear at the time that Fonda's public image, and hence her acting career, were being damaged by the propaganda campaign against her. But the actress never became so concerned about her future in Hollywood that she drew back from her political commitment. The commercial success of *Klute*, says Fonda, demonstrated that she still had drawing power. And as long as the public went to see films which she appeared in, Fonda believed, the film industry would offer her work. Besides, she told an international film gathering in 1974, risking her career for peace in Vietnam seemed like a small sacrifice.

But in the end she was never forced to choose between her career and her principles. Nixon fell, the war came to an end, and Jane Fonda was offered amnesty. "I'm told there is still a tremendous amount of hostility toward me," says Fonda. "At least that's what the polls say. But I don't feel it nowadays. I do a lot of traveling and speaking and I don't feel it. When I went to work on *Dick and Jane* in 1976, I really sensed that I had made it home. It was like we were right, we survived, we look good, and we are vindicated. And we can still act, and we can still do comedy, and we are alright. You know what I mean? And everybody knows it. That's when I finally realized that yes, I was not going to be blacklisted, their efforts had failed. But not only that, the balance of power is actually shifting...So I'm extremely happy that things have worked out the way they have. It's no accident that I've been redeemed in the public

---

machinations. In 1970, for instance, the FBI sent *Variety* a phony letter which accused Fonda of threatening President Nixon's life at a Black Panther fundraising event. According to FBI documents which were made public in 1975, the letter was sent "from a fictitious person" in order to "cause (Fonda) embarrassment and detract from her status with the general public." *Variety* did not publish the letter; but the FBI's antagonism toward Fonda undoubtedly found its expression in other letters, columns, and articles which did appear in print.

eye. I think that it is part of a larger process that is important to understand, because I think that it affects every area of our lives. To understand it is to understand what is possible politically. But looking back, I don't feel, 'Thank God I got through all that!' We did what was necessary. And we were right. And if we hadn't been right, and if we hadn't succeeded, then I'd be making other kinds of movies. I'd be getting together with independent filmmakers like Robert Kramer (*Milestones, Portugal: Scenes from the Class Struggle,* etc.) to see what could be done."

In the past couple years, the media have rushed to embrace Jane Fonda once again, to take back all the malicious remarks made about her in the heat of the Vientam conflict. There has been a barrage of magazine stories, all of which feature radiant photos of the actress and respectful comments about her acting abilities and her politics. She is, it seems, an exemplary citizen after all. "She's a fine actress," pronounced *Newsweek* in October 1977, "whose very behavior seems to mean something to us even before we connect it with the role she's playing. And despite her sometimes strident radicalizing that angered many Americans in a divided time, she's an image in the American grain—direct, clear, appealing, with the resilience of the old American optimism, good faith and high spirits in her movements and her voice."

In December 1977, the Hollywood Women's Press Club presented Fonda with their Golden Apple award for being the "female star of the year." Several years earlier, the same club had given Fonda a Sour Apple for "bringing disrepute to the entertainment industry with her unpopular views."* Fonda graciously accepted her Golden Apple from conservative actor John Wayne, who quipped as they stood alongside each other, "I'm surprised to find you on the right of me."

Fonda has appeared as award-recipient and mistress of ceremonies at various Hollywood functions in recent times (including the 1977 Academy Awards; the American Film Institute's Fifth Life Achievement Award, held in honor of Bette Davis; and the thirty-fifth annual Golden Globes). She

---

*In the words of *Variety*.

feels it is important to participate in the entertainment industry's public rituals: it is a way of legitimizing herself, she says, and thereby making her left wing views more palatable to the U.S. populace. Does her willingness to attend these glittering affairs signify that she has toned down her political convictions? Not at all, she insists. It's the film industry which has changed, she told *Variety* after picking up her Golden Apple award, not her.

*****

Fonda's determined effort to make progressive Hollywood features is part of a general strategy to influence U.S. culture and politics. Her return to commercial filmmaking coincided with her husband Tom Hayden's 1976 race for the U.S. Senate, and the subsequent development of the Campaign for Economic Democracy (CED), a statewide organization which has become a significant force within California's Democratic Party. CED lobbies in Sacramento for the passage of progressive legislation, while working to build a grassroots network of political activists. The organization's basic political theme is that corporate domination of U.S. society must be counteracted by extending public control over the nation's economy.

"We're talking about a vision whose time has come," says Fonda. "It's now possible for people who represent the politics of the sixties movements to begin to take political power. We're not interested in being protesters for the rest of our lives. We're talking about running candidates for public office. We're talking about sponsoring legislation. And we're talking about making progressive movies, because it's important to build a progressive culture and to open up people's minds. Ultimately we must concern ourselves with pulling out by its roots the decadence that controls our culture, the profit motive that controls our culture. But you can't do that unless you have power."

In order for progressives to operate effectively in the political arena, believes Fonda, they must learn the mechanics of campaigning, lobbying, administering, etc. And in order for progressive filmmakers to function effectively in the cultural arena, she insists, they must learn how to construct emotionally powerful movies with democratic messages. There was a time when Fonda dismissed Hollywood films such as *The Grapes of Wrath* (which starred her father, Henry) as "sentimental and bourgeois." But in preparing to make her own films, Fonda viewed many of these old populist movies once again and developed a new appreciation for them. Progressive film-makers, she says, must "not be afraid to pluck the old heartstrings."

We do not live in a politically sophisticated country, Fonda observes. So perhaps the best thing that movies can do at this point in history, she says, is stir people's emotions—anger them, fill them with sorrow, inspire them. "I don't believe that culture at this stage is going to be able to go too far ahead." Movies are primarily a visceral medium, Fonda believes. And there is only so much enlightenment which can be induced in an audience through visceral means.

Fonda is prepared to accept the aesthetic and intellectual limits of Hollywood movies and work within them. Com-mercial features generally lack depth, subtlety, nuance, and shading. Nevertheless, she points out, they are effective. "People in my generation all grew up hating Indians, objectify-ing women, fearing 'mobs' and all that. Those moviemakers really knew how to manipulate people's emotions. Well we have to do the same thing. We have to learn how to move people, but in other directions. We have to learn the tried and true techniques of moviemaking."

Fonda has also come to accept her role as a movie star. She went through a period of self-denial in the early seventies, when she attempted to blend in with other political activists and shed her celebrity status. But now she is determined to use her stardom for progressive purposes. Over the years, Fonda has developed a distinctive screen personality which seems to delight many moviegoers and draw them into her films. The actress describes her screen character as a satisfying mix of "vulnerability and toughness." "I think people like that com-bination—that kind of woman who allows the audience to care about her because she is fragile, yet who also has a very feisty streak. People like *chutzpah*. They like someone who is going to stick up for what she believes in. That seems to be my theatrical role as well as my role in real life. A number of people I run into say to me, 'I may not always agree with what you say, but I admire your candor,' or 'Hey, Jane, keep giving 'em hell.' It's a trait which Americans seem to admire."

Fonda acknowledges that the salaries which are paid to movie stars are much too high; but, says the actress, she does not use her riches solely for her personal pleasure. She plows much of her money into political projects (now, for the most part, those projects are CED-related). "The salaries we earn are just ridiculous. I think we should be organizing against the salaries we're given, it's just terrible. But since the money is there, I'm going to take it and use it (for political purposes)."

Fonda believes that it is very important for progressive people to work within political organizations. On their own, says Fonda, individuals have little power (even if they are celebrities). They cannot sustain their energy, they wander off in unwise directions. But smoothly functioning organizations provide their members with political direction, support, and stimulation. "The fact that I'm organizationally related makes a tremendous difference in my life. If you're working in the context of a political organization, you have criticism/self-criticism, you have people to bounce ideas off of and to help keep you in touch. You have to act in a responsible and disciplined way, instead of flailing around on your own. To have consistent, ongoing political work makes all the differ-ence in the world. If I didn't have that womb, that circle of dedicated political people within which to work, I think I would have dropped out—burned out—a long time ago."

In the beginning stage of her political development, which the actress characterizes as her "extreme sectarian period," Fonda often stumbled in the public spotlight. Anxious to impress her new political comrades, she frequently made statements to the press which were badly formulated and counterproductive. It is very difficult to transform yourself politically while the whole world is closely examining your every word and deed. The media made Fonda a spokesperson for the left wing movement before she had time to gather her thoughts. "During the first years of my political existence, I was so filled with self-loathing and contempt for what I represented that I couldn't function effectively. What got me into so much trouble was this attitude that, 'I'm not left enough, I'm not militant enough.' More left rhetoric came out of my mouth during that time—I didn't even know what the words really meant. I was trying too hard to prove my credentials, to prove that I was sincere. It was very bad, for both me *and* the movement. We must learn to recognize the importance of involving people like me, and find sensible ways of doing it. When I was first out there, I was so ridiculous; I just didn't know any better."

After several years of involvement in political organizations, however, Fonda now feels that she is qualified to speak on behalf of progressive causes. She is better prepared to handle the media; she can often use it to her own advantage, rather than being consistently victimized by it. Fonda recognizes that she is not a political leader in the traditional sense; she is a "visible figure." But visible figures play an important role in political movements too, she says. "I think that any successful movement has its visible figures. They are not necessarily the theoretical leaders, or the strategists, or the field organizers. But they're visible. And visible leadership is very important, especially in a country like ours where the media is so powerful. These people must be cared for, and tended to, and encouraged a great deal, because they are extremely vulnerable. They must not be led down garden paths, taken in directions where they don't want to go, pushed too far and too fast, or anything like that."

There are problems with the kind of visible leadership which Fonda—and Tom Hayden—have provided the left wing movement. When political figures are elevated by the media (and derive much of their power from their celebrity status), there is a tendency for them to become insulated and unaccountable. They are inclined to shape their political organizations too strongly in their own image. Many people on the left regard the Campaign for Economic Democracy more as a Hayden-Fonda political machine than as a grassroots, democratic organization.

Nevertheless, Fonda has gained respect for her willingness to work with other political activists. And her political organization has succeeded in focusing public attention on the excessive power of multinational corporations, and in projecting left wing ideas and candidates into the arena of mainstream politics. Fonda has concerned herself in recent years with becoming politically legitimate in the eyes of the U.S. public. In the process, she has toned down her angry (and rhetorical) speaking style; but she is just as committed to a democratic restructuring of U.S. society today as she was in the past. While many other well-known left wing dissidents have dropped by the wayside during the seventies, Fonda has maintained a consistently high level of political activity. She has gone on national speaking tours, raised money for progressive causes, engaged in electoral campaigns and—of course—participated in the production of enlightened Hollywood features.

How has Fonda's political activism affected her work as an actress? It has consumed time and energy which could have gone into further developing her acting abilities, she concedes. But more importantly, she says, it has allowed her to bring much more to her portrayals. Because it has made her a fuller human being. "Maybe I missed out on some development as an actress because I spent so much time speaking at antiwar rallies and so on—time which I could have spent in acting classes or something. Maybe. But it will all be lost in history anyway, except for the fact that the war ended—and the antiwar movement had something to do with it...Prior to becoming a political person, I was extremely alienated. I saw *Barbarella* or part of it awhile back at the San Francisco Film Festival. I was interested in seeing it because even some women friends of mine said, 'It's really not so bad.' So I went, but I couldn't stand it. It was like my voice was coming out of my ear. It was like there was no one home, and there wasn't. I could see that my performance was superficial, off the top. It was empty, vacant. When I began to come into focus as a human being, which was pretty late in my life, my acting started getting deeper. One of the reasons that *Klute* was the best performance I had given to date was that I was really getting involved in the women's movement. There is a scene at the end of the movie, where I'm listening to a tape of this murdered woman's voice, and the guy is about to kill me. When I heard that woman, her voice, as she was going into the hotel with him and eventually beaten to death by him, I began to cry. I would never have anticipated that reaction as an actress. I cried for all the women who have ever been brutalized and victimized. And for me it was like new doors were opening up...So anyway, I feel that the more complete a person you are—the more you have an understanding of social forces and how they affect people—the more substantial an actress you are...When you feel that you have a reason for living and you feel committed to something beyond yourself, I think you're a better artist."

Thom Mount

Thom Mount is a young executive at the leading studio in Hollywood—Universal, a subsidiary of MCA, Inc. He has been responsible for overseeing the production of such features as *The Bingo Long Traveling All-Stars and Motor Kings, Car Wash, Smokey and the Bandit, Which Way Is Up?* and *The Wiz.* Mount came of age during the 1960s, and his political attitudes and cultural tastes are in part a reflection of that dynamic period. Like thousands of other concerned students in those years, Mount played an active role in the antiwar and civil rights movements. He was also an enthusiastic fan of the rock 'n' roll culture which provided the decade with much of its driving power. The young studio executive's ideas about the business and art of moviemaking place him in the liberal wing of Hollywood's corporate leadership.

Mount believes that the first function of a Hollywood film must be to make a profit. In this, he is in concurrence with every other studio executive. But unlike some executives, he also believes that movies have a social responsibility. Commercial features, Mount says, should ideally have some dramatic substance, they should reveal certain truths about our existence. At the very least, he adds, they should avoid perpetuating negative cultural stereotypes.

Mount is proud of the fact that some of the pictures which he has supervised have been socially concerned as well as commercially successful. While *Car Wash* was designed primarily as an entertainment, he says, it also contains some insightful material about "the ways our culture acts upon poor black people in an urban setting." *Which Way Is Up?,* declares Mount, is essentially a showcase for the comedic talents of Richard Pryor; but it also accurately reflects the distrustful attitude which most working people have towards large multinational corporations. Furthermore, he says, the film is aware of the changing relationship between the sexes, and the changing role of black women in particular. "I think that no group in American society has been so touched by the feminist movement as black women. We wanted the picture to reflect their changing consciousness and we wanted Richard Pryor to encounter it. We thought it would be a very funny and revealing confrontation.

Bingo Long, says Mount, is also primarily a light-hearted romp. But in telling the story of a 1930s black baseball team which breaks away from the exploitative Negro National League and tries to operate as an independent collective, the movie raises some interesting social issues—in an almost off-handed way. "Since the central plot of the picture had to do with organizing a player-owned team, we tried to talk about the pains and frustrations of achieving that kind of union. We tried to talk about the way that profit oriented powers try to break up that kind of effort. And we tried to tell the story in personal terms—in terms of the relationship between the pitcher, Bingo Long (Billy Dee Williams), and the catcher, Leon Carter (James Earl Jones). Leon sees the enterprise in political and humanitarian terms. He is fond of quoting W.E.B. DuBois. Bingo, on the other hand, sees collectivism as a kind of hustlers' alternative to the club owners' system. We tried to explore the dichotomies between those two points of view. But to describe *Bingo Long* as a socially profound film is to fool yourself. It is essentially a comedy."

To what extent does Mount influence the ideological perspective of the movies which he is given the task of supervising? His position does allow him to get involved in many of the creative aspects of the filmmaking process. But, he asserts, his power to shape the social content of movies is actually very limited. "Filmmaking is truly collective," he says. "No one person is ever going to guide the course of an entire film. Films have a life of their own. As soon as you decide that you are going to make one and you hire someone to write a script—from that point to the moment it hits the screen, God only knows where it is going to go. (As the production executive) you do what you can to shape it along the way. The director has a major influence, and the actors have a certain kind of input, and the producers, and the technicians and everybody else. In the end it all adds up to something that is not exactly like what anyone had in mind."

Mount says that the political beliefs of studio executives are rarely a factor in determining the social outlook of Hollywood features. He has known executives with virtually no social conscience who turn out enlightened pictures. And he knows that executives like himself—who are more concerned about social issues than others—often make movies which are superficial and irrelevant.

For instance, Mount was responsible for supervising the production of *Smokey and the Bandit*, a 1977 Burt Reynolds movie that was built around one long collision-filled car chase. The picture turned out to be the top moneymaker for Universal that year. Yet it had remarkably little social or artistic value. In fact, it was as insubstantial a piece of entertainment as Hollywood makes.

Mount says that he does not regret his participation in the movie. While he generally prefers to work on films with more depth, he says there must be a place in U.S. culture for "unchallenging entertainment." "I happen to enjoy *Smokey and the Bandit* a lot. It is pure junk food, but I *like* Big Macs and Coca-Cola. They mean something to me...The film is a fantasy, it is a cartoon-like picture and it was supposed to be. We set out to have a good time and we had a very good time. I enjoyed working on it enormously and I wouldn't trade the experience for the world. I would not want to make that kind of film exclusively; I am aware of its limitations. But I don't feel a great need to defend it. I think it is what it is. It's part of the filmmaking business, and a part that I'm quite happy with."

Many film critics have charged that Hollywood consistently underestimates the sophistication of its audience. Mount disagrees: "There is definite audience resistance in this country to films that are too intellectual or aesthetically complex." He maintains that the movie audience in the U.S. seeks emotional stimulation above all else.

It is possible, Mount remarks, to produce films within the commercial system that are both popular and profound. Why then are so few of these films made? Not because of studio management, he says. There is no conspiracy in Hollywood's higher echelons to block films that are richly woven and socially provocative, says Mount.

"Studios will produce anything that they think will make money." The primary barrier to this type of movie, he contends, is not studio censorship but the creative limitations of Hollywood's workforce. "It's extremely hard to find a writer who can write a movie like that. I mean there are probably fifteen or twenty writers in this business who are capable of writing such a film during their lives. There are even fewer who are capable of doing it on a regular basis. And then there are maybe ten or fifteen directors in the business who can execute a script like that, and perhaps twenty-five or thirty actors who are capable of bringing the characters fully to life. So the odds against the right assortment of talent coming together at the right time and place are pretty high."

Mount admits that the movie industry has not done very much to nurture new creative talent. "I think the single most disheartening thing about the film business is the lack of training and opportunities for young filmmakers." Universal, he says, is the only major studio "that has an active policy of using first-time directors on pictures. Over the last ten years, Universal has used more first-time directors on motion pictures than all of the other studios put together." Studio executives, Mount says, are reluctant to employ unseasoned filmmakers because of the large amounts of capital which are invested in feature-length films. "It is a business risk. You just can't try somebody out and if he fouls up say, 'That's alright, he'll get it right next time.' This is not the record business, where you can write off the cost of producing an album, which is maybe fifty or sixty thousand dollars. If you botch a movie, you lose at least three or four million dollars. Studios are public companies, so the top executives have to answer to the stockholders once or twice a year. It can get a little embarrassing for these executives, not to mention damaging to their careers, if they blow too many pictures."

Mount believes that a film's ideological content must be submerged in a strong narrative, or the picture's impact will be lessened. Entertainment must be the filmmaker's first consideration, he says. He is sharply critical of films that are politically explicit or didactic. Mount asked the writers of *Bingo Long*, Matthew Robbins and Hal Barwood, to cut some ideological dialogue which he felt was inappropriate. "There were a couple of places in the script where the writers got carried away with political rhetoric. I think it is inconceivable that a 1930s baseball player with no political background would talk in a sort of New Left Marxist dialect. I think that kind of thing is inconsistent with good storytelling. And that's why we cut it out. I think that everyone involved in the picture agreed with the decision." Mount says that the script deletions which he suggested in no way diluted the social content of the movie.

Scenes which contained some pointed social commentary were also removed from another of Mount's films—*Car Wash*, a 1976 comedy about one day at an inner city car wash. The scenes involved a character named Abdullah, a bitter young black nationalist who works on the car wash line. "One of the major scenes that was cut," says Mount, "was a moment between Abdullah (Bill Duke) and the old shoeshine man (Clarence Muse) in the locker room. Abdullah is playing a saxophone, and you discover that he is not simply a caricature militant. He is in fact a very talented musician and he also has some deeply held political beliefs and he doesn't know what to do with his life. He's working in a car wash, he feels completely trapped and there doesn't seem to be a way out. And the character played by Clarence Muse talks to him about the nature of survival as a black person in this society. How you must be extremely resolute in your struggle because you can only triumph if you are strong."

Mount says that this scene and others like it were added by director Michael Schultz in order to flesh out "the dramatic and political aspects of the Abdullah character." But when the film was shown at preview screenings, says Mount, "the audiences got very restless (during these scenes) and ran for the popcorn stand." So these passages were eliminated. "The final arbiter in the editing of a motion picture should always be the audience. Because they are the people who are going to pay for it."

Schultz was not happy with the cuts and he battled for awhile to keep his film intact. But in the end, Mount says, the director gave Universal his permission to make the deletions. "Michael Schultz was a full participant in the cutting of this picture. Nothing was removed without his permission. We try not to do that to filmmakers. Studios do occasionally cut films without the creative people's input, but I don't approve of that. It's not an acceptable way to work."

Mount makes it clear that he was generally sympathetic to the social aims of *Car Wash*. While he did participate in the decision to cut some of Abdullah's scenes, he also made an effort to keep other meaningful moments in the movie. There were times when the executive "insulated" director Schultz from studio pressure. And there were times when he "exposed Michael to criticism because I thought it would be educational and beneficial for him to have to deal with it." There are limits to how far Mount can go in defending a filmmaker's creative perspective. "Obviously," he says, "to be able to defend Michael's interests, as I did on that picture, I had to remain employed. If I were fired and on the streets, I could be more vocal but I'd have virtually no impact. So it is a curious compromise that one has to effect."

It was not very long ago when Thom Mount and other student activists *were* more vocal and *were* making an impact on the system—from the outside. While in college in North Carolina during the 1960s, Mount worked as an organizer for the Southern Students Organizing Committee (SSOC), a regional campus oriented group with close ties to the Student Nonviolent Coordinating Committee (SNCC) and Students for a Democratic Society (SDS). SSOC's leadership tended to be radical in its political outlook, but the group's ideological perspective was general enough to attract a wide spectrum of students. SSOC's founding statement, "We'll Take Our Stand" (1964), called for a "rise of full and equal employment for all," "an end to personal poverty," an end to "public poverty" in such areas as schools, medical care and housing, "a democratic society where politics pose meaningful dialogue and choices about issues that affect men's lives, not manipulation by vested elites" and "a place where industries and large cities can blend into forms and natural splendor to provide meaningful work and leisure opportunities for all." During its five years of existence, SSOC made a commendable effort to adapt New Left principles and strategies to the unique Southern environment. The group's organizational symbol was a button which showed black and white hands clasped together against the backdrop of a Confederate flag.

Mount engaged in a variety of political activities during his years as an SSOC organizer. In 1967 he helped put together a "Peace Tour" of antiwar speakers which visited numerous college campuses throughout the South. Later Mount helped coordinate student support for striking workers at a textile mill in Greensboro, North Carolina. In 1968 he took part in a large scale student strike at Duke University in Durham, North Carolina. The strike was called to support the university's grossly underpaid non-academic employees (maids, janitors, cafeteria employees, hospital orderlies)—most of whom were black—who were fighting for higher pay and collective bargaining rights.

In 1970 Mount moved to Southern California to enroll in the film program at California Institute of the Arts. While attending Cal Arts, he became involved with the Indochina Peace Campaign (IPC), a Los Angeles-based antiwar organization founded by Tom Hayden and Jane Fonda. Mount helped put out the group's newsletter, *Focal Point*, and took part in organizing antiwar demonstrations.

After graduating from Cal Arts in 1973, Mount went to work as a story reader for producer Daniel Selznick. Within a year, he had become Selznick's associate producer. Later he went to work as a "packager" of movie projects for New York-based producer Hannah Weinstein. Throughout this period, Mount continued to participate in IPC activities. But his involvement in the organization came to an end in 1975 soon after he was hired as a Universal production executive. "The workload became so huge at Universal that I didn't have time for anything else. I barely had time to breathe...If I had the time today and there were another *Focal Point* being published, I would be working on it. I love to do that kind of stuff. But you can't do it and make a lot of movies at the same time. Both of them are very time-consuming."

Mount was taken into Universal by Ned Tanen, who is now president of the studio's feature production arm. Tanen, who joined MCA in 1954 when it was a talent agency, worked in the corporation's record division before shifting to film production in 1969. It was Tanen who decided to make *American Graffiti* (1973), the highly successful youth oriented picture which helped Universal gain a dominant position in the mid-seventies film market.

Since his arrival at Universal, Mount has steadily improved his position within the studio. All but one of his pictures have made a sizable profit. (*Bingo Long* broke even.)*Smokey and the Bandit* is one of the studio's all-time top-grossing movies. He has been rewarded with substantial salary increases, bigger offices, and most importantly from his point of view—more creative leeway.

How could someone who went through the 1960s and early 1970s as a student activist wind up filling an executive slot in a large entertainment conglomerate? It is a question which some of those who knew Mount in the past still find hard to fully answer. After all, there was a deep sentiment among young people in those years against corporate power and the commercialization of culture. Mount himself sees something of a logical progression between his past and present. One of the main things which attracted him to New Left politics in the 1960s was "the sense of energy and excitement surrounding it." To be politically involved in those years was to be in the center of action, "to participate with thousands of other young people in the reshaping of culture." After the mass movements of that period faded away, the power to "reshape culture" once again became the exclusive property of the communications industries. Nowadays, says Mount, to be working for a corporation like MCA is to be in the center of action. Story ideas, scripts, songs, cultural trends, talent—both raw and refined—all come flowing into these corporations' offices. Executives like Mount go sifting through all of this material and decide which of it is to be processed and distributed on a mass scale.

While Mount sees certain parallels between what he is doing today and what he was doing in the past, he is also aware of the glaring dissimilarities. He is no longer organizing students and workers to effect social change; he is wielding corporate power. He once belonged to a group which opposed "manipulation by vested elites" and worked for a democratic redistribution of power. He is now a junior ranking member of that elite group which controls the bulk of the nation's film output. Mount says that he has no regrets about what he has become. "American culture," he remarks, "is fraught with ironies and existential jokes. What can I say? I don't feel enormously guilty that I'm not involved in concrete left activities."

Mount now says that he identifies more strongly with the film business than with the left movement or any other social activity. "I think of myself primarily as a person involved in the making of pictures. It's fairly hard, for me at least, to relate to the left in the late 1970s as a cohesive body. I don't know what we're talking about anymore when we say 'the left.' I know a lot of organizations that are doing a lot of good things. And there are many people, for whom I have great respect, who are struggling in various ways to improve society. But in talking to them I don't sense much of a connection between any of the different groups. There is no common political program or philosophy which draws them together. And there doesn't even seem to be much mutual support."

Mount does not feel an overpowering need to justify his current line of work in social terms. (Perhaps this is in part due to the weakness of the left.) He finds it very personally satisfying and that seems to be enough. He did not go into the film business for social reasons. He went into it because it seemed like an enjoyable way to make a living. But Mount does believe that in the process of making Hollywood movies, one can make a social contribution. Movies can open people's eyes and replenish their spirit, he says. "It is important not to completely ignore mass culture. I think that most of my former colleagues on the left chose more narrowly focused and traditional left things to do with the rest of their lives. And those things are very important. At the same time, if you give up the film business or the record business or the newspaper business or the television business—or any other form of mass communication—to people who have absolutely no tendency to think humanely or act compassionately, then you sacrifice the possibility of keeping the flame alive."

Mount feels that if popular culture is to be managed by a corporate elite, it is a good thing there are some people with his social outlook among that elite. He is confident that he has the best interests of the public at heart. In a sense, says Mount, he reminds himself of his father—a Southern power broker who runs candidates for political office. Like his father, he wields power in a behind-the-scenes fashion. And though he is not directly accountable to the public, he is "always trying to do what I think is good for them."

While recent technological developments have greatly democratized the means of production in film and video, the means of distribution are still controlled by large economic interests. Leftists charge that this has a constricting effect on U.S. culture: it limits the range of ideas, subjects, and issues which receive general circulation. Mount agrees: "The major studios' tight control of distribution tends to discourage socially provocative and risk-taking filmmaking."

While Mount accepts some of the left wing criticisms which are directed at the entertainment industry he rejects others.

U.S. film companies market their products on a world-wide scale. The Hollywood movie occupies more than fifty percent of world screen time and accounts for about half of global film trade. "At every moment of the day," film industry analyst Thomas Guback has written, "an American picture is being shown someplace on the earth." Progressive and nation-alist elements in many foreign countries have tried with varying degrees of success to resist this massive cultural intervention. It has been frequently stated that the heavy influx of Hollywood products into these countries holds back the development of their own film industries. Mount, on the other hand, prefers to see the worldwide distribution of U.S. films as a form of cultural exchange rather than cultural domination. Foreign rentals, he adds, are a vital source of income for the U.S. film industry*—an industry, he says, which needs all the financial assistance it can get.

Most Hollywood film studios are now owned by large conglomerates which have interests in other media fields. MCA, which is one of the largest and most diversified entertainment conglomerates in the world, not only owns Universal Theatrical Motion Pictures but a TV production company (Universal Television), a record company (MCA Records), a company which is developing a video-disc system for home use (MCA Disco-Vision), a book publishing house (G.P. Putnam's Sons), and a magazine (*New Times*). As a result, MCA has the ability to exploit a theatrical film product in a

---

*More than fifty percent of the U.S. film industry's revenue comes from abroad.

number of ways: it can turn the film into a TV show, it can produce a soundtrack album, it can package it as a video-disc, it can publish the screenplay in book form, and it can turn it into a publicity item in the pages of its magazine. Many media critics fear that this development will lead to a further homogenization of our culture. The public, they say, will be presented with a much less diverse array of media products in a greater variety of forms. But Mount sees hope in it: "One of the great things about MCA is that it *can* exploit a film product in every conceivable way. This is one of the ways that the film business is going to survive. The studios are beginning to realize that when you make a film, it has many different ramifications. If you can turn a film into a TV series or release a soundtrack album, then you can lessen the financial risk involved in moviemaking. As the risk goes down, the studios can afford to be somewhat freer and more adventurous in deciding what movies to make."

While Mount's corporate position and his advocacy of Hollywood's business interests tend to place him outside of the left, he continues to hold progressive opinions on most social and political issues. He remains, for example, a staunch believer in civil rights and has helped raise money for the Southern Poverty Law Center. He is also building Hollywood support for the Film Fund, a national foundation which promotes the production and distribution of movies, slide shows, and videotapes for social change. So far, however, these are the only two projects outside of his studio routine in which Mount has become actively engaged. He takes an interest in left-liberal political campaigns, but has not yet participated in any of them. At this stage of his career at least, Mount is far less politically involved than some of his managerial colleagues.

MCA's top management has been—and continues to be—a very politicized group of men. Jules Stein, the corporation's retired founder, is a major contributor to the Republican Party, as was former MCA vice president Taft Schreiber until his death in 1976. Stein and Schreiber both played key roles in Ronald Reagan's rise to political prominence. Stein belonged to the circle of Southern California millionaires who put up the money for Reagan's gubernatorial campaign in 1966. Schreiber, who was Reagan's first Hollywood agent, became a close political advisor of his during the former agent's first term as California governor. Schreiber broke from Reagan in 1975 to become national co-chairman of the President Ford Committee.

MCA chairman Lew Wasserman, on the other hand, is a strong supporter of the Democratic Party. Over the years, he has given a lavish amount of money to Democratic candidates. He served as a trustee of the John F. Kennedy Library and the John F. Kennedy Center for the Performing Arts; he was a personal friend of Lyndon Johnson; and he has played host to Jimmy Carter. "I think the greatest crime of all is not participating in politics," Wasserman once told the *Wall Street Journal*.

In 1961, the U.S. Justice Department charged that MCA had become a "predatory" monopoly by operating both the nation's largest talent agency and the largest production facilities for show business talent. A year later, the government forced the corporation to dissolve its highly profitable talent agency (which represented more than half of Hollywood's top stars). Ever since then, it has been commented, MCA has played both sides of the political fence so it will have friends in Washington no matter which party is in power.*

Not all of the political activity which MCA executives have engaged in has been connected to the Republican and Democratic parties. In 1973, while Taft Schreiber continued to actively support President Nixon, MCA vice president Jennings Lang threw a fund raising party for Pentagon Papers

---

*MCA was accused of using its political influence in Washington to make sure that the Tax Reform Act of 1976 restricted movie tax shelters. Before passage of this legislation, many independent producers—as well as debt-ridden Columbia Pictures—drew heavily on tax shelter money to finance their movies. In October 1977, producer William Borchert (*Serpico, Dog Day Afternoon*) told the *New York Times*: "(If tax shelters had not been restricted), it would have made independent production very strong. The majors wanted to put the independents back under their thumb. They wanted to monopolize the industry. Universal's greatest disappointment was that the legislation didn't kill Columbia."

defendant Daniel Ellsberg—one of the top names on the Nixon Administration's enemies list. In 1977, Lang hosted a fund raising party for the left-leaning publication, *Mother Jones*.

Apparently there is room within MCA's executive offices for a fairly wide range of political beliefs. Over the years, the corporation's hierarchy had included both right wing conservatives and left wing liberals, as well as a large share of political centrists. When it comes to corporate fundamentals, however, these men are in complete agreement: they all believe in the necessity of making maximum profits, they all believe in exploiting MCA's cultural products to the fullest extent possible, they all believe in expanding MCA's share of the entertainment market. On these business related matters, they are all of one mind, including Thom Mount.

*****

Mount concedes that he has experienced a few difficult moments at Universal—moments when his social conscience and his corporate responsibilities have come into conflict. Mount's first assignment as a Universal executive was to cut *Bingo Long's* budget by approximately $500,000. One of the ways he did this was by moving the production to the South, in the vicinity of Macon, Georgia, where there were plenty of extras who did not have to be paid union scale. "The film was originally going to be shot in California, inside the Screen Extras Guild jurisdiction," says Mount. "And we were going to have to pay about $50 a day plus fringes for extras. So I moved it to Macon, where we paid $20 a day and found all the extras we needed." (Mount also picked the Georgia locale because it resembled 1930s America and because the state's film board offered the studio a generous array of services.)

Mount's decision to move *Bingo Long* southward made good business sense, of course. But it was hard for him to rationalize in social terms. In the 1960s, he had fought to help Southern workers win the right of union representation. Less than ten years later, he found himself shifting a movie production to the South, in part, to take advantage of that region's non-unionized labor pool.

Mount could not work up much enthusiasm for *Two Minute Warning*, a suspense movie which Universal began putting together in 1975. Mount felt that the picture, which was about a mad sniper in a crowded football stadium, was dramatically predictable and socially harmful. It would be a somewhat better picture, he told the studio, if the ending—which had the sniper brutally eliminated by a heroic SWAT team— was altered. Wouldn't the film be much more suspenseful, he suggested, if SWAT could not get its man and the football fans were forced to save themselves? There was also some positive human value in this, Mount felt, as opposed to a conclusion which simply glorified paramilitary police violence. A few other executives liked Mount's idea and the ending was shot in the way he suggested. But some time before the movie was completed, the studio changed its mind and in the final version of the film SWAT captain John Cassavetes destroys the sniper with savage vehemence.*

Incidents like these, Mount emphasizes, occur infrequently and are not troubling enough to make him reevaluate the course he has taken. He is very happy working at the largest studio in Hollywood, and he plans to stay there for some time to come. Universal once had a reputation for turning out uniformly bland, cost-efficient film products. But, says Mount, the studio now produces a wide variety of movies, including some which are thought-provoking and innovative and some which fit into conventional entertainment molds. "One of the nice things about Universal is that it makes a little bit of everything, which it needs to do in order to stay in business. I have a colleague at the studio who is in charge of the *Airport* series, and he continues to generate ideas for more sequels. There will be an *Airport 79* and there will be an *Airport 80-something* and so on. They are enormously popular with audiences, especially overseas, and it's important that Universal continue to make that kind of film. It's also important that Universal make pictures that break new ground."

Mount believes that Universal will continue to change

---

*Critics generally agreed with Mount's assessment of the film. *Two Minute Warning,* wrote *New York Times* critic Richard Eder," has the suspense, the compassion, the human vision, and the individual nuance you would expect in a movie about a foot stepping on an anthill." Nor was the film popular with moviegoers: Universal lost money on the picture.

with the times and respond to new cultural developments. He has great respect for his boss, Ned Tanen: "Tanen is the only studio president in Hollywood who has some sense of the street. It is easy for men in his position to become isolated, but he makes an effort to stay in touch with the culture. That is what makes him, in my opinion, the best studio head in the business. And that is what makes him a delight to work with. He has a real sense of what is happening, and he has not lost his ability to get excited and inspired."

Mount says that he too has successfully withstood the tendency to become isolated by his corporate position. He likes to get outside of his studio office and move around in different circles as much as possible. His ability to do this, says Mount, is one of the things which makes him a valuable person in the film business. "I travel around quite often and I have a lot of friends around the country left over from the experiences of the sixties. And whenever I go to a different city, I call up people and find out what's happening, go have lunch or dinner with someone and talk things over. Whereas most studio executives spend all of their time in New York on the corner of Fifty-ninth and Fifth, I spend most of my time in Soho hanging out with people I've known for ten or fifteen years, and they help a lot. They're very critical of what I'm doing, and I spend a lot of time defending myself. But that's good exercise."

Some old friends and acquaintances, Mount concedes, find it too difficult to get around the fact that he has become a studio executive. They either write him off as a sellout, or approach him for personal favors. Mount has no patience for dealing with people like this. He is the same person he has always been, Mount insists, "a child of American culture." His "power is largely illusory." "In general, the people who regard me differently because I work for a studio and am involved in making pictures, I write off. Because I don't have the time or patience to try to beat into them a real understanding of what's going on here. The people who were close friends to begin with are frequently still close friends—and they can still see me as I am. I don't dress differently, I don't cut my hair differently, and I still like to eat in greasy spoons. So it is still possible to be fairly normal."

Postscript:

In early 1978, Universal Studios released *Blue Collar*, the toughest and most honest Hollywood film about industrial life since the 1930s. The movie, which was co-written and directed by Paul Schrader, starred Richard Pryor, Yaphet Kotto, and Harvey Keitel as three hard-pressed, embittered Detroit autoworkers, who resort to breaking into their union's safe in order to stay economically afloat. As the workers' struggle to survive grows increasingly desperate, their interracial friendship cracks apart in jagged pieces. In the film's concluding scene, Pryor and Keitel exchange racial slurs and slash at one another with factory tools.

Like Schrader's other film work, *Blue Collar* is flawed by its deeply cynical attitude: the union is hopelessly corrupt, the rank and file passively accept the misery of the factory, the one worker who does loudly protest (Pryor) is bought off with a promotion. People are incapable of acting out of anything but narrow self-interest, Schrader seems to be saying throughout most of the film. And yet there are powerful moments of social insight in *Blue Collar*: moments which indicate that it's not human nature which is the problem, but rather the conditions which shape people's lives. As Pryor and Keitel attack each other in the final scene, they suddenly freeze in full fury, and we hear Kotto's voice repeating something he said earlier in the film: "Everything they do, the way they pit the lifers against the new boys, the old against the young, the black against the white, is meant to keep is in our place." The message here is clear: racism is a function of the social system, not simply an ugly human trait. It is not inevitable.

Hollywood filmmakers seldom employ didactic techniques such as this; rarely do they ask the audience to pull back from the action on the screen and think about what is occurring. But Schrader uses this technique with great effect here. One moment we are caught up in the racial violence which is exploding on screen; the next moment we are encouraged to examine its social roots. This, perhaps, is the film's most significant contribution.

It was Thom Mount who convinced Universal to distribute *Blue Collar* after the other major studios had rejected it. "I thought it was important to release the picture," he says, "regardless of whether it made money or not. Because it was a sign to the motion picture community that this studio is willing to take chances and is willing to distribute films that are socially engaging. I was very encouraged that Ned Tanen understood the importance of releasing this picture. If you look at our product over the next two years, you'll see this is a very new kind of Universal."

Post postscript:

In spring 1978, Mount was named executive vice president in charge of production. He is now responsible for overseeing Universal's entire feature film output.

III.
SLOW CHANGES
Preface
Hilda Haynes
Michael Schultz

Preface

Racism continues to be a major problem in the entertainment industry. In 1977, the U.S. Civil Rights Commission released a report on the status of women and minorities in television entitled "Window Dressing on the Set." The report, which was based on an evaluation of network programming between 1969-74 and employment statistics for commercial and public TV stations in the top forty markets, declared that minorities were still underrepresented both on- and off-camera. During the six-year study period, only 10.9% of all TV dramatic roles were played by nonwhites. "Minority men appear more frequently than minority women,"* stated the report, "but they are often typecast in ghetto roles and appear primarily in foreign or ethnic locales. Minority characters also appear as tokens in otherwise all white shows." The commission also found that the "overwhelming majority" of decision-making positions at local TV stations were held by white males.

According to the commission report, minorities did make some progress during the early 1970s, in the wake of the civil rights movement, but the TV industry is still far from being fully integrated at all levels. The picture is much the same in film. In 1975, the motion picture industry reported a total minority employment of 14.6%—a discouraging figure in light of the fact that minorities represent 30% of the work force in greater Los Angeles.

The following chapters examine the careers of two black entertainment artists—veteran actress Hilda Haynes and young director Michael Schultz. These chapters do not present a comprehensive picture of the black experience in Hollywood; but they do touch upon some of the problems which have confronted blacks and other minorities in the entertainment industry over the last thirty years. And they describe some of the ways that blacks have tried to deal with these problems.

---

*Minority women are so underrepresented in dramatic TV, declared the commission, they are "nearly invisible."

Haynes, who is a long-time civil rights activist, has worked for many years in black groups and entertainment unions to improve the status of black performers. She is convinced that organized pressure is the only way to fundamentally change the entertainment industry. There have been times during the struggle when she has grown weary and discouraged; but she realizes that if it weren't for the concerted efforts of older civil rights activists like herself, there would be no black feature film directors such as Michael Schultz today.

Schultz, on the other hand, prefers to operate individually. So far, he has shunned political involvement, choosing to channel most of his energies into his creative work. He has succeeded in becoming a director of films which are both popular and socially astute. There was a time when Schultz felt that his success would open the studio gates to many more black filmmakers. But this, unfortunately, has not occurred. It seems clear that the only way blacks and other minorities will achieve equal status in the entertainment industry is through the persistent and dedicated efforts of a great many people—that is, through an organized movement.

Hilda Haynes

"Life for me ain't been no crystal stair," actress Hilda Haynes declares, quoting the poet Langston Hughes.* "But," she adds, "I'm going to remain undaunted and triumphant deep inside of me."

Haynes began her career as a stage, television, and film performer in the 1940s, when opportunities for blacks in mainstream culture were still extremely limited. Black women appeared, for the most part, as loyal domestics, exotic sex objects, and tragic mulattoes (their "tragedy," film historian Donald Bogle observed, was that they were not born all white). Even these demeaning roles were hard to come by. Black actresses were not in big demand in the entertainment industry.

With the rise of the civil rights movement in the 1950s, this situation began to change. It became increasingly less possible to present the same blatant racial caricatures. Blacks were seen in a wider range of roles than ever before. But despite the significant strides made by black performers over the last three decades, the stereotypes have not yet disappeared and economic security is still a fleeting reality for all but a few. When black women try out for parts today, they are all too often confronted with casting directors and producers who have distorted and offensive notions of what it is to be female and black. And work is still scarce enough to make even the proudest actresses think twice before turning down a less-than-dignified role.

In spite of the burdens imposed on her as a performer because of her race and sex, Haynes has managed to develop a distinguished acting career. She has appeared in such major Broadway dramas as *A Streetcar Named Desire, Blues for Mr. Charlie,* and *The Great White Hope,* countless television shows (including prestigious specials, daytime serials, and situation comedies), and movies such as *Taxi, Stage Struck, Home from the Hill, Key Witness, The Pawnbroker, Gone Are the Days, Diary of a Mad Housewife, Let's Do It Again,* and *The River Niger.* Many of her roles

*Langston Hughes, "Mother to Son" from *Don't You Turn Back* (Alfred A. Knopf, 1969).

have been minor, but she has brought pride and sensitivity to each one of her characterizations. The acting credits she has accumulated over the years represent social as well as personal triumphs. Haynes has approached each one of her roles not only as an opportunity to display her considerable talents as a performer but also as a chance to chip away at the dehumanizing stereotypes which continue to permeate U.S. culture.

*****

Haynes' career as a professional actress got underway in 1946, when she understudied two roles in the New York production of *Deep Are the Roots* and appeared in summer stock presentations of *The Male Animal* and *You Can't Take It With You.* The following year, she was selected to go on tour with the road production of *Anna Lucasta.* The play, which was originally about a Polish-American family, had been adapted by the American Negro Theatre in 1944 with great success.

Haynes had done some acting as a youngster during the 1930s in church pageants and high school plays, but it was not until she joined the American Negro Theatre (ANT) in 1940 that she received her formal training as an actress. The ANT was founded by Frederick O'Neal, a young black actor from St. Louis, and playwright Abram Hill, whose formative years were spent in the Federal Theater. The group rehearsed and performed in the basement of a Harlem public library, where twenty years earlier W.E.B. DuBois' Krigwa Players had maintained their headquarters. The ANT was one of the most promising efforts to establish a black community theater which the century had yet seen. O'Neal explained the meaning and purpose behind the organization in this way: "The old portrayals of the Negro's way of life have had their day as fantastic caricatures. With few exceptions, plays about Negroes have been two grades above the minstrel stage—the cork is missing but the spirit is there. This has created an apathy on the part of the Negro, who is averse to patronizing the theatre which reveals him as a happy-go-lucky race in rompers. We of the ANT are trying to present a true conception of our lives and to emulate, if we can, the integrity and dignity of artists who have reached out for us: Paul Robeson, Marian Anderson, Richard Wright, Dorothy Maynor, Canada Lee, Langston Hughes and others."

The ANT made an effort to present plays about black life by black authors, but unfortunately it was not until four years after the group's formation, with *Anna Lucasta*, that they enjoyed a major critical success. A year after the play opened, it was moved downtown into a Broadway theater. Two ANT road companies subsequently went on tour with the play. Ironically, it was not long after *Anna Lucasta's* triumphant run on Broadway that the ANT disbanded. But before it did, it succeeded in launching Haynes and other black talents such as Ruby Dee, Ossie Davis, Sidney Poitier, Harry Belafonte, Maxwell Glanville, Clarice Taylor, Helen Martin, Isobel Sanford, and Alice Childress on their entertainment careers.*

When Haynes returned to New York, after the completion of the *Anna Lucasta* national tour, she took a job as a typist for an educational testing service to support herself and her young son. It was not the first time she had had to look outside of the theater for work, nor would it be the last. During the early stages of her career, when acting roles were low paying and in scarce supply, Haynes held a variety of odd jobs—so many, in fact, that she has forgotten some of them. She worked as a secretary, a saleswoman, a switchboard operator, a factory worker, a camp counselor, and during the Second World War—as a correspondence clerk for the federal government. As a result of these diverse experiences, Haynes remarks, she has become a "very versatile person."

Haynes did not have to remain with the educational testing service long, for soon after going to work there she won a part in *A Streetcar Named Desire*, the most celebrated play of the 1947-48 Broadway season. Her life was suddenly and magically transformed; it is these breathtaking twists of fate,

---

*Some observers have linked the collapse of the ANT to its successful move to Broadway. Once the group broke into the white-dominated dramatic arena, it has been said, the idea of an all black theater was undermined. "While such acceptance speaks well for the American democratic tradition," black playwright Loften Mitchell wrote, "it could portend the utter negation of the Negro cultural heritage. It could result in a loss of identity, an 'assimilation' into the dominant white majority of an important minority people." Social

she comments, which make the performer's life worth living. Haynes remembers every detail about the day she tried out for the role: It was fall, she wore a simple skirt and blouse, the producer's assistant made a joke but she was so serious and intense that she failed to enjoy it. She walked across the empty stage and sang a plaintive spiritual while the producer, Irene Selznick, watched silently from the orchestra pit. After she was excused, she debated whether she should take her son to the park or go straight home and await the producer's decision. She chose the latter course, and was at home changing her clothes when the telephone call came. Haynes' heart beat wildly as she went downstairs to take the call (there was no telephone in her apartment). When she heard the good news, she let out a loud scream. ("I thought she had fainted," the assistant producer would later tell people at cocktail parties.) The elated actress took hold of another apartment tenant and danced her across the floor, laughing and crying at the same time.

The role, which was made available when actress Gee Gee James left the play, was not a sizable one. In the script the character is referred to simply as "Negro Woman." She is one of the inhabitants of the low-rent New Orleans neighborhood which serves as the backdrop for the play. Nevertheless, Haynes was delighted to have the part. Broadway was thought of as the ultimate goal by black and white stage performers alike. And *Streetcar* was the dramatic event of the season. In Haynes' opinion, to be a part of the cast, which included Marlon Brando, Jessica Tandy, Karl Malden, Kim Hunter, and Edna Thomas was a great honor. "It was one of the most wonderful experiences of my career. (The members of the

---

critic Harold Cruse has written that the "ideological conflict over integration versus ethnic group identity"—which is a fundamental tension within many black cultural groups—also existed within the ANT. According to Cruse, it was the actors in the group—"for whom *any theatre* that provided work was acceptable"—who represented the integrationist tendency, while the playwrights—"for whom a Negro theater was mandatory"—leaned toward cultural separatism.

cast) remained close for a long time. I think we still are close. If anyone of us wanted or needed anything, the others would all come through. It was a closely-knit, beautiful company. Marlon is a wonderful person. (Everybody asks, 'Did he always feel strongly about civil rights?' Well I know that he did, because we used to talk all about it. He was interested in every aspect of what was going on.) I knew without a shadow of a doubt that he would go to Hollywood. He gave the most brilliant young male performance I had ever seen. The whole cast was superb. I'd often go out in the wings and watch them and I never got tired, even though I knew every line. Some scenes were electrifying! It's one of the great American plays."

After she had been with the play for awhile, Haynes was encouraged by some people to quit the show and take advantage of her association with it by getting a better paying role somewhere else. While her involvement with *Streetcar* brought her considerable prestige, she was only paid the minimum union wage. But Haynes decided to stay put; she knew how difficult it was for a black woman to find substantive roles in the New York theater. She remained with the play until it closed, 550 performances after she had joined the cast.

When *Streetcar* finally rolled off into theater history, Haynes found herself without a job. The leading members of the original cast immediately went on to other lucrative assignments, but Haynes did not receive any offers. She had been right about the dismal lack of employment opportunities for black stage performers. Four years would pass before she would find another opening in a Broadway show.

Haynes realized that almost all stage actors suffer periodic bouts of joblessness, but she also knew that it was especially hard for her because she was black. Haynes' racial awareness had developed within her at an early age. Her parents, whom she remembers as strong and loving people, instilled in her a deep sense of self-pride. Both of them emigrated to New York from the West Indies when they were young, and they never came to feel completely at home in their new country because of the virulent racism they encountered here. While growing up in Harlem, Haynes became involved in civil rights activities through her local church.* Churches have long been centers of social and political activities in the black community. But Haynes feels that the churches did not do nearly as much as they could have to advance the interests of the community. Only a few black ministers (like Adam Clayton Powell Jr.), she says, sought to raise the political consciousness of their parishoners. Haynes was deeply impressed by Powell's efforts to integrate Harlem workplaces in the years before the war. In 1941, she did volunteer work for the March on Washington which had been called by labor leader A. Philip Randolph to press for equal employment opportunities in the defense industries.** I have always been a civil rights person," Haynes says. "I began thinking and acting that way when I became conscious I was black."

Haynes carried her struggle for civil rights into the entertainment world when she became a professional actress. In the late 1940s, she and actress Fredi Washington established a hotel accomodations committee under the jurisdiction of the Actors' Equity Association to determine which hotels across the country would house traveling black performers. She and Washington typed and mailed out queries to hundreds of hotel managers; the responses they received were overwhelmingly negative. The names of the few hotels which responded affirmatively were recorded for the benefit of integrated road companies.

---

*Though Haynes and her four brothers were raised in what she calls "upper poverty," she has pleasant memories of her childhood. The family home was a warm environment where friends and neighbors of different ethnic backgrounds felt immediately comfortable and where holidays were drawn out festive occasions. Haynes' father worked as an elevator operator and a porter. Her mother kept house and occasionally took other part-time jobs, which, says Haynes, "she shouldn't have done because she was too frail a person—but she had to because there were five of us to support, and my father's salary was not a living wage."

**The march was called off in June 1941 when President Roosevelt signed an executive order, reaffirming the government's policy of nondiscrimination and establishing a Fair Employment Practices Commission to investigate violations of this policy in defense industries.

Haynes herself had experienced much overt racism during the *Anna Lucasta* road tour. While she and the rest of the black theater company played in Canada, they had no trouble finding comfortable accomodations. But once they entered the United States, they were forced to stay in people's homes or in the run-down hotels which catered exclusively to blacks. In Cincinnati, two light skinned members of ·the company managed to find rooms in a decent downtown hotel when the desk clerk mistook them for whites. The others checked into the Manse Hotel, which was located further away from the theater, in the black section of town.*

Haynes and the rest of the *Anna Lucasta* company also had great difficulty finding restaurants which would serve them meals. While they were performing in St. Louis, food was brought to them in the theater because no restaurant in the area would serve blacks. In Youngstown, Ohio recalls Haynes, "I had one of the worst experiences of my life." On their way to a performance one night, she and another actress decided to stop and get a bite to eat somewhere near the theater. It was winter, and they stood shivering in the bitter cold as they tried to determine which of the several restaurants in the neighborhood would allow them inside. Finally they picked a modest looking place with a windmill on top which served hamburgers and chili.

As the two women walked in and sat down at the counter, they were met with long looks of disbelief from everyone in the restaurant. Even the kitchen workers came out to stare. After the waitresses recovered from the initial shock, they went briskly about their business, but none of them came near Haynes and her friend. Haynes decided not to budge from her seat; from her bag she took out a half-finished afghan and began crocheting. Her friend was puzzled by her apparent

---

*Staying at all-black hotels did, on occasion, have its rewards, remarks Haynes. "At the Manse, there was the greatest congregation of black talent I'd ever seen. Duke Ellington and his band were there, and a host of other black performers. All because we couldn't get a place downtown." The Manse was one of the few good hotels which catered to blacks, she says.

nonchalance. But underneath her calm demeanor, Haynes was burning with anger and resentment. Finally she exploded. "As the waitress passed me by one more time, I bent over the counter and said, 'You. Stop right there! Are you going to serve us or not?' I had to hold tightly onto the counter to prevent myself from grabbing her. She said, 'Well, uh...' and she got away from me and went into the back. Then I started talking out loud so everybody could hear. I said, 'I came into this town with a theater company to entertain the people here and I can't get something to eat? Did my brothers fight and bleed overseas so that you could refuse to serve me? Must I go through this indignity just to get some lousy beans?' I went on and on and terrible accusing words poured out of me."

At last the waitress returned and began to clear away the dirty dishes in front of Haynes and the other actress. They were, it seemed, to be served after all. But Haynes got quickly to her feet. "I said, 'I don't want anything here.' My knees almost gave way as I stood up. I have never been so angry in all my life." After leaving the restaurant, Haynes and her friend complained to a policeman about the way they had been treated. He told them that Ohio had a civil rights law on its books, but since they were not going to be in the state long enough to take legal action, they knew they would have to let the outrage stand.

"That was the first time I was refused a meal. It made me sick. Then we went to eat in another place. We asked for some soup, and I still don't understand it, but when they brought the soup out there was a roach in it. Couldn't eat the soup. Had to get up and leave...I didn't get hungry for a long time after Youngstown. It was such a horrendous experience. You feel so hurt and degraded. Your whole system reacts to something like that. This was the kind of thing that black entertainers had to live through. Josephine Baker, Bert Williams, Nat King Cole, Louis Armstrong, Paul Robeson, Marion Anderson, and many other top stars—they all came up against it. 'Can't stay here, can't eat here, use the back door.' These things contributed to the heartbreak of Billie Holiday."

By establishing the hotel accomodations committee within the stage performers' union, Haynes and Fredi Washington made it clear that there was a problem and it had to be resolved. The time soon came when white members of integrated road companies began boycotting hotels if they refused to house black performers.

*****

With the rise of the television industry in the late forties and early fifties, a whole new job market opened up for under-employed New York stage performers. Haynes was eager to break into TV, since she had been unable to find more work on Broadway after *A Streetcar Named Desire* completed its run. To make ends meet, she had been working as a secretary and taken jobs in summer stock productions. TV roles for black women, however, proved to be in short supply. And the few roles which did open up generally conformed to the same stereotypes which had been popularized in film and radio. The characters Haynes played in the early days of television were almost exclusively house servants. Nevertheless, Haynes always made the best of what she was given. She refused to play domestic roles in a crude or demeaning fashion. "I always did maids as human beings, because there's no other way to do them. I simply would not play them the way they expected me to, as women who were not very smart or attractive. I brought dignity to every one of the maids I played. I did so because it was my way of saying to domestic workers, 'You are to be commended; because of the work you do on your knees, many black children have been able to go to college and become doctors, teachers, lawyers, and outstanding citizens of this country.' I honor these women."

It was the little touches she gave her domestic roles, says Haynes, which raised them above the standard characteriza-tions. On "The Goldbergs," the popular TV program which originated as a radio serial, she played the part-time maid in a way which showed the woman had a life of her own. "There was one episode," she recalls, "where I was supposed to dress up to go out for dinner after work. The wardrobe mistress went to Bonwit Teller's and bought a beautiful hat and a coat that looked very much like mink, and they did a whole scene around me as I was preparing to go out for the evening. As I put on these wonderful looking clothes, I sang 'Diamonds Are a Girl's Best Friend.' It was a fabulous moment, because it was the first time my family and friends saw me on national televison looking my best."

Haynes appeared in a variety of TV programs during the 1950s including "The Goldbergs," "Robert Montgomery Presents," "The Armstrong Circle Theatre," "Studio One," "Alcoa Theatre," and "Hallmark Hall of Fame." One role stands out for her above all the others: in 1958 she was cast as the young Mary McLeod Bethune in a TV drama titled "Light in the Southern Sky." The program, which told the life story of the famous black educator and social activist, was written by a young black writer named William Branch. It was broadcast over NBC as part of a dramatic series called "Frontiers of Faith." Haynes had long been an ardent admirer of Bethune. "She was one of the first people I had read about when I became interested in learning about my people. I read a book that is now out of print called *In Spite of Handicap*, which told of how she started Bethune-Cookman College with $1.50. She was my idol from then on. As the years went by, I met her several times. But then to be given the opportunity to play her...well it was a tremendous thrill."

The Bethune drama is a notable TV event because 1) it marked the second time that a black actress was featured in a half-hour, nationwide broadcast and 2) it is one of the rare occasions in TV history when the life of a strong, exemplary black woman has been given serious dramatic treatment. The day after the show was broadcast, Haynes was deluged with telephone calls from friends and acquaintances who told her how proud they were of her performance. Haynes still thinks of the program as one of the most uplifting experiences of her career.

Television, Haynes realized, had an unprecedented power to shape the American population's image of itself. But throughout the 1950s, racial minorities were almost entirely excluded from the TV airwaves. The world of fifties television was filled with a crazy assortment of fictional and nonfictional characters, from various ethnic and class backgrounds, but few of them were nonwhite. Early in her television career, Haynes became involved in organized efforts to increase the number of roles for blacks in TV. She was a founding member of a group called the Coordinating Council for Negro Performers, which attempted to make the broadcasting monolith more socially enlightened by applying pressure in a variety of interesting ways. The Council protested television's shallow and offensive portrayal of blacks by organizing a one-night "blackout" of TV. Members of the group walked the streets of Harlem and other black communities and urged people to express their indignation by pulling the plugs on their TV sets for one night. Later the group turned its attention to the lack of black performers in TV commercials.* They discussed launching a boycott against Ivory Soap or some other popular detergent in order to pressure TV advertisers into hiring more black actors and actresses. (Although the Council's efforts did not produce any concrete results, the group succeeded in focusing public attention on the plight of black performers. Their tactics would be adopted by a later generation of media reformers.)

Haynes ultimately became convinced that the best way to improve the lot of blacks in the broadcasting industry was through the unions. She played an active role in the Screen Actors Guild (SAG)—American Federation of Television and Radio Artists (AFTRA) joint committee on minorities, from its inception until a few years ago. The minorities committee monitored television to determine how often nonwhites were used in programs and commercials, and met regularly with network representatives to apprise them of their findings. The goal of the committee was complete, across-the-board integration of TV. "We wanted to be represented as we really are in the United States of America," says Haynes, "as we are in the workplace, as we are walking down the street, as we are in the grocery store. We don't all work as maids. We are magistrates, we are doctors, we are nurses, we are social workers, we are teachers, we are factory workers. Isn't that what's happening in real life? Well then why not put it on the

---

*Haynes made a personal effort to penetrate the lily white world of television commercials. She would walk into the offices of J. Walter Thompson, Young and Rubicam, and the other leading advertising agencies which were responsible for casting performers in TV commercials, and announce that she was available for work. "The typewriters would stop and people would look up in awe," Haynes recalls. "And I would put on a broad smile and say, 'I just came to leave my

television set? This is a multi-racial society we live in. So why doesn't it appear that way on the screen?"

Change came at a frustratingly slow pace, particularly in the early years of the committee's operation. Network officials would acknowledge there was a problem and promise to take steps to remedy it. But little was actually done. "There would be some token improvements," Haynes recalls. "One or two minority people would appear in commercials. And then nothing. Unless you kept constantly putting pressure on them, it would fall away again. They understood, they were concerned about it, but nothing substantial was done." Over the next two decades, the combined impact of groups such as the minorities committee and the civil rights movement in general would bring about noticeable changes in TV programming. But, says Haynes, the goal of total integration is still far off in the distance. "I don't want to make it seem like nothing's been done. It's been a long, hard process and there has been some general improvement. But a great deal remains to be accomplished. The proof of this, I think, is that the (minorities) committee is still functioning and still fighting the same old battles. So you see it's really a continuous (struggle)."

*****

Throughout the 1950s, Haynes continued to perform on the stage whenever possible. Television acting remained an economic necessity, but her first love was the theater. In 1954, she returned to Broadway in *King of Hearts*, a comedy by Jean Kerr and Eleanor Brooke which enjoyed a modestly successful run. The following year she appeared in Joshua Logan's *The Wisteria Trees*, an adaptation of Chekhov's *The Cherry Orchard*.

Haynes found her most satisfying roles during this period in two plays by black dramatists. In Louis Peterson's *Take a*

---

picture with the casting director, that's all. I know you're not ready to use my face, but I want you to have my picture. You never can tell." Nothing came of Haynes' numerous forays into these Madison Avenue offices. But, she says, "It was something which I felt that I had to do. I had to open those doors whether they were ready for me or not, and therefore I did it. I walked the streets. And I put my picture every place I went."

Giant Step, which was a success both on and off Broadway during the mid-fifties, she played the mother of a teen-aged boy who was growing to understand what it means to be black in a white-dominated society. In *Trouble in Mind,* Alice Childress' bitterly funny play about the experience of black performers on the Broadway stage, Haynes played actress Millie Davis—a character close to her own heart. Millie laments the fact that she is continually cast in stereotyped roles: "Wish I'd get to wear some decent clothes sometime. Only chance I get to dress up is offstage. I'll wear them baggy cotton dresses but damn if I'll wear another bandanna."—"Last show I was in," she adds, "I wouldn't even tell my relatives. All I did was shout 'Lord, have mercy!' for almost two hours every night." It must have been deeply cathartic for Haynes to utter lines like these after all she had been through as a performer.

"The dramatic pieces which I'm proudest of having been in," Haynes says, "were written by black writers, because they know how to write for and about their people. They have an understanding of our experience, and they present you as you should be presented."

While Haynes prefers to appear in black-authored plays which examine black life, she has always actively sought work in other types of plays as well—not only for economic reasons, but because she prides herself on being a versatile performer. At times in her career, she has even appeared in roles which were originally written for white performers. In 1952, the actress played the part of a Jewish mother in an off-Broadway production of Les Pine's *Monday's Heroes.* The play ran six months at the Greenwich Mews Theatre, a cultural adjunct of the Village Presbyterian Church and the Brotherhood Synagogue. In 1959, she and other black performers set out to demonstrate that they could play roles which were originally written for whites "with no noticeable distortion of artistic values." They organized an experimental showcase under the auspices of Actors' Equity and staged a variety of famous plays with integrated casts. Leading Broadway producers were invited to attend the performances in the hope that they would hire blacks to play roles written by white playwrights for white actors and actresses. Strong advocates of black cultural identity like Harold Cruse would later criticize this experimental showcase as an "integrated charade."* Efforts such as this, Cruse wrote, failed to take into account the significant cultural differences which exist between whites and blacks. But Haynes and the others felt that the showcase would be an effective way of breaking down the racial stereotyping which continued to limit their stage careers. If they could demonstrate their versatility as performers by playing roles that were always filled by whites, perhaps they would begin to win more and more parts which did not require them to wear aprons or dungarees.

*****

During the 1950s, Haynes appeared in several movies which were shot in the New York area. She won her first featured role in a motion picture in 1959, when she was hired to play a housekeeper in MGM's *Home from the Hill.* She was recommended for the part by her friend, Ruth Attaway. Director Vincente Minnelli picked Haynes after viewing her performance as Mary McLeod Bethune. Haynes was delighted to get the assignment because it brought her to Hollywood for the first time. Her stay in the film capital was marred, however, when she was turned away from several Hollywood apartment buildings. "I wanted to rent a place in the Hollywood area because I could not drive at the time, and I wanted to live where you could get around easily on buses. But it was pretty awful here in 1959. It seemed like there were no private apartment houses in Hollywood which would admit blacks. A friend and I drove all over trying to find an apartment one day and we got all kinds of excuses. It was infuriating. You talk of hurt feelings, but what does that actually mean? Nobody can ever describe how it feels when you call an apartment manager on the phone and he says, 'Yes, we have an apartment to rent;' and then you go see the place and he says, 'Well, you didn't sound black on the phone.' Or when a person tells you there are no vacancies even though there's a sign that says the opposite on the front of the building. I'll never forget experiences like these."

---

*Harold Cruse, *The Crisis of the Negro Intellectual* (William Morrow & Co., 1967).

After completing *Home from the Hill,* Haynes was put to work as Johnny Nash's mother in *Key Witness,* another MGM production. As soon as this job was over, she packed her bags and returned to New York. She would not move back to Hollywood until sixteen years later.

Haynes continued to find roles in movies which were filmed in New York. In 1963, she appeared in *Gone Are the Days,* the film version of Ossie Davis's Broadway play *Purlie Victorious.* The Davis creation was a boisterous satire of race relations in the South. It presented the familiar stereotypes with such comic exaggeration that the poison was taken out of them. As a play it did reasonably well, running more than seven months and attracting about 40,000 people. But the film version was a box office disaster. Like many "serious" black films, it received ineffectual distribution and faded away before it reached its audience.

It took the producers of *Gone Are the Days* an inordinately long time to find a distributor. In September 1963, they booked the film into a New York theater, hoping it would do well enough to attract a national distributor. When the film failed to catch on immediately during its limited New York engagement its chances grew even slimmer. Finally, almost one year after the movie's N.Y. premiere, the producers signed a distribution arrangement with Trans Lux. Nothing much was done with the film however. Two years later, it was re-released under the gimmicky title of *The Man From C.O.T.T.O.N. or: How I Stopped Worrying and Learned to Love the Boll Weevil.* By then, time had passed it by. *Los Angeles Times* critic Kevin Thomas wrote: "A picture that takes a comically trenchant look at race relations could scarcely be more welcome, yet, having been written during the civil rights movement's first burst of idealism, it no longer seems adequate for these disheartening days."

Black film historian Donald Bogle characterized *Gone Are the Days* as a "prodigious failure." Nevertheless, he wrote, it "was the first step in the evolution of the new-style all-black movie."* Haynes, who feels very fondly about the film, insists

---

*Donald Bogle, *Toms, Coons, Mulattoes, Mammies and Bucks: An Interpretive History of Blacks in American Films* (The Viking Press, 1973).

that it is destined to become "one of the classics."

Haynes' long years of struggle as an actress began to pay off in the 1960s, when she at last found steady work in film, television, and theater. She made a brief appearance in *The Pawnbroker* (1965) as one of the pawnshop owner's destitute clients. Five years later she played a housekeeper in *Diary of a Mad Housewife.* (Much to Haynes' dismay, her performance was cut to one scene when the movie was edited; later, however, the rest of her performance was put back in for the television premiere of the film.) Television was her bread and butter. She landed roles in numerous primetime series (everything from "Car 54, Where Are You?" to "The Defenders") and daytime soap operas ("The Guiding Light," "The Edge of Night," "As the World Turns," "The Secret Storm," "All My Children").

Her most gratifying work continued to be on stage. In 1965 she appeared in James Baldwin's *Blues for Mr. Charlie* on Broadway and at the World Theatre Festival in London. In 1967 she was cast as James Earl Jones' mother in *The Great White Hope,* which opened to great acclaim at the Arena Stage in Washington D.C. and later moved to Broadway. In 1968, she went to Chicago and London with Sammy Davis Jr. in the musical *Golden Boy.* During the 1972-73 season, the actress played in Alice Childress' *Wedding Band* at the Public Theater in New York.

Soon afterwards, Haynes toured in the national company of *The River Niger,* Joseph A. Walker's award-winning play about a proud black family beset with personal and social problems. Haynes played the part of Wilhelmina Geneva Brown, the family's tough, cantankerous matriarch. She regards it as her favorite role. In 1975, she was hired to appear in the film version of the play along with leading black performers James Earl Jones, Cicely Tyson, Glynn Turman, and Lou Gossett. Haynes was extremely pleased to be associated with the film project. She felt there was an urgent need for more non-exploitative movies about black life. Nineteen-seventies Hollywood seemed bent on depicting blacks almost exclusively as dope pushers, pimps, and prostitutes. "It's presenting the wrong images and ideas to our young people," she says. "They see these blaxploitation' movies and they think that's the way they should live their lives. You deal in dope, you drive a big fancy car, you dress in fine clothes, you wear a big diamond ring—you don't go to school, you don't get an education. The way you get ahead is by abusing other people... These movies never show black people loving one another. In a way what these movies are saying is that black people don't care for one another when in reality we're some of the most loving people in the world."

Haynes believed that *The River Niger* would help offset the negative images of the "blaxploitation" films. It depicted a family of black people who, despite being subject to enormous stresses and strains, still maintained deep feelings of love for one another. This view of black reality came much closer to capturing her own experience than any of the crude and flashy black pictures being churned out by Hollywood. Unfortunately, it was not nearly as bankable. For awhile, it seemed as if *The River Niger* film project would die for lack of financial backing. Producer Sidney Beckerman could not interest any of the major Hollywood studios in the project, despite his impressive list of commercial successes (*Cabaret, Earthquake, Jeremiah Johnson*). "There are major studios, major distributors who will not finance a (non-exploitative) black picture at this time," he told the *Hollywood Reporter* in June 1975. "They do have resistance to it. They resist black quality products based on the fact that their sales people probably can't book it as well in certain parts of the country as they can other films and they have let that slant their thinking in some way."

After the project was turned down by Hollywood, Beckerman linked up with Ike Jones, a black producer who had worked mainly in the nightclub field. Jones succeeded in getting money from a group of black businessmen who had never before invested in a movie.* The film was made for less

---

*The investors specified that the film crew should be composed of as many blacks as possible. Beckerman and Jones complied by hiring a black associate producer, assistant director, assistant cameraman, makeup team, hairdresser, and still photographer. "We would have hired more blacks," Jones told the *New York Times* in July 1975, "but it was shocking to find how few blacks there are in the unions. There

than $1 million. The principal actors agreed to work for a minimum salary and a percentage of the profits.

The critical response to the film when it was released in spring 1976 was generally unfavorable. Like many commendable stage dramas, it was remarked, *The River Niger* lost much of its power and credibility in the process of being adapted for the screen. Some of the criticism was politically motivated. John Simon, of *New York* magazine, for instance, raged against the film's militant social perspective. (He labeled it "another incendiary, white-hating movie.") But, for the most part, the negative reactions came from critics who were inclined to welcome a forthright examination of contemporary black life. Maurice Peterson, film reviewer for the black periodical *Essence,* complained that the dramatic emphasis was shifted away from the family's inner turmoils to "the crime and action aspects of the story in an attempt to appeal to movie mentalities."

The men responsible for bringing *The River Niger* to the screen—producers Beckerman and Jones, director Krishna Shah and writer Joseph Walker—were under intense pressure to make it a commercial success.   Black investors were watching to see if they should put more money into movie production. Hollywood was watching to see if serious black films could attract sizable audiences. Laboring under this weight, the filmmakers produced a movie which was neither as dramatically sound as it should have been nor as financially rewarding as they hoped it would be.

"The project had such tremendous potential," says Haynes. "We had a magnificent cast of people, so many fine black performers gathered together in one place." Unfortunately, she adds, some of the film's best elements were discarded in the editing process. "The movie was adapted by

---

are virtually no black electricians or black Teamsters working in Hollywood." Despite intense pressure in recent years from minority rights organizations, governmental agencies, and minority film workers themselves, the Hollywood craft unions remain overwhelmingly white.

the playwright himself. It was all in there, and it was all shot. But we (the cast) don't know what happened to all the work we did. Much of it did not remain in the final version." Haynes says that her role in particular was badly tampered with in the editing room. "They left me in it, but they took out the heart of the character. Her point of view about the world, how she lost her husband (a defiant Southern sharecropper who had been struck down in his prime)—these things were completely left out of the film...It seems to me that they focused on my grandson (Glynn Turman) and the gang—the business with the bad language, the dope and the violence. And they left out a large part of the relationships between the three generations in the family. They wanted to make it more commercial, so they put in more of the the stuff they think people want to see and hear. But I think that people are way past that now. They've seen so many of those films, that they are getting tired of them."

Haynes came back to Los Angeles to work on *The River Niger*. After the film was completed, she decided to rent an apartment in Hollywood (this proved to be a much easier task than it had been sixteen years earlier) and live there on a part-time basis. Her deepest emotional ties were to New York, and she refused to give up her place in Manhattan, but she realized that for economic reasons she would have to spend at least some of each year in Los Angeles, where TV and film production was centered. "You just can't afford to stay in New York," she says. "The studios used to send for you when they needed you, but not anymore. They just pick someone from the big pool of talent they have out here. So you have to come out here. You have to find a Hollywood agent, you have to get used to driving a car. You have to make a great many adjustments to live out here."

Once she settled in Hollywood, Haynes did find more work in television. She has appeared in the new style black situation comedies "Good Times," "The Jeffersons," "Sanford and Son," and "That's My Mama" as well as other primetime series such as "Family," "Rookies," "Executive Suite," "Starsky and Hutch," and "Ellery Queen" and TV movies such as "Sarah T. (Portrait of a Teenage Alcoholic)" and "The Boy in the Plastic Bubble." She is still is not in a position, however, where she can turn down a job if the pay is slim or the role is something less than she deserves. "We never make enough money. People think we do. When they see us on television they think we're making a great deal of money, but we're not. When a producer offers you a job, you only get a little more than minimum salary. And you are never financially secure enough to say 'I don't work for that anymore.' This is something that gets you at the core. Because you would like so badly to turn down some of these offers, but you can't. You always have bills to pay and so on. When you become a star, *maybe* then you can make demands. But most performers are never in a position to say, 'I won't do it.' The roles are so scarce that you can't afford to say it. You're boxed in and the producers know it and they use it to their advantage. So you take the money and run—not to the bank, but to pay some of your bills. And you say to yourself, 'Maybe next time.' "

One of the most aggravating aspects about working in the "the New Hollywood" for a long-time civil rights activist such as Haynes is that blacks (and other minorities) are still being cast in stereotyped roles which have been only modified by the passage of time. There are moments when she wonders just exactly what the last three decades of struggle in the entertainment industry have accomplished. She has discovered from personal experience that many of those in charge of the Hollywood casting process still have narrow, deeply ingrained ideas about the way black women should speak and appear. "We are seldom thought of as natural women, as black women. We are buxom and loud, we are old and wizened. Or we are super women, all sex and action. We are rarely called upon to look or act like ourselves. Sometimes they say to me, 'Well you're refined, you have class, that's not exactly what we're looking for.' And I say, 'I'm an actress. I'm glad I am refined and I'm glad that I have class, and nothing in the world is going to change that. But if you give me some lines to read, I'll read them the way you want them read.' Which is generally with a thick Southern accent. They're always looking for down-home country types, or something close to it. They just can't seem to get past that 'mammy' image.

"And another thing they don't understand is that black women do not age like white women. When they call for someone around sixty years old, they expect you to come in all wrinkled. But black women who are sixty are in the prime of their life and don't have a wrinkle on their face unless they have been ill. You can't get this over to them. We don't age the same way...These are the kinds of things that a black actress is up against."

Several years ago, Haynes stepped down from her position on the SAG-AFTRA joint minorities committee. The incessant struggle to make TV and movies reflect the rainbow coloration of America finally became too much for her. "I reached the point where I could not go on with it anymore. It was running my blood pressure up. I would go over the same problems again and again. One day I turned the doorknob to go into a meeting and I couldn't bring myself to go into that room I went back home and got into bed, because it made me ill. I told myself, 'You cannot be sick over this question anymore.'...I'd been on the battlefield my whole life, and I had to get away from it."

Though Haynes has slipped away from the front lines, in a sense, she still feels the urgency of the battle. Pressure must be continuously applied on the networks and studios, she says, if the goal of total integration of the mass media is to be achieved. She still believes that the entertainment unions are the key to success. If their full power could be brought to bear on corporate Hollywood, major changes would be effected, declares the actress. Unfortunately, however, the memberships of these unions are not entirely convinced that more steps should be taken to integrate the entertainment workforce. "I think that the majority of union members now feel that because there are some black shows on TV and more black faces on the movie screen and some successful Broadway plays with black casts, enough has been done. They feel, 'Well, they're on their way, we don't really have to do anything more about it.' But they forget that it took some thirty odd years to get this far. None of these things were happening thirty years ago. We were on the outside during those times while the others were working all the time. And even today, the situation hasn't improved that much for many of the 'grassroots' people who are not stars. My friends here are not working as often as they should be. A talented person should be working every other week or so in this field. But months go by before many of us get another job. And that's because we're not totally integrated into the mainstream of Hollywood. If we were, we wouldn't have to keep protesting."

*****

The acting profession, declares Haynes, is "the most difficult (one) in the world to choose." The life of a performer is filled with frustrations and rejections and spoiled dreams. There are countless occasions when you desire a role so badly "you can taste it," says Haynes, only to see it slip into the hands of one of your many competitors. You are continually called upon to prove yourself, to display your virtuosity, to make yourself into the exact image of somebody else. You rarely ever feel in control of your life. "We are like puppets. Everyone tells us what and how. We don't have a life of our own...We're powerless as actors. We're the only ones in that position. The artist can always paint, the writer can always write, but we must wait long periods of time for our chance to perform."

What makes it all worthwhile? The soaring moments, the highlights, the unforgettable performances before genuinely appreciative audiences. Haynes' career is not devoid of experiences like these. "I am very fortunate as a black woman to have done some really wonderful things that I'm very proud of." An actress can be locked into a long, grim stretch of unemployment and then be suddenly and joyously released by one telephone call. "You can be sitting at home and the phone can ring and you can be off to London, England just like that. This is the magic of it. It's often happened to me. The phone can ring and your whole life can change."

In between these high moments, Haynes has been sustained by her inner strength, her deep sense of self-worth. Some performers she knows have turned to drugs and alcohol during the low points; she has drawn consistently on her own resources. "I have built-in faith," she says. Haynes has withstood the misfortunes and injustices of the past thirty years with grace and dignity. She never allowed the entertainment industry's treatment of her to shape her self-image.

Recently Haynes set down her philosophy of life on paper: "Courage is my life's blood," she wrote. "It is one of the most important assets, especially if you are an actress, a black, and a woman. Without it I could not function as a mother, an artist, or as a human being. I have persisted for over thirty years through disappointment, heartbreak, and almost daily rejection and discrimination. But to live on and to go on is called survival. I am optimistic, and I think in terms of being triumphant over all the negative. I believe in holding onto my dreams no matter what. To win, one must stay on top of such things as fear, frustration, discouragement, depression. All artists suffer from these things a great deal. For when one is not creating, one is not fully alive."

Michael Schultz

Michael Schultz is something of a cultural phenomenon. He is the only young black feature film director who works regularly in Hollywood. Each of his first four movies—*Cooley High, Car Wash, Greased Lightning,* and *Which Way Is Up?*—focused on black protagonists, but they managed to "cross over" (in the film industry's jargon) and attract white as well as black moviegoers. Schultz's screen work has a slick, commercial veneer, but none of his films is exploitative in the same sense as *Shaft, Superfly,* or any of the other black films spawned by these two box office hits. Schultz broke into the film industry in 1975, just as the "blaxploitation" film cycle of the early seventies was exhausting itself. His movies demonstrated to Hollywood that black experience could be successfully dramatized on screen without resorting to extemes of sex and violence.

On the eve of his debut as a film director, Schultz made it clear what he wanted—and did not want—to accomplish in Hollywood. "I want to be able to do things as a director that are more than just one dimensional," he told the *Hollywood Reporter* in April 1975, two months before the premiere of *Cooley High.* "I've turned down many black exploitation-type films for this reason...There's more to movies than just selling violence and sensationalism. People are looking for guidance as well as entertainment, especially in view of the present economic and political situation." Some months later, in an interview with the *Los Angeles Times,* Schultz criticized Sidney Poitier for making tame, inconsequential pictures. By attacking both blaxploitation and Poitier-style movies—the two dominant trends in black commercial filmmaking—Schultz made it known that he would be charting a new creative course in Hollywood. "My theory," he told the *Hollywood Reporter,* "is that you can make just as exciting films by dealing with reality, not fantasy."

Over the last few years, Schultz has indeed succeeded in creating a distinctive body of film work. While his movies share some of the crude and exaggerated elements of the blaxploitation cycle, they also display a sensitivity and insight which was missing in those films. And though it cannot be said that Schultz's movies are deeply rooted in social reality, they are certainly more genuinely reflective of the urban black experience than the vast bulk of Hollywood's current screen product. In Schultz's work, one can plainly see the efforts of a filmmaker who is determined to be both conscientious and commercial. He has not been consistently successful, yet he deserves respect for making the attempt. The deficiencies in his work say less about his abilities as a filmmaker than about the creative limitations of Hollywood.

Schultz grew up in a black working class neighborhood in Milwaukee. He and his brother, says Schultz, were the products of a "so-called 'broken home.'" They were raised by their mother, who worked in a meat packing plant during the Second World War and later in an aerospace factory. "I was very removed from the realities of life," recalls Schultz. "I didn't even know that I lived in a black ghetto, that's how naive I was." The idea of becoming a filmmaker never occurred to Schultz during his early youth. Creative ambitions like this, he later told *Sepia* magazine, simply were not nurtured in his social environment: "In the fifties if you had a desire or aspiration to be outside the ghetto, people looked at you as if you were crazy. The possibilities of channeling your individual talents into a (meaningful) life endeavor (were) limited. If you had aspirations to be a writer, it was ridiculous. To be a director was even more ridiculous."

Nevertheless, Schultz began to follow his creative instincts while enrolled in college during the late fifties and early sixties. He transferred from the University of Wisconsin, where he was majoring in engineering, to Marquette University, in order to become involved in the theater arts program. In 1964 he moved to New York and began working at the World's Fair as an assistant stage manager and actor. Later that year, after appearing in two productions for the American Place Theatre, Schultz decided that he did not have the psychological make-up to become an actor. Not wanting to abandon the theater, he turned his efforts at that point toward becoming a stage director. His work at Princeton's McCarter Theatre brought him to the attention of Douglas Turner Ward, artistic director of the newly formed Negro Ensemble Company, and he was hired as a staff director for the NEC's 1967-68 season.

It was during his stint with the Negro Ensemble Company that Schultz firmly established himself as a directorial talent. The NEC was founded in 1967 by playwright Ward, actor Robert Hooks, and producer Gerald Krone with a large grant from the Ford Foundation. There had been several attempts to establish theaters of black identity since the collapse of the American Negro Theatre in the late 1940s. But none of them was as well organized or as well financed as the Negro Ensemble Company.

The NEC came to life during a highly politicized period. The civil rights movement was in the process of splintering into a variety of integrationist, nationalist, and socialist tendencies. There were heated debates about what the role of black cultural institutions should be in the overall black struggle. Soon after the NEC was founded, it came under criticism from some establishment quarters as too separatist. As their first season of plays was presented, the theater company was rebuked by these same critics for being too propagandistic and overly concerned with black themes. Some leading black cultural figures, on the other hand, attacked the NEC for being too white-influenced. "...We are 'against' Negro Ensemble Company," wrote Imamu Amiri Baraka in *Ebony* magazine, "not because they take the devil's money...We are against NEC because they also accept the devil's ideas with that money. That poor mouth little integrated nigger-O (theater) expresses nothing so much as the capture and manipulation of the African personality by white people."

Douglas Turner Ward felt compelled to answer the theater company's critics in angry interviews and newspaper articles. He strongly restated why there was a need for an autonomous black theater: "There has to be a place where Negroes can control and examine their own possibilities in the theater. Are we supposed to wait for that ideal time when total integration has taken place?...It's perfectly obvious how limited a place there is now for Negro talent in the (Broadway) theater, and whatever the case may be in fifty years, those of us who want to realize our capacities now will be dead by then. That's why we have to stake a claim for ourselves in the theater while we're here." In answer to the criticism from black nationalists, Ward declared: "The NEC has never worn its black consciousness on its sleeve, not because it lacks it, but because its spokesmen are more interested in letting what it does speak for itself rather than in indulging in grandiose rhetoric and postures." The NEC's strength, Ward further stated, derived from the fact that it was "not restrictive, not ideological."

Schultz did not choose to project himself into the controversy which surrounded the NEC during its formative years. He quietly and diligently went about his business as the theater company's staff director. Nor did Schultz become involved in any of the larger political struggles which shaped the 1960s. He did not take part in civil rights or antiwar demonstrations, or join any political organizations. The theater was his life. "I was really removed from all of (the political upheaval of the sixties). While everybody was marching in the streets, I was learning what made human behavior happen."

Schultz tended to see the major political confrontations of this period as "an extension of the theater." The mass marches on Washington, it seemed to him, were skillfully choreographed dramas, designed to make the maximum emotional impact on the public. Schultz particularly admired the grandstand politics of media-conscious groups like the Yippies. They understood the modern era of mass communications better than anyone else, thought the young director. This conception of political struggle as a dramatic spectacle would inform some of Schultz's later work as a film director.

While Schultz regarded political events from a distance during his years with the Negro Ensemble Company, his theater work was, by and large, powerfully partisan. During the NEC's first season, he directed two plays for the company—Peter Weiss' *Song of the Lusitanian Bogey* and *Kongi's Harvest* by Wole Soyinka. The first was a searing, poetic denunciation of Portuguese oppression in Angola, Mozambique, and Guinea-Bissau. The play interwove imperialistic sermons with bitter vignettes about life under the Portuguese colonialists. His work on this production won Schultz an Obie Award for best direction. The second play was a political satire about the perils of an emerging African nation. It was written by a widely acclaimed Nigerian playwright who was, at the time of the NEC production, a political prisoner in his own country. Schultz's direction again won praise from the critics. "(He)...stages (the play) with the fireworks brilliance of a Tyrone Guthrie," remarked the *New York Times*.

The NEC opened its second season with another Schultz-directed play, *God is a (Guess What?)* by a new black playwright from Georgia named Ray McIver. The play was a biting, comical statement about race relations in America: it featured a devout black man, two white Southerners who are dead set on lynching him, and a suave gray-hued God who intervenes at the last moment. This God urges militant resistance rather than meekness, submission, or any other Christian virtue. "You get wiped out with that other-cheek kick," he declares. "Force! That's what they understand!"

In 1969 Schultz took a leave of absence from the NEC and made his directorial debut on broadway with *Does a Tiger Wear A Necktie?*, starring Al Pacino and Hal Holbrook. His work on the drama, which was based on playwright Don Petersen's experiences as an English instructor at a rehabilitation center for young drug addicts, brought Schultz a New York Drama Critics Award and a Tony Award for best direction.

The following season he returned to the NEC to direct Douglas Turner Ward's *The Reckoning*, a "surreal Southern fable" about a confrontation between a crafty white racist governor and an even craftier black pimp. Using his knowledge of the governor's backdoor relationship with a black prostitute as a lever, the pimp succeeds in wresting money and political concessions from his opponent. "...Schultz..." stated the *New York Times*, "orchestrates the actors with deftness and intelligence."

In 1970 Schultz staged Sam Shepard's *Operation Sidewinder* at the Lincoln Center's Vivian Beaumont Theater. The play, which dealt with the escalating political conflicts in U.S. life, was distinguished from the other dramas in which Schultz had been involved by its deeply cynical attitude. The picture it presented of Black Panthers and white radicals was as disparaging as the one it gave of the military/scientific complex. The play recommended a form of spiritual abstention from the world's raging battles based on Hopi mystical teachings. *Sidewinder* had been scheduled for production by the Yale

Repertory Theater the year before, but it was withdrawn when black students objected to its characterization of Panthers as cold-blooded thugs. When the play was presented at the Lincoln Center, it drew complaints from Native Americans.

Schultz's final contribution as a New York stage director, before moving to Los Angeles, was *Dream on Monkey Mountain*, which was presented by the NEC in 1971. The play, which was written by the Trinidadian dramatist Derek Walcott, was a bittersweet allegorical tale about black identity and colonialism. It centered upon a poor, aging Caribbean black man who receives a vision and sets out in search of his African homeland. Once again, Schultz's work met with the critics' approval.

The following year the young director decided to go west and try to break into the film industry. He had resisted making this move for some time. His conceptions of Hollywood were, predictably enough, overwhelmingly negative. "The whole California atmosphere," he says, "seemed to be directly opposed to anything that smacked of culture or the intellect." But in the end, the film industry's commercial allure proved to be too powerful. "Money, money, money," declares Schultz with a grin, was the reason he came to Hollywood. "I don't think Hollywood is the place where you come to make socially meaningful statements. I moved here out of economic necessity. My family was getting larger, and the theater—which I love dearly—was not supporting us in any fashion. My bill collectors were becoming more numerous than my friends. I said to myself, 'I better go do something else and make some real money.' "

Schultz was confident that he would soon establish himself as a moviemaker. " 'Look,' I told myself, 'if all these turkeys out here are doing it, I know that I can do it.' " And though the products which Hollywood turned out seemed to be, for the most part, shoddy and uninspired, he felt that he might be able to create something once in awhile of which he could be proud. "When you come out here, you see all these people who have copped out along the way, all these people who no longer try—they just put in their eight hours and do their thing and don't really care about anything...But what I decided to do was to stick it out and see how far I could go and what I could do."

Gaining a foothold in the film industry proved to be somewhat harder than Schultz had anticipated. Though he brought with him from New York a reputation as a first-rate stage director, he discovered this meant very little in Hollywood. "Coming out here from New York was like starting all over again. I had done some work in the theater which I thought was very artful. But when I made the rounds here looking for work, they said, 'Who are you? What did you do?' They were not interested in hearing about New York or the stage."

Eventually Schultz found work in the Universal Studios television factory. He directed installments of various police and detective shows like *Toma, Rockford Files,* and *Baretta*. But he did not adapt well to the assembly line pace of television production. "They told me, 'You'll never make it in television. You're too slow.' I said, 'Well it really pains me to see it done wrong.' "

Fortunately for Schultz his stint as a TV director did not last very long. While working at Universal, he was approached by producer Steve Krantz with a film script called *Cooley High,* which was based on screenwriter Eric Monte's high school experiences in Chicago's black ghetto during the early 1960s. Schultz had been recommended to Krantz by a film editor who had worked with the director on a film version of Lorraine Hansberry's *To Be Young, Gifted and Black* for WNET in New York. Schultz initially turned down the project: "I realized after reading the script that it was unique. There had not been any films about black kids in high school during that period. It had a lot of love in it, and I am drawn to positive films. But it was a total mess." Krantz was persistent, however, and Schultz finally agreed to rework the script with screenwriter Monte. (Schultz later learned that the confusion in Monte's script was due to the fact that a less knowledgeable person had been rewriting it.)

The picture was eventually sold to American International Pictures, Hollywood's leading manufacturer of "trash" movies. *Cooley High's* unsensational, poignant treatment of black experience made it a strange selection for AIP, a studio which had reaped large profits with blaxploitation films like

Coffy, *Black Caesar*, and *Slaughter*. But as AIP chief Sam Arkoff explained to the *New York Times Magazine* in August 1974, this cycle of supercharged movies was "not a novelty anymore." In Arkoff's estimation, the black teenage audience was now ready for a more subtle reflection of itself. Just in case he was mistaken, however, the studio executive decided to put only $750,000 into the film.

During the making of the movie, Schultz came under strong pressure to "white-ify" the film in order to make it palatable for white moviegoers. "They said, 'You can't do this, it's too ethnic.' (he laughs) I said, 'What are you talking about? You want to make these kids white, right? You want to give them white attitudes and everything. That will destroy precisely what makes it interesting for a white audience—(the characters' distinctive ethnic traits)...' I said, 'No way, what we're talking about here are human beings and what's really interesting about these people is what makes them who they are and how they operate and all that. And by exploring their unique characteristics, you find that which is universal, that which is common to all people.'"

The AIP hierarchy wanted to hedge its bets even further by including more sex and violence in the film. But Schultz objected adamantly to this as well. In the end, the strong-minded film director prevailed. *Cooley High* was filmed essentially the way he wanted it to be. "The film corresponds very closely to what I had conceived and what I was able to do during the twenty-five-day shooting schedule."

While *Cooley High* is not culturally exact in its depiction of ghetto life (has there ever been such a Hollywood film?), a great deal of sincerity and sensitivity shines through the movie. Schultz and Monte were clearly intent upon presenting black teenagers—their aspirations, exuberance, silliness, awkwardness, and despair—in a more understanding way than any other Hollywood filmmakers had before them. In this, they were indisputably successful.

The movie focuses on several members of the 1964 graduating class of Edwin G. Cooley Vocational High School in Chicago. These adolescents are shown in the final moments of their innocence (and, the film suggests, the decade's final year of innocence), as they prepare to venture into a world which will not treat them generously. Jack Slater, a staff writer for the *New York Times*, has written: "*Cooley High*... remind(s) us, almost incidently, of who we once were, reminds those of us who grew up black during the fifties and early sixties of the sense of self we managed to achieve during those years, before job hunting became a futile exercise, before feeding our newly established families became a daily battle, before the knowledge slowly dawned that our children's education would be more of a mockery than the one we had received—before all of it (including the collapse of civil rights) forced us to caricature ourselves as victims..."

There is no reference in *Cooley High* to the larger civil rights struggle which was then building to a crescendo. This deprives the characters' experiences of an important historical context. And the ghetto's harsher edges are, for the most part, presented in a softened light. But *Cooley High* is not a simple, nostalgic flashback like *American Graffitti* (a film with which it is often compared). The grim economic and social realities which haunt black youth are the frame which surrounds the picture. In an interview with *Sepia* magazine, Schultz remarked: "Eric and I wanted to turn the audience on to the love and joy in the kids of that time and underplay all the hard realities. Not to deny them, but it all comes out subliminally. Looking at the film, I clearly saw the horrors of the ghetto."

Film critics, in general, responded favorably to *Cooley High*. Kevin Thomas of the *Los Angeles Times* was particularly exuberant: "*Cooley High* is a landmark movie, one of the year's most important and heartening pictures, that shows what the black film can be when creative talents are given an opportunity free of the strong sex and violence requirements of the exploitation formulae." And even more importantly, from the standpoint of Schultz's career, the film proved to be a major box office success as well. The picture grossed over $8 million, or more than ten times what it cost to make. Schultz too regarded the movie as a worthy achievement. "I took what could have been *American Graffitti* in black face and turned it into something that I think has more value."

Schultz thought that the success of *Cooley High* would encourage Hollywood to produce more "soft" black pictures and open the industry's doors to aspiring black directors. This was not the case, however. The film failed to expand the range of possibilities for black filmmakers in general. But it did launch Schultz on a promising movie career. After *Cooley High* was released in summer 1975, Schultz was hired by Universal Studios to direct *Car Wash*, a disco musical comedy set inside a Los Angeles car wash operation. According to the *Hollywood Reporter:* "The concept for *Car Wash* had been developed in 1973 by producers Art Linson and Gary Stromberg as a stage-album project similar to *Jesus Christ Superstar* and *Tommy*. When Ned Tanen, executive v.p. of Universal became involved, a mutual decision was made to bypass the stage and go right into film production." Joel Schumacher (*Sparkle*) was signed to write the screen play.

Schultz envisioned the structure of *Car Wash* as a sort of double helix. He wanted to carefully thread "a very serious, realistic—you might call it 'social'—dramatic line" through and around the picture's comedic backbone. "I felt that both threads were needed to support the film; the two really went together. The audience is not stupid or rigid. You can do a lot with them. You can make them laugh, and then you can make them think, and then you can make them laugh again." But Schultz says that those in the studio hierarchy, with one or two exceptions, saw the film in much simpler terms. "They didn't expect anything but bubble gum comedy," he remarks.

Once again, Schultz found himself in the position of having to continually defend his creative perspective. He was beginning to realize that this was a process which he would have to go through on each one of his movies. It begins, says Schultz, during the scriptwriting stage of the film when you struggle to keep important scenes and dialogue intact. "You might put a lot of minor things into the script which you know are going to be cut. So that you can fight the battles over the less significant stuff and finally emerge with something close to what you wanted."

During the production stage, says Schultz, the main pressures on the director are related to "time and communication (i.e., getting the actors, cinematographer, and the multitude of other people to put the image that you have somewhere in your head on film without having it too badly defiled)." The production schedule on each of his first four films was very tight. He was given only twenty-eight days to shoot *Car Wash*, but he wound up taking ten more in order to complete it. "I said, 'Look, I'm not finished, what can I tell you?' "

During the editing stage, there are more battles with the studio management over various elements of the film. "I may concede something during the scriptwriting stage and then go ahead and film it anyway. I tell myself, 'When they see it on film, they'll realize I was right.' (he laughs) Sometimes they do, sometimes they don't. But at least you give yourself another chance to win. Between the time the script is written and the time the film is edited, the studio can change its mind— depending on what other films flopped at the studio, or what the weather is like, or who had a fight with whose wife, or who's winning in the power struggle within the studio at that particular time. All of those things can change the way they relate to your particular little insignificant project, which is really very important to you as a director. So you fight for the things you want all over again during the editing process. If you don't have final cut, then you win some and you lose some. By the time your picture is finished and playing in the theaters, if as the director you have managed to get eighty percent of what you originally conceived into the film, then you have done superlatively well."

Schultz says that the final version of *Car Wash* represents only seventy-five percent of what he wanted the movie to be. "I lost bigger fights (on *Car Wash*)," he remarks. Nevertheless, says the director, the movie still "has its values." "It introduced audiences to a certain (social) element whom they knew little or nothing about. People go through car washes all the time, but they seldom relate to the minorities who do the work there. *Car Wash* explored the dreams and desires of these guys, and portrayed them as human beings." This is the main strength of the picture. Though it falls far short of capturing the full interior reality of a car wash, it does present the operation's Third World workforce in a warm and appreciative manner. The car washers resist the drudgery of their workday by playing pranks, weaving elaborate daydreams, pulling off minor acts of sabotage, and giving each other moral support— when this doesn't work, they just turn up the radio to a blaring volume. As one left wing critic noted, "The joy of the film is in the immense survival spirit of the workers..."

But despite its occasional insights into the culture of the workplace, *Car Wash* is largely a superficial piece of film-making. The gags and comedic sketches tend to be trivial and unrevealing, and the characters lack substance. Politics appears in the form of two Hollywood stereotypes: the boss'-son-turned-revolutionary who tries to inspire his father's employees with readings from Chairman Mao's Little Red book, and a young black nationalist named Abdullah who masks the pain inside him with a surly, contemptuous attitude. They are both treated with amused tolerance by the rest of the car wash crew (which is perfectly understandable, given the absurd posturing of the two characters). The relationship between workers and ideological commitment is a rich and fascinating area to explore, but rather than making the effort to do this, the film simply exploits these two characters for some easy laughs. (Schultz says that some key scenes involving Abdullah and Lonnie, one of the older car washers, were cut at the studio's insistence. "I had a very strong relationship between Abdullah and Lonnie, but it eventually got whittled away until it was just a hint of what it was supposed to be.") Perhaps Abdullah would have seemed less a caricature if these scenes had remained.

Car Wash received a mixed response from critics when it was released in summer 1976. Pauline Kael labeled it "the movie equivalent of junk food." "I guess that Schultz is trying to make life rise up out of these schlock ingredients," she observed, "that he's trying to show that soul food can come out of junk food, but don't all purveyors of junk food claim that it's nourishing?" Charles Champlin of the *Los Angeles Times,* on the other hand, "found it particularly refreshing because it seemed to work within the conventional studio wisdom of the moment—that movies ought to be entertaining and untroubling and leave a pleasant aftertaste—but was also able to stay in touch with observable reality." And Maurice Peterson of *Essence* magazine wrote that *Car Wash* proved Schultz "to be the most stylish Black film director around."

Audience reaction to the film was overwhelmingly positive. The picture, which had been produced for $2 million, made $10 million in the domestic market alone. Sales of the soundtrack album brought MCA a few million dollars more.

Schultz says that both *Cooley High* and *Car Wash* could have done even better business than they did if they had been properly marketed. "They were both classified as 'black movies,' which placed certain limitations on them. The film industry has made it so that 'black movies' are synonymous with 'rip-off,' 'exploitation,' 'low-quality'—everything that has a negative connotation." Schultz also states that his films met some resistance from theater owners. "There are exhibitors all around the country who are basically racist people. Some theater owners in suburban white neighborhoods don't want black audiences coming into their theaters because they feel it will scare away their business... So therefore they say, 'We can't show this movie. We don't want to drive away our customers.' It's a very insidious and very entrenched kind of thing."

After completing *Car Wash*, Schultz began preparing a second feature for Universal titled *Which Way Is Up?* He interrupted his work on this film to replace Melvin Van Peebles as the director of Warner Brothers' *Greased Lightning*, the story of black race car champion Wendell Scott. Van Peebles, whose *Sweet Sweetback's Baadasssss Song* set off major repercussions in the movie industry during the early 1970s, had been fired by producer Hannah Weinstein while in the process of shooting the film. ("Creative differences," that favorite industry expression, was cited as the reason.) Ironically, Van Peebles was one of the few Hollywood filmmakers whom Schultz respected. In an interview with *Sepia* magazine, Schultz labeled *Sweetback* as "the only revolutionary black film." He said it reminded him of "some brilliant cinema from South America, crude but still brilliant. It's the only black film with substance, with an artist's integrity behind it. It told people not to be sheeplike, but to stand up for one's humanity."

Schultz estimates that he re-shot eighty percent of what Van Peebles had already photographed, but he feels that *Greased Lightning*" is not really my picture—even though it has my name on it." Schultz says that the film is less reflective of his aesthetic perspective than it is of producer Weinstein's. After he finished shooting the picture, says the director, he was forced to return to *Which Way Is Up?*, and therefore could devote only half of his time to editing *Greased Lightning.* Weinstein, he says, objected to the way he was cutting the picture and fired his editor—the same person who had edited his two previous films. "See, everything about moviemaking," he remarks, "is very political. Because I wasn't there all the time to fight the political battles, to impress upon her my own ideas, I lost out."

Weinstein, like Schultz, is a strong advocate of minority rights within the film industry. *Greased Lightning* was the second film turned out by Third World Cinema,* the New York-based production company she helped establish in 1969 to expand opportunities for minority film workers. There were no differences of opinion between Schultz and Weinstein over the movie's forceful pro-civil rights content. It was Weinstein's stylistic approach which Schultz disagreed with. "She had in mind what I call the soap opera style of movie-making—she wanted a lot of emphasis on the family and on the boring points of the picture. I had cut it in a very modern form, all flashbacks. I had the movie open as Scott begins his championship race, and then it flashed back to how he got there. It was very interesting, or so I thought. (he laughs)...But they took it and put it together in this archaic fashion, which I hated. (Weinstein) is in her fifties or sixties and the film has that kind of feeling about it. When I saw it with an audience, I said, 'Well, the spirit of the film survives, but it could have been so much better.' "

In spinning the tale of Wendell Scott, who was the first black champion in the world of stock car racing, *Greased Lightning* makes all the right points: blacks can and do act heroically, blacks can and do have strong, loving family lives, commercial interests often exploit racial hostilities, alliances between poor downtrodden blacks and whites make a great deal of sense. Unfortunately, these points are somewhat dulled by the fact that the picture, as an overall effort, is sentimental, plodding, and predictable. The film's attitude toward Scott is overly deferential; the result is that he comes off as a bland,

---

Claudine, starring Diahann Carroll and James Earl Jones, was the first.

one dimensional figure (despite Richard Pryor's animated performance). "In a funny, old fashioned way," commented Don Morrison in the *Minneapolis Star,* " "*Greased Lightning* is the spiritual cousin of, say, *The Glenn Miller Story* or any of the scores of similar 1930s to 1950s film celebrations of white culture heroes. Such pictures set up the principal character as a flawless icon almost from the first frame.

There is an interesting sidelight to *Greased Lightning:* the film marked the debut of Pam Grier, the queen of blaxploitation pictures, as a "serious" actress. Grier, who had been featured in movies like *Coffy* and *Foxy Brown* as a super-sexual, super-physical black dynamo, played the part of Scott's wife. She proudly told the *Baltimore Afro-American* that her role in *Greased Lightning* marked the end of her career as a female *Shaft.* But Grier's part in the racing picture proved to be just as limited, in its own way, as her previous roles. She was reduced to playing the woman-behind-the-man, cheering her husband on to victories and listening attentively to his grand dreams.

While *Greased Lightning* was appearing of the nation's movie screens during summer 1977, Schultz was completing work on *Which Way Is Up?,* another vehicle for actor/comedian Richard Pryor. *Which Way* was based on Lina Wertmuller's *The Seduction of Mimi,* the story of a vacillating man who can choose neither corruption nor social commitment. Producer Steve Krantz had conceived the idea of transferring Wertmuller's film to the American social situation during the making of *Cooley High.* The idea intrigued Schultz, and over the next year he proceeded to develop it. Schultz decided to set the story in the context of the California farmworkers' struggle: the *campesinos* and their labor organization would represent the forces of social enlightenment; the forces of evil and corruption would be represented not by the Mafia (as in the Wertmuller film) but by agribusiness. Wavering in between would be a tragi-comic black fruitpicker named Leroy Jones (Richard Pryor).

Schultz realized that the film would be probing a social controversy which was still very much alive and which he had no firsthand knowledge of. He was determined, therefore, to bring people into the project whose ethnic backgrounds and political experience would make them more sensitive and informed than the average Hollywood film crew. Schultz insisted that Universal hire cinematographer John Alonzo and his Chicano camera crew, even though they were generally paid considerably more than union scale. Universal had a longstanding policy against paying camerapeople more than scale, but they grudgingly complied with Schultz's request. The director also decided to involve El Teatro Campesino, the talented and dedicated farmworkers' theater troupe, in the project. Again the studio was resistant: it was pointed out to Schultz that they had no previous Hollywood credits. But the director's arguments finally prevailed. "I quietly and matter of factly told them that in order for the film to be realistic, I had to have these people's help. I said, 'Look, I don't know anything about the farmworkers, I haven't been active in that movement. I don't want to do a phony representation of what it is all about and neither do you. Because if you do, then theaters are going to get burned.' That changed their tune. (he laughs)...One finds oneself playing all kinds of funny games (with studio management) simply to win things which should have been agreed to at the very beginning."

El Teatro, which had been dramatizing the farmworkers' struggle for a dozen years, initially was reluctant to get involved in a Hollywood movie. "They were upset about the knife-carrying hoodlum-type roles that they always seem to see on the screen," Schultz told writer Louis Torres in the *Los Angeles Times*. "What persuaded them to do the film was that it was a chance to do something that showed a very real part of the Chicano-American experience." According to Torres: "The Teatro's main contribution, aside from providing actors for the film, was in reshaping portions of the script dealing with the Chicano characters.* They also provided an ongoing link to the nuances of Chicano lifestyle. During an evening break in the filming, members screened a print of their documentary film about the farmworker movement, *Fighting For Our Lives*, and afterward answered questions from the

---

*The script for *Which Way Is Up?* was written by black novelist Cecil Brown (*The Life and Loves of Mr. Jiveass Nigger*) and screenwriter Carl Gottlieb (*Jaws*).

cast." On the whole, their participation in *Which Way Is Up?* was apparently a gratifying experience for the theater troupe. Daniel Valdez, who serves as Pryor's moral conscience in the film, became fully convinced that "the time for the Chicano in TV and films is now. I used to feel that the time was ripe a few years ago, but now I know that we have the right experience to along with the opportunities. The time is now."

Which Way Is Up? is Schultz's most overtly political movie to date. It is also raucous, crude, and highly entertaining. Of his first four films, it is the most successful fusion of political content and commercial aesthetics. Cesar Chavez and *La Causa* are presented with a kind of respect and care which Hollywood rarely bestows upon progressive social movements and their leaders. (Chavez is called "Ramon Juarez" in the film and is played by Luis Valdez, the founder of El Teatro; the United Farmworkers is referred to as "the Affiliated Farmworkers.") Members of the farmworkers movement are shown to be dedicated, nonviolent, hardworking, and just.

Agribusiness, on the other hand, is presented in its full villainy: smashing peaceful union organizing efforts with club-wielding thugs, attempting to assassinate the Chavez-like leader of the farmworkers union, and exerting its corrupting influence throughout society. (In the film, agribusiness takes the form of a fictitious, vertically integrated corporate behemoth called Agrico Industries, Inc. Agrico, whose slogan is "If it's in your mouth, Agrico put it there," is run by a cold, ruthless executive whose white hair and white suit give him the appearance of a Southern plantation owner.)

But the film's main strength does not lie in its overt politics. The political antagonists in the film essentially operate as symbols, and the farmworkers' struggle is more of a backdrop than a central focus. The movie's primary contribution lies in its comic and insightful examination of Leroy the fruitpicker, a man who wants everything he can get out of life but without having to work for it. He wants the respect and admiration of his farmworker friends, but he refuses to join their struggle. He wants the status and material comforts which Agrico can give him, but he finds it difficult to serve the company's cause. He wants the love and devotion of two women, but he cannot find the time or energy to maintain a relationship with either one of them. *Which Way Is Up?* nicely conveys the pain and absurdity of being unable to commit oneself to anything or anyone.

Some critics attacked the film for reviving the stereotype of the shiftless "coon." But the stereotype here is put to a political purpose. The audience is asked to laugh at Leroy because he consistently refuses to take a stand against the white corporate order and become his own man. Furthermore, with racially astute Pryor playing the role, the audience is continually made aware that they are watching a social satire. In the end, Leroy finally breaks out of his stereotyped role by telling off his corporate overseer in strong "street" language: "You got the wrong nigger for this job, because I quit. I'm at the bottom of my life, and the only way is up. And if you don't like that, you can shoot me in my ass, 'cause that's the only part of me you're gonna see, motherfucker." With that, Leroy turns on his heel and strides down the highway, gaining more confidence with each step as he realizes he is not going to be shot. It is a liberating moment.

Which Way Is Up? also features some interesting sexual politics. Leroy repeatedly tries to take advantage of the women in his life, only to have them turn the tables on him. Leroy tries to discourage the sexual advances of his wife out of deference to his mistress, but one night he winds up playing the victim in an outrageous bondage scene. When his wife sleeps with the local preacher, Leroy sets out to even the sexual score by seducing Sister Sarah, the preacher's wife. He lays an elaborate trap for the woman, but when the fateful night arrives, it is she who takes control. "Alright I'm yours," says Sister Sarah with a gleam in her eye. "I hope you're ready for me, because I've been waiting for this for a long time. I hope you got a strong back." Sister Sarah's counterpart in Wertmuller's *Seduction of Mimi* was presented as an object of ridicule—her fat body was photographed in such a way as to evoke laughter and disgust. But this cruel element was missing in the scene which Schultz composed. Sister Sarah comes across simply as a righteously angry and lustful woman.

The major film critics, almost without exception, assailed *Which Way Is Up?* when it was released in fall 1977. Some of the strongest criticism came from critics who are close to the industry and was aimed primarily at Pryor and his biting comedic style. *Variety's* Art Murphy commented that "Pryor's career seems now at a crossroads, where his increasingly annoying brand of reverse racism must be tempered and matured, or else the fragile public coalition of his audiences will vanish." Charles Champlin of the *Los Angeles Times*, whose reviews are usually generous to a fault, called the film "racially offensive" and suggested—in so many words—that it be picketed by the NAACP. *Which Way Is Up?* appeared at a time when there was something of a media backlash against Pryor. The backlash seems to have been due, in part, to the performer's controversial NBC variety show (which was the source of much anxiety for the TV network) and his hostile appearance at a Hollywood Bowl gay rights benefit in September. Despite the critics' overwhelmingly negative response, the movie did well at the box office. It failed to draw a substantial white audience, but black filmgoers went to see it in large enough numbers to make it a hit.

Before *Which Way Is Up?* came out, Schultz was hired by Robert Stigwood Productions (makers of *Tommy* and *Jesus Christ Superstar*) to direct *Sergeant Pepper's Lonely Hearts Club Band*, a rock opera built around twenty-nine Beatles' songs. The picture, which featured 1970s pop stars Peter Frampton and the Bee Gees, seemed to represent a further commercialization and debasement of sixties culture. But Schultz, whose first four movies had all dealt with black experience, welcomed the opportunity to break into a new film category. Throughout his brief film career, Schultz had resisted being "typed" by the entertainment industry. "I'm *not* a black director," he told the *Hollywood Reporter* in May 1977, "I'm a director." He frequently declared that his aim was to make movies which explored a variety of dramatic topics and appealed to a wide range of people. Schultz realized that the *Sergeant Pepper* assignment was an important and necessary step in terms of his Hollywood career. Hollywood finances the production of so few "serious" pictures about black experience and generally attaches so little significance to them, that a black director would soon fade away if he/she limited him/herself to making only black films. The black director must either go outside his/her cultural experience or face extinction as a Hollywood filmmaker.*

Schultz hoped that his directing credit on *Sergeant Pepper* would make it easier to secure financing for screen projects which held more meaning for him. "Before you can jump out and do something which you deeply care about, you must get some credentials. Someone like me needs more credentials than a director like George Lucas. Because the films I want to do, when you really look at them, are threatening in a way. They have never been done before. They are not just fantasy trips. So in order to get the people who control the money to put their trust in me, I have to put together a very impressive list of credentials."

Schultz has built his Hollywood career in a very thoughtful fashion. He has carefully tried to avoid making the same mistakes which proved to be the downfall of other black filmmakers. At one point he considered forming an independent production company with Gordon Parks Sr. and other black directors "who are really doing something," but he later decided this would not be "a cool move." "It would have drawn negative attention," explains Schultz. "It would have been too easy a target." The movie industry, says Schultz, tends to react with undisguised hostility to those black filmmakers who "make waves." "So what I have essentially done," he says, "is assume a very unthreatening stance.** I simply go about my

---

*Gordon Parks Sr. (*The Learning Tree, Shaft, Leadbelly*) is among those black directors who have come to realize this. "Black directors have got to stop thinking about doing only black films," he commented in a Fall 1977 interview with *Cineaste*. "They've got to address Hollywood to that. I do it to my agents all the time. I say 'Don't just bring me black films. Bring me *Ryan's Daughter*. Let me refuse it if I want to. Let me refuse *The Exorcist* or take it if I want to. Bring those things to me.

"The white directors are doing films that black directors could best do. So what's left for black directors? Develop themselves as fine directors and forget the fact that they're black so they can do any film they want to. Because after awhile there's going to be a limit to what you can do out there."

**Schultz's policy of maintaining "a low profile" includes refraining from political activity. He is not involved in any political organizations, nor does he publicly support any specific causes. He says that he has chosen to influence society through his creative work alone.

business and direct pictures. But meanwhile I'm developing these wonderful ideas for the future."

For the past few years, Schultz has talked about making the film biographies of two intriguing historical figures—Alexander Pushkin, the great nineteenth century Russian poet, and Toussaint L'Ouverture, one of the principal leaders of the slave insurrection that eventually led to the independence of Haiti. Pushkin (who, Schultz points out, was a descendant of an Abyssinian prince) was forced to do his creative work under the careful supervision of the Russian autocracy. As a low ranking member of Czar Nicholas I's court, he enjoyed certain privileges but also suffered great indignities. "Pushkin was at the same time a pet and an enemy of the Czar's," Schultz remarks. Schultz's position in Hollywood, as a favored black director, is not altogether different from that of the Russian poet. He strives to maintain his creative integrity, while taking pains not to offend his patrons. "Oh yeah," laughs Schultz, "things don't change, people just put on different costumes."

So far Schultz's two film ideas have not evoked much enthusiasm in studio offices. Movie executives fail to see the drawing power in stories about a controversial nineteenth century poet and a black Haitian revolutionary. Schultz, who has consistently maintained that politics and entertainment are entirely compatible, finds the studios' cultural prejudices extremely vexing. The story of Pushkin, he tells them, is not just about artistry under political constraints—it is about romance, jealousy, personal intrigues, and violent passions. For the poet did indeed live a flamboyant life and he died a tragic death. And the story of Toussaint and the Haitian Revolution is not just about the collapse of colonialism, slavery and the old world order and the coming of a new contradictory era. It is about war, heroism, treachery, and defeat. Because Toussaint *was* a brilliant military strategist and was finally brought down by the duplicity of his enemies. When talking with studio management, it is these elements of the stories which Schultz emphasizes. "Because," he says, "when you're dealing with the beast, you have to wring things around a little bit."

Schultz is confident that he will eventually get to make the important movies which he has within him. He is a strong believer in the power of the individual. "I'm a firm believer that we are the instruments of change. And if anybody tells you otherwise, they're just trying to maintain the status quo."

While he is fully aware of the problems of operating within a commercial mass medium, Schultz is determined to continue working as a Hollywood filmmaker. He plans to return on occasion to the theater, because working in a smaller, less commercial context "keeps your creative juices flowing." But he has come to feel that it would be "a gross mistake"—in social as well as financial terms—to abandon Hollywood altogether. "The film industry has the power to disseminate ideas and information to a huge audience. No artist who is worth his salt would leave that instrument in the sole possession of the empty-headed. If the more thoughtful artists were to leave the film industry, it would result in a creative vacuum, and that would be unconscionable. What I say is, 'Get in there and do battle with the dragon.' "

"Every artist, no matter how devoted he is, wants to reach the greatest number of people," Schultz declares. "The trick is to avoid reaching them with a diluted product." It is a trick which Schultz is still struggling to master. But at least he is making the effort.

IV.
UNFINISHED BUSINESS
Preface
Carol Chaka
Lynda Calhoun
Patti Bereyso

Preface

With the rise of the women's movement in the early 1970s, a number of organizations sprang up around the country to advance the interests of female clerical workers. Among these organizations was the Inter-Studio Feminist Alliance, a coalition of Hollywood office workers which formed in summer 1972. The primary goal of ISFA was to open up career opportunities for women in the entertainment industry. Women had long been excluded from Hollywood's creative, managerial, and technical echelons.* The vast majority of Hollywood's female workers were lumped in clerical positions, from which there was virtually no hope of advancing. ISFA also concerned itself with Hollywood's screen products. The group protested the entertainment industry's perpetuation of negative sexual stereotypes and called for the production of truer, more intelligent films about women's experience.

The Inter-Studio Feminist Alliance grew out of a short-lived rank and file movement within Local 174 of the Office and Professional Employees International Union, which represents office workers at most of the major studios. The rank and file movement, which was led by Universal secretary Carol Chaka, was geared towards making the union more responsive to the needs of its female membership. When this effort collapsed, studio office workers Lynda Calhoun and Patti Bereyso organized ISFA as an independent pressure group. ISFA was launched on a powerful wave of women's discontent. For three years the group haunted the corridors of Universal studios, demanding a release from mind-numbing office work and striking fear into the hearts of Universal's

---

*A 1974 Screen Actors Guild study found that only 28.2% of the TV roles during prime time hours were played by women. A Writers Guild study, conducted between October 1973 and September 1974, found that female writers accounted for only 10.8% of prime time TV credits at ABC, 8.4% at CBS, and 8.2% at NBC. Barbara Searles, chairperson of the Directors Guild women's committee, told a California state commission in 1975 that none of the guild's female members worked regularly as Hollywood directors.

male leadership. By 1975, however, the group no longer had the strength or the numbers to carry on.

What are the factors that contributed to ISFA's demise? The most obvious one is the stiff resistance which the women encountered from Universal management. The studio was unalterably opposed to the office workers' attempts to intervene in the creative and managerial process. Secondly, the women who took an active role in the ISFA campaign and the Local 174 uprising which preceded it were not experienced opponents of corporate power. Their strategy was largely improvised as they went along, and they were probably not as prepared for a long, drawn out battle as they should have been. Thirdly, the group was unable to develop strong links with other feminist and labor struggles inside and outside of the entertainment industry. The women's isolation tended to reinforce their sense of powerlessness.

Finally, there was a fundamental flaw in ISFA's political outlook. The group was not mainly concerned with improving clerical work itself, but with catapulting clerical workers into high status, high income job categories. Because of the way Hollywood is structured, however, there is room for only a few at the top. The vast majority of female office workers can never become high ranking Hollywood figures, no matter how ambitious and hard working they are, because the industry is simply not organized that way. ISFA might have attracted more women if it had focused its efforts on making office work more interesting and fulfilling. The only way to do this is by giving office workers more creative and decision-making authority. This would, of course, blur the distinctions between executives, producers, writers, and their secretaries— but that is precisely what is needed. The hierarchical structure of the entertainment industry must be broken down, if the majority of Hollywood employees are to derive pleasure from their work.

Despite its failings, the office workers campaign was a significant development in recent Hollywood history. It was part of a general upsurge of feminist activity which has brought about major changes in the entertainment industry. Women are located in a wider variety of positions in Hollywood than they were in the early seventies. And the images of women in TV and film have also changed considerably over the last several years. "...Women are once more the center of numerous Hollywood films," wrote feminist film critic Joan Mellen in 1978, "and (they) are being treated as persons of substance rather than as mere decorative objects."

And yet much more needs to be accomplished. Most of Hollywood's female employees are still concentrated in dull, unsatisfying clerical positions. And the progressive depictions of women in features like *Julia* and *An Unmarried Woman* and TV dramas like "Breakup" and "See How She Runs" are continually offset by a plethora of sexist fantasies. There is a need for a new wave of feminist activism in Hollywood today, in order to protect the gains of the past and to go beyond them.

Carol Chaka

Secretaries, Carol Chaka says, are the "drones" of the entertainment industry; their daily drudgery is what keeps the dream factory going. Between 1957 and 1972, Chaka worked as a secretary for various producers, associate producers, and television writers. While she answered their telephones, took their notes, did their typing, coordinated their schedules, and occasionally hosted their parties, her bosses engaged in the more creative and stimulating process of manufacturing network television shows. It was Chaka's fervent hope that she might one day be relieved of her office duties and promoted into the industry's higher ranks.

Hollywood has always nurtured ambitions like Chaka's; countless films and television programs have featured lowly unknowns who through diligence, luck, and charm finally become Somebodies. But the dreams which the industry produces for the screen, Chaka discovered early in her secretarial career, rarely come true in its offices. In fact, the possibility of succeeding in Hollywood seemed so remote that Chaka did not even dare tell her fantasy to her friends. "To think of being a producer was so out of the question, nobody ever mentioned it," Chaka recalls. "I mean it would have been embarrassing. They would all laugh at you. You sit down and have lunch with your three girlfriends (and tell them) and they would laugh."

As a young woman coming of age in Cleveland during the 1950s, Chaka felt that her career options were extremely limited. It was assumed that she would follow her mother's example and devote herself early in life to housekeeping and raising children. "I was never encouraged," she says. "I came from a working class background. Nobody in our family had ever been to college—much less a woman. I had taken tests and all that; I had a 148 IQ, which didn't impress anybody in the family. It sort of impressed me, but I didn't know how. But nobody ever took me aside and said, 'Well, you've got a great brain, you've got this potential, you know...What are you interested in?' "

Most of her girlfriends married soon after they graduated from high school, but Chaka did not want to settle down right away. Music was high among her interests at the time; she remembers reading an item in a *Downbeat* column one day which reported that a Los Angeles jazz company was looking for a secretary who genuinely appreciated music. Chaka was unable to reach the company by telephone, but she was confident she could find an exciting position somewhere in the record industry and in 1957 she left Cleveland for the Coast. As it turned out, however, the young woman went to work in another entertainment field: "It was kind of a fluke that I started working (in television) at Warner Brothers because I went on an interview at Capitol Records (at the same time), but they were so cold and...so busy impressing me—'Oh you'll be talkir.g to celebrities all the time on the phone'—like this was going to be worth $60 a week!...And the people who interviewed me at Warner Brothers I liked much more. They were very nice, warm and seemed interesting...so I wound up getting into television instead of the record business."

During her first year in the entertainment industry, Chaka felt she was going to make significant progress. She had escaped Cleveland and the domestic career for which she had been programmed. Hollywood seemed to hold infinite possibilities: "when I was young, twenty years old and starting out in the business, things were wonderful. And I was bright and I was complimented all along the way for everything that I did because I did it so well. That was the last time that I had the active thought, 'God this is wonderful!' You know, I thought I would just go right up the ladder. People would be so thrilled to have me working for them that I would be rewarded for my abilities."

Chaka soon figured out, however, that her employers liked having a "bright, wonderful secretary," and had no intention of helping her advance. "They'll pick your brains and never pay you for it," a friend told her, and Chaka's experience in the industry verified it. "I was reading scripts and making synopses and giving opinions and coming up with suggestions and all that stuff," Chaka remembers. "And they said, 'Oh wonderful. That's wonderful. You're such a good secretary.' Always the compliments come to reinforce your position, keep you where you are."

During her first years in Hollywood, the young secretary worked for the men who produced "The Bell Telephone Hour" and "The Dinah Shore Chevy Show." In 1963, after a brief period of freelancing, she transferred to Universal Studios where she performed clerical chores for the producers of shows such as "The Virginian," "Arrest and Trial," and "The Kraft Suspense Theatre." Chaka made a continual effort throughout this period to learn more about the mechanics of television so she could eventually move from behind her desk into the world of production. From time to time, she would slip out of her office to watch "dailies" (film from the previous day of shooting), or quietly observe her bosses' creative sessions. But her secretarial duties invariably interfered. "Your job is to be at that desk, to cover the phone. You're not supposed to be flitting around, so you don't have too much of a chance to acquaint yourself with things. If the head of the steno pool calls the office and you're not there for ten minutes, or your boss says 'I'm not getting my calls. I'm sorry you can't go to the dailies today—there's no reason for you to be there anyway.'...well, that's just the way it goes."

Chaka still managed to teach herself about television production, but her skill and initiative went unrecognized. She once asked one of her bosses, a producer for whom she had worked five years, to give her a production board so she could demonstrate that she knew how to "break down"a shooting script (i.e. schedule the filming of a project so that it costs the least amount of money to produce). "I did my board and I was so thrilled," recalls Chaka. "And it went into (the producer's) closet. He said 'Well, I'll look at it someday' and he never did."

In 1971, her eighth year at Universal, Chaka was assigned to the office of Bill Link and Dick Levinson, a highly successful television writing team. The secretary found her new bosses, who were co-creators of the TV series "Columbo," to be "very bright, sharp, and articulate;" the atmosphere in her new office seemed to be charged with more excitement and creativity than the other posts on the studio lot where she had been stationed. But once again Chaka was denied access to the creative center. "They were very interesting guys. But I felt very left out because they had each other, you know. I really was there just for phone calls and memos and stuff. Every once in awhile I could slink in and sit on their couch and listen—they are just fantastic guys and they write like crazy!...They would try to include me. But they were so bright they didn't need anybody."

Chaka was enormously disappointed by her failure to advance in Hollywood. She had been working in the entertainment industry for fifteen years and had acquired a considerable amount of knowledge about the television production process but she still found herself confined to routine office chores. Her self-confidence was steadily eroding; she came to believe it was her own personal limitations which held her back. "I figured it was because I don't have a college degree, or I haven't the moxie, you know. You just feel like it's your own fault."

By the opening of the 1970s, however, the newly revived national women's movement was starting to have an impact on the entertainment industry. Female television and film workers who for years had accepted their low status in the industry as a part of social reality began to vehemently protest. In 1970, a woman film cutter who had worked at MGM since 1955 filed a complaint with the Equal Employment Opportunity Commission charging that the studio refused to promote her because of her sex. The same year a woman who had tried unsuccessfully for seven years to become a member of the Hollywood local of the International Photographers union filed a lawsuit to gain admission to the union. (Her attorney later subpoenaed statistics from fifteen Hollywood craft unions which indicated that women represented less than thirteen percent of the workforce in those craft categories.) In spring 1971, a women's group was formed within the Writers Guild of America-West to discuss job discrimination and screen sexism. "When we pooled our knowledge and shared our experiences," wrote the group's chairperson, Diana Gould, in the November issue of the Guild newsletter, "we found there were shows we could not write for, men who would not hire us and stories that could not get made. (When was the last time you saw a woman leave a man at the end? And not get slaughtered as a result?)" The same year, a women's conference committee was organized within the Screen Actors Guild under the leadership of actress Kathleen Nolan.

Nineteen seventy-two was a watershed period in Chaka's life. Early in the year, she began having conversations with other women office workers which were different than any she had had before. It had always been difficult for the secretaries at Universal to establish close ties with one another. "At the studio they tried not to encourage friendship," says Chaka. "They wanted to keep people on their toes, afraid of each other, afraid that anybody might turn them in for an infraction of the rules. You know, if somebody wanted to leave work ten minutes early and someone said, 'I'll punch out for you'—I mean if anybody caught you, oh God! Little things like that. Or 'I'll cover your phones for you'— whatever. You just couldn't do friendly things like that for each other." But as the social atmosphere changed, Chaka realized that the ways she and some of her co-workers related to one another were also changing. They shared confidences, they discussed their jobs. Each discovered she was not the only one who harbored dreams about breaking out of the clerical ranks.

They had often aired work related grievances before. "We would all complain about our bosses and different things," recalls Chaka. "We just figured all workers complain." But this was different. Now they were considering changing their lives. "For us to even talk about wanting to be more than a secretary was a very intimate admission to make to each other —very. It was very, not disloyal to the job, but just not part of, you know, answering phones and everything. So that was a breakthrough, just the fact that we all got into this discussion. That gave us a lot of solidarity."

The secretaries' casual conversations with one another were followed by formal gatherings. In late February, Chaka organized a meeting in a public hall across the street from Universal to discuss the clerical workers' status within the company and how to improve it. Some of the thirty or forty women who gathered in the hall that day wanted to fight for greater career opportunities; others were less interested in escaping from office work than they were in making it more tolerable. They all agreed that sex discrimination was a built-in feature in the entertainment industry and had to be aggressively opposed.

Several different methods of applying pressure on the industry were discussed at the initial meeting, including affiliating with a more militant union and establishing a new one altogether, but in the end the women decided to work within their existing labor organization, Local 174 of the Office and Professional Employees International Union, AFL-CIO. Chaka and the others were aware that OPEIU's existing contract with the studios was scheduled to expire on January 1, 1973. Their first step was to compile a list of demands for the union to include among its proposals when it negotiated the new contract. "We put down everything we ever wanted in the world," says Chaka, including: a thirty-five hour work week, screen credits for production secretaries and secretaries to the producers, career ladders to insure that secretaries could become executives and producers, low cost day care for all studio employees, elimination of the "dehumanizing, demeaning" time clock, free studio parking, a clear statement of their right to strike, termination of janitorial duties, cost of living raises, better savings and bonus plans, and a comprehensive medical plan.

The activist secretaries encountered opposition from the management of Universal Studios as soon as they set out to distribute copies of their twenty-four proposals. "We had to (distribute the proposals) through individuals," says Chaka. "We would give them to a bunch of people who would try to hand them out individually. One time we left them on a bunch of desks in one department at Universal and the boss came in early and confiscated all the copies. They were very worried. They were very worried that the union was getting active. They wondered what this subversive thing was going on, this wave going through the studio."

A few copies were handed out in the offices of Columbia Pictures, where the Universal women had some contacts, but for the most part their agitational efforts were confined to their own studio. They soon realized, however, that they would have to convince a sizable number of the 1800 members of Local 174 to join them if their contract proposals were to be endorsed by the union. This was no simple task; Local 174's membership was scattered among a variety of studios, film laboratories, film exchanges, and independent production companies in the Los Angeles area. Just a small percentage bothered to show up at union meetings. The only certain way of reaching everyone in the local seemed to be through the printed records of these meetings which were routinely distributed to the entire membership. So the Universal secretaries decided to make an appearance at the next union meeting, which was scheduled for April 17, in order to read their proposals into the minutes and let their fellow office workers know where they stood.

Chaka was chosen to represent the small pressure group at the April 17 meeting; when union president Herman J. Pope asked that evening if there was any new business, she immediately stood up to read aloud the twenty-four items. At first Pope refused to recognize her. Chaka, he said, should submit her proposals to the contract negotiating committee in a few months. But she insisted on her right to speak: "You accuse us of not participating in our union. We want to participate. We want the membership to know what we've been doing for the last several months, that we are interested." As she argued her point, she noticed a man coming down the aisle toward her. "They weren't going to hit me or anything like that, but I was like a rabblerouser. I mean, they wanted to give me the hook and get me out of there, shut me up. And I wouldn't shut up!" While Chaka fought to read the proposals, several dozen secretaries who had come to support her cheered her on. Finally she was allowed to proceed, and the secretaries' recommendations for a new contract were duly recorded in the minutes of the meeting.

Much to the activists' dismay, however, the twenty-four point list failed to elicit a strong response from the clerical rank and file or an endorsement from the Local 174 hierarchy. The union deemed only one of the group's proposals legitimate enough to take up with studio management—the secretaries' request to be relieved of janitorial or "office wife" duties such as washing coffee pots and cups and defrosting refrigerators. Universal secretaries had been instructed to take over these chores as an "emergency measure" in 1970, after the studio announced it was laying off much of its janitorial staff due to financial difficulties. For secretaries like Chaka, who were striving mightily to upgrade their professional status, "it was the final humiliation." In their contract proposals, the women noted that MCA (Universal's parent corporation) had reported a twenty-six percent increase in profits in 1971. "We think it is safe to assume that this emergency no longer exists," they concluded.

Soon after the April 17 meeting, the union fired off several sternly worded letters to Universal's industrial relations office declaring that kitchen chores were not part of the secretarial function. Studio management took a different view but offered to transfer discontented secretaries to "non-coffee assignments." Chaka felt the union was trivializing the secretaries' concerns by focusing on the coffee cup issue to the exclusion of all the others. In her opinion, the primary problem was the secretaries' lack of advancement opportunities; she was demanding a way for secretaries to free themselves from dead end clerical positions and become part of the creative and managerial force which shapes Hollywood's products. The union apparently felt this was outside its domain.

The secretaries began to realize it would take more time, planning, and effort than they had anticipated to get the union behind their cause. Chaka, who had become the prime mover in the secretaries' struggle, found there was always too much organizational work to be done. The office where she worked was transformed into the secretaries' command post, much to the displeasure of her two bosses. "You've got your army in here all the time," they complained. "The phone never rings for us anymore—it's always you and your union business." In the heat of the battle, there seemed to be little opportunity to pause and develop a coherent plan of action. "There wasn't time for it," says Chaka, "because I always had to make twenty-five phone calls to get people to do something right away. We just jumped in and that was that. There wasn't really time to share (information). Everything just seemed so...we had to move, we had to move, we had to move."

After the union turned aside their contract recommendations, the secretaries considered various courses of action. For awhile they discussed running a slate of officers in the next union election, but they finally decided that they lacked the necessary experience. Chaka found it difficult to picture herself in the role of a union leader. "It scared me. They wanted me to run for business manager and I thought, 'Oh my God, I don't want to become that. I don't want to be some sharkskin suit sitting head to head with the Universal labor relations boys who are out to kill us.'" In May, as the nascent feminist movement within Local 174 began to falter, Chaka went off in a different direction. Hearing that the AFL-CIO had begun to lobby against the Equal Rights Amendment in California, she decided to file a sex discrimination complaint with the EEOC charging that the giant labor organization had failed to poll its membership or take women's interests into account. At the time, this move seemed like a logical extension of the secretaries' fight for better union representation, but Chaka later came to feel it was "far off target. We had not set out to revolutionize the entire union structure. We just wanted to create some opportunities for women."

In the end, the EEOC complaint drained Chaka of whatever organizational energy she still had. "We were trying to do the union proposal thing and then we got involved in the ERA issue and all this time you're holding down a full-time job. I was exhausted. By June I was absolutely exhausted." When Chaka's strength gave out, the union movement came to a halt. "Chaka was really almost the whole guiding spirit of that union movement," declares one of the clerical activists. "We had had our grumblings all along, but I think there's a great possibility that if she hadn't gotten the whole thing rolling it may never have happened."

Its failure to win wider support within the studio offices proved to be the downfall of the brief secretarial uprising. Chaka and her circle of friends simply could not keep the momentum going by themselves. "It was really hard. Nobody wanted to take a stand. The guys you have to serve coffee to are the guys you have to look at every day. Some of the women were older and didn't want to risk rocking the boat. They had their pensions at stake. And most of the older ones had been active in bringing the union into the studio so they felt they were better off than they had ever been. They were grateful for what they had. Some women were supporting their children, they couldn't risk losing their jobs. Some women liked the way things were. They were very happy being secretaries. They accepted that way of life and that was it."

Chaka also feels that the unique atmosphere within the entertainment industry makes it particularly difficult to draw studio office employees into the labor arena. "It's a funny thing," she remarks. "You're secretary to a producer and it's a glamour business. And a union is kind of tacky. Unions are for workers and you don't think you're quite a worker...Secretaries and all the office workers are the drones who keep it going... But when you're secretary to a producer and you're dealing with these television actors and the casting, you're so close to the glamour that you still have your dreams going. You're so close to the glamour that you don't want to think of yourself as a union member, a worker, or somebody like that. You want to go out with some doll, go to a disco or something like that. That's your self-image. Your self-image is so peculiar when you're secretary to a producer."

Chaka had developed a different attitude about labor activism while growing up in Cleveland. Her grandfather was a one-time member of the militant Industrial Workers of the World, and her father was an active participant in the struggle to establish the United Auto Workers. Chaka remembers walking on picket lines as a small child with her father, who was the editor of his union newspaper, *The Eyeopener*. "He really had a lot of courage," she says. "He stuck his neck out and was very outspoken."

Chaka's view of labor unions is ambivalent. She respects their democratic traditions and ideals but, as she told her father during the office workers' uprising, "they are no longer what they were supposed to be." Even before her run-in with the leadership of Local 174, she had come to believe that unions were bureaucratic institutions which were sadly out of touch with the rank and file. Her experience inside the office employees union reinforced her opinions. "They gave us the fast shuffle," she says. "...The union wasn't acting in the interests of the workers. It didn't care what we thought, it was totally removed."

In retrospect, Chaka concedes that the secretaries were making a somewhat peculiar request of the union by asking it to help them break out of the clerical ranks. "It's very strange for a union member...I mean I think back to my dad. My dad refused to be a foreman because he wanted to be with the workers...and to be a foreman would put him with management. Here we were saying that we wanted to get into the fame and glamour and goodies—the big money. So it was a strange position...Now looking back I see that it's almost a contradiction to become more active in the union because you want to get into management. That is basically the contradiction which I didn't have my finger on at the time." It probably would have made more tactical sense, says Chaka, to have used an instrument like affirmative action programs to open up career opportunities for women in the industry. But at the time she was unaware of that option.

The secretaries' call for career ladders was a strong, innovative demand to make of an industry which lumps most of its female work force in clerical positions. Young men who start out in the studio mail rooms are often groomed for more prestigious jobs, but as a rule women who begin their Hollywood career as office workers end them as office workers. Chaka and the others insisted that the people who did the typing and filing had a right to ultimately become those who made the creative decisions. The insurgent secretaries, however, stopped short of challenging Hollywood's system of hierarchy. They accepted the fact that power was concentrated at the top in the entertainment industry; what they demanded was access to those higher levels.

During the secretaries' campaign, says Chaka, her writer-bosses urged her to concentrate on building her own career "instead of trying to light a fire under 1800 women." In summer 1972 she took their advice and left Universal in search of success. "I feel regrets," she remarks, "that we couldn't carry it further, really carry it on...But I was just so utterly frustrated after nine years at that company, that I just couldn't hang in there anymore. I just had to get away from there and that crippling kind of oppression." Chaka managed to find a secretarial position at Spelling-Goldberg, a television production company, which afforded her more creative opportunities than she had before. Later she landed an office job with the Jerry Lewis Muscular Distrophy Telethon and she finally succeeded in breaking out of the clerical ranks by becoming a talent coordinator for the annual television marathon. Today she works as a freelance production assistant on various television projects.

It has been four years since Chaka worked as a secretary, and yet she remains vaguely insecure about her status in the

industry. She finds that she picks her jobs carefully to avoid
sliding back into a secretarial slot. "It's a funny thing. Having
started out as a secretary, I react very strongly against doing
anything that resembles secretarial work. The further I get
away from that period of my life, the less it bothers me. This
year, for instance, I didn't mind getting somebody a cup of
coffee. But two years ago, it would have made me furious."

Chaka still has not realized her dream of becoming a
producer; sometimes she wonders whether the struggle to
reach a high-level industry position is really worth it. It is easy
to get intimidated and discouraged along the way, she says.
She misses the support she used to get from other women
during the secretaries' campaign. "I find it hard to beat down
doors by myself. That was one good thing about that particular
time—we could draw from each other...I hope there's a closer
community of women in Hollywood in the future. You need it
for moral support."

Postscript:
In summer 1977, Chaka left the entertainment industry
to become a real estate agent. She says that she has no regrets
about her decision. Too much of her time as a freelance film
worker went into tracking down jobs, and not enough into the
work itself. "The amount of money you make in real estate is
directly related to the amount of energy you spend. (As a film
worker) I was always having to play politics, to maneuver
around, in order to get jobs. I'm making a better living now,
and there's less pressure."

Though she herself no longer aspires to be a Hollywood
producer, she is deeply gratified by the advances which
women in the entertainment industry have made over the last
several years. "Women are holding more different positions in
Hollywood than ever before. I feel that I was part of the
change which took place. If all of us had not made our individual and collective efforts, nothing would have improved.
There seems to have been something happening on a universal
plane during that period—everybody was moving at once—
and our group was part of it."

Lynda Calhoun

Among those office workers activated by Carol Chaka's campaign within Local 174 of the OPEIU were Lynda Calhoun, a casting coordinator at Universal Studios, and Patti Bereyso, a secretary at Paramount. Like Chaka, Calhoun and Bereyso deeply resented the way that women in the entertainment industry were concentrated in low paying, dead end clerical positions. "Lynda and I had been doing office work for so long," says Bereyso. "You'd do your boss' job, and if he got promoted you'd train the next guy who came in and then he would leave and you never got any credit. You could never move anywhere. This was something that really needed changing."

In July 1972, not long after Chaka quit her secretarial job at Universal, Calhoun and Bereyso met for lunch and decided to keep the women's campaign going by forming a pressure group which they called the Inter-Studio Feminist Alliance (ISFA). Instead of relying on the union to open up career opportunities for clerical workers, ISFA would use the power of federal law. Title VII of the 1964 Civil Rights Act prohibited discrimination based on sex in all employment practices. Executive Order 11246, issued by President Johnson in 1965, required all firms with over $50,000 in federal contracts and fifty or more employees to develop and implement affirmative action programs (i.e., blueprints for upgrading the status of women and minorities). "...Employers are not abiding by these laws, " declared ISFA in its statement of purpose. "Therefore ISFA will...arm itself and its members with women's rights under the law for equal opportunity and equal pay."

ISFA vowed not only to fight for the rights of women who worked "behind the scenes" in Hollywood, but to improve the roles of women "on the screen." The entertainment industry, charged the group in its opening statement, abused its enormous power as an image maker by consistently stereotyping and degrading women. Females were habitually cast in roles of "servant, sex object, and second class citizen." ISFA proposed that its members monitor films and television programs and advise "those in authority" how to improve the portrayal of women.

Although ISFA co-founders Calhoun and Bereyso hoped to make an impact on the entire industry, they decided that initially the group would focus its attention on one studio—Universal (which is owned by giant MCA, Inc.). "That was our territory," explains Bereyso, who worked there before moving over to Paramount. "We thought if we could make an inroad on the biggest studio in town, we'd have the problem licked." MCA was a formidable target: it was the nation's leading supplier of network television programs, it operated the world's largest motion picture studio (a 420-acre spread), it had interests in records, music publishing, real estate, recreation, mail-order gifts, and savings and loans. Over the years, its television and film divisions had gained a reputation for ruthless efficiency and less than inspired creativity. "MCA's introduction of computers and tight cost controls into television production," stated the *Wall Street Journal* in 1973, "resulted in the nickname, 'the factory' for the company's television production center." MCA, Inc. was an empire on the rise; big, bustling, prosperous, and highly cost-conscious.

Despite the awesome size and character of their corporate adversary, Calhoun and Bereyso were unintimidated. The Inter-Studio Feminist Alliance was launched in a burst of optimism and exuberance. Announcements of the group's first meeting, recalls Calhoun, were sent out to "a number of women who we knew were just generally marvelous complainers...At that initial meeting we discussed what we would like to do and there was great enthusiasm...We thought that we would form this group and have great success and really be a tremendous force in the history of this business...We were really going to start a great movement!"

During the first year of its existence, ISFA received an endorsement from the National Organization for Women (NOW) and formed a loose alliance with several feminist organizations in the entertainment industry, including Cinewomen, Creative Women of America, and the Women's Conference Committee of the Screen Actors Guild. Members of the group met regularly in each other's homes, helped produce women oriented programs for KVST (a publicly supported TV station in Los Angeles) and published a newsletter called *Ms. on Scene* which was circulated among known sympathizers inside and outside of the industry. *Ms. on Scene,* which began appearing in spring 1973 on a quarterly basis, was the main instrument ISFA members used to break through the confinement of their nine-to-five studio jobs and establish communication with women who shared their concerns. The mimeographed newsletter was filled with accounts of ISFA's latest activities, tips on how to win promotions and sell scripts, interviews with industry feminists, articles on legislation affecting women, statistical reports on the status of women in Hollywood, movie and book reviews, and announcements of women's cultural events in the Los Angeles area.

Calhoun was an indefatigable contributor to *Ms. on Scene* and its pages probably reflected her spirit and perspective more than anyone else's. The media industries' latest assaults on women elicited outraged responses from the Universal office worker. She greeted each new advance by women in Hollywood with heartfelt enthusiasm, whether it was a new television series with a leading female role or the admission of another woman into a craft union. Since her childhood, Calhoun had been an ardent movie fan and collector of screen memorabilia. *Ms. on Scene* gave her a forum to express her opinions about films and develop her critical abilities. Calhoun found the bulk of Hollywood's recent products to be fairly shameful. She chastised director George Roy Hill (*Butch Cassidy and the Sundance Kid, The Sting,* and *The Great Waldo Pepper)* for using women in his films only to assure audiences that his leading male characters were "normal." "The women (in Hill's movies) just put their time in," wrote Calhoun. "Hill likes the twosome to be males. Women are only a necessary inconvenience." The *Ms. on Scene* film critic found more to recommend in older Hollywood pictures like *Mannequin,* a "soapy" 1938 MGM production starring Joan Crawford. Calhoun found the plot to be "conventional" but applauded the "right-on liberated dialogue" which the film contained. ("Men are strong, women are weak," remarks Crawford with considerable irony. "My mother spent a lifetime of strength trying to prove that.")

It was Calhoun who became the leading activist in ISFA's campaign at Universal. She initiated meetings, mapped out group strategy, and solicited outside support and advice. The office worker's strong advocacy of women's rights made her a somewhat controversial figure in the studio. Not long after

ISFA was organized. Calhoun discovered that the young male employees who worked in the studio mailroom (commonly referred to as "mailboys") were technically considered "management trainees" and were offered regular training sessions during company time. Calhoun dashed off a letter requesting the studio to either open up the training sessions to female clerical workers or develop a separate program for the women. Universal management responded by cancelling the training sessions altogether. Stories linking Calhoun's letter to management's decision spread throughout the studio, and a contingent of angry mailboys stormed into the casting department where the ISFA activist worked carrying an obscene poster of "Women's Libbie Calhoun." She tried to explain to the young men that she had not intended to shut down their training program. ("I wish I had that much power," she quips. "It would be terrific to be able to tell management to do something and have them hop right to it.") She just wanted the studio to offer its female employees the same opportunities. But for a period, the young "management trainees" refused to deliver mail to Calhoun's desk.

The conflict with the mailboys was an unpleasant experience for Calhoun. "There were an awful lot of rumors going around that I hated men and all this kind of stuff. That hurt me in a personal way and in a job related way. It made it difficult to work with some people." Management's decision had forced the aspirations of the clerical workers and the mailboys to collide head on. "It was just a big breakdown in communication," says Calhoun. "The mailboys should have come and talked the whole thing out with me."

In November 1973, management agreed to meet with ISFA and listen to the women's grievances. ISFA assembled a delegation of Universal office workers and spokespersons from various feminist organizations in the entertainment industry and Los Angeles community; the corporation was represented by three executives—Joe Hiatt, Gareth Hughes, and Elliot Witt. Calhoun opened the session by reading a short statement and then turned it over to the other women, who gave brief accounts of their experiences in the industry. The twelve Universal office workers who were present told the corporate managers of the discrimination they had been subjected to while working at the studio. The remarks made by one of the twelve—a secretary who wrote for television in her spare time—were particularly moving, remembers Calhoun: "She was very nervous and had been afraid to come to the meeting. She got started talking and her voice was shaking badly because she was so scared and excited and everything all at once. And she proceeded to tell her story; she knew she had talent, she told them. She was extremely admired by all the people she had worked for. And other studios obviously felt she had talent because they had optioned her work. But she couldn't get the time of day a Universal. 'It's very disillusioning,' she said to them. She was thinking of leaving the industry."

After the women completed their personal accounts, ISFA members tried to determine precisely what MCA was doing at that moment and planning to do in the future to end sexism on the screen and in its offices. The women directed a series of questions at the three executives: Which Universal films and television pilots this year star women? Who are the women working behind the scenes on these films and TV shows? What is Universal doing to change the screen image of women? Are there progressive stories in the making? Does MCA offer training programs for women? What scholarships are available to female employees for cinema classes on company time? Who are the creative and decision-making personnel at MCA and its studio? Are women being moved into top corporate positions? Will MCA appoint a female vice president to oversee the hiring and promotion of women?

None of these questions, ISFA members felt, were adequately answered that morning; but, says Calhoun, there was an "implied promise" of future meetings and the women came out of the session in high spirits. "We put the fear of God in them somewhat," declares the feminist office worker. But in the weeks that followed the November meeting, management adopted a hard line toward the progressive group. One of ISFA's primary goals was to set up a major summit meeting with all people in charge of creating Universal's entertainment products—executives, producers, casting directors—in order to discuss the studio's treatment of women. Justicia, a Chicano community group, had been allowed to present its case against racial discrimination at a similar studio meeting the year before. In a phone conversation with a labor relations executive on November 23, 1973, however, Calhoun was informed that the ISFA women would not be granted such a hearing. Furthermore, stated the executive, the studio was upset by the fact that ISFA had brought outside women supporters to the November meeting. Never again would management take part in sessions which included non-Universal women, Calhoun was told. Finally, the information regarding creative and decision-making personnel which ISFA had requested was confidential, according to the executive, and could not be put in writing.

"The only concrete thing that honestly came out of that November meeting," says Calhoun, "was that management asked me to send them resumes of women who were interested in advancing. So I sent over quite a number of them, several dozen resumes and letters of recommendation. I don't think any of those women ever got jobs though. We were just spinning our wheels...Management probably put in their report to the federal government— Oh, yes, we had all these interviews with women!' "

Through phone calls and urgently worded memos, Calhoun continued to press the studio to agree to a summit conference and to release the information ISFA sought. But management's position remained the same. Calhoun grew increasingly angry and frustrated with the studio's uncompromising attitude. "Who does he think he is!" wrote Calhoun in her personal records following a December 5 phone call with a labor relations executive. "He once again turned down a Justicia-type meeting. He insisted on having meetings with just Universal women. He once again brought up our going to the Producers Association. He feels that would be our most effective action. He doesn't understand why Universal should be singled out. He put across the point that other studios have the same problems. I indicated that Universal is in a unique position as the largest employer and its position with the federal government (Universal does a sizable amount of film business with the government). He wanted to know what my facts were. That he didn't feel I could say that It was not a friendly conversation. I told him that I was very busy and that my time was limited and that phone conversations were inconvenient for me, etc. He indicated that I was welcome to meet with him in his office at any time. Would I let him know and keep him informed of my decision to meet with him? I'm afraid I was rather short with him. He infuriated me so. I feel like this is a type of harassment. Go to his office alone! Never!"

ISFA's requests were perfectly legitimate; the women were simply trying to ascertain whether or not the studio was complying quickly and fully with federal law. But the group lacked the sufficient size and strength to get what it wanted from Universal. Calhoun and Bereyso had a spectacular vision: they saw a legion of secretaries, filled with deep dissatisfactions and righteous anger, jumping up from their desks and demanding more out of life. But the movement they envisioned failed to materialize. "What Lynda and I wanted," Bereyso declares, "was a mass of women to go out on strike, to stand up and shout, 'Hey! All of us, down to the last person, are sick and tired of being treated in a subservient way! This second rate, second class citizen time has got to go. Let's all stand up and shout, and if the people at the top don't like it they can lump it!' If every secretary in the world walked off their jobs, industry would collapse. The economy would collapse. It would be incredible. If all the secretaries left, forget it. The world would come to a screeching halt. And that's what we wanted to do. But you can't do it with six people. Six people will only get fired and be replaced."

Calhoun and Bereyso made a strenuous effort to bring more studio office workers into their organization. They scheduled regular meetings at members' homes and mailed invitations (at their own expense) to everyone who received their newsletter. When this failed to produce results, they tried to lure people with the promise of wine and cheese, and chips and dip. "We'd call these meetings," remembers Bereyso, "and we'd ask this other gal if she would donate her house that night, and we'd run over to her house which was close to Universal and we'd sit around and wait for nobody to come. When we started using bribes, some people—a few here, a few there—would show up. They'd come once. Then they'd say, 'Gosh, I've got to get home and make dinner for my husband!' or 'Gosh, I'm going out tonight, I've got a date' or whatever. Everything took precedence over what they were doing...It got down to the point where I'd be taking minutes at meetings and keeping files and I'd be dragging around shopping baskets full of materials to all these meetings and there was nobody to take advantage of them. Nobody there to help us with them."

ISFA did not appeal to those women who for various reasons had resigned themselves to a clerical career. And, by and large, those who aspired to higher status positions in the studio seemed to feel they did not need the collective assistance of groups like ISFA in order to move upwards. In a sense, this was true. By 1974, feminist groups within the industry and the women's movement in general had created an atmosphere in Hollywood which made it necessary for studios to promote a token number of females to high-level positions. Some of the women who benefited from this atmospheric change had never been involved (or were only marginally involved) with the groups which helped bring about the change.

It disturbed Calhoun to see more and more women in Hollywood set out to make it on their own, independently of their sisters. She wrote an impassioned plea for collective action in the fall 1974 issue of *Ms. on Scene:*

> Have you noticed that women are back into individual action rather than group action within the industry? There seems to be a lessening of action on all fronts...and that's just what industry management wants. They hope we'll give up so they can get back to their unprogressive ways...Women in the media must regroup...all the work cannot be done by just a few. Media action must be led by media women. We must continue to exert pressure, make waves. ISFA's main interest has been to assist and encourage media women to move up the studio/industry ladder into positions of influence...influence that will lead to the change of women's image onscreen...ISFA hopes that women won't give up their principles in that long, mostly slow trek to the top. If management can convince women to stop being advocates of women's rights within the industry then there is reason to believe that when those women make it they'll be the same I-made-it-on-my-own-you'll-have-to-do-it-too type of human being. Remain committed...don't fall away...continue to exert pressure...work for yourself and others. Fight for equality now!

As Calhoun saw it, the purpose of the feminist movement in Hollywood was not to place a select group of women in top echelon jobs but to make creative and meaningful work a real possibility for all women in the industry. She had felt embarrassed at the November meeting with management when a few women attempted to snare jobs for themselves. "Don't give plugs for yourselves," the ISFA organizers had told the women's delegation before the meeting. Nevertheless, says Calhoun, "several individuals went right ahead and said 'Use me.' Not 'Use all of us, use more women writers, use more actresses' but 'Use me.' "

Organizing is a particularly troublesome task in an industry like Hollywood which is fueled by the burning ambitions of its work force. "The women and men here are not really used to putting other people in the same light as themselves," remarks Calhoun. "We are all very success oriented, very concerned about our personal success. I think that is the great obstacle in the way of the equal rights movement in the industry, the fact that people think of themselves first. It is that type of industry. Me first, screw you. If you don't like it, buddy, that's your problem. It's not an industry that encourages group action."

Calhoun had quiet hopes of someday becoming a professional writer, but her career was not her primary concern. Her goal in life, she says, is to be "as decent a human being as possible...I know that sounds corny and old and cliched, but success for me means becoming the best person that I can." Among her friends at the studio, Calhoun was known as the kind of woman who considered others' welfare before her own. There is a good possibility that if she had put as much effort into advancing her career as she put into ISFA activities, she would have arrived at a higher niche in the industry. But Calhoun feared that she might violate too many of her principles if she gave chase to the Hollywood dream. She felt that she made enough compromises in her daily routine as an office worker.

The orientation and pace of the workday in Universal's casting department prevented Calhoun from being as human and caring as she wanted to be. "There is that conflict," she says, "between your humanitarian feelings and just having to work hard and get the job done...You're expected to do things without conscience. If you've got a conscience, you've got a hard road in this industry and that's all there is to it." One of her tasks as a casting coordinator was to answer countless phone calls from actors and actresses who were searching for work. She would "give them this little spiel— 'Send in your photos and resumes etc.,'" hang up, and continue with the rest of her work. "It's awful! You would like to be able to have the time to talk to people, even to those persons who call in and just want to be Somebody. They want to have a chance at life, to do something they think will be fascinating and interesting. But generally you don't have the time to be sympathetic."

Cynicism is an occupational hazard in Hollywood, says Calhoun. You fight it when you can with a kind personal gesture—by taking the extra time, perhaps, to answer one of the thousands of letters which pour into the studio from people all over the country who aspire to a Hollywood career. Calhoun calls it "humanizing the industry." " 'The thing you nave to remember,' " she would write, " 'is that there's very heavy competition in this industry and if you feel that you can't take it, then don't enter it.' You have to tell them that. Someone has got to warn them. Because it's not a loving industry. It's a hard industry."

*****

Calhoun was not unique among Universal's clerical employees in complaining about her work. But her way of understanding job-related problems was somewhat different than her fellow workers'. What made life miserable for most studio employees, Calhoun was convinced, was the fact that the entertainment industry was operated on a profit basis. The system was set up to squeeze as much as possible out of its labor force in order to produce the maximum amount of money. It was that simple; there was a cruel logic to it all. "The whole division between management and labor has to be brought out a little more," she says. "Labor is really exploited. A lot of people don't believe it. They work everyday at Universal and come in and crab about everything, but they don't realize that fundamental truth. Management is exploiting them and getting as much out of them as it can and for as little compensation as possible and giving all the profits to the stockholders. Rather than giving it to the people who actually do the work, they give it to the people who don't. I object so tremendously to that kind of system...Management has got to realize that we are no longer going to be put on the bottom.

That's really what we had going for us during the first year of ISFA's existence—the fact that we were really letting management know that we were a working force which was willing to go to many ends to get what was our due."

Calhoun looks forward to a day when popular culture will be publicly subsidized and entertainment workers will cooperatively own the institutions in which they work. "Wouldn't it be marvelous to have a film company where everything was reordered and the workers were partners? Maybe the guy who founded it might get a little bit more money because it was his idea, but not that much more. I don't have any objection to that, that type of thing is fine with me. It's just that they have to realize that they wouldn't have a product if it weren't for the workers."

The inspiration for Calhoun's social visions comes from her devout Christian upbringing and her reading of socialist history and literature. As a girl she was active in her church's youth group. At home she was encouraged to be outspoken and committed. Later, while studying history at Mt. San Antonio College near her hometown—Chino, California— she read with interest about Norman Thomas and the Socialist Party. "I think I've probably always had socialist leanings," she remarks. "It may be my sense of justice, which I've always seemed to have."

Calhoun feels that her religious and political beliefs are entirely compatible. "Within my socialist philosophy, I incorporate a great deal of Christian feeling—the really true Christian feeling, not the exploitative kind that has killed off millions all over the world since Christ came. But the whole feeling of loving your neighbor, and of working together to really do good...I feel that my socialism is totally synonymous with my Christian feeling. I'm probably a socialist because I'm a Christian. The first Christians were cooperative, they lived together, they banded together—not only for safety, but for comfort and encouragement."

Calhoun once registered as a member of the Socialist Party; she has signed a number of petitions to help put various left wing parties on the ballot. But Calhoun finds none of the socialist organizations in existence today appealing enough to join. She is particularly critical of the kind of politics practiced by the U.S. Communist Party and the Soviet government. Her own brand of socialism draws on the divergent philosophies of her three heroes: consumer advocate Ralph Nader, socialist author-activist Michael Harrington, and turn-of-the-century anarchist-feminist Emma Goldman—a type of socialism which celebrates the freedom and dignity of the individual.

*****

In late 1974, the Inter-Studio Feminist Alliance changed its name to the Alliance of Media Women. The new title subtly reflected the group's lowered expectations. An industry-wide movement for office workers' liberation no longer appeared imminent. There was talk of intensifying the pressure on Universal by filing a sex discrimination suit against the studio. But the activists within the studio lacked the time and experience it takes to package a legal complaint. And their outside supporters in the Los Angeles feminist community were not organizationally prepared to assist them. By 1975, the Alliance had only enough strength to continue publishing *Ms. on Scene*. The responsibility for putting out the newsletter eventually fell almost entirely on Calhoun's shoulders. There was no point, Calhoun decided, in carrying on a one-woman crusade against the industry so in fall 1975 she suspended publication of the newsletter and the Alliance of Media women was, in effect, dissolved.

The collapse of the group forced Calhoun to reevaluate her plans for the future. After the spirited and purposeful days of the clerical workers' campaign, the nine-to-five routine in Universal's casting department seemed more boring and unfulfilling than ever. During the winter of 1975-76, she considered several different courses of action, including leaving Universal and landing a job with a smaller, warmer Hollywood company; running for political office; and going to work for a nonprofit service or religious institution.

As time went by, the idea of staying in the entertainment industry grew less and less attractive. "I really do like to write," she says. "I thought at one time that I'd like to go into associate producing and then into some other area where I'd be able to use whatever writing talent I had. But I came to the conclusion that unless you want to totally dedicate yourself to what they want you to do on film—and I mean devote every single living minute to it—you're not going to get anyplace. I decided that the other portions of my life are much too important to be devoting that much time to the industry. And what you have to do! I mean devoting your life to garbage! Learning to write formula and doing just endless trivial work."

Calhoun also concluded that, in all likelihood, the industry would never promote someone with her politics to a top ranking creative position. "I think that any woman or man who is deeply and truly concerned about changing this society so it's less profit oriented and more humane has very slim chances of getting ahead in Hollywood. It's virtually impossible for anybody with that kind of consciousness to move up. I really believe that. They tag you quickly."

Furthermore, she decided, no high ranking progressive could accomplish anything of major consequence unless he or she was supported by a strong social movement. "Individuals get lost if they're in the hierarchy. You get somebody who is to the left and more often than not they are so lost that they never can do anything, because they are not in a position to have final say anyway. Unless you have a large group that is backing them and forcing the hierarchy to give in, they really don't have much of an opportunity. I personally think the only way to really go is with a group. An individual can only really get ahead and maintain their principles by having a group behind them."

But Calhoun's group no longer existed. In spring 1976, she decided to drop out of the entertainment industry and go to work as a secretary at an Episcopal church in Santa Monica. Her new job paid fifty percent less than her old one but she found it much more socially rewarding. It gave her the opportunity to work for various humanitarian causes— hunger relief, orphans, Chilean refugees, women's rights. Through her work at the church, Calhoun found the kind of personal fulfillment which was missing in the daily studio grind. "It's really been wonderful to be able to put my faith into action. It's very liberating, both spiritually and personally. You can get deeply involved in women's issues at the church because that's the raging question among Episcopalians now— women's right to be ordained. So I'm never going to be leaving the women's movement. You can always find some little thing no matter where you go."

Calhoun still feels that Hollywood is a crucially important arena in the struggle for progressive change, but she does not regret leaving the industry. "I don't think I will ever go back to Universal. I *would* like to work on more meaningful films some-day—something either in a religious vein or documentaries about social topics. I don't think I'd be interested in going back to the everyday production of television series. But I think I would by very interested in doing something with media. I haven't been disillusioned to the point where I don't care anymore. I do care very much about the commercial film product, what is shown on the screen, and I'd like to see progress in the industry as far as the workers go. But that's really only one aspect of what I've always been interested in—mainly justice and human rights."

Patti Bereyso

To Lynda Calhoun, Patti Bereyso is a "doer" and a "fighter," one of the few women she knows who succeeded in pushing her way out of the clerical ranks into the male-dominated world of television production. "Bereyso went out and really fought for herself and finally got somewhere," says Calhoun. "When you look at the overall situation and see how few women get anywhere after years and years of trying, she clearly is a kind of success story. Not that many secretaries break out of their routines like she did, not that many become anything else in their lives."

Bereyso herself, however, is not at all satisfied with the way her career has developed so far. "I understand her feeling," says Calhoun. "She knows she's got the talent and she wonders, 'What's coming off here? I'm beating my brains out and not getting what I want.'...We consider her to be a success story. She considers herself to be a semi-failure. It's sort of a difference in perspectives...Other people look at you and say, 'Gosh, that's really terrific, you're doing great.' And you say, 'Oh, that's nothing compared to what I could be!' "

Bereyso came to Hollywood from the Midwest in 1965 to pursue a career in musical comedy. She acted in various small-scale theater productions around Los Angeles, but after a year she gave up on the idea of becoming a professional actress. The commercial acting scene, found the young woman, was nothing like college theater. "In school," she says, "we had a group of people who really cared about each other and worked for one another and helped each other out. Everything was done in a cooperative spirit. You might not be right for a certain part, but you were encouraged to try it anyway. It was fun and we all learned a lot...But out here (in Los Angeles) it was dog-eat-dog. You'd get on stage and the other actors would do everything they could to make you look bad and make themselves look great because some big agent was in the audience. It was no longer, 'Let's all be friends, let's all have a good time, let's put together the best show we can.' It was 'What can I do to be better than you so that I can get to the top quicker, so that I can make the most money and be the most famous.' I don't like to work that way and I don't like to work with people who do. It was just so discouraging I finally got out of it."

When Bereyso was growing up, her mother advised her to take secretarial courses in school in order to "have something to fall back on." Nothing about secretarial work appealed to her; she wanted to do more with her life than take care of other people's paperwork. But as her hopes of becoming a stage performer dimmed, she reluctantly went in search of office employment to pay her monthly bills. She worked for over a year in an insurance company and then in a talent agency which booked acts into Las Vegas nightspots. In 1968, she joined the secretarial pool at Universal Studios, where she was eventually assigned to the office of James McAdams, producer of the television series, "The Virginian." The following year, McAdams moved over to Paramount and Bereyso went with him. Clerical work proved to be just as tiresome as Bereyso expected it would. "I was deeply frustrated as a secretary...I wanted to do more. I was vegetating. I was unfulfilled. I was unsatisfied. I wanted to be challenged. I wanted to be creative. I wanted to make more money. I wanted a chance. And that's when ISFA came along."

Clerical workers who were interested in advancing their careers were in desperate need of an organization like the Inter-Studio Feminist Alliance, felt Bereyso. She had seen too many incompetent men promoted into high ranking positions, while their more experienced and intelligent secretaries stayed locked into the same routines. Bereyso took an active role in developing ISFA and keeping the organization going in its early days, but she decided not to rely solely on the group to break out of her secretarial role. On her own, she began to look for ways to expand the range of her job activities, for ways to assume more creative responsibility. "I began to read scripts that would come into the office," recalls Bereyso, "and I would write critiques on them before I put them in my boss' briefcase. And he read my comments and liked them. So I said, 'Great, let me do this on a regular basis for the story department then.' He agreed, and he helped me get promoted to story reader. Then I began working for all the production companies on the (Paramount) lot."

Bereyso's work made an impression on television

producers Tom Miller and Ed Milkis—her creative judgment, they said, was similar to their own—and they asked the studio to assign her to their company. The two producers put Bereyso to work on their new TV series, a situation comedy set in the 1950s called "Happy Days." Bereyso's new position, which was officially titled "assistant to the executive producers," included a wide variety of duties. "I served as the technical advisor. I was in charge of researching and approving everything that went on the screen. I checked out the sets, the wardrobe, the hairstyles, the props, the cars, the lingo—all the slang phrases that were used—everything like that. To make sure it was authentic and of that period. I also helped in the post production end of the show—supervising the sound effects, the dubbing, the scoring sessions. I also worked on merchandising, trying to hustle T-shirts and combs and pencils. And finally, I helped coordinate the publicity—putting tours together, arranging personal appearances and radio spots. There were a lot of different things that I did on the show."

As Bereyso's responsibilities grew, so did her self-confidence. "I am a woman," she wrote in the Winter 1973 issue of the ISFA newsletter *Ms. on Scene,* "who has happened to have the good fortune and the good timing to be in the right place at the right time with the right champion at my side helping me to make it up and out of the secretarial pool at one of the major studios in town and into the swim of things, production-wise—from first a secretary to a junior executive and then one more additional rung up that legendary 'ladder,' all in the span of one short year."

In the process of moving out of the traditional sphere of female employment, Bereyso developed new, ambitious goals for herself. She was determined to make it to the top of the television production hierarchy; she would settle for nothing less than becoming a producer. By succeeding as a producer, felt Bereyso, she would demonstrate to the men in control of the industry that women were capable of wielding decision-making authority, and she would serve as an inspiration to all the female office workers who yearned to do more than typing and filing.

It was important to Bereyso that more women follow her example and force their way out of clerical positions into more rewarding areas of work. In her Winter 73 *Ms. on Scene* article, which she titled "Two Feet in the Door," she urged the women in the offices of the entertainment industry to be aggressive and create their own opportunities:

> Many secretaries that I have spoken with in the past year have found it difficult to take the first step to a promotion— to go to the big man, the man who has the power of money, (the power) to say 'yes' or 'no,' and tell him of their desires to be more than just a secretary and to be of more value to the company. It is no easy task to muster up all the courage and strength and faith in yourself and beat down the doors to do a smashing sales job on yourself to someone who can do something about it. Regretfully, women aren't brought up to think in those terms...But that is the *only* way you're going to get anywhere. Sure it helps to have help...and to have people backing you whenever possible; but in the final crunch it's just going to be you and him. And no amount of memo writing and working through spokespersons is going to work. Go see the man and tell him how you feel and tell him what you expect in the way of a job with the company... Let him know that you are intelligent, capable, responsible, willing to work hard, and willing to work hard to make his department and his company better because *you* will be put to better use—you will be doing a more valuable job. Don't forget, the greater your input, the greater their output. The more you do for them, the better quality of their product. It's as simple as dollars and cents and don't let them forget it.

In the early days of the Inter-Studio Feminist Alliance, Bereyso believed that a multitude of secretaries would begin to shake off the fear, despair, and numbness which had kept them in place for so long, and begin actively pursuing exciting Hollywood careers. But when ISFA's organizing efforts ran aground, Bereyso grew demoralized and gave up all hope of activating office workers on a mass scale. The vast majority of secretaries, she concluded, were simply not interested in career advancement. "If you're organizing secretaries," she remarks with some bitterness, "you are dealing with women who are daytime wives to their bosses, who don't want to make waves. So maybe out of a hundred secretaries, you'll find ten who want to do something. And maybe they'll come to your meetings or maybe they won't. They might have a date that night, that's what often happens. The other ninety you can't count on at all, because they've got to pay those bills, they've got to pay those property taxes, they've got to get their kids into college. They've got to do all those things so they don't want to make waves. They don't want to make a career, they just want to get over the hump. It's impossible to organize people for change who really don't want change. And if you don't have a lot of backing, you might as well give up. You're not going to do anything for women as a whole unless you have their complete support."

Bereyso decided to withdraw from ISFA and concentrate on her career. She would continue to help those women who came to her for encouragement and advice, but she was convinced that efforts to mobilize office workers in general were an exercise in futility. Bereyso continued to find her work interesting and she remained hopeful about making further progress in the industry. "Happy Days" had turned into a hit television series and her bosses gave her additional work on another show they were producing called "Petrocelli." If most of those in the secretarial pool seemed content to stay where they were, at least she was going places. Bereyso had some vague misgivings about the climb toward success. "I have discovered many interesting things," she wrote in her *Ms. on Scene* article, "not the least of which is that my frustrations did not end once the shackle of the time clock was lifted...I'm beginning to realize that this feeling I had as a secretary, this feeling of trying to get ahead, of wanting to be recognized and appreciated, of wanting to be utilized and valued and fulfilled and rewarded—this will never end." Nonetheless, she continued to pursue her career with single-minded devotion.

Then, in February 1975, she was laid off. The steady progress she had been making in television came to a sudden grinding halt. Bereyso's assumptions about how one got ahead in Hollywood were severely shaken by this unexpected blow. "In the beginning," she says, "I thought it was possible to keep doing a good job and keep getting merit promotions. I'm doing this work so give me the title; now I'm doing this work so give me this title and so on. I just assumed that I could simply be myself and do a good job and keep working hard and go as far as I wanted to. 'Be a good little girl and you get rewards.'

Wrong! That's so wrong. It doesn't work that way."

Bereyso was out of work for five months. During that period, she recalls, she did a lot of thinking about her career. She began to review her decision to become a producer in the light of everything she had learned during her ten years in Hollywood. At one time, the sizable amount of creative decision-making authority which was concentrated in the producer's hands had made that role seem extremely attractive to Bereyso. But now the drawbacks of becoming a producer grew increasingly clear in her mind. Was it really worth all the sacrifice and effort, she asked herself.

So many of the producers in Hollywood, it seemed to Bereyso, were "evil" people. "They probably started out with ideals and values of some sort," she says, but in the course of pursuing their careers they changed. At some point they became obsessed with their own survival and prosperity and coldly indifferent to the people around them. "I had seen very nice, very bright people turn into vicious lunatics as they came closer to the creative center. It frightened me and made me not want to be part of that (process) anymore. I knew some guys who became so engrossed in their own self-importance that they started ordering people around and treating them like dirt. There was one fellow who I swear would've hired someone to wipe his bottom if he could've found such a person...This man was always, 'I want, I want, I want,' and nothing was too good for him."

From what Bereyso had observed, it appeared as if producers were more involved in wheeling and dealing and manipulation—what she refers to as "politics"—than they were in the creative phase of television production. "The politics of the job really bothered me," she remarks. "It seemed to me that a producer's success had almost nothing to do with their ability to make movies or television shows, to cast the right actors, to find good directors or anything like that. It was whether or not they could handle the guy at the top. Could they get the money (to finance the project)? Could they sit down with an actor who's throwing a tantrum and say 'Everything is going to be alright, baby'?...Ninety percent of a producer's job, it seemed, was dealing with people, keeping them all appeased, saying 'yes' to all the right people and saying 'no' when it was appropriate. That sort of work was not very appealing to me."

The fact that producers earned breathtakingly high salaries did lend a certain attraction to the job, Bereyso admitted to herself. But she was not the kind of person who romanticized wealth. Their money, felt Bereyso, could not insulate them from the intense pressures of their work or from the mundane problems which everyone faces. "They have ulcers, they self-destruct...All you get out of being a producer is money. That's all. So instead of buying a $4,000 car they buy a $14,000 car, but it still has mechanical problems, you know. Instead of living in a little $140 a month apartment they live in $140,000 homes, but they still have to call someone in to fix the waterheater."

Bereyso also recognized that success and prosperity were not permanently guaranteed in Hollywood. Television producers could command a network show one year and be out of work the next. Like everyone in Hollywood, they were subject to long bothersome spells of unemployment. "Work in this industry is so tenuous and seasonal, that you can easily spend many months each year out of work, regardless of who you are. And the longer you're out of work, the harder it is to get hired. Because if you're not at work, you're not viable, you're not on the scene, you're not in there plugging away—and that means you're a nobody and no one wants to hire a nobody... There are only so many jobs and there are hundreds if not thousands of producers. How many television series have come and gone? Plenty. Each one of those shows had a producer who is an experienced, skilled person—and a lot of them are out of work. Because there is only enough room on the air for a few series each year. There is a pool of producers that is scattered around town, sitting there, waiting, hustling, calling all their friends. 'What's going on? Let me get something going. Give me some money.' They're all living off their savings. At one time they were making forty or sixty thousand a year. Let's hope they banked a lot of it because that was the last year they're going to make that kind of money for a long, long time."

Finally, Bereyso came to realize that TV producers did not enjoy creative autonomy; their control was subject to constant interference from above. "I worked for this one producer for about four years," she comments, "and even he didn't get to do what he wanted. And he was a man. And he was dealing only with men. But even he didn't get to go on the air with what he wanted. He would say that maybe once in a television season you'll do one nice moment that you'll really be proud of—but that's it. The rest of the stuff is schlock. That happens to be the nature of this industry. Schlock. So no matter who you are, no matter what you do, you're always answerable to someone. Even producers. They have to fulfill the expectations of the network and the sponsors. And the network bosses have to fulfill the expectations of their board of directors. And the board of directors has to fulfill the expectations of the major stockholders...So there's no end to it. You're always fulfilling other people's expectations."

For all these reasons, Bereyso decided at last, she would no longer sweat and strain to become part of the production hierarchy. Instead, she would simply try to find a "niche" somewhere in the industry where she could do relatively satisfying work and make a decent living. In the summer of 1975, Bereyso mailed her job resume to over sixty Hollywood producers. As a result, she received three offers to become a production secretary and a fourth to become a music coordinator on "The Young and the Restless," a CBS daytime soap opera. Bereyso accepted the fourth offer. She had absolutely no desire to return to the secretarial ranks; perhaps the soap opera position, she told herself, would be moderately interesting. Perhaps it would allow her to use a modest amount of creative judgment.

Bereyso soon found out, however, that her duties as a music coordinator were fairly limited. There were no scoring sessions to take part in the way there had been on "Happy Days;" the music which was played on "The Young and the Restless" was all pre-recorded. Her job consists of selecting the right snips of tape for the right dramatic moments. "I read through the script and I figure out where the music should be played and I figure out what kind of music should be played. Then I write the music cues into the script and give it to the engineer. He pulls the cartridges and he puts them in the machine. And I sit behind him with a stopwatch and I squeeze him on the shoulder when it's the exact moment to play."

It did not take long, says Bereyso, to become acquainted with the entire music library and everything about her job. After that her work grew increasingly dull and monotonous. "My job would be much more interesting," she remarks, "if I were not locked into existing pieces of music which I cannot chop up. There is no editing in live television. There is no opportunity to play around with the soundtrack. In nighttime television, it's different. You can say, 'Alright, I'm going to take that cymbal from there, that oboe from over there, this drum, and that piano and I'll put them all together and I'll make a new piece of music and I'll put it in at that precise moment, as this actor lifts his hand and touches his cheek. You can do anything you want when you're tracking nighttime television shows. It's wonderful. There is creativity. Everytime is new.

"Nobody (on 'The Young and the Restless' production staff) sees the show as a creative outlet. They see it as a weekly paycheck. There is one advantage to working on a soap opera. Where else in this business do you know that you're going to work fifty-two weeks a year? But the work is only a challenge until you know what you're doing and until you get as far as you can. I got as far as I was going in three days. And that was it. There's no movement from where I am. It's another dead end job."

The tediousness of Bereyso's work is aggravated by the fact that she has little interest in the program itself. "The Young and the Restless" seems to her to be just as silly and vacuous as every other soap opera. "Have you ever watched a soap opera?" she demands rhetorically. "Would you ever want to? I mean is that really the highlight of your life? We do the same show four times a day. We do a camera blocking, during which we rehearse. We do a run-through, during which we rehearse. We do a dress rehearsal, and we do the actual tape. So we do it four times a day! The same show! Sometimes I feel like, 'I've had it up to here! I want out—let me out of here. This is torture!'

"Half of the things in the show have no basis in reality. Some of the things are nice, some of the dialogue, some of the speeches are really super. But usually the characterizations and the story lines are stupid. They're ridiculous, as in any soap opera. I don't know why people watch it, I really don't...

Our stories are so corny that we even have people breaking into song. Like on today's show, for instance, this lonely gal walks out of this deserted nightclub which her sister owns and standing there is an ex-boyfriend whom she had an affair with in Europe, and he's plucking away on his guitar. And as she starts to walk away, he begins singing, 'It was just one of those things.' And she turns around and says, 'Just one of those now and then things.' This is what happens on the show! And once, there was this gal praying over her dead husband's grave and the same guy comes up in the background and starts singing, 'When you walk through a storm hold your head up high.' Need I go on?"

Bereyso says that the show's writers do make a periodic effort to work contemporary, provocative subjects into the narrative. But unfortunately there is often a strong element of sensationalism in the way these subjects are treated. When two of the female characters in the show became lovers, there were complaints from women in the cast and crew. "The women on the show felt it was just exploitative," explains Bereyso. "The lesbianism was just being done for exploitation, for rating. It didn't really fit in with the characters. The story couldn't really go anywhere. (The writers) were just going to touch on it and tantalize the audience. It was silly. It made the characters look stupid."

Bereyso is also critical of the show's traditional view of women's roles. Occasionally, a "token" female professional appears upon the scene, says Bereyso, but generally the women in "The Young and the Restless" are "wives, mothers, lovers, or service people." They stay at home and tend to domestic chores and matters of the heart. They rarely venture into the world of money and power.

Bereyso lays much of the responsibility for this on the audience itself. "The Young and the Restless," in large part, reflects the desires and expectations of its viewers, she asserts. Fan mail is the one kind of input which the show's writer-creator pays attention to, says Bereyso. "The women who watch soap operas are the women who are at home during the day. They are not working women; they are women who are stuck in stereotype situations—diapering the kids and making the school lunches and sending their husbands off to work and getting ready for the PTA and having the bridge club over. Those are the women who are the audience out there for daytime television, and soap operas are what they want to see. They want to see themselves reflected. They want to see the kind of feelings and concerns they have as subordinate, oppressed people reflected on television. I'm sure they have a lot of suppressed hostile feelings because they are not able to do what they want, but all they see on TV are the same old images of what it is to be a woman. It's just a vicious cycle. That's what they want to see, so that's what we give them."

How would Bereyso change soap operas if she were given the opportunity? "The only change I'd like to see," she replies with conviction, "is to have that sort of thing totally eliminated from television."

Bereyso cannot resign herself to a work routine so devoid of creative stimulation. Soon after being slotted into her position on "The Young and the Restless," she began looking for ways to escape. While working as a secretary at Paramount, she had taken up television writing in her spare time. Now she intensified her efforts to write and sell TV shows. If she could just sell one script, she reasoned, she could secure a writing credit, join the Writers Guild, and launch an entirely new career as a television scenarist. Bereyso and a female writing partner carefully watched the television series "Rhoda" over a period of time, clocking each scene, noting how many set changes occurred during the show, and studying the dramatic conventions which were used to move the plot along. With this information in mind, they constructed their own "Rhoda" episode. "It was about Rhoda's efforts to save her old school," says Bereyso. "It didn't really have a very strong woman's theme." Bereyso and her partner similarly tried to decipher and imitate the dramatic formula of "Petrocelli." In their "Petrocelli" script, the wife of the series' hero is arrested and imprisoned for a crime she did not commit. "One of the things I wanted to show in the story," Bereyso remarks, "was how difficult it is for a woman when she's put into a jail. Any one of us could be picked up tomorrow for something that we knew nothing about." The two women also wrote a television pilot about two newspaper reporters—one female, one male—which they submitted to NBC.

Bereyso had high hopes that their efforts would pay off. She felt that she and her co-writer worked very well together. "She was the creative one as far as mood and dialogue and all that," comments Bereyso. "And I was the structure person. I would sit down and set up each scene. I would say, 'This is what is going to happen here,' and then she would fill in the dialogue. She was very good at that and I was good with structure. So it was a nice collaboration." Bereyso had built up some useful contacts in the TV production hierarchy over the years, so their scripts were passed to the right people. "That's the only way you're going to get anyplace in this business. If you're not the son of it, you're going to have to know it." But the sale which Bereyso was counting on to change her life was never made. Not one of their scripts was purchased. Bereyso eventually grew so demoralized that she gave up the idea of becoming a writer. She was not going to continue producing material for a system which apparently would never buy it.

"I got shot down in every direction. You know, writing is not the most pleasant thing to do in the world. I mean ask any writer if he or she likes to write. If you're making it big, fine. Once you get into a writing routine, you just keep going. It's hard to sit down at first, but once you get into it for a month or two, you're just churning it out. But if you're churning it out for no one to buy, it's just utter frustration all the way, it's really awful...To write for this business, to have a bunch of men read the scripts and a bunch of men approve the work—that doesn't appeal to me at all."

After her series of setbacks as a writer, Bereyso began to seriously consider leaving the entertainment industry. If all the industry could promise her was a lifetime of tedious labor on superficial TV programs, she was not sure that she wanted to remain a part of it. "I want to do something that *matters* during my life," she says with vehemence. "The world is not going to stop or go on the fact that I put the laughs into 'Happy Days' or the fact that I put the music into a soap opera. Who cares? When World War III comes, nobody is going to turn around and say, 'My God, we can't let her go to war—she's putting the music into a soap opera!' No they won't do that. I mean, who cares? Are they going to etch it on my gravestone? No they're not."

For awhile, Bereyso contemplated going into broadcast journalism. As a reporter, she felt, she would be directly in touch with "what is going on in the world." In her free time, Bereyso began working as a volunteer in the news department of a local, nonprofit radio station. Later she enrolled in a class on television newscasting. But the idea turned sour when Bereyso started to recognize the extent to which commercial values influence electronic journalism. "I found out that TV news was just more hype, more entertainment, more sensationalism. More of the same thing that I was already involved in."

So, for now at least, Bereyso continues in her post as music coordinator for "The Young and the Restless." People tend to think that the entertainment industry must be an exciting world to work in, says Bereyso. The daily contact with stars, the continual spinning of fantasies must make this world of production infinitely more enjoyable than the others. But for Bereyso, the excitement she once felt has worn almost entirely away. "It's a job like any other job. There is that glamor to it, there is that sparkle to it—but I don't usually see it. The only time I see it is through someone else's eyes. Those are the only times I feel good and I feel special about working here. Like when I visit my sister in Tennessee, the phone never stops ringing and people are always coming in the door: 'What's happening on the show? Do you really know Lance?' and all that. And I think, 'Well, I guess there's more to this than I really thought' (she laughs). But, you know, to me it's just nice people and a steady job. I go to work every day in the same old place and do the same old thing. It can't be anymore exciting than going to work in a bank."

Bereyso does not feel like a creative person; she feels like a salaried worker. Her job is limited and specialized and allows for little independent thinking. Even her freedom to choose from the catalogue of pre-recorded musical pieces is sometimes abrogated. If higher authorities on the show dispute her choice of tapes, there is nothing she can do about it. They have the final say about what goes on the air. "I'm so tired," says Bereyso, "of always having to turn around and answer to someone else. 'Oh yes, that's what you want. Oh no, that's not what you want.' "

Bereyso is not the only one in her work environment who feels deeply dissatisfied about what she or he does for a living. Many of her women friends who work alongside her are equally frustrated, she says. "Most of my women friends nowadays are technicians, because I work with technicians upstairs (at CBS Television City). CBS is a big bureaucracy. I get down and kiss the floor every night and thank God that I don't work for CBS. The CBS mentality is so limited and so unimaginative, it's incredible. Utilizing people to their best ability is the furthest thing from their mind. Their attitude is simply, 'Let's get a bunch of people in here and let's just arbitrarily assign them jobs. Here's the list of jobs we need filled, and here's the list of people. Now let's plug them in.' What they should be saying is 'This person's forte is sound mixing, this person's forte is boom.' But they've got audio mixers pulling cable on 'The Price is Right.' They have no concept of what's really going on. They have no idea what people really want to do, or what they can do. And so, of course these women are very frustrated at CBS. Very frustrated. Because they came here after having experience as mixers or audio people in little radio stations and television stations somewhere else in the country. And they arrive here with big expectations. CBS! Network! Hollywood! And what are they doing? They're pulling cable, they're playing music for the audience as it files in to watch the Dinah show. I mean the whole thing is ludicrous."

What do these television workers do with their frustrations? They "sit on them," says Bereyso. They think about freeing themselves from the network bureaucracy and becoming freelance technicians. Do they ever consider taking up these issues with management at the contract negotiating table? Would they seriously contemplate walking off their jobs to improve the quality of their work? "Nobody ever fantasizes in that direction," responds Bereyso. "the only time they do, it's for money. 'We want more money. We want better hours. We don't want to have to work twelve hours straight. We want to have a lunch break built in after every five hours. We want better insurance.' Those kinds of issues."

What does Bereyso plan to do about her work related frustrations? There was a brief period in her life when she felt that her salvation lay in collective action. If enough women came together and demanded better job opportunities, they could escape the bleak futures which the industry had planned for them. This dream was put to rest, as far as Bereyso was concerned, by the demise of the ISFA. Recently, her longing to have control over her work, to find a satisfying way to make a living has taken a new form. She fantasizes now about opening her own shop and becoming her own boss. Never again, says Bereyso, would she have to spend her days "fulfilling other people's expectations." "That's what I would love to do someday," she declares. "To open up my own store and really be my own boss. I wouldn't get myself a franchise, because that means I'd still be answering to someone else. I've got to go out and just buy myself a store and run it the way I want to. Then the only person I'll have to answer to is myself. And if I hire anybody, they answer to me. But I won't have to turn around all the time and answer to somebody else."

V.
THE WHOLE WORLD IS WATCHING

Preface
Mark Rosenberg

Katherine: The Making of an Exception
Bruce Green
Mike Gray
Jesus Salvador Trevino
Lynn Phillips

Preface

The following people were all active participants in the great, sweeping efforts of the 1960s and early 1970s to radically transform American society. Like their political forerunners in the 1930s and 40s, of whom they knew little, they were determined to create a new social system based on peace, justice, and equality. There was no facet of American life, no major institution which did not draw this political generation's critical attention. It was all called into question. When it came to theory and programs—for specific ways to remodel society—the New Left was generally lacking. There were some elements which fell into the old trap of adopting ready-made solutions and foreign models. But, for the most part, this generation of left wing activists shared a simple and deep faith in the ability of the American people to devise their own sensible plans for the future.

The New Left's attitude towards Hollywood was one of unmitigated contempt and distrust. "(Our) argument," Lynn Phillips recalls, "was that there was no effective way to work within the culture industry. It was stronger and would always prevail; it would dilute or turn a strong oppositional statement to its own advantage." The reason why sixties radicals could not imagine working inside Hollywood lies partly in the fact that they grew up during a period when the film industry was purged of leftists. The films and TV shows of their childhood were the products of an industry whose social conscience had been temporarily suppressed. As Norm Fruchter, co-founder of New York Newsreel, remarked in a 1968 interview: "None of us are old enough to have any illusions about infiltrating the mass media to reach mass consciousness and change it—we grew up on TV and fifties Hollywood."

The New Left concentrated on developing alternative cultural projects: film and video collectives, guerrilla theater troupes, newspapers, poetry groups, musical bands. But as the Movement began to fade in the early 1970s, so did the hope that these forms of activity would become a serious alternative to the dominant culture. Meanwhile, the dominant culture itself began to reflect many of the values, customs, and styles of the sixties (often in distorted ways). Suddenly, centers of mainstream cultural activity like Hollywood became more attractive to young radical filmmakers.

New Leftists entered the entertainment industry in the 1970s for the same reasons they went into other mainstream institutions. These institutions can support them economically and they affect the lives of a broad spectrum of people. Those who are profiled below have come to reject the idea that nothing of social value can be produced in Hollywood. They have varying opinions about how far one can go within Hollywood's commercial boundaries.* But they agree that the left cannot afford to dismiss the idea of working inside the studio gates. Pursuing a socially rewarding Hollywood career, they say, is a difficult and complicated process. But they have concluded that it is worth the effort.

The 1960s activists who are now employed in Hollywood are not a cohesive political force. Some know each other personally; some work or have worked with one another. But their contacts are rarely of a political nature. Generally speaking, they are primarily concerned at this point with their careers. The spirit of zealous competition which infects all Hollywood life shapes their lives as well. Only a few have managed to find the time and willpower to stay politically active.

Until these people, and other concerned Hollywood employees, create a political context within the entertainment industry—a context which allows them to meet regularly and discuss their lives and work in political terms—the industry will continue to influence them more than they influence the industry. Only by working together in an industry-wide organization, in conjunction with media pressure groups and independent film and video makers, can Hollywood leftists democratically restructure the industry and make it more responsive to the public.

---

*The following section includes a chapter about the making of a 1975 TV movie titled *Katherine*. The film, which is an abbreviated but sympathetic study of sixties radicalism, is a good example of what can (and cannot) be accomplished in commercial television with a maximum amount of effort and dedication.

Mark Rosenberg

There was a time when Mark Rosenberg, like many other student activists, felt "the revolution" would go on and on. "Everyone had this romantic vision of being a middle class urban Che Guevara and spending their entire lives organizing people," he says. Throughout his college years, Rosenberg concerned himself more with political activities than with his studies. His life then was making sacrifices, taking risks, putting his body on the line. Failing a course, dropping a semester were negligible losses compared to those the Vietnamese were suffering.

In fall 1967, Rosenberg helped organize a draft resistance union at Bard College in upstate New York; soon afterwards, he and a contingent of Bard war resisters trekked to Washington to turn over their draft cards to the Justice Department and take part in the massive siege of the Pentagon. The demonstration outside the center of American military might took the antiwar struggle to a new level; thousands of protestors swept past lines of armed and dangerous soldiers, pitched camp on the Pentagon lawns and raised an NLF flag in place of the Stars and Stripes before they were finally driven away. Rosenberg was arrested and briefly interned, and when he came back to Bard there were two FBI agents waiting to quiz him about his missing draft card. These were the risks involved in throwing yourself against government policies, but Rosenberg was one of those willing to take them.

The following year, Rosenberg and the woman he was living with transferred to the University of Wisconsin "because we were history majors at the time and Wisconsin probably had the single best history department" and, even more importantly, "because politically it was clearly one of the four or five leading campuses in the country." By this time Rosenberg primarily thought of himself as a Movement activist. He joined the Students for a Democratic Society (SDS), took part in a university-wide strike to support black student demands, protested the construction of the Army-Math Research Center, and fought to prevent recruiters from Dow Chemical Company (the leading manufacturer of napalm) and the Central Intelligence Agency from coming on campus. "That year," he says, "Madison was an incredibly tumultuous place to be. The political activities were just never ending."

While at Wisconsin, Rosenberg came to regard the war in Southeast Asia as a logical outgrowth of the country's political and economic policies. The system functioned in such a way as to produce racism and poverty at home and neocolonial wars abroad. He began to view the campaign against the war as part of a wider effort to radically change the system itself. Universities like Wisconsin were an important arena in this general struggle, felt Rosenberg, because they were closely bound to corporate and political power and were deeply involved in the war effort. Near the end of the school term in 1969, however, student activists shifted most of their attention to the relatively narrow issue of curriculum reform and Rosenberg lost interest in the university. "At that point I thought the struggle was much bigger than that."

At the conflict-torn SDS convention that summer, Rosenberg sided with the newly formed Weatherman faction. Weatherman was one of three rival groups fighting to win control of SDS. According to Weatherman's analysis, the principal struggle going on in the world was between U.S. imperialism and national liberation movements. Vietnamese, blacks, and other Third World peoples, therefore, represented the "key revolutionary force." It was the duty of all white revolutionary youths in the United States, declared Weatherman, to shed their "white skin privilege" and come to the aid of these embattled peoples by "bringing the war home." Weatherman would build a disciplined shock force which would meet the unrelenting butchery in Southeast Asia and the growing repression of blacks at home with increased violence against police and oppressive institutions.

"I lined up with Weather," comments Rosenberg, "because the other major factions within SDS simply did not want to reinterpret the traditional Marxist concepts. They tended to idolize the industrial worker. The Weather analysis was appealing to me because it attempted to revise that nineteenth century view. My cultural background was such that if I idolized anybody it was those who were nonwhite.

That probably came in part out of my Jewish guilt—having been raised by a black maid—and also out of having gone to public school with a lot of blacks and being very much in touch with that experience. My decision to support Weather also had to do with my objective perceptions of the world. It seemed clear to me that blacks, Indians, and Puerto Ricans were more oppressed as a group than white workers. It *still* is clear to me that Third World people inside and outside of America are the most oppressed people on the face of the earth. And since my politics were motivated largely by a sense of morality, I felt that I had to find a theory of political struggle which centered around those who were most oppressed. Weatherman supplied that theory."

In the fall, Rosenberg joined a New York Weather collective. He had quit school and was making money by driving a cab. Like the other knots of Weatherpeople across the country, Rosenberg's collective put its efforts into organizing for the "Days of Rage" demonstration which was scheduled to take place in Chicago during the second week of October. The wild street actions, which pitted a few hundred helmeted demonstrators against the full fury of the Chicago police force, were designed to test the fighting spirit of the Weather cadre and to show the country how combative certain sections of the Movement had become, how far they were prepared to go. The demonstration was Rosenberg's last episode as a Weatherman. "It was madness," he says. "People said, 'We're all gonna die. It'll be good if we die—we'll set an example etc., etc.' About one-tenth of the people who were supposed to show up actually showed, or that we were told were going to show up. And it was a mess. Fortunately, because of cowardice and luck combined, I did not get busted or beat up too badly. And I got back to New York and decided that I had had it with Weather collectives...It scared the shit out of me. And it seemed like why should I have the shit scared out of me and risk my body when we weren't being supported by a large number of people. We were sort of like a sliver on the floor of the world, you know, a little splinter."

While Rosenberg was put off by the sacrificial nature of Weatherman's tactics, he still believed in the fundamental importance of militant action. President Nixon, in his first year in office, was making the war his own by doubling the tonnage of bombs dropped on Indochina. COINTELPRO, the secret FBI program begun in 1967 to "neutralize" the activities of the black movement, was picking up speed. (During 1968 and 1969, more than thirty Black Panther offices around the country were raided by police.) There was a growing sense of rage and frustration throughout the Movement, a widespread feeling that the escalation of the war and the crackdown on the Panthers demanded highly charged responses.

In early December 1969, Fred Hampton, a young charismatic Black Panther spokesman, was murdered in his bed by a raiding party of Chicago policemen. The radical community charged that the raid was part of the federal government's bloody vendetta against the Panthers, an allegation which was substantiated years later when evidence of the FBI's involvement in the assault was revealed. Rosenberg and the other former Weatherpeople who made up a New York group called Mad Dogs vowed to strike back in the quickest, most emphatic way they knew how—by taking their fury into the streets. "We wanted to bring the spirit of Fred Hampton to New York," says Rosenberg. On the night of December 9, as President Nixon was honored by the National Football Foundation in a ceremony at the Waldorf-Astoria, a group of howling demonstrators went rampaging as far as Radio City, smashing windows in Saks Fifth Avenue and five other stores along the way. Sixty-five people were arrested, including two of Rosenberg's friends, who were severely beaten by policemen after being taken into custody.

The increasing militancy of this period, remarks Rosenberg, stemmed from the Movement's sense of powerlessness, its apparent inability to affect the course of national events. "Everyone would now admit that the Movement had an effect. Our activities helped bring about the collapse of both the Johnson and Nixon Administrations. But at the time we didn't feel our power. If you did, it was only for a fleeting moment, then frustration would come the next week. No one could really be sure we were having an effect. I think that we might have believed it in an intellectual way; we recognized on some level that we were now part of the political world because we were on the news and Walter Cronkite was talking about the Movement. But were we having a real effect? No, we didn't think so...When you feel that you have so little control over your life and society in general, you naturally get very angry. And if you're angry, you've got to show your anger—by fighting, screaming, throwing rocks, etc. Militancy was, in a sense, a way to release emotions. It felt good."

Rosenberg, like many other radicals at the time, also believed that militant action made strong political and moral sense. He felt that it was important to "punish" those in power for their crimes, even if it was only symbolic retribution. He was also convinced that militant demonstrations captured the public's attention and could, if properly executed, attract more people into the radical ranks. "Up to a certain point, when repression became very severe, highly militant activity tended to draw in a wide base of support. Now it was a base that was not reliable because it was largely composed of students and street people and so forth. It was not a base that involved the key class, in Marxist terms, that is the working class. But it did attract numbers."

Soon after the December 9 demonstration, Rosenberg and several other Mad Dogs formed a new group to give ongoing militant support to the beleaguered Black Panthers. The December 4 Movement (D4M), named for the day of Hampton's death, established a presence at New York University, City College, and particularly Columbia, where it attempted to revive the spirit of the '68 strike. D4M demanded that the Columbia administration post bail for the New York Panther 21 to make up for the university's displacement of black and Puerto Rican people in the Morningside Heights neighborhood. The group held rallies, seized buildings, smashed windows, and lit bonfires to back up its demand. "...A strike in 1970 is not going to be the same kind of tea party that a strike in 1968 was," declared a D4M leaflet. "Repression has escalated and we must escalate our level of struggle." D4M's springtime campaign culminated in a large march and assembly in Central Park which called for the release of the New York Panthers, who were accused of a bizarre assortment of conspiracy crimes. (The defendants were freed the following year after a jury found them innocent of all charges.)

Rosenberg hit his peak as a militant activist during the

D4M offensive. On several occasions he was selected by the group to address campus rallies. "I would get up in front of crowds at the Sundial," he recalls, "and urge people to take strong action in defense of the Panthers. I was a fairly good inciter." But the limits of militancy as a political strategy were becoming tragically evident. In March 1970, three young radicals (including Ted Gold, one of the leaders of Rosenberg's old Weatherman collective) were blown up in a New York townhouse explosion when a bomb they were assembling accidentally went off. "All the fatal flaws of the left were brought into sharp focus by the townhouse explosion," says Rosenberg. "...It was politically senseless as well as self-destructive. The three people who died were all exceptionally bright and exceptionally privileged people whose lives were snuffed out—and it's a hard thing to say, but it's true—not because of the enemy, but because of themselves. Because of flaws within their movement and their thinking and themselves."

When summer vacation brought the campus based December 4 Movement to an end, Rosenberg and two other D4M activists went to New Haven to help mobilize support for Lonnie McLucas, a Black Panther accused of killing a suspected police informer. Following the McLucas trial, the government planned to prosecute Black Panther leaders Bobby Seale and Ericka Huggins on murder conspiracy charges stemming from the same incident.* The New Haven Panther trials raised the issue of equal justice for black activists. Yale President Kingman Brewster declared in spring 1970 that he thought it was impossible for black radicals to get fair trials in the U.S. Leftists asserted that the trials were part of a systematic government attempt to eliminate the leadership of the Panther organization. "I went to New Haven," says Rosenberg, "because I believed that the Black Panther Party was the only revolutionary group within America at the time which had any semblance of power. I believed they had correctly analyzed the political situation of blacks in this country and they had

---

*McLucas was eventually convicted of a lesser charge. Seale and Huggins were freed after their trial resulted in a deadlocked jury.

chosen brilliant ways to implement their programs. Brilliant because they exposed the way that power functioned in America. Brilliant because they catalyzed and made cohesive a large number of young blacks—mostly males—who had been street junkies of one sort or another. They were the only black group with a socialist analysis of society which was taken seriously in the black community...I believed that the Panthers were in a sense the center of the left, and it was absolutely essential for white radicals to work on their defense. By defending them you were defending the leadership of your Movement. They were being totally wiped out."

Rosenberg put a great deal of time and effort into the McLucas case, but by fall he felt too worn down to continue working on the New Haven trials. He decided to return to New York and temporarily reduce his involvement in political activities. "I was just tired. The work had been very difficult and there was a lot of factionalism within the Panther organization...It was also hard to develop personal relationships and still maintain some sort of leading or active role in politics. Because everything you did in the Movement during that period was constantly questioned—not wrongfully so, and in many ways rightfully so—but nevertheless you were on the line every moment. You were not only on the line politically but personally as well, you know, in terms of doing the dishes and changing your attitudes toward women. Anyway, there was constant pressure and it finally became just too much to bear."

Rosenberg's loss of momentum paralleled a general decline in activism on the left. The antiwar movement—the core of the New Left radicalism—was beginning to disintegrate, partly because of the Nixon Administration's repressive tactics at home and Vietnamization abroad ("Changing the color of the bodies from white to yellow") and partly because of the Movement's own failure to develop a long-range strategy for radically changing U.S. society. Rosenberg re-entered the political fray to take part in the 1971 May Day demonstration in Washington. The attempt to shut down the nation's capital briefly revived the antiwar movement but after May Day Rosenberg felt "it was all over."

Suddenly, the main task confronting young radicals like

Rosenberg was not that of making history but that of finding work and making a living. The question no longer was whether "the revolution is possible or not," says Rosenberg. The question was, "What are we going to do in our everyday lives?...All of us had to find something to do with our lives that wasn't simply organizing twenty-four hours a day...You know, one of the things you felt while you were in the student movement was that you did not have the same responsibilities everybody else did. You didn't have to go to a traditional nine-to-five job,you didn't have to provide for a family, you didn't have to deal with the IRS, you didn't seem to worry about your yearly medical check-ups. You lived and operated in a world which was outside of the mainstream of society. But as that world started to collapse, you were faced with a whole new set of problems."

Rosenberg solved the job problem temporarily by going to work as a business manager for a left wing New York publication called *University Review*, which two of his friends had purchased. "What *UR* was trying to do," he says, "was to provide a place for five or six or eight of us to work everyday, let us make some money—if we could—and give us the opportunity to say something and reach people with our ideas." Rosenberg felt that the writing in *UR* was excellent: "We printed intelligent political analysis. I remember an extended piece by Tom Hayden about the bombing of Hanoi and the mining of Haiphong which was particularly good.We also ran investigative stories. A woman named Deborah Larned wrote an article on women's health care in New York which blew the lid off these rip-off abortion clinics." But the publication was beset by serious financial troubles; the *Rolling Stone* advertising revenue which the staff had hoped to attract failed to come in and efforts to find wealthy investors proved unsuccessful. Although the magazine was distributed free on New York college campuses, its circulation remained discouragingly low. Rosenberg grew increasingly disenchanted with the venture and in fall 1973, one year after joining the publication's staff, he decided to quit. "We were kidding ourselves," he says. "The magazine was reaching ourselves and our friends and our friends' friends. It wasn't reaching anybody else. At the very least, a confrontation with the police in the middle of the street in a big city reaches twenty times more people than *UR* was reaching. People see it on the news and they have to have an opinion about it. When Abbie (Hoffman) was on top of the Wall Street stock exchange and threw the money away, boom! You had to to have an opinion one way or the other, and millions of people heard of it. *UR* was just taking too long and it wasn't reaching enough people."

His stint at *University Review* was Rosenberg's last experience with an alternative institution. As the Movement wound down in the early seventies, thousands of young radicals got involved in women's health clinics, printing collectives, child care centers, film cooperatives and the like. But Rosenberg found that he was temperamentally unsuited for that kind of work. "I'm much better under pressure and I feel better when there's a risk. I think the whole thing about life and politics is that you have to take risks. Alternative institutions are a risk on the one hand, but they're a real womb in another way." It was confrontation politics which he was cut out for, says Rosenberg, but those days were over.

Rosenberg had fallen in love with movies while he was at the University of Wisconsin, one of the leading centers of film studies. During the days of *UR's* decline, he went to the movies more frequently than ever. "My interest in movies escalated," he says, "as the Movement and all that other work went down...I find the idea of sitting in a darkened theater with a movie that totally envelops me to be *extremely* attractive. It's entertaining, it's escapist. I don't think there is anything absolutely evil about escapism. Everybody has troubles of a psychological and material nature, and there's nothing wrong with getting away from them for two hours." Rosenberg's taste in films ranged from Clint Eastwood Westerns to Third World revolutionary cinema. The more pictures he viewed, he says, the sharper his critical abilities became. He came to recognize what worked in a feature and what did not. As his infatuation with film grew, Rosenberg began to discuss the possibility of making political documentaries with Paula Weinstein, a fellow New York radical who produced street fairs for the Lindsay Administration. None of the projects they talked about got off the ground, but the fantasizing filled an important need for both of them. In early 1973, Weinstein moved to Hollywood where she found a job as a script reader and later as an agent.* Near the end of the same year, Rosenberg came out to visit and decided to stay.

The movie business seemed like the ideal line of work for someone with his personality, skills, and interests. He was quick-minded, fast-talking, and self-confident. And he was genuinely intrigued by the creative and social potential of film. High quality features enlivened and enriched people's everyday experience; they commanded the public's attention in a way which nothing else did. Rosenberg concluded that if movies were to be his trade, Hollywood was where he must settle. "I never did anything without being at the center of it," he remarks. "One of the psychological reasons people joined the Movement was to be at the center of what was going on in society. Now I had to locate myself at the center of film production." Rosenberg's goal was to find an interesting job somewhere within the industry, the kind of job which would bring him into contact with a variety of people and give him insight into the ways in which the production system worked. And perhaps after he had been at it long enough and accumulated enough experience, he would reach a position in the industry where he could produce his kind of movies. Entertaining features that had something to say about the human condition.

After working as an advertising man and a script reader, Rosenberg found a job at International Famous Agency with the help of his friend Paula who had been hired there some months earlier. "The idea behind becoming an agent," he says, "was that agents are integrally involved in almost every film, at least at the preliminary level. So you gain a great deal of visibility. They represent the artists who execute the film, they're involved in packaging the creative elements that make up the filmmaking team. They make the deals, which is an essential part of the filmmaking process." But IFA, which was one of Hollywood's largest talent agencies at the time, turned out to be a disappointment. Rosenberg felt that the firm's rigid

---

*Weinstein is now vice president of production at 20th Century-Fox.

corporate character allowed for too little cooperation between agents and not enough personal contact with clients. After half a year, he quit to join Adams, Ray and Rosenberg (no relation), a small agency which represents an exclusive stable of Hollywood writers.

Rosenberg finds that deal-making comes easy to him. "I've always been a *handler*, as they say in Yiddish. What I did in the Movement, among others things, was raise money because I'm good at that kind of salesmanship. In fact, I overdo it, if anything. I'm too effusive." There are occasions when he gets to use his skill to sell socially relevant scripts. One of his clients has written a screenplay about an Applachian coal strike which the young agent calls "a brilliant masterpiece, comparable in tone to Steinbeck's *Grapes of Wrath*." But that kind of material rarely crosses his desk. Only a handful of his agency's clients are inclined to write scripts with exceptional social content. Most, for reasons of economic survival, stay well within the conventional dramatic limits of commercial film and television. "A lot of our clients simply must take whatever television assignments are handed to them. They have little or no control over what they're working on. When they do write their own scripts, they are generally guided by what they feel the studios will buy. Since these people make their living from writing, they can't take the liberty of writing whatever they please too often. They can't afford to ignore the realities of the marketplace."

So Rosenberg spends most of his time marketing standard Hollywood goods. Even though Rosenberg does not find the bulk of what he sells to be socially or aesthetically inspiring, he pursues his work with diligence and care. "It would be folly for me to say that every piece of material I sell is something that I am totally in love with and absolutely enthusiastic about. Some screenplays come along which I would not go to see as movies. This is a subjective business and I have opinions like everybody else. But the job of the agent is to serve the client's best interest; therefore even when I'm handling a script which is not terribly appealing to me, I still have to find a way to do the best job I can, and to submit the script in the best possible fashion. I don't find that obligation hard to take, because after all I'm being paid by my clients to perform a service. You have to be a professional and do the best job you can."

On two occasions in the past, Rosenberg was handed scripts which offended him so strongly that he decided he could not market them in good conscience. One was a spy thriller with a zealous Cold War perspective. The other featured a female character who was drawn in such savagely unfavorable terms, felt Rosenberg, that even the market would find the script too misogynist. "It was written with such venom and had such a stench about it that I just couldn't see myself going out and convincingly saying this is a piece you should buy...I am not somebody who takes a hard radical line in judging material, but since it was so offensive to me I was certain that it would be offensive to the buyers." But these kinds of scripts turn up so rarely, says the agent, that they do not pose a major problem. "Generally, the studios won't buy stuff that is too repugnant, because they're afraid of alienating a large share of the audience."

Thousands of movie and television scripts by unknown scenarists are written each year. As a rule, Adams, Ray, and Rosenberg will not read material written by non-clients unless it comes recommended. But on rare occasions, Rosenberg has made exceptions. One day, a nervous black writer came into the agent's office with a script which Rosenberg found sufficiently interesting to read. "It was a horror story with a sociological twist, a King Kong-like tale about a Jamaican monster who comes to the United States where he is regarded as a vicious, dangerous creature although he really isn't." Rosenberg felt the story itself was "all out of whack," but he thought the writing showed talent.

"So I called the writer for a meeting; and he was unbelievably inarticulate. He couldn't put two words together—not because he didn't know how, because I saw that he knew how. But because he was so nervous. He was one of those people who you can see develop a sweat. He was sweating and nervous and didn't know what to say and couldn't get his thoughts together. I really didn't know how to deal with him. I couldn't say that I'd sign him because it simply wasn't that great a script. It was just good interesting writing. So I asked for another script, and the same thing was true with the second script. And all this time, all my feelings of what I *should* do came welling up. Because I knew in general that this was a 'pass.' I mean 'Get him out of your hair,' you know. The line in most agencies would be, 'Who needs new, untried black writers—they're too hard to sell.' And I live with that all the time, but that's another story. Anyway, I finally showed the script to someone else in the office who agreed with me that it was way out of whack, that it was hardly saleable, but the writing was very interesting. So slowly I'm working this guy in; hopefully he'll become less nervous."

But Rosenberg's meetings with new writers rarely have this upbeat a conclusion. "I had a black woman come into my office at IFA with silver thigh-length boots, a mini skirt that had to be an inch and a half long—if that—a halter top with exposed nipples and teased hair. Clearly a hooker...She had under her arm a huge manuscript, 1200 pages. And when she told the story it became obvious that it was her story: of having a boyfriend at age fourteen, knocked up, getting an abortion. The boyfriend beats her up but she still loves him. He throws her out of the house. She finds him in bed with another girl, she throws bottles at him. She goes back, he takes her back, he beats her up again. She finally kills him, in a rage, and goes to jail. Comes out and decides that the only way to cut it is as a hooker...And you realize there's a human experience there, and if you ever caught it on film, if you could catch it impromptu on film, it would be dynamite! But who's going to read through 1200 pages of manuscript? You can't do it, you'd never get through it all.

"I just had to say, 'Look, I'm very sorry...' I started feeling very guilty, very very responsible. I said, 'I'm very sorry, you've got to go home. You can't bring in anything more than 300 to 400 pages, and even that's too long. And it can't be handwritten, or badly typed on lined paper, because no one is going to go through the pain to read it, despite all the pain that you went through to write it.' And that's the reality—it's a harsh reality, but it's true."

"People come in, they figure the way to break out of their life is to write stuff down, to keep a diary, to fictionalize their experience. They figure that's the way to break out of the anomie of their existence. And they do it and you know that it's not good. You know that it's not publishable or filmable and what do you say to them? What do you say to someone who has at least made the attempt to break out of that shitty existence? It's a rough situation; it really makes you focus on the way that the structure of this business puts people at odds with one another. Because I'm in a position of power, and they're put in the position of being supplicants. They're saying, 'Please, please, please' and you're saying 'No, no, no.' And there's no way they can walk out of that place sympathetic with you. No way. No matter how reasonable and nice and sympathetic and warm you are. They can't because there's that deep resentment that runs underneath it all...It's emotionally the most difficult part of being an agent...saying 'no.'"

*****

When Rosenberg went to work in the entertainment industry, he entered an environment with an entirely different value system than that of the 1960s student left. Here everything was measured in terms of its profitability rather than the contribution it made to society. The most illuminating and artfully done pictures could drop forever from circulation unless they sold the proper number of tickets. The makers of movies were only as highly esteemed as their latest box office grosses. It seemed to Rosenberg that the industry would exploit any subject, tell anyone's life story, dramatize any social event if it could be convinced there was enough money to be made. One way to preserve a critical sensibility in an environment like this is to develop a wry sense of humor. "Paula and I used to go to these IFA staff meetings," says Rosenberg. "And you have to realize that they think they're IBM, not IFA—you know, mahogany rooms and everything. They would announce, 'We're going to do something on Cuba.' And Paula and I would nudge each other and say, 'Yeah, we'll sign Fidel to a two-year contract in movies, television, and recordings."

But Rosenberg has found only a few people in Hollywood who share his political assumptions and can put the industry in its proper perspective. And some of these friendships are marred by the intense professional rivalry which predominates in Hollywood. "There is a certain amount of tension," observes Rosenberg, "between those of us who started at the same point in terms of income, status, and power. Because some of these people have risen faster and higher than the rest and that generates competition. And competition is anathema to me. I hate it. And if the other people involved don't hate it—or thrive on it—the situation becomes even more uncomfortable...One tends to feel very much alone in this business. Its structure demands individual competition, it demands individual aggressiveness. There's a never ending battle for good creative material, for better jobs, for more money. The emphasis in the sixties was on collective action, we tried to downplay individual achievement. To be in a business where there's a constant aura of wild competition takes some getting used to."

His deepest friendships continue to be those he developed in New York during his days as a political activist. "There's a reason for that," he says. "Because in the course of that political struggle there developed a deep trust between all of us. Now that trust breaks down somewhat when you move away. I'm sure that when I talk to my friends on the phone, they sometimes say to themselves, 'Who am I talking to? What is going on?' But from my point of view, anyway, I feel much safer calling up my friend Louis in New York and saying, 'God, I'm so depressed' than any of the people I've met here. Because I feel that I went through a lot of turmoil with him and he was there with me...and we went through it together and came out the other end. And that kind of trust is hard to find."

Agency business takes up most of Rosenberg's time; there are always stacks of scripts to read, phone calls to return, and meetings to attend. He would like to keep up with world and national news more than he does, but he cannot find enough leisure moments in his busy schedule. Rosenberg is strongly dedicated to his career; he is hard working and success oriented. Yet he remains somewhat uncomfortable about having become an established Hollywood businessman. He knows that the industry does not put a premium on ethical business behavior. "It tends," he says, "to reward hustling and aggressiveness." But he rejects the idea that one has to be "cold, calculating, and deceitful" in order to get ahead. He prides himself on the fact that his own ambition drive is "somewhat curbed by my moral code." "Like I stated earlier, if a piece of material is completely repugnant to me, I step back from it. I don't feel bound to be a whore. I don't accept lying from others and I won't breach my word even if it would further my career or my client's career."

There is something in Rosenberg which rebels against the process of growing up and getting involved in the grim world of commerce. Life in the seventies, he often feels, pales in comparison to his youthful experience in the sixties. "The sixties," he says, "were Oz. The fifties were that dark hurricane outside that drove you into the storm cellar that Judy Garland's family went into. And the sixties were Oz. And the seventies are coming out of Oz and realizing that you're back on the Kansas plain and that's all there is. When you've had the experience of going through Oz, you don't want to deal with that barren plain anymore."

But, he readily admits, he would have found it impossible to maintain his sixties subsistence-level lifestyle indefinitely. "Six years ago, I distinctly remember saying, 'I don't need more than a hundred bucks a week to live on.' Well, that's just bullshit. I grew out of that one fast...It's an amazing thing to say to oneself. It's so naive. To think that's all you needed!...I'm sure it's still possible, that if you had a hundred dollars cash every week you could make do and sort of bum around and subsist—but that's not a decent kind of life to lead. I mean most people in the world who live on that amount of money want a lot better. The reason that there's any political struggle at all is that they want something better. So I mean to think of that as a dream is insanity."

Rosenberg enjoys the material comforts and the sense of security which working in Hollywood has given him. "I have great desires in terms of my lifestyle. I need a certain amount of money to live and will need more money to live. And there are things that I like which I don't want to do without—like vacations, and a nice place to live, and a nice car, those kinds of things. And that makes me middle class and bourgeois in a lot of ways. But I accept that...Where Weatherman politics erred was that it did not properly identify what the enemy is. The enemy is not the desire to live life well. Everybody has that desire. The lowest peasants in the most oppressed countries in the world all have the desire to live well. Exploitation is the central problem, not material comforts."

Living and working in a commercial environment with values and customs so different than those of the Movement subculture can be profoundly alienating, concedes Rosenberg. But he is prepared to make certain psychological sacrifices in order to reap the benefits of a Hollywood career. "The sacrifices I must make because of the course I took are sacrifices of the mind," he says. "They are abstract sacrifices. You either have to pay your dues here (he points to his head) or somewhere else." Those who decide to remain in the alternative environment, says Rosenberg, generally suffer the physical hardships of low income living. He is simply not willing to forgo financial security and the ability to raise a family in a comfortable manner, he declares.

There are rare moments when his two worlds do not seem so extremely far apart, when Hollywood actually seems capable of understanding his sixties experience. These are the special occasions which give him new hope about doing meaningful work in the entertainment industry. When he first heard that young writer-director Jeremy Kagan was preparing a television movie for ABC based on the life of Diana Oughton, one of the Weatherpeople who died in the New York townhouse explosion, he became indignant. This was *his* history that Kagan and the network were tampering with. Television had already presented one distorted drama on a Movement subject that year—a CBS television movie, which Rosenberg felt was "absolutely execrable," about the killings of civil rights workers James Chaney, Andrew Goodman, and Michael Schwerner. He was convinced that Kagan's movie, which was titled *Katherine*, would be equally deplorable. "Whenever I spoke to my friends in New York," says Rosenberg, "I would complain about this guy who was going to exploit the Weather Underground for television. I really resented it." But when he finally saw *Katherine*, which aired in fall 1975, he was surprised by how warm and sympathetic a portrayal of sixties radicalism it was. "I was amazed that something like that could be done on television, something that sensitive to the subject. It had a big emotional impact on me."

Looking back, Rosenberg recognizes there were some significant flaws in *Katherine*: the character modeled on Weather spokeswoman Bernadine Dohrn was too much of a radical stereotype, certain political issues and events were given too abbreviated a treatment. But, in general, Rosenberg feels that *Katherine* helped expand the public's understanding of the sixties. Ten years ago, he says, the general population only took in negative images of radical activism. Now, through dramas like *Katherine*, television and film audiences are getting new information about the social struggles of that period and gaining new insight into the people who participated in those struggles. Mass culture is rapidly assimilating the political content of the sixties, a process Rosenberg finds very encouraging. "Unless you're prepared to give up on three-quarters of the population, just say to the winds with them, you better hope that the mass media absorb some progressive ideas."

*****

Rosenberg is impressed by the immense drawing power of movies such as *Jaws* and *Star Wars*. "The fact that a movie makes $150 million or more domestically means there is something there that people want. I don't care what anyone says anymore, I believe that. It is impossible to say that they are forcing them into the theaters. We know enough about television and the marketplace to know that people would rather sit at home than go out. So if they go out and pay four dollars to see *Star Wars*, there's got to be something there." The left, he says, could benefit from paying more attention to successful films and figuring out what specific needs in people they satisfy. Some of these needs are "legitimate," some are not, but in either case they should be analyzed and understood, he believes, if one is interested in building a popular movement for social change.

"I feel that *Death Wish* spoke to very base needs in its audience," Rosenberg remarks. "The need for revenge at any cost, blind irrational revenge. The story unfolds in a contemporary urban setting filled with terrible random violence—it's a setting the audience is painfully familiar with. But rather than addressing why that violence exists, the film simply indulges the audience's desire to lash out at street criminals in a wanton, unthinking kind of way. The film also reinforces certain stereotypes, which makes it even worse. The avenger is a white, upper middle class professional and the sinister people he goes around knocking off are all poor, black, and Puerto Rican—street people and subway urchins."

"*Rocky* was an altogether different kind of film, a much more positive film. I'm actually not the biggest champion of the film—it was built around a very simple formula—but it certainly was very effective. Because it spoke to the need for love, the need for respect. Even if you're some average Philadelphia working class guy, you can make something worthwhile out of your life...Here's a guy who only wants to be a contender. I mean he doesn't even dream of being a winner. He just wants the gratification of lasting fifteen rounds. Well, who doesn't want that, whether it's in the boxing ring or some other arena?"

"The point is that both those films made a big impact on movie audiences; the first because it gratified the audience's baser instincts, the second because it spoke to people's higher aspirations. The popularity of those two movies tells you a lot about the public's hopes and fears. All those who are interested in keeping their fingers on the pulse of this country's population would do well to examine these kinds of films."

Many left wing critics have assailed Hollywood movies for overwhelming audiences with such a torrent of sights and sounds that viewers have little intellectual room to reflect on what is happening. Rosenberg acknowledges that the Hollywood style of movie-making tends to "reinforce audience passivity," but he balks at the idea of changing the industry's cinematic approach. "The magic of film as an art form, it seems to me, is that you have a submissive audience, you have an audience which will willingly suspend their disbelief. You have an audience in a dark room with a screen that is as wide as the ocean, with incredible color and stereosound and beautiful photography and larger-than-life characters. I don't think that should be done away with."

Rosenberg's primary criticism of Hollywood features has to do with their content rather than their style. The dominant attitude in the industry, he says, is that movies with social substance are not commercial. Rosenberg points to the box office successes of five pictures which were released in recent years—*Dog Day Afternoon, One Flew Over the Cuckoo's Nest, Taxi Driver, All The President's Men,* and *Network*—to show that this belief is unfounded. Each one of these films made a powerful social statement, says the agent; each one explored a "dark and seamy" side of the human experience, each one was "downbeat" in its attitude. And they all drew large numbers of people into the movie theaters. "The success of those five pictures—and there are at least one or two like them every year—seems to indicate that it is possible to make pictures which entertain people as well as make a statement. 'Message' films are not necessarily uncommercial."

Nevertheless, Hollywood continues to make a strong distinction between "message" pictures and "entertainment" pictures. Entertainment pictures are those which combine the proper commercial elements—a "big name cast," a director with a good track record, a tried and true dramatic formula, a certain amount of volatile dialogue and visual pyrotechnics." These films are thought by the studios to have "built-in audiences." Message pictures, on the other hand, are always thought of as commercial risks. And studio executives are not inclined to take risks. "Studio executives' jobs depend on the film decisions they make. They know that if they choose to go ahead with projects that have the right commercial elements and these projects flop at the box office, they probably won't be blamed. They can always say, 'It wasn't my fault—after all, it had Clint Eastwood in it.' Or 'It wasn't my fault—it was about a burning skyscraper.' But if you try to make a *Cuckoo's Nest* on the strength of your beliefs and it fails, then you're in the toilet. Because the industry will say, 'He should never have gone ahead with something that difficult.' So the fear on the part of the executives drives them to do things that are safe, that have enough 'insurance.' "

Rosenberg is critical of the industry's inclination to produce only "surefire" movies with a guaranteed audience. He does not believe that all pictures should be turned out in such a way as to fit into a ready-made market. The industry's marketing approach should be much more creative, he says. "I believe that you should make your picture and *then* go out and find your audience. You should go into movie-making with the attitude that *every* picture has an audience, and then develop advertising techniques—ways of communicating with the public—that will bring your audience into the theaters." There is a market for socially meaningful films, Rosenberg insists; the studios simply must take the time and effort to locate the audience and engage its interest.

Rosenberg is not asking anything more from Hollywood than he thinks it is capable of delivering; he does not expect the industry to produce films in the political mold of *Battle of Algiers*. He simply believes that Hollywood should turn out more truthful, humane, and intelligent features than it does. "In Hollywood, it's not a question of radical vs. liberal vs. conservative movies. It's a question of cartoon-like movies with cardboard characters vs. more honest pictures in which people are portrayed in a fairly sophisticated way. It's a question of Woody Allen's *Annie Hall* vs. Mel Brooks' *Blazing Saddles*. *Annie Hall* is simply a much richer film than any of Mel Brooks' comedies because it examines human experience and talks about personal relationships in sensitive and insightful ways. I mean I liked *Blazing Saddles*, I laughed a lot. But I would never go back to see it again. It just doesn't have the resonance that *Annie Hall* does. Now *Annie Hall* will not make as much money as *Blazing Saddles*, because it's not as broad a film— it's geared to the educated, urban population. But I hope the industry makes more movies like it. I'd rather see movies which confront reality, which tap something inside you—that's my personal taste."

*****

For more than five years of his young life, Rosenberg thought of himself as a political agitator, a mover of events, an active participant in history. He tried to "make people uncomfortable" and push them to take stands—"that's what it amounted to," he says. Often, he and the radical groups he belonged to tried to accomplish this by "taking exemplary action," in the words of the day, by engaging in daring and militant confrontations. But he is unsure about how one demonstrates his or her political commitment in today's political climate. There is no longer a mass movement for social change, and there will not be one, he is convinced, until a political issue on the scale of the Vietnam War again emerges— an issue which clearly exposes the fundamental flaws of U.S. society. Major issues, deep conflicts are beginning to come into focus, but as yet it is all too murky and undefined; the situation is still too ambiguous to suggest a definite course of action.

"I believe that it is only possible to organize people on a

mass scale when the system in which we live creates issues that are terribly pressing and terribly difficult to solve through the normal political mechanisms. That's when radical alternatives become important. That has happened in a limited fashion since the sixties. The energy problem seems to be getting out of control; it's a hot issue because it reveals major weaknesses in the system. Ecologists are a strong progressive force in that area. But it has not yet reached a critical point. And I don't believe a mass movement can form until a crisis of some sort develops."

Rosenberg also feels that there is little hope at this point in history of building a broadly based reform movement within the entertainment industry. "In the three years that I have been working in Hollywood," he says, "I have not seen one issue which could bring together the disparate elements of this industry in a common struggle." What about the chronically severe unemployment in Hollywood? It seems like it would be possible to build a coalition of entertainment workers to push for more film and television production. But Rosenberg sees little sense in putting pressure on the studios for more movies. Audience demand determines how many films are made each year, he says, not the studios. And Rosenberg thinks there is no way to convince the TV networks to broadcast fewer reruns and increase television production, because they will not tolerate a decline in profits. The long-range solution to unemployment among film and television workers, he says, lies outside the commercial system; full employment will come only with the creation of a massive public subsidy program for the arts.

Rosenberg's inability to recognize organizing possibilities may be due in part to the position he occupies within the industry. Once you reach his occupational level in Hollywood, comments the agent, organizing becomes a highly problematic venture. Individual career advancement tends to be the primary goal among his professional and managerial colleagues rather than improving general industry conditions. "If I were to call up a couple agents that I know, and a couple writers that I know, a studio executive or two that I know, and maybe a director, and we all sat here and discussed the political and economic problems within the industry, you'd find that there would be a lot of tension in the room. Because the writer would think, 'Gee, that agent over there represents writers who are better than me or who are doing better than me and maybe I can get him to represent me.' And the agent would be thinking, 'My God, that writer is someone I would like to represent.' Or the writer is thinking, 'That studio executive can give me $50,000 to write a script.' So you would find that the roles, at least in the beginning, would overwhelm the people, would inhibit their ability to talk openly and freely and make strong commitments."

Rosenberg says that he continues to think of himself as a radical. "My critical faculties have not diminished," he remarks. "I may be more critical of some things now than I was back in the sixties and I may be less critical of other things. But my general perspective remains the same. I still consider myself to be in opposition to much of what goes on in this country." He still believes that the political and economic system must be radically transformed if society is to become truly just and equitable. But his opinions about how and when this transformation is going to occur have changed considerably since the sixties. He no longer has an "apocalyptic" view of history, says Rosenberg. He now tends to think of social conflict and change as part of the general flow of time rather than the immediate prelude to revolution.

"I no longer believe that everything is going to happen overnight. That was the sixties image of revolution. And even if there were a revolution, I'm not sure that all its goals could be achieved in my lifetime. It's clear to me now that major changes in society take a great deal of time to occur. There is a good possibility that changes of a fundamental nature will not take place in my lifetime. Now that doesn't mean that people should not be critical and active and do all the things they feel are right to do. What it means is that we must have a long view and put things in perspective. History is not just a constant series of explosions. The apocalyptic view that we used to have—that feeling of always being on the brink—is wrong. If one has that narrow view of history, it seems to me that one gets easily frustrated or one gets involved in factional disputes and political conflicts which have no real bearing on power or the way things function in society."

Because the left is not part of the mainstream of U.S. life, it is very difficult for individual radicals like himself to integrate their politics with their everyday worlds, says Rosenberg. "Radicalism in America has never been the moving force it is in Europe. In France and Italy the environment is much more politicized. When left wing workers go out on strike there they paralyze the country. In an election, they are heard from, they win seats. It's part of life. If you see Italian films by Bertolucci or Wertmuller or others, the characters are always talking about socialism or communism or fascism. It's embedded in their culture. Not in America. The left here is outside the main arena."

If a major social crisis were to develop in this country in the future, says Rosenberg, he is confident that he and other concerned people in the entertainment industry would find some way to take a stand. "When something really serious happens, people always find the time to do something— whether it is circulating a petition, taking out an ad, or going to a meeting." But Rosenberg does not feel compelled during this relatively quiescent period to take time away from his demanding business schedule and participate in political activities. He has invested himself entirely—for now at least—in his career. "When you are involved in a business like this, you are *really* involved. It takes a great deal of time and energy, too much. Success is based in many ways on being compulsive about your work. And if you're a compulsive worker, that doesn't leave a lot of room in your life for much of anything else."

Because of his past political involvement, however, because of the ideas, assumptions, and instincts which became part of him during the 1960s, Rosenberg approaches his work in a somewhat different frame of mind than most Hollywood businessmen. His creative judgment is slightly unique, his sense of ethics is distinguishable from the norm. No matter how deeply immersed he becomes in the commercial realities of the entertainment industry, says Rosenberg, he will always carry with him the visions of the New Left. "The sixties was a decade which was like a bomb, it was an explosive era. It was an explosion which made a profound impact on me, because it made me a very thoughtful and critical person. It still affects me today, so that when I look at a screenplay or go about doing something else, I put to use the critical tools I developed back then...There were hundreds of thousands of people who went through experiences similar to mine. Once you go through something like that, it affects you for the rest of your life. So whether you become teacher or a writer or a cab driver or go into the movie business, you bring that experience with you. There is now a group of people in this business who were tempered by that decade, so the effect of that period will be felt in the movies as it will be in other cultural areas. I hope that means there will be better movies and more of them. Maybe there will be, maybe there won't. You can't say for sure."

Postscript:
In April 1978, Rosenberg became a vice-president of production at Warner Brothers.

"Katherine": The Making of an Exception

The fall 1975 TV season was distinguished by two rather remarkable made-for-television movies. On October 2, CBS broadcast *Fear on Trial*, a "docu-drama" about the 1950s blacklisting of radio personality John Henry Faulk. What made the movie particularly noteworthy was the fact that it was WCBS, the network's New York flagship station, which had fired Faulk in 1957 after he was labeled "pro-communist" by a right wing organization. Over the years, CBS steadfastly maintained that Faulk had been banished from the airwaves simply because his ratings had slipped. The network refused to acknowledge that there had been a blacklisting system in the broadcasting industry throughout the Cold War. But eighteen years after Faulk lost his job, CBS decided to set the record straight by airing *Fear on Trial*. It was an unburdening of the corporate conscience which was only possible in a political climate such as the post-Watergate period.

Three days later, on Sunday October 5, ABC broadcast a TV movie called *Katherine*, which was aesthetically superior to the blacklist drama and in some respects more politically astonishing. *Katherine* starred Sissy Spacek as a 1960s radical activist whose growing militancy and moral outrage compel her underground as a Weatherwoman and finally to her death. The movie, which was loosely based on the life of Diana Oughton (one of the three Weatherpeople killed in a March 1970 New York townhouse explosion), took a surprisingly favorable attitude towards the political activism of the sixties and treated the heroine's descent into the underground as a tragic mistake rather than as a heinous crime or an act of insanity. Never before on television were radical characters depicted with as much understanding and feeling as they were in *Katherine*. While *Fear on Trial* asked the TV audience to extend its sympathy to a man who had suffered because he had been inaccurately labeled a pro-communist, *Katherine* evoked a warm, compassionate reponse for a young woman who was unmistakably dedicated to the radical transformation of U.S. society.

Katherine was the work of a twenty-nine year old writer-director named Jeremy Paul Kagan. Kagan, the son of a rabbi, grew up in a New York suburb and attended Harvard from

1963 to 1967. As a student, Kagan was sympathetic to the New Left, but he did not join SDS or any other political groups. "I'm not a group joiner," remarks Kagan. "Though friends of mine were members of, and organizers of, SDS and Weatherman, I was not there. That's not the route I chose." While at Harvard, Kagan devoted himself primarily to theater work and film studies. His thesis was on Russian director Sergei Eisenstein, one of the giant figures in cinema history. Kagan admired Eisenstein's masterful style and his political passion.

After graduating from Harvard, Kagan enrolled in a New York film school called the Institute of Film and Television, where he made an assortment of student movies. None of them was particularly political, but they were imaginative and they won praise and awards for Kagan. In 1969, Kagan joined the first class of the American Film Institute in Beverly Hills. When Kagan arrived on the West Coast, he was much more under the influence of European and Russian films than Hollywood movies. He knew little about Hollywood history and he had no ambition to become the next John Ford or Howard Hawks. "Sam Fuller could have been a brush sales- man for all I knew," says Kagan. He was much more taken by directors like Godard, Pontecorvo, and De Sica.

Kagan felt that a film's first duty was to hold the audience's attention—"that is my definition of entertain- ment"—but he also believed that filmmakers had a respons- ibility to inform people and "raise their consciousness." In May 1970, Kagan was invited to participate in a student film exhibition sponsored by the Television Academy. A few days before the event took place, Ohio National Guardsmen opened fire on student demonstrators at Kent State Univer- sity, killing four and wounding nine. Kagan, deeply affected by the shootings, turned the panel discussion which followed the film screenings into a debate about the social responsibilities of the Hollywood movie community. "I started yelling and I started accusing—I couldn't get Kent State off my mind," recalls Kagan. "A few people said, 'We're here to talk about movies.' And I said, 'Bullshit! What's the point? We're just trying to pretend that we can exist in this little protected world of filmmakers. We're responsible to those people who died.

We're responsible for making sure that doesn't happen again. Those are the films that we should be making.' "

The audience, in general, took Kagan's outspoken remarks in stride. "Let's face it," he says, "the major part of the Hollywood community has always been to the left. Writers and artists are more that way than not. What I said appealed to their sense of guilt. And then they probably knew much more about me than I did. They realized, "Well, he's here in Hollywood and he's going to end up like us sooner or later. He'll be supporting and cheering the Tom Haydens, but he won't be there. He'll be part of the industry.

Variety's report on the forum put less emphasis on Kagan's political comments than on his filmmaking abilities. *Mate Game,* one of the two Kagan films which were shown that night, "was a demonstration of a fully developed filmmaking... talent," commented the trade paper. As a result of that plug, Kagan acquired a Hollywood agent and the young filmmaker was on his way to becoming a member of the industry.

Kagan's agent introduced him to writer-director Frank Pierson, who was overseeing a TV series called "Nichols," starring James Garner. Pierson gave Kagan a chance to direct a "Nichols" segment and that assignment led to more television work. He directed a "Columbo" episode, a "Bold Ones" installment, and an ABC Afterschool Special, before graduating to television movies. *Unwed Father,* his first TV movie, dealt with a seventeen year old boy's battle to win custody over his pregnant girlfriend's unborn child. *Judge Dee in the Monastery Murders,* starred Khigh Dheigh as a seventh century Chinese detective.

Kagan put an unusual amount of care and effort into each one of his directing assignments, even if the material seemed fairly routine. A TV director's involvement with a program generally begins when the script is completed and ends when the shooting is over. But Kagan made a point of getting involved in each stage of the production. "I feel that I am responsible from the minute I become associated with a project. Even if it is not my script, I will make sure that the script is as right as it can be. And I will not be finished with a movie until an answer print is made."

Kagan prided himself on giving his TV dramas a certain

amount of stylistic distinction. He photographed parts of *Judge Dee* to look like a Chinese silk screen. He tried to give his "Nichols" episode the appearance of "a Kurosawa Western." By the end of 1974, Kagan had developed a reputation as a hard working and creative television director. Cecil Smith, TV critic for the *Los Angeles Times*, labeled him "one of the American Film Institute's brightest young men."

Soon after completing *Judge Dee*, Kagan was asked by producer Jerry Isenberg if he would be interested in making a TV movie about the Weather Underground—a project which the producer had been contemplating for several years. It sounded like a rare opportunity to do something out of the ordinary on television, and Kagan enthusiastically accepted the assignment. Kagan wanted to make sure the movie would reflect his point of view, so he decided to write the script himself. Kagan's knowledge of sixties radicalism was somewhat limited. He had not *lived* that experience. The passionate struggles of that period had not become part of his personal identity the way they had for activist oriented members of his generation. But he had enough sympathy and respect for those who *were* deeply involved in radical activities to honor their experience. And he was dedicated enough as a filmmaker to put long hours of research into the project. He gathered an abundance of material, including "piles and piles of articles from the underground press," books, position papers. The research, he says, included just about everything which had been written on the subject. Kagan also talked to old friends who had been—and still were—"totally radically committed." People who would come through L.A. every now and then and visit with him.

The script that finally emerged was a moving and—by television standards—intelligent tale of a young woman's personal and political transformation. The story, which covers eight years in the life of Katherine Alman, is told through flashbacks and interviews with the woman's family and friends. Each year of her life from 1964 to 1970 is marked off at the beginning with a news footage montage of some of the events which characterized that year. Each segment is closed by Katherine's own comments on that period in her life; she sits on a stool in an all white "limbo room" and speaks directly to us.

   We see Katherine as a college senior, full of energy and promise, and a vague desire to better the world. She winds up going to Peru as a Peace Corps volunteer, against the wishes of her wealthy parents who want only the best for their well-bred daughter. "I grew up a princess in a fairy tale," Katherine tells us, "—no misfortunes, no suffering, no hardships. It's a good life—everyone should be so lucky...but they aren't...I'd been in a protected shell so long, you see, and...I felt I had to do something about it." In Peru, Katherine witnesses terrible poverty and suffering first hand. Her humanitarian efforts seem useless in the face of such widespread misery. Armed violence is still too drastic a measure for her to accept, but she agrees to supply local guerrillas with food and medicine. When the government finds out, she is promptly deported.

   Back home, the distance between Katherine and her family grows wider and wider. "I don't want my comfort and well-being to depend on somebody else's hardship," she tells her father. She goes South to teach black children and learns how deep and bitter the divisions between blacks and whites are in the U.S. She comes to realize that "my white skin has given me a lot of privileges in this society." Later, she and her boyfriend become traveling organizers for SDS. They are both beaten and arrested during the tumultuous antiwar demonstration outside of the 1968 Democratic National Convention. The brutal police reaction to the demonstration convinces Katherine that the struggle for political change is entering a new militant phase. "The revolution was no longer imaginary, it was real, now," she comments, "...and it was clear that the police state wasn't gonna give up without a battle—I mean there was blood in the streets—I won't forget those images. They're burned into my head forever. They changed my life— If we were gonna win, it would take all our strength."

   Katherine sides with Weatherman when SDS splits apart, and not long afterward she goes underground. She accepts the logic behind blowing up symbolic targets. She is in the process of carrying out one such mission when the bomb goes off prematurely, killing her instantly. In the final letter to her family before her death, Katherine writes:

> Too many of my generation have already sold themselves to
> the false dreams—but I refuse to follow that path. I believe
> with all my being that what I am doing is both right and
> necessary. Perhaps you will not see it now, but in time, I
> hope you will. I know I haven't ever fully expressed my
> fondness for you and I have often been too rigid in my
> actions. I know you have not always understood me, but I
> hope my family will never be ashamed of me, for what I am
> doing is right—and I am proud of it. I have loved you all very
> much and always will, even though I can never be the
> daughter you once had. With these words I give you all an
> embrace from your obstinate, prodigal Katherine.

Kagan's teleplay was unique because, unlike other TV
programs about radical activists, it never denigrated or
downplayed her political commitment. Kagan acknowledged
the power and validity in Katherine's criticisms of American
society. Even when she was en route to planting the bomb—an
act which Kagan clearly deplored—he tried to put what she
was about to do in some perspective by focusing in on a
newspaper headline which read "Cambodian Bombing Continues." Her death was meant to leave the TV audience with a
sharp sense of loss. She is alive in the final scene, sitting on the
stool and looking into our eyes, and suddenly there is a jump
cut and the chair is empty.

"I wanted to make a movie," says Kagan, "which would
truly be accepted by all of my radical friends." He was also
aiming for the other tens of millions he knew would be
watching television the night *Katherine* aired. All those people
who associated radicalism with lunacy. He wanted to raise the
possibility with these people that the radicals of the sixties
were battling for just causes and that even those few among
them who chose the ill-considered and disastrous tactics of
Weatherman were "well-motivated human beings." It was not
Kagan's intention to convince Americans of the merits of
radical ideology, but rather to promote understanding
between the generation of political activists who came of age
in the 1960s and all those who were profoundly alienated from
them. "I wanted as many Americans as possible," he says, "to
realize that people who are radicals are human beings, their
children...and they love them. That's what I wanted to have

happen." It was a call for political harmony which seemed wholly appropriate in the cultural ambience of the post-Nixon period, after the administration which had tried—with considerable success—to discredit and destroy the New Left had itself fallen in disgrace.

The final draft of *Katherine* was completed in May 1975 and production began soon afterwards. Kagan was given only eighteen days to shoot the TV feature. Actress Sissy Spacek, who played the lead role, found the tight production schedule very frustrating. She felt that it did not give her enough time to get fully into her character. Spacek had marched in peace demonstrations, but her personal knowledge of the radical left was slight. Shooting began just three days after the young actress was awarded the role, so there was little time to assimilate new information. She was given a stack of research material to read, but, says Spacek, she was told that the most important thing she had to do was lose her Texas accent, so she spent most of her time on that. Among the few things she was able to read were Jerry Rubin's *We Are Everywhere* and Susan Stern's *With the Weathermen*, neither of which brought her to a closer understanding of her character. "I didn't agree with a single thing Susan Stern said," remarks Spacek. "She was more or less just a girl along for the quick lays, which is fine, but that was not my character. Jerry Rubin, it seemed, just wanted to get stoned all the time and he was into seeing freaks hanging from the White House. But Katherine was much more serious." Astonishingly enough, Spacek had no idea she was playing a character who was loosely based on Diana Oughton until "about three-quarters of the way" into production when someone handed her a copy of Thomas Power's book *Diana: The Making of a Terrorist*. "Had I known about Diana Oughton," says Spacek, "it would have been *so* much easier."*

---

*Even though she disliked the process in which *Katherine* was made, Spacek was glad to be associated with the final product because of the statement it made. "It was a very gallant and brave step for the producer and director—them more than anyone—much more than it was for me. And for that I think they're pretty great. You gotta do what you can, when you can, and they did."

Despite the limited intellectual grasp she had of her character, Spacek turned in an outstanding performance. She played Katherine with a rare sensitivity and passion. She was supported by a first-rate cast, including Art Carney in the role of her father; Jane Wyatt as her mother; and Henry Winkler, who stepped out of his "Fonz" mold long enough to give an admirable performance as Katherine's boyfriend.

Even though Kagan was pressed for time, he managed to create a feature whose production qualities were far superior to the standard TV movie. Not only were the performances accurate, but the visual imagery was carefully composed and convincing. For the first time in dramatic television, a street demonstration looked like something more than a small gathering of extras carrying nearly identical signs.

But it was the ideological content of *Katherine* which set it off most clearly from the rest of television. The TV movie provoked a strong response from television critics when it was finally aired by ABC in the first week of October. Mary Murphy of the *Los Angeles Times* praised it as "a courageous work for television." She noted that "the tendency in television movies about politically sensitive subjects has often been to cop out at the end, coming down hard for balance or effect." But wrote Murphy, "at no point (in *Katherine*) do the filmmakers feel compelled to apologize for the principal character's radicalization."

New York Times TV critic John J. O'Connor acknowledged the aesthetic merits of *Katherine*, but was greatly alarmed by the political content of the TV drama. The fact that such a program was aired on national television, remarked O'Connor, clearly demonstrated that the TV networks were bent on self-destruction. "The details and structure of *Katherine*," he wrote, "were ingenious and the quality of the production was far above the average encountered in a made for TV movie. But the notion of presenting a sympathetic portrait of a terrorist committed to the overthrow of most American institutions, presumably including commercial television itself, is ludicrous."

O'Connor exaggerated the political significance of *Katherine*; it is doubtful that the TV movie seriously undermined the commercial medium in which it was presented as well as "most other American institutions." While *Katherine* did elicit strong emotional support for the lead character, it did not present a well-developed intellectual argument for radicalism. As Murphy commented in her review, the filmmakers chose to explore Katherine's political evolution "in human rather than philosophical terms." Nonetheless, O'Connor was correct in perceiving something extremely unusual—by television standards—in *Katherine*. It *was* a phenomenon of sorts for network television to depict a radical opponent of the established order with simple human compassion and respect.

How *did* such a movie get on national television? It was not easy. There were compromises to make and obstacles to overcome. And in the end, it was a news event over which Kagan and his producer had no control which won the movie an air date.

The ABC executives who were in charge of overseeing *Katherine* asked Kagan to make some significant deletions in his script. Kagan fought to keep in everything he thought was essential, but he was forced to give up some of his material. One of the things taken out of *Katherine*, says Kagan, was specific information about the radical underground: "how people get around from place to place, how people make false identities..." ABC told Kagan it was cutting this material out "for dramatic reasons." "So," says the writer-director, "there was some logic to it other than political logic and I was able to deal with it and even accept it."

The network also objected to the documentary news footage which was used to put Katherine's life in the context of the times, and the limbo room scenes in which Katherine speaks directly to the audience and explains her actions. "Their reasoning," says Kagan, "was it was too jarring and didn't add dramatically (to the movie)." But Kagan adamantly refused to surrender these sections of his movie. In the end, all he lost of the news montages were a few images (like those of Walt Disney and Mickey Mouse) which he could not get legal permission to use and two lines from the first limbo room scene. This scene was meant to show that Katherine's radicalism was motivated, in part, by the love she felt for her country. The lines which Kagan was told to cut from Katherine's speech were: "I remember reading once that Thomas Jefferson said 'God forbid this country should go twenty years without a rebellion.' I think of myself as merely carrying on that tradition." Presumably, the network did not want to see a member of the Weather Underground ideologically linked with one of the founding fathers.

The most serious cuts ABC dictated involved scenes in which political strategy was discussed. "What they made me cut," says Kagan, "would have made the film a little more politically sophisticated. In terms of (showing) the political growth of a number of individuals. You would have watched scenes where they discussed political approaches. Tactics would have been verbally debated, rather than just visually shown. You would have seen much more information about what was expected to happen in Chicago (during the 1968 Democratic convention). There was an entire scene about that." That scene, says Kagan, would have shown that SDS initially opposed the Chicago demonstration, and then later decided to go in order to organize the large numbers of young people who were expected to be there—*not*, says Kagan, in order to provoke a violent confrontation with the Chicago police.

One of *Katherine's* more regrettable defects was its failure to clearly convey that Weatherman was just *one* tendency within the New Left. The underground path which Kagan's lead character chooses to follow was not the one taken by most of her brothers and sisters. Weatherman's political perspective was vigorously debated within the antiwar movement and in the end was repudiated by the vast majority of radical activists. But *Katherine* only hints at this. During the one strategy meeting which did appear in the movie, a young man rises to his feet to denounce armed violence as "counterproductive." It is advocated, he says, by those who "don't want to do the hard political work of changing people's minds. We've got to educate the public to what's going on. Once they see what's really happening, then they'll join us." This is all we hear in the way of left wing opposition to Weatherman.

Kagan agrees that the movie did not "give enough attention" to the debates about Weatherman within the left. The scene in which armed struggle is politically discussed was much longer and more developed, says Kagan, in his original script. "In the original, the split (between pro and anti-Weatherman factions) was much more delineated. The two sides were much more clear." But ABC felt that the TV audience would be bored by a substantive strategy discussion. "I had to fight to make sure that one line (about educating the public) stayed in," remarks Kagan. "I mean it was at a level where I said, 'If that line doesn't stay, I don't stay.' It was only a line, I realize, but it's one of the most important lines for me...in the entire film."

Even after tampering with *Katherine*, ABC was still nervous about broadcasting it. The TV movie was originally scheduled to air on September 26; but soon after it was pre-screened for Fred Silverman, ABC's new head of programming, it was pulled from the network's fall lineup and tentatively rescheduled for December. "In (Silverman's) mind," says Kagan, "the movie would get low ratings, and it would cause a great deal of controversy. He had just come over to ABC, and he wasn't going to be responsible for having a radical film on the air."

Kagan, fearing that his movie would become a victim of network timidity, went to friends of his in the press to alert them to the problems which *Katherine* was encountering. But before it became necessary to argue the case for *Katherine* in public, a major media event occurred which changed ABC's mind: on September 18 Patty Hearst and her two Symbionese Liberation Army companions, Bill and Emily Harris, were captured by the FBI in San Fransisco. The newspapers ran banner stories, the eyewitness newscasters could talk about little else. In the ABC hierarchy's simple-minded view, the fictional tale of Katherine Alman bore a distinct resemblance to the true-life adventures of Patty Hearst—enough anyway to allow them to capitalize on this new flurry of publicity. Two days after the arrest, ABC slipped *Katherine* back into its fall schedule. Political considerations gave way to commercial ones. Silverman had vowed to make the number three network into number one, and he was not about to pass up an opportunity for high ratings like this.

Katherine, in fact, did perform well for ABC. It won a substantial share of the audience, against the tough competition of "Kojak." "*Katherine* got on the air," says Kagan, "because by putting themselves down (politically) they got an audience. Because the radical left to America is a great adventure."

Because Kagan was the son of a rabbi who marched for peace and civil rights, because he had gone to college during a period when it was exceedingly difficult for concerned students not to be affected by radical ideas and activities, because he was a serious craftsman who took pride in the integrity of his work...Kagan's movie about 1960s activism was *not* crudely drawn and sensationalistic. To his credit, he refused to make a TV drama which was essentially exploitative.

After *Katherine* was aired, Kagan's career entered a new stage. He began receiving numerous offers to direct theatrical features. "I don't think I will do just any feature film," commented Kagan, as he surveyed his future. "I have strong ambitions, but I'm not Stephen Speilberg. I don't just want to be a movie director, although that's an enormous thing to want to be. And Speilberg can do it and he's terrific and I admire his talent enormously. But then I feel a different kind of responsibility. Now maybe I'll lose that, maybe I'll replace it and rationalize it. But I doubt it. *Katherine* makes me think there's so much more to know. There are more films like it in me that need to be made."

*****

In July 1977, more than twenty-one months after *Katherine* was originally aired, Kagan had yet another run-in with ABC over his controversial TV movie. The network announced that on Friday July 22 it was airing *Katherine* back-to-back with another TV feature which was first shown in October 1975, and cutting down each of them from their original two hours to ninety minutes. Kagan reportedly "freaked out" when he learned that one-quarter of his movie was going to be chopped out, and together with producer Jerry Isenberg, he confronted ABC vice president Brandon Stoddard. After what *Variety* called "a mild duel in (Stoddard's) executive suite," it was announced that the truncated version of *Katherine* would be replaced by another TV feature. Kagan had successfully withstood one more attempt to gut his carefully constructed social drama. "I'm really impressed," Kagan told *Variety*, "that every now and then when you confront the system with your own beliefs, they'll bow to them when they see your beliefs are right." According to Kagan, the ABC brass acknowledged they had made a mistake and apologized for it. It was one of those rare occasions when network power gives in to the will of its creative personnel. Said Kagan: "They recognized that this particular film, because it's one of the few political films that they dared to make in the first place, was so well balanced in its own construction that to take a quarter out of it would be to maim it beyond recognition. They admitted it and immediately got working on it, and I'm very pleased. I find this exception enormously encouraging."

Postscript:

Kagan made his debut as a screen director in late 1977 with the movie *Heroes*, starring Henry Winkler as a Vietnam war veteran. The film received poor critical notices, but performed well at the box office. His next assignment was *The Big Fix*, which features Richard Dreyfuss as private detective Moses Wine—a man, says Kagan, "who grew up in and gained his identity from the sixties. It was an era of idealism that is now over and Moses Wine is adjusting."

Mike Gray

Mike Gray was running a television commercial production company in Chicago called the Film Group when the social movements of the sixties began to have an impact on him. Gray interrupted his commercial work at various key moments to make documentary films about the period. In the summer of 1966, Chicago became the site of a major civil rights confrontation when Martin Luther King and other black leaders launched a drive to end housing discrimination in the city's all-white neighborhoods. Gray accompanied civil rights protestors on a harrowing march through the segregated suburb, Cicero, and recorded the experience on film. Two years later, Gray and his film unit went into the streets again to film the demonstrations outside the Democratic National Convention. The filmmakers' original intention, says Gray, was to show "what really happened" in the summer of 1968, but it was subsequently decided that the convention should not be treated as an isolated event. So the film's focus shifted to the city's poor communities and the ongoing battle against police harassment, bad housing, and unemployment. The seventy-five minute feature was released the following year under the title *American Revolution 2*.

After the Democratic Convention, Gray became involved with Movement activities on a day to day basis. The filmmaker felt that he was part of the events which he was covering. "I was no spectator," he remarks. But Gray did not think of himself as a political filmmaker working in the service of the Movement. "I thought of myself as a political filmmaker in the service of justice, which has always been an obsession of mine. And the Movement certainly expressed my sense of justice much more clearly than any other structure in society. However, I have never considered myself to be in the service of the Movement. There are certain limitations there." Radical filmmakers in the 1960s, declares Gray, too often became enmeshed in "political considerations which had nothing to do with communication, and which tended to obscure their understanding of where people were really at. We (in the Film Group) had a terrific advantage in that regard because our commercial work forced us constantly to deal with people who were outside our political context...We were forced to have this continuing contact with people outside the Movement and it kept us a little clear. However, we succumbed in our own ways. I mean we put a lot of stuff in one film that was politically motivated, and not motivated by a sense of communication. But life was like that; I can't really criticize that in the movie."

In the course of filming *American Revolution 2*, Gray became acquainted with Fred Hampton, the young chairman of the Illinois Black Panther Party. "He was an incredibly dynamic human being," recalls Gray. "He stopped us all dead in our tracks. He was one of the first people I'd ever known who was unafraid, and that has a remarkable effect on people." Before *Revolution* was completed, Gray and his associates began making a movie about Hampton and the local Panther organization. Gray and his crew had shot about 50,000 feet of film when, on December 4th 1969, they received a phone call telling them that Hampton and another Panther had been killed by the Chicago police during a pre-dawn raid on the Party's headquarters.

Plans for the bloody assault had been set in motion weeks earlier when the FBI supplied the Chicago police and the Cook County state's attorney's office with a detailed floor map of the apartment where Hampton slept. There is evidence that Hampton was drugged the night before the raid to make sure he would offer no resistance. None of this was known at the time however. The official version was that the police had gone to the Panther apartment to conduct an authorized search and had been subjected to withering gunfire from within. It was a miracle, state prosecutor Edward V. Hanrahan told the press, that there were no police casualties.

Gray and his associates did not accept the authorities' explanation of the killings and their film at that point became an unofficial inquest. The filmmakers carefully photographed Hampton's bullet-ridden and blood-stained apartment soon after the raid. This footage was then assembled with interviews with survivors of the assault, the testimony of a ballistics expert, and TV newsfilm of Hanrahan's press conferences and a police reenactment of the incident. The resulting film, which was titled *The Murder of Fred Hampton*, effectively unravels the lies and contradictions which hold together the official version of the raid. Bullet holes which were allegedly caused by Panther gunfire are shown to be nailheads or the result of incoming police fire. Hanrahan, scrambling to maintain his credibility, denies making statements we have just seen him make.

The Murder of Fred Hampton is somewhat marred as a film by its unquestioning, devotional attitude toward the Panthers; this problem is particularly evident in the first half of the film which is composed largely of scenes from Panther rallies and demonstrations. Gray and editor Howard Alk let too much militant posturing and suicidal rhetoric go by without comment. But the film's significance as an expose of official violence and illegality is undeniable. "My interest in the Black Panther Party was motivated strictly by a sense of respect for the Constitution," says Gray. "The injustices perpetrated against them, as we now see quite clearly from documents out of J. Edgar Hoover's own filing cabinet, were quite monumental. A staggering amount of the FBI's energy was focused on these people, and it finally snuffed them out."

The December 4 police raid grew into a raging public controversy. "Hanrahan was inundated with criticism," says Gray. "He had misinterpreted the situation. He had thought that Hampton was just another 'loud-mouthed nigger,' and they'd been blowing away 'loud-mouthed niggers' in Chicago since time immemorial—with very little consequence. And all of a sudden, here are bankers and businessmen and responsible leaders in the community who are outraged and saying so on editorial pages. It was quite unexpected." Gray became deeply involved in the events which followed the raid. Part of his film was shown to a Chicago Grand Jury which eventually returned indictments against Hanrahan and the police officers involved. He worked hard to defeat Hanrahan during the state's attorney's 1972 reelection bid. Gray's production outfit offered to make TV and radio commercials for any of the incumbent's opponents who wanted them. "We went in there with hammer and tong and concentrated all our energies and managed finally to beat him."

The Murder of Fred Hampton was completed in 1971. Because of the film's powerful and topical subject matter, Gray and his colleagues were hopeful that it would receive wide distribution. There was no alternative film network capable of distributing the documentary on a mass scale so Gray tried selling it to Hollywood distributors. The film's chances were boosted by a successful screening at Cannes Film Festival and favorable reviews in a number of publications, including the *New York Times* and *Variety*.* Producer Bert Schneider, who was politically sympathetic to the film, helped introduce Gray to some key business figures in the movie industry. Warner Brothers executive John Calley at one time expressed an interest in the film, says Gray, but the studio later vetoed it. In the end, Gray's efforts to find a major Hollywood distributor for *The Murder of Fred Hampton* proved unsuccessful. "The thing that I was impressed by here in Hollywood," remarks the filmmaker, "was the questions on the part of the distributors: 'Why isn't the film in color? Who is this guy Hampton? What other movies has he played in?' and so on. I began to notice a pattern. There is no question that the political content of the film was frightening to certain people. But, in general, the main reservations about the film seemed to be related to these other questions.

The Murder of Fred Hampton was eventually picked up by a distribution company in New York called Videotape Network, but the audience it drew was discouragingly small. The film stayed within the general distribution boundaries of the average political documentary. "I remember I went back to Chicago shortly after I had moved to Los Angeles," says Gray. "It was December 1973 and there was a memorial service for Hampton at the Church of the Epiphany, which is on the South Side of Chicago. It's a big old Gothic structure that was put there when the Catholic Church reigned supreme in Chicago. It has an eighty or ninety foot rise to the top of the

---

*"Although it is unabashedly biased and it is flawed in technical execution," wrote the *Times* critic, "it emerges as a disturbingly somber illustration of some of the ills that beset us and our social system." Declared business-wise *Variety*: "(The) film probably will become an underground blockbuster and will clearly do extremely well in many black communities and on campus."

vault and seating for a thousand or two—a big cruciform
Gothic cathedral. And in the room there were maybe forty or
fifty of the faithful, most of the faces recognizable. Way up in
front there was a tiny screen, you know. And a little Kodak
Pageant projector with a little internal speaker, and *The Murder
of Fred Hampton* was playing. And these images that we had
labored over at the laboratories for countless numbers of
hours were little wavering shapes, indistinguishable on this
tiny screen. And the sound was wafting off into the marble
vastness and echoing back and all you could hear was this
waaar-waaar. But it didn't make any difference because everybody there had seen the film maybe two or three times
already.

"That is the inherent problem of the political documentary. I sensed it at the time we were making the film, I thought
it was going to be a problem. But it was not possible to do
anything about it. We were simply committed to a course of
action and had to see it through to its conclusion. Given the
same information, the same set of circumstances, I would
unhesitatingly do exactly the same thing again. You're stuck,
you know—but you don't have to keep doing it."

After *The Murder of Fred Hampton*, Gray began to reexamine
his decision to make political documentaries. Independent
nonfiction filmmaking seemed to raise insoluble distribution
problems. Television would not broadcast the type of documentaries he wanted to produce, Gray was convinced. And
large audiences could not be lured into the movie theaters,
unless some way could be found of making documentaries
entertaining. How could nonfiction films be made to be as
dramatically engaging as fictional features? This was an
artistic puzzle for which Gray did not yet have an answer. "I'm
really not certain that *Murder of Fred Hampton* could have been
successful with any distribution system," comments the
filmmaker. "Because I think there is a very real consideration
here which we must address ourselves to, and that is the
extreme difficulty of assembling an audience which will pay
money to see a film like that, one which is going to depress the
hell out of them. I mean the movie has a heavy impact, and
everybody who sees it is glad they saw it, but they walk out of
the theater like they've been smacked in the face with a two-

by-four. I have come to believe that the reason the vast majority of people go to the movies is to be entertained. Now that doesn't mean that it can only be The Three Stooges. Even Hollywood has risen above that. But those considerations must be attended to; it's something that I grew very sensitive to."

The more Gray dwelled on the importance of reaching a mass audience, the more his thoughts focused on Hollywood. No cultural artifact had more power and mystique, it seemed to him, than a Hollywood motion picture. In November 1973, Gray moved to Los Angeles with his mind set on becoming a writer and director of feature-length movies. "I believe that here in Hollywood is the key to the problem," he says. "At the very moment that the culture has become fragmented, we have the tools handed to us for re-forming it and reshaping it and bringing it back together and making sense out of it through the communications engine that exists in this town. What goes down here affects—and *has* affected, we now see clearly—the course of world history...This is where it's possible to actually get a hand on the throttle, as it were— there's no other place you can do it."

Gray's decision to enter the movie industry was based on the assumption that one could make features with socially provocative content if one could master the Hollywood style of storytelling. He rejected the idea that a progressive film-maker's work had to be "totally pure and have brand new form as well as new content." Those political filmmakers who put strong emphasis on developing a "revolutionary style," be-lieved Gray, generally had trouble communicating with a broad audience. Their style was too self-conscious and distracting. His films would present alternative viewpoints in the traditional Hollywood forms—forms which were readily accepted by the masses of movie-going Americans. "I'm looking for the most natural way to get the story in front of the audience," remarks Gray, "a way that leaves me appar-ently out of the picture altogether."

Soon after he arrived in Los Angeles, Gray began "re-tooling" himself, i.e., "learning those crude fundamentals that these shoe salesmen out here have discovered to be infallible—conflict, resolution, character development, sus-pense, and dramatic thrust—whatever you call it that holds the fucking audience riveted to their chairs and leaves them wanting to see more of it, and going out and telling people 'You gotta see it!' Not something you *should* see, but something you *have* to see." Gray had never written a fictional feature before, so he had to learn the dramatic structure of Hollywood movies from scratch. He taught himself screenwriting by soliciting advice from a twenty-six year old University of Wisconsin graduate who had just sold his first script and by carefully studying the works of past masters. "I read somewhere that Hemingway had learned to write by writing all the great novels, he wrote them out in longhand. He would sit there at his desk and copy *Madame Bovary* word for word. So I decided to sit down with James Agee's script, *The African Queen,* which I felt was one of the more remarkable in terms of its flow, its structure, its description, and do the same...It only takes a couple days, you know, but once you've done it you walk away with an entirely different comprehension, one that you cannot get from simply reading it, no matter how carefully you read it. It has to do with the words flowing back through the fingers to the brain."

After a brief and disappointing adventure in network television, Gray began researching and writing a feature-length screenplay on the subject of nuclear power. He spent one year traveling around the country, interviewing scientists and public interest lawyers and visiting nuclear power plants. He spent several more years shaping and reshaping this raw information into a suspenseful drama which he titled *The China Syndrome.* The plot revolved around an accident in a nuclear power plant and the attempts to cover it up. It raised ominous questions about the safety of nuclear technology.

The central message of *The China Syndrome* was new and different but the script contained many of the traditional dramatic elements of the Hollywood thriller as well, including, says Gray, "tits and ass, guns, and a chase." When asked to justify his use of these elements, the filmmaker fell back on a standard defense—the audience (and hence, the industry) demanded it. "I was explaining the movie to some twenty-one year old revolutionary a short time ago," he remarks, "—and I must say in his defense that he didn't know my political credentials, he didn't know where I was coming from at all. He just heard the words and jumped to the wrong conclusion. I was telling him about this movie that I was making, and I said, 'It's going to have tits and ass, a chase scene, guns, etc.' And the guy *jumped* up from the table and started swearing at me and calling me a low-life Hollywood creep and a sellout and everything like that, you know. Now that kind of knee-jerk reaction does not serve us well. Because you must relate to people where they're at. I mean if society consisted only of followers of Nietzsche, for example, or there were only erudite English literature majors out there, then our problem would be infinitely different. But that's simply not the case."

What lifted his screenplay above the normal Hollywood fare, Gray believed, was what it had to say about nuclear power. "The content basically is about something that actually matters a great deal in terms of the survival of humanity," he says. Gray had difficulty selling the script, in part because of its controversial subject matter and critical perspective. One producer, says the filmmaker, bluntly stated in his rejection letter that he refused to be associated with "this political sabotage of the nuclear power industry."

The sale was complicated even more by the fact that Gray insisted on also directing the feature. Gray had never directed a dramatic film before and no producer seemed willing to take a chance with him. But the filmmaker was strongly reluctant to relinquish control of the material because he knew it might be badly altered if it fell into the wrong hands. "There is a danger of turning it into a science fiction movie...I mean every facet of the story is just incredible. Every piece of information is stunning. But I can substantiate all of it. People will have a tendency to say, 'That can't be true.' So it's extremely important that the film look like reality on every level. The little details are absolutely essential. For example, the guys who operate nuclear power plants do not wear white smocks at all. They wear everyday clothes like yours and mine and their union badges—the International Brotherhood of Electrical Workers. It's the same union that wires your house. The entire training that they've had for operating a nuclear power plant probably comes from a gig in the Navy and six weeks at General Electric. And their comprehension of what's going on downstairs is marginal at best. So when they throw the wrong switch, to them it's just the wrong switch, the same as it would be at any other power plant, although in this case the consequences may be catastrophic. These workers must be shown as real people. But Hollywood's inclination is to exaggerate them and make them larger than life."

Finally, in 1976, after a long and frustrating search, Gray struck a deal with Michael Douglas, the young co-producer of *One Flew Over the Cuckoo's Nest*. Gray's contract did not stipulate that he must be given the directing assignment on *The China Syndrome*, but Douglas verbally promised to do as much as he could to get Gray the job. Gray felt that was sufficient: "I said I believed him because when Michael Douglas says that he's going to make his best effort, I have a sense that he means what he says." After signing with Douglas, Gray set about revising the screenplay, with the help of the producer and a rewrite man, to get it ready for production in mid-1977.

When he first began marketing *The China Syndrome*, the filmmaker had serious doubts about the willingness of the movie industry to manufacture such a "politically sensitive" film. Yet a couple years later, the film was scheduled to go before the cameras with a budget estimated at $2.3 million. What made Hollywood willing to produce a feature about the hazards of nuclear power? First of all, responds Gray, public awareness about nuclear power has steadily grown. "The nuclear power industry is on the defensive," he says. "They cannot make the audacious kinds of moves they were able to in the past, when, for instance, they would try to get critics fired from their jobs and things like that. Also there have been a lot of thriller stories in the press and on television about this subject...The point is it's no longer possible to keep the damn thing out of the public eye." Secondly, says Gray, the film was carefully designed to be "apparently non-political." By this Gray means that the film focuses its blame on out-of-control technological forces rather than corporations and individuals. Gray believes that everybody—including those who run the energy industries—has in some way been victimized by the shift to nuclear power.

"There was the initial decision on my part to make a true story about nuclear power, and that in and of itself is political," says the filmmaker. "But the film itself does not take the posture that one might expect; in other words, this is not an environmentalist diatribe. Rather it is a movie about a series of events in which there is no villain. Everybody in the movie is heroic in his own way. Everybody is confronted with overwhelming problems. This is true of the power company; they're confronted with staggering problems which they do their damndest to deal with. But they simply cannot overcome the inherent flaws of nuclear technology. So the film illustrates the kind of situation we face today, where everyone doing the very best job that he can within his own specific area combines to bring about disaster."

In the course of working in Hollywood and putting *The China Syndrome* into production, Gray has come to various conclusions about what is and is not possible in large scale commercial filmmaking. It is not possible, he says, to make features whose social perspective is considerably more advanced than the consciousness of the mass audience. "The distance you can take your audience in terms of the new information that you're going to give them is inversely proportionate to the size of the audience. In other words, you can do a film like *The Murder of Fred Hampton* that has an overwhelming effect on a very small audience. Or you can do a broader picture on the same issue for wide distribution. But it must be more attenuated in what it says or else you'll lose your audience... You will always find a narrow audience for some shocking truth. But that same shocking truth will be too shocking for a broader audience... There are certain kinds of things that people will go for, and there are certain things that they won't."

So the audience itself, asserts Gray, imposes its own set of ideological constraints on the Hollywood filmmaker. As for the producers, he says, their overriding concern is profit. There is a limited number who will object to socially provocative scripts for political reasons, comments the filmmaker, including the one who rejected *The China Syndrome* because of its perspective on nuclear power. "But," says Gray, "I'm convinced that in general the people in charge of this industry couldn't care less about the subject of the picture as long as it makes money."

Gray acknowledges that producers' ideas of what will make money are largely shaped by what has been profitable in the past. "If the story material you submit to them falls totally out of the framework of anything that they've known before," he says, "then you have a more difficult problem." Stories whose profit potential is not immediately recognizable may be passed over completely. This is a form of censorship which occurs commonly in Hollywood—it's not "political" in the strict sense of the word, but "economic."

Nevertheless, maintains Gray, the range of subjects, issues and ideas that can be explored on the screen is still remarkably broad. The fact that *The China Syndrome* is going into production is a clear indication to him that the system is not closed to progressive filmmakers, that there is room inside in which to maneuver. "Here's the point," he says, "—in the next few weeks a major studio is going to be giving us more than two million dollars—an amount of money I've never seen before—to make a movie that is at the very least extremely controversial. And why are they going to do that? They're going to do that on the basis of one man's word—Michael Douglas. A man who happened to see something in my script. That's the way it works."

*****

Communication—the free flow of ideas—is the key to a truly democratic society, Gray believes. That is why Hollywood—the capital of television and film production—represents, in his opinion, "the focus of struggle. It's why everybody is here. I mean this is L.A.'s moment." Gray feels confident that Hollywood's production machinery can be converted to the manufacture of humane dreams. He thinks of himself as part of a growing wave of progressive filmmakers which will eventually succeed in becoming the dominant force in the movie industry. "More conscientious filmmakers are emerging all the time," he says. "Younger people are coming out, the business is going to be taken over by people who feel a sincere (social) responsibility, as opposed to (director Sam) Peckinpah who admits gleefully that he's a whore. I mean those people will always be around, you'll always have whores. But there are going to be other people whose ideas and commercial success will be just as spectacular, but whose responsibility to the culture, to humanity is a much more sincere commitment."

The creative achievements of this new wave of socially concerned filmmakers, predicts Gray, will surpass those made

in Hollywood during the highly charged 1930s. The dissolution of the old studio system, he feels, has given creative
filmmakers a measure of freedom which they did not enjoy in
those years. "The significant difference between then and
now is that the situation is much less controlled now, from the
establishment's viewpoint. At that time, if a handful of
powerful people said 'That idea is not going to emerge,' it
simply did not emerge. It was totally suppressed. That is not
possible now—power is more dispersed."

Gray concedes that it will not be easy for progressives to
climb into the industry's top creative levels. It is difficult
enough to master Hollywood's dramatic forms, he says,
without trying to infuse them with some deeper social
significance. But he regards the future with a sense of
"tremendous optimism." There will come a day, he feels, when
people with his social perspective will be as adept at fabricating
Hollywood fantasies as anyone ever was. "Hollywood can be
taken over, simply because the people who are in the operating
positions are not that smart. They just try not to rock the boat
and they're able to adapt the forms and use them for their own
personal commercial advancement. There is no reason that
we cannot do precisely the same thing, with a slightly different
motivation. As long as we don't lose our focus, and don't lose
our nerve and don't become overwhelmed and discouraged,
we can succeed."

Postscript:

In spring 1977, Columbia Pictures decided to finance the
modestly budgeted *China Syndrome* with Mike Gray as director.
Richard Dreyfuss, Jack Lemmon, and Michael Douglas agreed
to play the leading roles for considerably less money than they
normally receive. Shortly before the film was to go into
production, however, Dreyfuss asked for his standard salary
of $500,000 and the budget suddenly climbed. Columbia
refused to put up the extra money, because Gray had no prior
experience as a Hollywood director, and the film project
collapsed. "A motion picture deal is like a house of cards," says
Gray, "until the cameras start rolling. If the slightest thing
goes wrong, the whole structure can fall apart."

At this point, Jane Fonda entered the picture. For some
time, the actress had been trying to put together a movie based

on the life of Karen Silkwood, the woman who died while trying to expose the unsafe conditions at an Oklahoma plutonium plant. Columbia rejected Fonda's screenplay (which was written by former *Rolling Stone* reporter Joe Eszterhas) but suggested that she get involved in *China Syndrome*. The actress agreed and *China Syndrome* was rewritten to give her a starring role.

As soon as Fonda became involved in the film project, it turned into a major production. Michael Douglas fought to keep Gray in the director's chair. But, says Gray, "The studio told Douglas, 'You're crazy if you think the bankers in New York will put up $5 million for a picture with an unknown director.' " In the end, Gray was removed and James Bridges (*Paper Chase*, *Sept.30, 1955*) was given the directing assignment. The movie went into production in February 1978.

"The mistake I made," says Gray in retrospect, "was in tackling too big a project as my first film. It was always in danger of getting away from me because of the elaborate sets and high production costs." His next screen project, says Gray, will be so small scale that he can maintain control of it.

Although he is disappointed that he was not allowed to direct *China Syndrome*, Gray says it will still be a provocative and realistic movie. "All of those connected with the film are doing their best. I think everyone is gripped by the importance of the subject."

Gray remains deeply convinced that Hollywood is the right place to be for progressive filmmakers. "Everything works by the numbers here. Once you learn how to press the buttons, you've got it made. This industry is bubbling over with talented, concerned people—many of whom have arrived here recently from the East. It's very exciting to be here right now."

Bruce Green

Bruce Green was not burning with the same ambitions which torment most film school graduates when, in 1973, he began looking for work in Hollywood: he did not yearn with all his soul to become a director, a studio titan, a producer, or a screenwriter. He was, in fact, uncertain about his future. Some of those he had known at the California Institute of the Arts were already laying the foundations for successful film careers (including Thom Mount, who is a former roommate of Green's). But Green had no carefully worked-out plans. For awhile, he considered returning to New York, where he had grown up, to seek work in the documentary news division of one of the major TV networks. But Hollywood's allure proved stronger. He decided to stay where he was and explore employment possibilities in the entertainment capital. Green donned a suit and made the rounds, offering himself to more than thirty producers, executives, and publicists at various movie studios. He expected to be given a menial assignment and to be paid little money for long hours of labor (in short, he expected to be taken advantage of). But he was young and inexperienced and he had no guardian angels in Hollywood's highest offices, so there was really no alternative.

"I was looking for anything," remembers Green. "I told people that I would fetch coffee, deliver mail, things like that. I knew enough not to be the kind of obnoxious film student who comes in and announces, 'I want to direct feature films,' or 'I want to be an editor.' I was looking for anything. I wanted to make $125 a week, enough money to pay the rent and cover living expenses, and just kind of feel my way around and see what the situation was."

For the average young person starting out in Hollywood, however, even "anything" is hard to find. "I was told things like you have to be the son of a director to get a job in the mailroom," says Green. Finally he landed a job as a "production assistant" on an industrial relations film. For $90 a week, the film school graduate picked up McDonald's lunches for the crew and performed a variety of other chores. Although Green was pleased to be working, he felt uncomfortable about the content of the film which he was helping to make. The purpose of the documentary, says Green, was to teach foremen "how to manipulate their workers, how to compliment a worker and how to bawl out a worker so that he or she still works hard for you and doesn't resent you...It was really awful."

But the young man soon found a way to relate to his work which allowed him to keep on going. "I stopped worrying about being a hypocrite. I snapped into the frame of mind of an anthropologist, and I said to myself, 'Here I am in this completely alien world and I'm just watching it from a distance and learning about it.' " If he had not developed this faculty, he would have found it much more difficult to make a living in Hollywood.

The next job Green found was in a small, non-union film lab. He worked the night shift, preparing prints of the old "Mod Squad" TV show for nationwide syndication. It was tedious and meaningless work, and Green sought to liven it up by using his creative imagination: he sometimes removed the frames which indicated where the commercials were supposed to go, he occasionally reversed the order of the scenes. "It wasn't a conscious political act on my part," says Green. "I was just doing it because I was really bored and it was such a terrible job. 'Nobody in the world should have to do this,' I thought. And I really resented the people who ran the place. It wasn't a union job, so they didn't pay decent wages. So I became very creative. I decided I was going to get back at them and have some fun." The lab management failed to appreciate the whimsical touches which Green brought to his work and he was promptly dismissed. "You know, ever since then I've had the hope that someday I'll be in a motel in Kansas or someplace and I'll be watching an episode of 'Mod Squad,' and all of a sudden the actors will come on the screen upside down. That would make me feel wonderful!"

After hustling a few other odd jobs, Green joined with a friend from Cal Arts to set up an optical effects business. Though the two had no capital to invest, they managed to gain possession of a reasonably priced optical printer which they arranged to pay for over time. They soon became skilled at creating optical and special effects with the sophisticated machine. During the first year they were in business, Green and his partner earned Academy Award consideration for their work on *One by One*, a documentary about Grand Prix race car drivers. They also worked on major motion pictures such as *Hearts and Minds* and *The Trial of Billy Jack*.

But building a successful "optical house" did not interest Green for long. "I didn't want to own my own company," he says. "It was emotionally and creatively too much of a burden. I found that the majority of my time was going into hustling people, you know, being a salesman. 'Use us, use us, use us.' I would take a reel of our film around town and visit four or five people a day; I'd show them the effects and talk with them and try to get them to give us work. The rest of my time went into other business chores like accounting, figuring out how much to charge people for effects, and so on. I realized that if I stayed with it, the best I could hope to become was a very successful owner of an optical effects company—which meant that I'd be an employer, a member of management. I'd become everything which I resented."

After leaving his promising enterprise, Green went back to working as a production assistant—this time for Dove Films, a television commercial production company owned by cinematographer Haskell Wexler and Cal Bernstein. Again he was the person responsible for providing the crew with coffee and donuts and running errands. But after a short time in this role, Green worked his way into production. He held slates, announced the scene and take numbers, kept camera reports, and helped maintain the camera equipment—tasks generally performed by the second assistant cameraperson. But because Green could not get into the International Alliance of Theatrical and Stage Employees (IATSE), Hollywood's exclusive craft union, he could not officially become a second assistant cameraperson. He could only do the work and learn.

Green was delighted by the comfortable salary which Dove paid him. For the first time in his life, he says, he was making $200 to $300 a week. "It was more money than I ever dreamed of, and I was enjoying it," remarks Green. Though the company produced commercials for giant corporations like General Motors and Coca-Cola, Green's conscience did not disturb him. A young worker like him was in no position to be discriminating. He was new to the industry, he lacked the union's protection, he was one of many thousands who were scrambling for a place in Hollywood's production force. If he threw this job away, who knew how long it would take to find another? And what were the chances of someone like him finding a job in Hollywood which was any more socially commendable than this? His job at Dove afforded him the opportunity of working with talented and agreeable people and learning a great deal about the technical aspects of filmmaking. This was as much as one could expect under the circumstances.

"I learned more about filmmaking in one year at Dove," declares Green, "than I had learned in four years of college. Mainly because Haskell Wexler was very generous with his knowledge. He would set up a light on the set and I would go up to him and ask him why he did that. And he would say, 'Well, I did this because of such-and-such. This is the kick light and this is what it does, and this is the fill light, and this is the ratio of lights; and I'm using this to reflect that light instead of this because this is the look I'm aiming for. Why don't you come to the dailies and see what this stuff looks like.' He was just a great teacher. I feel very, very lucky that I got to work with him."

There were other first-rate cameramen at Dove Films besides Wexler—Conrad Hall, Laszlo Kovaks, and Vilmos Zsigmond among them. Being around these skillful craftsmen and watching them work made Green want to become a cinematographer. On the sets where he worked, it was always these men who seemed to be the creative centers of production. It was they who seemed the most stimulated by their work.

Soon after Green's first year at Dove had passed, Wexler decided to leave the company and devote himself entirely to dramatic features and political documentaries. As a result, business dropped off and most of the production workers were laid off, including Green. After a year of economic comfort, Green was again in the position of having to scramble for freelance assignments. He got a temporary job testing camera lenses for the Academy of Motion Picture Arts and Sciences, he worked on a film about a PGA golf tournament, but he could not find anything more. He had been out of circulation during his tenure at Dove—people did not know him, no one thought of him when they had a crew position to fill. Green tried to find ways to keep himself occupied until something came along. On Saturday mornings he and a few friends went to a camera store to study photographic equipment; he took up screenwriting, a favorite pastime among the underemployed in Hollywood. "I wrote a script, just because everybody writes scripts in Hollywood," he remarks. "Not for any important reason. I wrote a silly exploitation script to keep myself from looking for work."

While he was unemployed, Green became more conscious of the gaps in his life. It seemed that all he had been concerned with since leaving Cal Arts was making a living. While in high school and college during the sixties and early seventies, he had been active in the antiwar movement. He knew what it was like to be part of a mass struggle for social change. But since going to work in the entertainment industry, he had become disconnected from political activities. Was this all a natural part of growing up and entering the marketplace? Green didn't think so. He expected more out of life than most young people who were plotting courses in the entertainment industry in the mid-seventies. He wanted more than money and creative recognition. He wanted to regain that sense of social fulfillment which comes from being involved in a cause grander than your career. "I began to strongly feel the need to become politically involved," says Green. "It's hard to explain exactly why. I felt a lack of purpose in my life. Hollywood is not a very purposeful kind of place. At that point I saw Hollywood simply as a place where I could earn my living—but it was not a place that *moved* me. It was not a place where I felt very fulfilled."

Green started doing things he had not done since college: he went to the theater, he attended poetry readings, he took in underground films. At one cultural event, Green bumped into an old acquaintance from Cal Arts, who was wearing an intriguing political button. In red lettering, encircling a red star, the button proclaimed: "Everybody is a Star—The Socialist Media Group." "I was delighted," Green recalls. "The button said, 'Here's a left wing group with a sense of humor and an orientation towards Hollywood.' What more could I want? So I asked the guy about it and he invited me to come to a meeting."

In the fall of 1975, Green began attending Socialist Media Group study sessions on the history of the U.S. left and its relation to culture. The SMG had been founded a year earlier with two basic purposes in mind: 1) to provide a supportive environment for media workers and consumers who felt estranged from commercial culture and wanted to exercise their creative abilities in new ways, and 2) to directly challenge corporate control of the entertainment and news industries. Besides sponsoring study groups, the SMG staged public forums on the media, published pamphlets about the Los Angeles power structure, and helped coordinate publicity for local political events and demonstrations. Regular meetings, which featured film and video screenings and guest speakers, were held in a Santa Monica loft which doubled as the offices of a political film collective. Among the many independent films which were shown and analyzed were: *Union Maids*, a moving documentary about the lives of three veteran labor organizers; *Home Movie*, and *Six Unnatural Acts*, satirical comedies by lesbian filmmaker Jan Oxenberg; *Men's Lives*, a documentary about male socialization; *Last Grave at Dimbaza*, a documentary about South Africa; *Fidel and Cuba*; and *Loose Ends*, a dramatic feature about the dreams and daily frustrations of two garage mechanics. Speakers included filmmakers Haskell Wexler and Shirley Clarke and social activists Dorothy Healey, Stanley Aronowitz, and Stan Weir. The freewheeling discussions which took place during these meetings often centered around fundamental questions such as: how does mass media function as an instrument of social control? who controls the media industries? what can those who are employed in the communications industries do to change the content of their work as well as their working conditions? how can alternative culture be created and nurtured in an environment like Los Angeles which is so completely dominated by Hollywood aesthetics?

There was a loose and amiable quality about the group which set new members at ease. At the beginning of each meeting, everyone said a few words about him or herself and the work in which he or she was involved. Even the most serious and intense discussions were sprinkled with jokes and wisecracks. Those who regularly attended meetings numbered only a few dozen, but the group had grand visions about organizing all those who felt crushed by Hollywood's impoverished imagination.

Soon after discovering the group, Green became an active participant in it, helping to plan its meetings and social events and bringing in new members. "The Socialist Media Group gave me a place where I could meet and talk with other Hollywood craftworkers, and not feel competitive with them. Usually when you meet other people who work in the industry—over lunch or in the street—and one person starts talking about some job, everyone's ears perk up and everybody wants to know about it because there are just not enough jobs to go around. It's kind of cutthroat and you wind up competing for jobs with your best friends. The SMG was set up as a haven from all that.

"There was a real diversity in the group. For the first time, I could sit in a room with film editors, screenwriters, actors, and sound technicians as well as people who worked in other areas of communication—like radio broadcasters, magazine journalists, teachers, novelists, and video-makers. It was really quite a wonderful experience for me; most people in the industry never get anything like it. And the group wasn't so politically single-minded as to alienate people. There were many political tendencies represented in the group, those who identified with the liberal wing of the Democratic Party as well as those who considered themselves Marxists. But the common denominator among these people was that everyone was concerned with the media and wanted it to be much more responsive to the people in this country. So it was a very democratic group and it seemed very appealing to me. I became very involved in it and it filled a big vacuum in my life."

Ever since he had gone to work in Hollywood, Green had been aware of the tremendous disparity between the rich and varied dreams which *could* be produced there and the flat, predictable ones which *were* turned out. But as a lone, struggling craftworker, there seemed to be no possibility at all of making an impact on the industry. Perhaps someday through an organization like the SMG, he could help open up more creative opportunities in film and television.

In a larger sense, becoming involved in a socialist group meant identifying himself with generations of working class struggle. "When I'm active in socialist politics," says Green, "I feel that I am making history. I feel that I am doing the things I read about in history books as a kid." It meant he was unalterably opposed to a system in which his and others' labor power was bought and sold like a commodity, a system in which he had virtually no control over what he produced. "I believe that we in the working class are destined to eventually gain control of our lives. Working people in this country will sooner or later decide that they shouldn't allow the world to be run by others against their interests." Socialism, to Green, meant the liberation of human potential.

When he first entered the entertainment industry, Green did not clearly think of himself as a member of the working class. He had grown up in a middle income milieu and been educated in expensive schools. Classmates of his were on their way to becoming part of Hollywood's creative and managerial elite. He was not sure what his position within the industry would eventually be. At various times he tried his hand at screenwriting and running a small business, and even considered producing a low-budget feature. Collective consciousness among Hollywood craftworkers is weak. It was not until he became involved in the SMG that Green became fully aware of the history of the Hollywood labor movement.

As time went by, however, Green grew increasingly sure of where he fit in the overall structure of the industry. "I saw the direction I was going in. I was becoming a craftworker. I didn't think I was going to become a producer. I didn't have illusions about reaching the lofty position where I could make something like *The Battle of Algiers*. I saw that I was a worker."

Despite his growing working class consciousness, Green was still barred entry to the major union which represents craftworkers. As a result, he was forced to work on non-union productions to make a living. It was a situation which Green found maddeningly ironic and unjust. "I would have loved to have been in the union, to go to all the meetings, to pay my dues, to pay my initiation fee, to become a loyal member. I went to the union office and told them that. I told them, 'I'm strongly pro-union, I come from a union family, I really want to get in.' And they said, 'Tough.' So I felt resentful. I felt the union didn't care about people like me. It seemed like the IATSE was some sort of exclusive fraternity."

Green's dilemma was not unique. There were thousands of other young people who could not find their way into the union. The IATSE is set up to protect the interests of an elite segment of Hollywood's workforce—a segment which is composed largely of older white males. After talking with many people in his same situation, Green decided to do something about exposing the union's exclusivity.

In the winter of 1976, Green produced a one-hour radio documentary titled "The Hollywood Film Unions: Getting In" for KPFK, a publicly supported FM station in Los Angeles. The program, which was first broadcast on March 18, was made up largely of interviews with film workers who had run up against the IATSE's barriers. One person told Green that when he tried to join the union, he was informed there was a two-year waiting list just to obtain an application. Haskell Wexler stated that he had to wait six years to get in the Hollywood cinematographers local of IATSE even though he was already a skilled cameraman. Irving Lerner, who helped establish the New York film editors local of the IATSE during the 1940s, was told when he moved to Los Angeles that he would have to go through an eight year apprenticeship as an assistant editor before he could work in Hollywood as a union editor.

Green's documentary explained that in order to get into the IATSE, a film worker has to work a certain number of days for a producer who is a signatory of the union contract. But no producer who runs a union company will hire someone who does not belong to the union, unless all the union members in that job category are already employed—something which rarely happens in Hollywood. It is a classic catch-22 situation. You have to work on a union film in order to join the IATSE, but you cannot work on a union film if you aren't already in the union.

Green acknowledged the importance of maintaining a seniority system. How else can a union protect its older members, when young workers are invariably given preference during hiring? He also noted that union members have good reason to fear unregulated competition with other workers. A business agent of one IATSE local reported that there were 18,000 film students enrolled in 1976, and only 1500 people in his local—many of whom were unemployed. As long as there are more trained filmmakers than there are jobs, others observed, the rank and file of the IATSE will be very anxious about letting new members into their union.

In his conclusion, Green offered some answers to the problem:

> ...the problem is not people taking jobs away from other people, but one of not enough jobs. The union could be lobbying in the Congress for tax incentives for low-budget filmmaking and demanding that the studios produce more films per year instead of relying on a few blockbusters and many re-issues. Most importantly, the unions could de demanding a percentage of the profits these films bring in. Residuals for crew members who help make these films successful and percentage points for the locals could fill health and welfare and pension funds far beyond their present levels.

> But the union doesn't fight for the rank and file this way. Instead it fights other workers who want to join. Local 659 (of the IATSE) alone has spent over $100,000 in court cases to keep out qualified workers. They have lost all these cases. If the union were democratic and membership were based on talent instead of one's connections or...birth (rights), it would be much stronger.

After completing his program on the IATSE, Green continued to work (out of necessity) on various non-union films. He was employed as a camera assistant on some, as a production assistant on others. Between jobs, he lived off his unemployment checks. In many ways Green's first years' experience in Hollywood typified that of the young, unestablished film worker. He jumped from job to job, labored long hours—often seven days a week—and made relatively little money. Weeks of employment were broken up by stretches of unemployment. When he was out of work, he was always scanning the horizon for forthcoming assignments. The long hard hours, the irregularity of the work, and the insufficient pay might have been enough to drive a person with more personal and economic responsibilities out of the film industry. But Green, who was young and single, found the Hollywood work schedule suitable to his tastes. "Hollywood's a decent place to work, " he says. "It gives me as much money as I need to live, I have a lot of time off, and it can be fun at times...I can't survive in a nine-to-five job. I have tried that before. The film lab was sort of like that. I prefer to work eighteen hours a day, seven days a week for a couple months and then be free for a long time, rather than to work every weekday of the year and get Saturdays and Sundays off."

Green also liked the variety of experiences which freelancing in the film industry provided him. He was not chained to the same desk or machine day in and day out. There was a fresh quality to each new assignment. As wage labor went, film work was fairly interesting. "When you go from job to job in the movie industry, you're always meeting new groups of people and encountering new situations. Some people say that all films are the same—and there are certainly lots of similarities between films—but there are also differences. And every new film is a challenge because there are always new technical and creative problems to solve—and that's fun. It's not like working on the line in an automobile plant where every car comes by the same way and you do the same thing every day. There are not that many occupations in the world that afford you the diversity of experiences which those in the film industry do."

In April 1976, Green landed a job as a production assistant on a low-budget movie called *Cannonball!* It was his first crew assignment on a feature film. Two weeks into the job, Green was promoted to assistant editor. *Cannonball!* was a product of New World Pictures, the film company ruled by B-movie king, Roger Corman. Like its predecessor, *Death Race 2000*, it starred David Carradine as a daredevil driver who goes all out to win a grueling cross-country road race. The picture had just as little artistic and social merit as most Corman productions, which were shot and edited at breakneck speed for less money than anyone else thought possible. Though the picture was indeed "resourcefully made" and boast(ed) competent performances," a critic for the *Los Angeles Times* was to remark, it "is nonetheless just another of New World's spate of mindless destruction derbie(s) that feature mammoth car wrecks above all else."

Nonetheless, Green was grateful for the opportunity to work on the feature. Corman is a figure of almost mythic proportions in Hollywood. Stories abound about all the young, struggling filmmakers who have gained entry to the dazzling world of Hollywood movie-making by working on Corman's "exploitation" features. It is said that Jack Nicholson, Martin Scorcese, and Francis Coppola—among other Hollywood luminaries—got their first breaks from Roger Corman. To Green, breaking into a Corman movie was like getting into postgraduate school.

Green was employed on *Cannonball!* for over three months. He worked an average of eighty hours each week, for a weekly salary of $200. "I don't think I ever worked so hard in my life. I was doing it for the experience—not for the money. I would have made more money as a migrant farmworker...I looked at it as an education. I got a chance to work with some top notch editors and sound effects technicians and I learned quite a lot. I got badly exploited, but I was 'paying my dues' and I was making contacts—which is very important in this industry if you want to keep working."

Despite the highly exploitative nature of low-budget film work, says Green, there is a manic and freewheeling quality to these productions which makes them interesting to work on. "The attitude on the set is 'We're all being abused, but let's make this movie the best we can make it.' And that's what happens. The energy on the set is feverishly high. It's more exciting in some ways than working on big, union productions because there's more creative work going on. Necessity, after all, is the mother of invention... The producer has given you half the amount of money you need, and a third of the time, and has told you that if it is not completed on schedule he will shoot you. So you go out and you do it, and somehow you finish it within budget. I don't know how it happens, but it always turns out that way. It's like everybody's on a sinking ship and you all must pull together to make it through."

Cannonball! was supposed to conclude with a giant auto collision. But there was not enough footage to make the pile-up look sufficiently catastrophic. "So," recalls Green, "the producer came into (the editing room) and told us to use every crash three times. So we took this one piece of film showing a car going from left to right and crashing into another car and we used it once. Then we cut a bunch of other shots together. And then we took the same piece of film and flipped it over so that the car came from *right to left* this time before it crashed. And then we took it and enlarged it and put it on the lefthand side of the screen with another shot... You know, in Europe Corman is famous. People see this kind of stuff and say, 'He's brilliant! He's a genius!' Well, I was in the cutting room when we did it, and I know the reason we did it was because it was a low-budget film and we didn't have any time and money and the picture had to be a certain length to satisfy the distributors... The serious limitations meant that the technicians had to be very creative."

Green says that he was surprised to find out that craftworkers' expertise is valued on Hollywood productions. "I had assumed that I would be treated like a nobody—that no one would ever talk to me. But on every film that I've worked on, I have come to know the director. I've had directors ask me my opinion about various things and they seem to be genuinely interested in knowing what I felt. How often do workers on a GM assembly line get asked by their bosses, 'Hey, what do you think about these cars you're building?' "

The advice which directors solicited from Green was almost always limited to technical matters. But there have been rare occasions, says Green, when he has influenced a film's ideological content. The young film worker proudly asserts that he was responsible for eliminating a sequence from *Cannonball!* which he felt degraded women. In the sequence, a race car driver fondled his stickshift and then slid his hand onto the thigh of the woman sitting next to him, who tensed at his touch.

Green argued that this brief mechanical interaction made the driver, who was supposed to be a sympathetic character, seem lecherous and unappealing. As a result, he said, his death later in the film would not have the emotional impact on the audience which it should. According to Green, the director found this a convincing argument and the sequence was removed. If he had presented his case in more explicit political terms, says Green, he would not have been successful. "Ninety-nine percent of the people who make films in Hollywood, " he remarks, "think of their films simply as entertainment. They don't believe they are doing anything which has a political or social impact. I think that all films are political—all films make statements of some sort—but they don't see it that way. The big question they always ask is, 'Does it work?' They cut a scene into a picture and they ask themselves, 'Does it work?' That doesn't mean, 'Does it put across a certain ideological perspective?' What they mean by that is 'Does it hold the audience—are they still interested in the plot and characters?' "

While Green feels politically estranged from low-budget, action movies, he still enjoys going to watch them—largely, he says, because he likes viewing the products of his and his friends' labor. "I went to that kind of movie most often when I was working on them, mostly because when the credits came on, half the names listed would be friends of mine." His identification with his work was strong enough at one point to compel Green to buy a special license plate for his car which read "B Movie."

If you are to get through your workday, says Green, you cannot let your mind dwell on the flaws in these movies. There are so many and they are so pronounced, you would soon become throughly discouraged and cynical. "If you work on a film for three to six months, even if it is complete drek, you've got to convince yourself that it has some merits or else you're not going to survive. You've got to. If I'm going to work at an editing machine day in and day out over a long period of time, the only way I can maintain my sanity is to keep telling myself that there are some good things about the movie. Because if I were to sort of step back from my job and say, 'This film is one-hundred percent garbage and should not be made,' well then, what I'm saying to myself is, 'Bruce, you're wasting six months of your life.' And I can't do that. So when I'm on a film, I find things that I think are good. On *Cannonball!* there were two or three lines of dialogue that were really priceless and these are what I try to remember."

Not long after his stint on *Cannonball!*, Green was hired to work on a major 20th Century-Fox production. The director needed someone who had experience both as an assistant editor and as a special effects technician and Green fit the bill. Because there was close to full employment among union film editors at this time of year, and because the movie's associate producer intervened on his behalf, Green was finally able to get into the IATSE film editors local. Suddenly, the young film worker's income quadrupled. "It was incredible," he says. "I jumped from making $200 for an eighty hour week to $800 for a seventy-five hour week."

The movie which catapulted Green into the union was *Star Wars*, the $10 million futuristic fantasy written and directed by George Lucas. Green was one of a vast army who were given the task of transforming Lucas' visions into a reality through the magic of optical effects. Green was personally responsible for supervising the production of approximately 300 optical effects shots. Most of the effects were fairly simple ones—freeze frames, reverse action sequences and the like. But a few were more complicated. "Lucas once came in with a shot of a car—only it's called a 'land-speeder' because it's a space movie—and he said, 'I want this car to look like it's floating above the ground. Magically. So I want you to get rid of the wheels, get rid of the shadow, so you can see clear through underneath it.' So I took the shot and I went around to four of five optical effects houses and I got their opinions about it and I got different budget estimates and time estimates. And I decided who I thought could do the best work. Then I went back to the director with this information and told him my decision. And he said, 'Go ahead with it if that's who you think is best.'

"So my job was to pick the optical houses and make sure the work was done correctly and on time and try not to show the director until it was close to being perfect. There were certain creative decisions which only he could make, but I did have some control."

His *Star Wars* assignment put Green in a higher position within the Hollywood labor hierarchy. He was paid more money than ever before and he was given more responsibility. As a supervisor of one small segment of the multi-million dollar film, he was in charge of a budget which was more than half the entire budget of *Cannonball!* He worked immediately

below director Lucas and had frequent interactions with the
top man, whom he came to know and like. "George is a wonderful guy," says Green, "He's not one of these young punks
who thinks he's God's gift to cinema. He's just a very down-to-
earth kind of guy. I was very happy to work with him."

Despite all this, Green somehow managed to maintain a
critical detachment from the movie. In some ways, he is more
critical of *Star Wars* than he is of the low-budget action pictures
he worked on. Green is put off by the idea of spending so much
time, labor, and money on a space adventure which follows
conventional dramatic lines. "We're talking about millions and
millions of dollars!" he exclaims. "You could probably build an
entire hospital; I don't know how many teachers or doctors
you could train for that much money, or how many health
services you could deliver or how much food you could grow.
But it seems to me a complete waste to spend so much money
on a film, especially a film which glorifies combat and heroic
individualism."

When he was working on *Star Wars,* friends constantly
asked Green if it was going to be a good film. "I didn't know
how to respond. I really didn't know if *Star Wars* was a good
film, in aesthetic and ideological terms. I always answered by
saying, 'I don't know, but I *do* know that its going to make a lot
of money.' In the film industry, everything is box office. So
what's good about *Star Wars* is that it turned out to be a
fabulous money-maker. That's all Hollywood cares about."
Film workers and viewers are not likely to benefit from the
enormous financial success of *Star Wars*, adds Green. Twen-
tieth Century-Fox will use its vast profits from the picture to
acquire new corporate properties, he says, rather than produce more movies.

Movie production should not be governed by commercial
considerations, believes Green. A film's worth should be
judged by social and aesthetic criteria. "The main question
which should be asked before a film is given the go-ahead is
not, 'How much money is it going to make? ' The questions
should be: 'Will this film add richness and meaning to people's
lives? What will this film do for the workers who produce it?' "

Green also believes that decision-making authority in
Hollywood should not be concentrated in the hands of top

level studio executives. There are those who contend that it is moviegoers who have the ultimate power to determine which pictures get made in Hollywood by flocking to see certain types and staying away from others. But Green thinks this form of "control" over film production is largely illusory. He believes that the many different constituencies which make up the movie audience should all have *direct* input into the decision-making process. Green would also like the men and women who work on movies to have a significant degree of control over film production.

Film is just too powerful a medium to be left in the control of a few major corporations and banks, says the young film worker. There is much more to dramatic features than simple entertainment. "Hollywood manufactures ideology and mythology," he remarks. "The whole world learns about itself through Hollywood's film products. These products shape our consciousness." As long as the means of film production and distribution are owned by large blocs of private capital, states Green, movies as a whole will reflect the values of the status quo.

Green finds Hollywood's attitudes about love and sexuality, and ambition and success particularly objectionable. Human interaction is depicted by most commercial moviemakers in crude and oppressive terms. "Hollywood movies tell you that if you're a man you should be hard to women and that women like being treated roughly, and that your best friends are always going to be other men and that in the long run they will also cut your throat. They teach women that men expect them to be neo-Playboy bunnies. I'm interested in the subtleties of relationships. I'd like to see films in which the relationships have depth and shading, films in which both men and women are vulnerable and real, films where men and women carry within them the potential to change and act more sensitively toward one another."

Green calls the Hollywood hero "a destructive role model." Movies which are centered around a dynamic individual who battles against terrible odds to achieve a solitary victory, he believes, reinforce people's competitive and individualistic attitudes. "I would like to see films that encourage people to cooperate and work together rather than films which romanticize the lone figure who sets out aggressively to make it on his own."

Green's political consciousness sets him apart from most people who work in the entertainment industry, including his fellow craftworkers, the very people he is counting upon to someday group together and radically change Hollywood. It is deeply dispiriting for someone like Green to live in a politically quiescent period and not be in ideological harmony with his co-workers. "We do not live in a politicized country. We do not live in a country where you can walk onto a bus and hear people debating current political issues. I know there are places in the world where that happens. But here people talk about sports and sex, cars and sex, and sex and sex. Everybody talks about sex all the time. That's the number one topic at work. And its talked about in pretty awful ways. I don't generally participate—I try not to—though every once in awhile I lapse back into sexist ways. But I try not to participate, and when it seems appropriate, I try to raise questions and educate people. Sometimes someone will make a sexist or racist joke and everybody will laugh except me. Then someone will say, 'Why aren't you laughing?' And I'll say, 'Because I don't think that such and such is funny,' and I'll leave it at that. Then nobody will talk to me."

Backward sexual and racial attitudes are bound to predominate in a labor movement like that in Hollywood which has frozen in its tracks. Film workers, says Green, cannot become a force for progressive change in Hollywood until those inside the union realize it is in their interests to join hands with those who have been kept out (namely the young, women, and minorities) and until the craft barriers which now divide them are knocked down. "Right now," he says, "there are separate IATSE locals for camerapeople, grips, electricians and so on, and separate talent guilds for actors, writers and directors. This promotes divisions between workers. There is this terrible syndrome on Hollywood sets during lunchtime. The grips go one place to eat, the camera crew goes another place, and the key actors go off with the director somewhere else. Everybody divides up along craft lines. Each group makes a different salary and each has a different status. I think there should be one big industrial union in Hollywood to represent all film workers."

Without benefit of a dynamic, cohesive labor movement, Hollywood film workers have become competitive and entrepreneurial. "Cinematographers and editors operate like enterprising businessmen," observes Green. "They will undercut other people in the same union to get jobs. They'll make deals with producers to defer their pay or to work Saturday for free. This stuff goes on all the time. A cameraman will say: 'If you hire me , I can't work for less than union scale—but I do own my own camera and I will rent it to your company for fifty percent less than the going rate.' Editors will say: 'I have a movieola (an editing machine) that you can use for free,' or 'You can forget about paying me overtime.' Everybody is hustling all the time to get work and everyone is competing with each other. You wind up seeing other film workers as your principal enemy instead of the producers and the studio executives who have placed an artificial limit on the number of films which are made each year."

Despite the lack of solidarity among Hollywood workers and the current listless mood which hangs over the country, Green remains deeply committed to building a socialist movement in the United States. What gives you the determination to keep pursuing your goals, we ask him, after he has enumerated all the problems which face him as a political activist. "Blind faith," he replies with a laugh. "It can't get much worse. And there are certain developments on a world scale which I find encouraging. The gains of the Italian and French left make me hopeful. The victories of the people in Mozambique and Angola make me hopeful. The imminent victory of the people in Zimbabwe makes me hopeful. All these things give me strength.

"In terms of the United States, I'm a little more existential. I mean I just don't think I have a choice but to be hopeful. That's the only way to express it. It's like I've *got* to believe—it really comes down to faith. I *have* to believe things are going to be better because if I don't I'll just get very depressed. I don't want to live in the kind of situation I do today for the next fifty years. I'm twenty-five years old, and I'll probably be alive for the next fifty years, and if I thought the country was going to be like it is today—or worse—in fifty years, I'd go kill myself. I don't need this grief. So the one thing that makes me hopeful is that I have hope. It just seems to me that it's got to get better, it simply has to get better, okay? And I'm willing to work day in and day out to make it better, But it really is in a lot of ways like blind faith. I hate to say it, but maybe I have this fundamentalist streak." (he laughs)

Postscript:

When Green finished working on *Star Wars*, he left the United States to join a friend who lived in England. He wanted to travel, meet people, and learn more about the European political situation. He was not sure when he would return. Temporarily, the difficulty and complexity of organizing in Hollywood was left behind.

In early 1978, Green wrote a letter reevaluating his Hollywood film career in light of his overseas experience: "Things have changed quite a bit since we last talked. I've lived and worked in England for a year now. I've married and we're thinking of having a baby (one day). I've been making films with the London Newsreel Collective. I'm a year older and I've changed. We are coming back to Los Angeles to live and work in the film industry and I'm nervous about it. In London, many of our friends are non-film people. Our lives don't revolve as much around film. Filmmaking is a way to make a wage and occasionally express something you believe in. It is not the be-all and end-all of life. The world got along okay for thousands of years without it, and it's just not worth destroying yourself for. I want to work in the movie industry, but I also want to spend time with my family and friends, to do non-film activities, and have an existence outside of the industry. I don't know if that's possible in Los Angeles. The industry seems to demand everything of you. I've met so many older film technicians who have drinking problems, whose marriages are on the rocks, who just seem trampled. I know many younger film workers who are snorting coke to keep going and are finding it equally difficult to maintain personal relationships. I think about what I'll be like after twenty years inside the studios and it scares me.

"I'm concerned about the oppressive character of the film-making process. I'd like to see the film unions do more to improve the working conditions that lead to the emotional and physical ills which affect so many workers. But a union is nothing more than its members banded together in solidarity. If we aren't active, if we leave it to the other person, nothing will ever change. The producers, as a group, feel no responsibility for film workers, who give the industry the best years of their lives and have nothing but ulcers and debts to show for it. If you start to slow down or your health fails, you're booted out and replaced by some eager film school graduate wearing a sign saying, 'Exploit me.' When I return to Hollywood, I'd like to become active in my union and help create a film industry which respects its workers and responds to their needs."

Jesus Salvador Trevino

The Hispanic community (people with Spanish surnames) is rapidly becoming the largest minority group in the United States. In the Southwest, people of Mexican origin already constitute the major minority bloc. Yet so far the entertainment industry has failed to adequately communicate this people's experience to the general population. The demeaning stereotypes which characterized an earlier period (bandits, sleepy-heads, and loose women) have been virtually eliminated; but 1970s Hollywood has not produced a single major film about the country's Spanish-speaking citizenry and only one TV series, the silly and irrelevant "Chico and the Man."

Now, however, a generation of filmmakers who grew up in the *barrios* of America is beginning to emerge: filmmakers who are dedicated to interpreting the history of their people in richer and truer ways and who are intent upon making an impact on mass consciousness. Among this new wave is Jesus Salvador Trevino, a young, talented Chicano writer-director-producer. In the last several years, Trevino has created an artful and politically incisive body of film work. His list of credits includes the documentaries *Soledad* (1971), a one-hour film about Chicano and black prison inmates (which he co-produced); *America Tropical* (1971), a half-hour film about the controversial work of left wing Mexican muralist David Alfaro Siqueiros; and *Yo Soy Chicano* (1972), which has been hailed as a "definitive filmic statement on the Chicano experience." He has also written and directed a dramatic feature about labor conflict along the U.S.-Mexican border, *Raices de Sangre* (1977), and served as the executive producer of *Infinity Factory* (1975-76), a nationally broadcast children's TV series. He is currently involved in writing and producing a dramatic series on Latino history for PBS.

Almost all of Trevino's work to date has been done for public television. While public TV does not skirt controversy quite so assiduously as commercial television, its programmers still must work within distinct ideological limits. Trevino's films have consistently pushed against those limits and have often succeeded in expanding the range of creative possibilities. "My approach," says the filmmaker, "has been to

345

go for the opportunities that exist within the system and try to make the best of them, at times changing them, subverting them. I've been successful at doing this in certain areas."

*****

Trevino grew up in a working class family in East Los Angeles, the nation's largest Chicano *barrio*. He went through Occidental College on minority scholarships, graduating in 1968 with a degree in philosophy. That summer he enrolled in a government-funded training program called New Communicators, where he learned basic filmmaking skills. When the program came to an end, Trevino was hired by Los Angeles public TV station KCET to work on "Ahora!," a nightly talk show which was broadcast from the Mexican-American community. Trevino was kept on as a staff producer after the show went off the air in 1970. During the next few years, he produced a series of remarkable specials for the station, foremost of which was *Yo Soy Chicano* (*I Am Chicano*), which aired originally in August 1972.

Yo Soy is an elegantly composed history of the Chicano people from the Spanish conquest of Native American civilizations (and the subsequent birth of La Raza) to the social struggles of the 1970s. Key figures and events are summoned from the past through the skillful use of old drawings, photographs, and sepia-toned dramatizations. We are brought face-to-face with heroes like Juan Cortina, Ricardo Flores Magon, and Reies Lopez Tijerina: men who led struggles to regain the land and dignity which was lost after the Mexican-American War. We are reminded of painful incidents like the Zoot Suit riots of 1943, when large groups of servicemen invaded the east L.A. *barrio* and assaulted the flashily-dressed Chicano youths known as "zoot suiters." And we see the latest manifestations of the Chicano struggle: the efforts of the United Farm Workers to organize the fields, and the fight to take over the political machinery in urban areas such as Crystal City, Texas where Chicanos form a majority of the population. *Yo Soy Chicano* is a powerful tribute to the courage, resilience, and grace of La Raza.

Trevino's development as a filmmaker paralleled the rise of the Chicano movement in the late sixties and early seventies. Several of his early films chronicled the major political events of that period: the 1968 high school "walkouts," which were called to demand better education for Mexican-American students in Los Angeles city schools; the 1970 Chicano Moratorium antiwar demonstration, which was brought to a violent conclusion by club-wielding L.A. county sheriff's deputies; the inquest into the death of Ruben Salazar, the widely respected Mexican-American journalist who was struck and killed by a tear gas projectile during the protest; the 1972 national convention of La Raza Unida Party, a political organization which has attempted to unify Chicano forces outside of the two-party system. These documentaries tended to be professional in quality, and partisan in tone. For Trevino was not merely an observer of the Chicano struggle, he was an active participant in it. (In addition to filming the Raza Unida convention, he also served as the national media coordinator for the event.) Recording these episodes on film was one way of furthering the Chicano movement; like most oppositional struggles, it needed all the sympathetic media coverage it could get. "I was very committed to the political activity that was going on in my community," says Trevino, "and I was committed to using the media as a way of expressing the concerns, aspirations, and strategies of that community."

Television documentaries initially seemed to be the best vehicle for getting these ideas across to the public. Public service TV programming also happened to be one of the few areas in the electronic media system that was open to minorities. But as the years went by, Trevino became increasingly interested in fictional filmmaking. In 1976 he was given his first opportunity to direct a dramatic feature when the Mexican government agreed to finance *Raices de Sangre* (*Roots of Blood*), which the filmmaker had written the previous year. *Raices* was one of several films produced by Mexico's national film corporation to promote greater understanding of the Chicano experience. It was the only one written and directed by a Chicano.

"The film originally was not going to be about Mexicans at all," Trevino recalls. "It was just going to be a love story about Chicanos that would entertain the Mexican audience and give them some understanding of what the Chicano reality was like. Because there is a lot of prejudice against Chicanos in

Mexico, they see us as lower class people who do not speak Spanish well, are not educated, and are essentially the dregs of society. Chicanos have also adopted a lot of American culture, so we tend to be viewed as *agringadus*—assimilated into the worst of American society, drug addicts and the like. The idea originally was to present Mexicans with a positive image of who we are. But once I got into the project, I saw the need to have it work both ways. To have the film deliver a message about Mexicans to Chicanos, as well as the other way around. Because we are no less guilty of prejudice against our Mexican brothers and sisters."

Raices emphasizes the commonality of the Chicano and Mexican peoples. It is set along the Mexican-American border, where hundreds of U.S.-owned assembly plants have sprung up in recent years to take advantage of the region's low paid, non-unionized labor pool. The story line involves two couples—a pair of Chicano activists, and a Mexican working class couple. Although their paths never cross, and their lives are played out on opposite sides of the border, it is clear that their struggle is the same.

Trevino feels that the *Raices* assignment was a rare opportunity. "The Mexican film industry, which is an arm of the Mexican government, funded a film that I think is highly controversial—and not uncritical of the United States. And the fact that it would do that, and the fact that it would involve Chicanos in the project, is quite exceptional. I think opportunities like that do not come along every day. I'm not sure that Mexican film directors would have been given the kind of creative leeway that I was given if they had tried to make a similar statement about their own country."

Soon after finishing *Raices* in summer 1977, Trevino began work on a multi-part dramatic series on Latino history for public television. Like *Yo Soy Chicano*, the series will cover the 500-year period from the Spanish colonization of the New World to the present. "We plan to focus on the important events and people who have formed our reality today. Who were the trend setters and who were the people caught in pivotal moments that really made a lot of difference? Once we choose those individuals and those historical events, it will be up to the writers to develop believable and interesting stories."

Trevino does not expect the historical series to be as politically direct as *Raices*. "It's a different situation. I must keep in mind the audience which PBS reaches. How to relate several hundred years of history that is so filled with injustice, manifest destiny, and other forms of aggression against Latinos by the U.S. government, and how to allow people to feel it, and not make it boring. This is my task. I think this is where I get to explore how to be subtle and artful."

So far in his career, Trevino has concentrated on interpreting the Chicano experience. "Eventually I want to do stories that are not necessarily Chicano or Latino; since I'm bilingual and bicultural, I'm as much a part of the American reality as I am of the Hispanic reality. But my interest right now lies in exploring this particular area, because not enough has been done on it and because an artist invariably draws on what he or she knows. The reality that I know best right now is the Chicano reality."

Trevino wants to construct his ethnically based film stories in a way that gives them universal appeal. He insists that this can be done without flattening out characters, dialogue, and milieu as popular filmmakers generally do when dealing with ethnic subject matter. "I think you have to begin with a story or event that is not necessarily Anglo or Chicano or black, but simply a human story. And then you develop it, drawing on your knowledge of the cultural environment in which the story takes place. The problem has been that the people writing about the ghetto or the *barrio* have tended to have little or no firsthand knowledge of those environments. They have attempted to give their stories some ethnic color by adding a few Spanish words here and there or sprinkling the dialogue with some black vernacular. That's not good enough. They inevitably come out looking like white films, which is what they are. The ethnic material must be fully integrated into the narrative. I'm confident I can do that, because my point of view is fundamentally Chicano. That's who I am, and that's how I was raised."

Trevino continues to place strong emphasis on developing his artistic skills as a filmmaker. Several years ago, at the height of the Chicano movement, this seemed like a luxury. Political events were happening so fast and with such intensity, that socially committed filmmakers were hard-pressed to simply keep up with them. There was a need to quickly produce emphatic screen statements and to document the explosive events of the period. Ideological concerns tended to take precedence over artistic concerns; but Trevino has consistently tried to establish a balance between the two. "Many Chicano artists have come from a highly political background; because of this, our work often tends to be very specific and obvious. And yet if we are to achieve true artistry, our works must be more subtle, they must have universal elements. And so I'm interested in exploring the artistic dimension of filmmaking, and I know other filmmakers who are doing the same thing. We've come through the first phase of our politicization. In the past, there was so much pain and so much need to proclaim our newly developed ideas, that we were very forceful and direct. But I think that we're now getting to a place where we can be more introspective, where we can take more time to consider our work so that it has higher quality."

Trevino is honing his creative skills by carefully studying the work of other filmmakers and writers, and devoting more time to his own work. "I used to go to a movie or read a book for the pleasure of it. Now it's more like work. I analyze them; I try to identify what works and what doesn't. How did the filmmaker or novelist handle this creative problem? It makes a difference. You can learn a great deal by doing this."

Trevino is not neglecting his political growth; he continues to read political literature and participate in community events. But his artistic development is receiving special attention during this period. "I owe it to myself as an artist to do this; because otherwise I'm going to wind up as a propagandist. And I've done enough of that." Trevino wants to create films that continue to have relevance over a long period of time; for it is pictures like these, he says, which ultimately make the greatest social impact.

As Trevino's reputation as a film artist continues to grow, he will indoubtedly be offered jobs by Hollywood studios. Although he is cognizant of the movie industry's creative limitations, he is not opposed to the idea of working in this intensely commercial realm. He has great appreciation for the entertainment value of Hollywood products. "Hollywood movies are known for their fast pace, their emphasis on action and so forth. They don't allow the audience much room to reflect on the overall meaning of what is happening on the screen. That may come later, but right now you want to see if the good guy is going to get killed or not. I don't think I'm opposed to that cinematic style... I've worked in the Mexican film industry and to me Mexican films drag because their pacing is so slow. I ran into this problem while editing *Raices*. Working with a Mexican editor was difficult for me, because I wanted the film to move along briskly and he wanted it to go more leisurely. You see this in many European films as well, this slow and meandering style. But like it or not, Hollywood is setting the pace worldwide. And I would rather be part of that creative momentum than outside of it. I see no need in doing films that are not exciting, merely because Hollywood makes exciting films. Not everything that is done in the Hollywood style has to be superficial."

Trevino also accepts the Hollywood screen pattern of focusing on one dynamic individual. He would, however, like to make that hero/heroine more representative of the common people. "The American tradition is to focus on one major figure, who is generally a male, and revolve everything around him. The lives of the other characters become a backdrop to his reality. That approach has been criticized a lot by left wing commentators, who say it glorifies the individual and downplays the common experience of humanity. Well I think that individuals' stories are interesting in and of themselves. But I think that what we must do is change the social character of that hero or heroine. Instead of being a member of the traditional elite, he or she should be more like the average person...I guess that ever since the days of fairytales, we have followed the lives of kings and queens and other members of the ruling class. You see that pattern throughout the history of film. And I do think there are creative ways of dealing with those people. But I think that much more has to be done to explore the lives of everyday people. Films like *Grapes of Wrath* and *Salt of the Earth* have done this. But there is a need for much more."

Trevino is deeply aware that as he pursues his filmmaking

career—particularly if he does enter the Hollywood system—
he will come under intense pressure to relinquish his social
values.

He has seen this happen with depressing regularity to
progressives and minorities: they enter the entertainment
industry with the best intentions, they are continually frustrated in their efforts to do meaningful work, and finally they
succumb. It is a process, says Trevino, which has repeated
itself throughout history. "I'm a student of history, and I've
read many stories of people who begin their lives as radical
firebrands, dedicated to changing the world, and wind up
becoming part of what they were trying to overthrow. The
fortunate ones die before this happens (he laughs) and their
good names are preserved. There are some people of course
who don't sacrifice their beliefs: people who are honest and
principled and effective to the end of their days. But this is
enormously difficult to do. You are continually confronted
with decisions in your work and life that put your beliefs to a
test. And ultimately each individual makes these decisions by
him or herself.

"I spend a lot of time thinking about my career and the
direction in which it's going. It's the way I keep myself
straight. I ask myself, 'Is this something you will later regret
having done? Is it part of what you are about.' I think these
kinds of questions are important.

"I remember a line from a Salvador Diaz Miron poem:
'There are birds who cross the swamps and manage not to soil
their feathers. My plummage is of those birds.' I used to think
that perhaps one could be like those birds, maneuvering
through the industry without getting one's feathers soiled.
Well, reality has taught me differently, it has taught me that
you may have to get a little dirty if you're going to get anything
done. It's too easy to sit back and be ideologically 'pure ' and
not take chances, and wind up speaking only to yourself. Sure,
it's important for me to ask these hard questions of myself, but
it's just as important not to be afraid to take on projects. The
key for me is not losing sight of why I originally became a
filmmaker, or losing sight of the kind of world we can and
should bring about. If your works are to help in liberating the
human spirit, a little dirt on your wings is the price you
sometimes have to pay."

Lynn Phillips

Criticism of TV as a cultural institution was once the exclusive preserve of left wing theoreticians and conservative guardians of high culture. But throughout the 1970s, more and more people have come to regard television as mind-numbing, exploitative, and degrading. Audience discontent with TV has manifested itself in a variety of ways: in the popular response to the 1976 movie, *Network,* a scathing satire about media manipulation; in the dip in TV viewing which took place during the 1977-78 season; in the proliferation of pressure groups which have attempted to influence television programming. Criticism of TV is also surprisingly widespread within the creative community which produces it. But it is not an organized opposition. It is rarely even active. Most television writers are hushed by the money, or are stymied by their individual irrelevance in the face of so expansive a problem. TV writer Lynn Phillips sees herself in the latter category.

"It isn't often in commercial television," she says, " that you see a new possibility, something that's truly popular *and* accurately complex. When you see an opening like that, the only thing to do is go for broke; put everything you've got on it and ask your friends to help you pray." When "Mary Hartman, Mary Hartman," Norman Lear's offbeat television serial made its debut in 1976, Phillips recognized the program as unique. "It defined its audience differently," she says excitedly. Instead of making everyone respond to one thing one way—the monolithic mass approach—it provided a focus which different clumps of people could see and respond to in simultaneously different ways. The joke in America has always been that we're *socially* individualistic—that is, it's every small fish for himself or herself—but *culturally* we're like a military parade in Moscow. It's the worst of both worlds. The Lowest Common Denominator is a definitionally degenerate way to program a mass culture. Nobody ever gets to learn more about what they know best or think more deeply about it. The LCD is a dead weight, and we're the sinking bag of kittens."

Phillips says she can imagine various ways around this traditional problem of mass communications, but believes that the industry is slow to take risks and too jumpy about early failure to work out kinks in possible solutions. But in "Mary Hartman, Mary Hartman," she found a temporary relief from the headache and tedium of LCD programming. "It was a doubletake kind of humor," she explains. "A step more layered than 'All in the Family,' which is an ironic show in the sense that the show's creative intelligence keeps an affectionate distance from Archie's attitudes and views. 'Hartman' continued with that ironic attitude towards its characters, but it also introduced *formal* ironies. It was self-critical. 'Hartman' would run along in the conventional groove and then leap out, and start toying with its own conventions. There were some moments when several perspectives would be proposed at once—like the episode in which Mary worried about her 'waxy yellow buildup' while a mass murderer was terrorizing the neighborhood. That was one of those crystalline moments when three or four insights are embodied in one image. She was the self-centered fool in all of us who's honed in on her petty personal problems (her insecurity about the appearance of her floor) while the sky falls down around us; she was also that part of us that's too shellshocked by the dimensions of contemporary problems to feel any impulse other than withdrawal; she was the media victim in us who can't believe the evidence of our own eyes (yellow buildup) against the claims of our packages ('no buildup'); she was a parody of the innumerable 'housewife' ads on television which (incredibly) show a race of humanoids whose passions are most readily stimulated by the state of their kitchen floors. Louise Lasser, the actress, played the part with a 'knowing' innocence, which let you, if you wanted, read the situation all of these ways, flavored with the individual character's 'buildup' of personal sexual frustrations, moral confusions, and good intentions. It was a moment of richness, subtlety, and complexity that's rare in *any* art form—and it was seen by thirty million people, all of whom had a chance to enjoy it in any one or combination of its dimensions. *And it was funny each way.*

"The reason for going into this at length," Phillips sighs, "is that it's an example of the opposite of the kind of structuring which the Lowest Common Denominator strategy requires. That is, usually in television, you pick one button—terror, suspense, pathos, desire, pity, humor, derision—and lean on it for all it's worth. Ads often have a layered and dimensional texture, but programs rarely do—or they strenuously try to conceal them when they do—so that you end up with a subtext—a 'hidden' story—and a main one, rather than a frankly complex moment. This is every bit as true in "high class" PBS-type anglophylic television as it is on the commercial networks. The aesthetic objection isn't that television is a bad world, or a stupid or violent or dishonest or commercialized or plastic world—it's that TV land really *is* flat, filled with 'appropriate' responses to every imaginable situation. It's never untrue. It's always half true. A monocular mind in a binocular body politic."

What effect does this have on the viewing public? Phillips says she cannot presume to say. She liked "Mary Hartman" enough to get a job writing on it during its second and final season. When it evolved into the less successful "Forever Fernwood" in the spring of 1977, Phillips moved on to look for the next beam of light at the end of the Tube. In general, Phillips' experiences in the TV industry have neither made her feel at home nor made her feel like looking for another home elsewhere. "The *real* irony," according to Phillips, "is that mass culture has never been so good for so many before in its history as it is now. TV beats dancing around in a circle celebrating somebody's ritual clitoridectomy, and it's much more various and exciting kind of feudal art than the stained glass window. More people can enjoy it than could *ever* read well, and the things it does—its soaps and series and game shows and sports spectaculars, its news and most especially its ads—it does masterfully. But even though it's a better-than-ever cultural dispersal system, it's more *inadequate* than ever before, because the level of our technology is at a relatively higher *ratio* than ever before to the psychological preparation, conceptual training, and plain information, not to *mention* the political power of our ad-soaked, thrill drenched, and increasingly illiterate mass population. So we *feel* like we're being made stupid by TV, though what's really happening is that we're not being made smart enough fast enough.

"And the irony of *that*," she grins, "is that the people who keep the learning pace slow think it's elitist and undemocratic to speed it up—as if what people choose to watch is the same as what they *want* to choose to watch. Which it isn't. The pose of

'We're just giving the people what they want' doesn't wash. It's a front for the real motive—which is to exploit our weakness for sensation to get us in a receptive mood for Bounce, Trix, Exxon, and (did we ask for it?) Toyota."

An appreciation of the ironies of 'the business' is built into Phillips' background. "My mother was a legal executive at ABC in New York," she smiles, with a mixture of admiration and regret. "She helped lay the legal groundwork I get screwed by today. And she did it so that I could have a better life! It's what in older businesses, like saloonkeeping, is known as a protection racket. And it took a lot of courage, brains, and guts to do it as well as she did."

Lynn also found contradictions in the liberal attitudes she encountered as a student in New York City's special public school system: "What they kept suggesting was, basically, that you were better than those insensitive scumbags in the lower classes, because you were capable of appreciating the beauty and poignancy of their spirits. And they themselves weren't. So the best thing to do was to slip 'em a couple of bucks for a movie matinee before they stole your last red cent. Then you'd better run for the nearest museum and look at 'artifacts of the human quest,' because the hoods and bigots and other lunkheads were too stupid to come looking for you there. I, of course, being young and innocent, bought the whole snobby package. So in addition to being young and innocent, I soon became arrogant, world-weary, lonely, pretentious, and otherwise cute and talented."

While attending Harvard University in the mid-sixties, Phillips abandoned the idea of becoming a painter and began working in *cinema verite* documentary. After graduating in 1966, she went to work as an assistant editor for Richard Leacock, D.A. Pennebaker, the Maysles brothers, Bill Jersey, and other New York documentary filmmakers. "I was very alienated at the time, and filmmaking seemed to me a safe— and by that I mean a distanced—way to get reinvolved with the Great World."

In late 1967, Phillips joined New York Newsreel, an organization of filmmakers, artists, intellectuals, and inspired madpeople which believed that the Vietnam war, social inequality, meaningless labor, and inverted national priorities were in the best interests of an international corporate elite, which it would be in everyone else's interests (here and around the world) to supercede. Phillips had no prior experience in left wing politics, but she admired the film work which had been done by some of the group's founders and she was intrigued by the idea of film as a tool of social change.

Among the Newsreel films Phillips worked on were *Columbia Revolt*, a fifty minute documentary about the 1968 student strike at Columbia University, and *The Jeanette Rankin Brigade*, a film made in 1967 with an all-woman crew, documenting a women's peace march on Washington.

Columbia Revolt, which Phillips edited from over ten thousand feet of amateur footage, was Newsreel's most popular early film. It was seen by close to a million people and precipitated riots when shown at some colleges. It explains how Columbia's ties to the military-industrial complex plus its expansionist building program in black Harlem led to the SDS-organized student takeover of university buildings. The film's most effective scenes are those which show students forming an alternative community within the occupied buildings. The community is quickly destroyed, however, when the New York City police retake the buildings with brute force. "My sense of the Columbia strike," Phillips says, "was, 'Here is this bunch of middle class kids who are involved in an Eisensteinian-scale historical event. They're cupcakes. But they're grand. They're actually *making* history. Well...almost. It was that mixed tone that I went for in the film, and I think I succeeded."

Newsreel members, including Phillips, generally dismissed the idea of working within the Hollywood system. "The New Left's argument," recalls Phillips, "was that there was no effective way to work within the culture industry. It was stronger and would always prevail; it would dilute or turn a strong oppositional statement to its own advantage. We used to dismiss good moments by saying that they consoled everyone for the unbearable scarcity of good moments."

The hope at the time, says Phillips, was that radical groups like Newsreel could create a culture of opposition and that the opposition would create conditions in which a more humane culture could develop. "We didn't see ourselves as an alternative, superior culture," she says. "At least not in sane moments. We were a state-of-emergency force. We had a task. We refused to entertain. Entertainment is only amusing when all is well, which it wasn't, or when rapid social progress is blocked. Entertainment is amusing now. It wasn't then."

Phillips thought the late sixties offered an opportunity to transform exploitative relations at their root level. "It was a long shot at best," she smiles. "But it was crazy not to go for it. It was like one of those game shows. You could have the known factor—a lettuce spinner and a year's supply of Band-Aids—or try for the Eldorado that was possibly behind the curtain. Everyone I knew with a heart, a backbone, and a *real* sense of pleasure and entertainment went for the curtain— even if it meant being boring for a few years."

Newsreel rejected the ideological content of Hollywood pictures as propaganda for the status quo. The group denounced the undemocratic way in which they were produced and distributed, and was prepared to sacrifice the slickness of professionalism if a sloppier look allowed a wider range of people to participate in creating the American Culture. Newsreel's organizational style, both on and off camera, was confrontational. Its films confronted audiences with raw statements about U.S. racism, imperialism and economic injustice. They were films which demanded more than a passive response.

As part of its plan to engage rather than entertain audiences, Newsreel often sent out speakers with its films to initiate post-screening discussions. "Some of our best films," Phillips remembers, "were awful, but they provoked really hot discussions which more polished, more lucid, more balanced films wouldn't have elicited." Newsreel made a clear issue out of the context in which its works were shown. "We don't want to show our film in commercial cinemas or on TV," stated one member, "where they risk being directed by a system of consumerism and would not create the kind of political effect we seek." Newsreel managed to establish an independent system of distribution which was internationally reciprocal and at times quite effective.

But, while the organization acquired a certain amount of internal political influence among leftists it never became a cultural force comparable to, say, the underground press. "It wasn't that we were too naive. It was that we were too sophisticated. The leadership's aesthetic was philosophically, rather than practically, determined. It said that what we want is a cinema of action, a cinema of participation; and this rough-hewn, anybody-can-do-it, I'm-running-in-the-street look was the *right* one, the necessary one, and that to please, to cajole, to advertise, or to persuade would be manipulative, would perpetuate the passivity of viewers, impede their development as whole human beings. Which is all very noble and all *very* hard on the eyes. Remember that it's Stalin, Hitler, and Sarnoff who insist on 'music the workers can whistle to.' Culturally, we rejected them all—but we had as much contempt for the worker *liking* to whistle as Stalin, Hitler, and Sarnoff had for the worker. It was Norman Lear who figured out that the American public could think and whistle at the same time. I think both are necessary. One without the other in most historical circumstances causes brain-death. Preciousness and pandering are the Scylla and Charybdis of left culture. Newsreel, to avoid the pandering of 1930s nice-guy sentimentality, lapsed into a muscular kind of French intellectualism; and for all our trashy surface and rough posturing, I think we got as precious as, well, *Waiting for Godot*, or Godard. Waiting for Godard."

Phillips left Newsreel in late 1969. "I didn't go away mad," she explains. "I just went away. I'd been sent to work with the part of our group stationed in the South, where I spent three months touring around with films made on the coasts. And I found out that audiences in Atlanta read those films entirely differently than people in other parts of the country. Our strategies were often inappropriate, or worse, dangerous. Our ideas of things were provincial and presumptuous. What we thought of as a peaceful demonstration looked to kids in a small town in North Carolina like a mass revolution. And I learned that there were some things that just couldn't be recovered in discussion afterwards. The idea of going back to New York and trying to explain, 'Hey, fellas, we're living in a bubble...' was out of the ball park. I'd lived in that bubble all my life myself. Besides, the women's movement had grown a great deal by then, and there was too much in the feminist critique of the left leadership that was too true and too slow to change."

Phillips left New York and temporarily lived in St. Louis, where she became increasingly interested in mass cultural forms. She was drawn to the soap opera form for many reasons: "It's ongoing, a concordance with everyday life; it allows for character development over time, a sense of *process*; it's interior as well as active; it gives scale and importance to people's real concerns—betrayal, love, faith, evil, etc.; and it has multiple climaxes instead of one big hyped-up blow-out, like Greek tragedy or death. It's a female art form." But she could not imagine herself fitting into the ongoing soaps then playing on network television. "They were changing and progressing; they were modernizing at the time, but too slowly for me."

So, instead, Phillips and some friends began producing a soap opera of their own on a local, nonprofit FM radio station. The show, called "Winds of Change," was launched on a weekly basis in 1972. Phillips wrote eleven twenty-minute segments. "We had a bunch of people who, after work or school or childcaring, would get together and vamp it up. Then we'd lay in all kinds of silly music and effects and that was it. It was crude, but clever. The plots were very local. It was part of the regional idea. We'd put local issues and characters into the scripts, like the ward boss and the local alderman, or a pending welfare bill. Will Radish, the father, was away in Jefferson City a lot, knocking up Elizabeth Bender, his secretary. She would dream of power while lying supine beneath him, and his wife would worry about their daughter's affair with Roger the draft dodger. We had a narrator who got tired of narrating everyone else's life and decided she needed a life of her own. She was played by a woman who, in fact, *did* get tired of playing second fiddle to her left-intellectual boyfriend's academic career (books on Gramsci) and went forth to make a career for herself in New York. So much for regionalism. Still...it was great doing that show. It was lovely, silly, and, in a small way, consequential."

After "Winds of Change" came to an end, Phillips moved to San Francisco where she wrote a screenplay about the 1960s. The script failed to sell, but it brought her some additional work and, even more importantly, "appreciation and support from people whose opinions I respected." She began to think seriously about moving to Hollywood, but she doubted whether she had "the stamina to brave it out. I was still too alienated, too left, too argumentative to come down here and charm my way into the business." Then "Mary Hartman, Mary Hartman" went into production.

"When I heard of it," says Phillips, "my jaw dropped. At first I felt a strong pang of jealousy and regret. I felt like, 'Aw, I missed the boat.'* That lasted for five minutes. Then I tried to be spiritually correct; that is, I tried to be glad that what I cared about was being done. It freed me of the obligation to lose time, energy, and sleep doing it myself. But as the show began appearing, I said, 'Well, my goodness, I've *got* to be part of this. I belong down there, at least as a traveling pilgrim, at least for awhile."

Phillips sat down and wrote about two months worth of story lines for "Mary Hartman." Out of the story lines she drafted a complete script. Then she flew to Los Angeles and presented this material to Ann Marcus, the show's original head writer, whom she had met at a women writers' conference a month earlier. "I sort of threw myself at her feet. I told her that I thought what she was doing was literally great, which I sincerely did and do, and asked her which bone in my body I had to break to get a shot at it. Fortunately, she let me go on believing that one broken bone would be enough.

"I don't know how to say this so that it comes out sounding right. But Ann Marcus is an extraordinary person.

---

*Since moving to Hollywood, says Phillips, she has met a number of people who "are very pleased with themselves for not having become politically involved in the sixties." They are proud of the fact that they were never diverted from their primary goal of building an entertainment career, she says. But Phillips makes it clear that she has never had sustained feelings of regret about her past political involvement. "Personally, I don't feel that my time was wasted, I don't feel a sense of loss. I think I gained a great deal (in the process of being politically active). I don't feel that I've been cheated or misled. I never had utopian illusions about a perfect world or an inevitable victory—just utopian desires."

Open in a really rare way. Interested in people who aren't like her. Fair, kind...and tense. It isn't mush. She's not a softy. She knows the price of being good, the risk. It's a ferocious show of strength, hanging onto that much kindness. I'd given her my stuff on a Friday. She called me *Saturday night* to tell me she liked it and was going to recommend that I get a chance to write a trial episode. She must've known I'd be sitting there, waiting. It's the kind of torture a lot of types in this clever place really like to drag out, slooooow. They've got some weird, twisted, slithering, stinking habit in their lower brains. But she just skipped the entire Age of Reptiles and got up and walked upright at me. Amazing."

Phillips dashed back to San Francisco and waited. To-wards the end of the show's first season, Marcus called and asked her to come down. "It was during dinner. I put my roast chicken in a jiffy bag, grabbed a bunch of asparagus, a bottle of Polish vodka donated by friends, and hopped aboard a plane. The next day I read about a thousand pages. In the next two days I wrote a script. Ann liked it, (story consultants) Oliver and Betsy Hailey liked it, (creative supervisor) Al Burton liked it, Norman Lear liked it. They took me on. They took the chance even though I was a complete stranger. They were impressive, generous. I fit into a category they called 'new blood.' "

Phillips feels that her entry into the TV business was relatively free of personal ambition. "It wasn't that I *didn't* desperately want to write the show. It was that I *didn't* des-perately want to *be* a creature called 'Hot Writer.' I adored the show and liked the company's record. Norman Lear politicized American television and was attempting to set up a real alternative to the networks through syndication. It was all so worth doing, it didn't matter what it was worth, or how much of my 'new blood' I'd be shedding."

The world depicted by "Mary Hartman, Mary Hartman" was a cockeyed one where work held little or no meaning (and was often dangerous), where political corruption ran rampant, where people's private lives were completely overrun by an odd assortment of media hucksters, and where TV's values continually threatened to replace people's own judgment. It was, in short, a world very much like our own, except the madness was exaggerated sufficiently enough to give us distance from it and make us laugh. The "function" of "Mary Hartman," says Phillips, was not to change viewers' minds but to reinforce a certain perception of the world which was already shared by many people. 'I don't think its function was to radically change people or do anything spectacular or push them in a certain direction. But I think it was a kind of spiritual maintenance—an airing out, an ordering. It was housework of the soul."

The principal characters in "Mary Hartman" were continually searching for ways to transcend their Fernwood routines and lead fulfilling lives. In the process they often became embroiled in bizarre predicaments and made fools of themselves. But, says Phillips, the characters' deep longing to break out of their confining existences was always treated with respect by the program. "The show did speak to that comedic sensibility which likes to see people fall on their faces. But at the same time, it honored the characters' intentions. Their desires to communicate, to be good, to find meaning were always cast in a sympathetic light. No matter how ridiculous things turned out in the end, the characters were shown to be well motivated. In fact, that's what allows you to say about "Mary Hartman" that the problems it depicted were not problems of human nature but of the society—or rather of people in relation to society, and their inability to deal with it. The fact that what they want is so very clearly something other than what they've been handed."

Phillips says that it is difficult to generalize about her creative contribution to "Mary Hartman" because the organization of the writing process changed several times. She was one of four dialogue writers who would be given a story outline each week and asked to complete a script. Sometimes they had input into the outlines and sometimes not. The outlines themselves varied in length and in specificity. As the year went on, Phillips feels, the show became increasingly "packaged" and "pre-formulated." "The schedule was so grueling that I guess it was the only choice. But an element of freshness left the show. Every scene would start predictably with a little gadget, a little surprise. Slow stretches, which were used in the past to build, were sped up, more densely plotted, eliminated. It was all theoretically justifiable: the builds didn't always work in the past, sometimes they just sank. But the fast pace had a monotony of its own; mixed with irony it undercut a feeling of sincerity. With hindsight, I'd say it was the kind of show that people watched *because* it took risks and that its getting better—in the sense of more refined, polished, mastered—didn't agree with the audience's expectations. No matter how crazy the situations, they began to feel redundant. It was a rebel show. It wasn't good at holding on to its power, only in wresting it. But it was truly a very great show, an important moment, and I'm unshakably glad to have been a part of it. The people were brilliant and charming and difficult. The insecurity was agony. The problems were excruciating. It was like living in an earthquake. No insurance policy was covering you. And we'd all do it again, of course. It was worth it."

After "Mary Hartman," Phillips began writing other TV programs on a freelance basis. She prefers television to films because she feels TV has a better recent record in portraying women, and because the television audience in general is "less snobby." How TV viewers respond to Phillips' shows is almost impossible to determine. Unlike playwrights or screenwriters, TV writers are generally unable to sit with large groups of people and watch their work being performed. Trying to get in touch with the vast, invisible television audience is "like a meditational exercise," says Phillips. "I try to imagine the audience sitting out there, and figure out who they are. They're in their homes, in front of the box, watching these shows and hearing canned laughter. Are they laughing too? How do they feel about being part of this whole process? TV watching is sometimes talked about as a kind of ceremony of social unity. At any given moment, a sizable percentage of the nation's population is tuned into the same program. I'm aware of that. I'm not quite sure what it all means in terms of my work. But it's something I definitely think about."

Some conscientious TV writers, says Phillips, try to "treat the audience as if it's the same as them. They feel that if they approach their work this way, they won't be guilty of condescension." But Phillips believes there are undefinable differences between her and the TV audience. "I think that most of the audience has not gone to college, and a lot of it has not completed high school. The audience has not had the same experiences and options that I've had. They have different interests, needs, and concerns. They spend their time differently, they watch TV differently too. So what I like to say is that parts of the audience are very different from me, but I'm no better. And when it comes to writing a TV script, there are some things which you want to see in it and there are some things which others want to see in it. And you try your best to satisfy everyone. It's the art of cooking for a large family rather than for a lone gourmet."

Something is usually lost, however, in the effort to satisfy a network-size "family" of 25 million or more. Program content cannot be too specific or controversial; program style cannot stray too far from conventional television forms. Phillips hopes that cable TV, public television, and "fourth network" syndication* will expand the medium's possibilities. She looks forward to the day when there will be a greater diversity of programming geared towards more differentiated audiences. "Every element within the mass audience should have its own TV programs," declares Phillips. "I've always been a very ardent democrat, interested in a culture of differences—a culture able to enjoy the differences between people and less able to enjoy the differences in privilege and power that come between people and prevent or corrupt an innocent enjoyment of differences."

There is one television genre, says Phillips, which she would find extremely difficult to work within—the police/detective show. The baser elements of commercial entertainment, she feels, are concentrated within this particular TV genre.** "The mere fact that the entire moral analysis of modern civilization has been encapsulated in the police genre

---

*This is the way Norman Lear distributed "Mary Hartman" when the three major networks refused to buy the program. He sold the show directly to local TV stations throughout the country, thereby putting together his own independent network.
**Phillips says that the TV show "Columbo" is something of an exception: "The tone of Peter Falk's performances in 'Columbo' feel

is enough to keep some of us in bed all morning. I mean there are days when I don't want to go outside, because—according to these shows—the world is filled with nothing but cops, criminals, and victims. There are good cops and bad cops, liberal cops and fascist cops. And the rest of society is composed of criminals and victims, or potential criminals and victims. The cops are there to keep people from killing each other, because that's all people will do if you're not constantly shooting them down in the street (she laughs). It's an entertainment system that is based on a very virulent vision of humanity—and overall it has terrible effects on the audience. No one show has that much power, of course, but I think these shows as a group generate a climate of unpleasantness and fear and mistrust and discipline and obedience and witlessness that I just can't abide. And the use of suspense as the kind of emotional mechanism with which you propel the audience through this hideous world is, to me, criminal. It's a criminal use of the muse. Cowboys weren't much better, but at least you had the cows grazing in the background. The police are a *naked* metaphor of power."

Phillips feels strongly that "cultural climate" is politically critical in the long run. "I think that pleasureful experiences give people the strength and spirit for change. If people are dangerous slime, who needs a new world for 'em? You're better off with a strongbox and a good lock. I think there's too little real pleasure in the media; there's too much suspense, too much shock, too much humiliation—and not enough real satisfaction. Like the real satisfaction of fighting and winning a new set of conditions, as opposed to the fast and false satisfaction of arresting a suspect in a case of burglary. 'Messages' don't mean much either: audiences see things and respond to things in a show that its creators never fully understand, until later. Does 'Kojak' romanticize the law? Or

---

right to me—even though it is a crime show. I feel that his problems are real, that he is an actual person, that he has a life which he must bear, that his limitations are limitations created by the hardship of life and not a failure on his part. So even though it's a police detective show, his character is interesting, it isn't brittle."

does it romanticize emotional control? For me it's always been the latter. It's about sucking a lollipop instead of screaming or finding happiness. A lollipop is no satisfaction, just consolation. And it's bad for your teeth...It's the tone, attitude, and scope of media that shape our vision of the world over long periods of time. And if these things are all emanating from a bunch of money-hungry, super-competitive, testosterone-crazed Gucci addicts, you develop a sense of The Norm and of Human Nature which always distorts to the right. And it will do that for years and generations, no matter who or what's in power. That leaning will haunt us all."

Phillips is reluctant to define her TV career as a vocation for social change. "The word 'change' is so huge, and I feel so modest beside it." But she does say that she has "certain aesthetic objectives that I think are socially progressive." "Today and ultimately," she states, "one hopes to find ways to battle alienation, to be part of the human community, to contribute to its well-being, or to at least slow its degeneration."

Phillips believes that progressive media work can at best help establish preconditions for social change. "Real egalitarianism, real democracy won't come about as a result of the Movie of the Week." In the final analysis, she says, "our major problems can only be resolved by large numbers of active, committed people working together with a sense of reality and humor in cohesive groups under certain conditions of struggle." But no such conditions or mass organizations exist in the United States today, or none that have captured Phillips' imagination. So like thousands of other like-minded individuals, she goes about her business on her own, without a formal political affiliation. "I always operate from a long-term strategic sense of 'Best Available Direction,' even when I seem to be dozing. But what's available to a solitary female TV writer isn't often momentous. My words reach millions. Somewhere between eighteen hours of guest panelists and six hours of Ultra-Brite. Now, is that power, or a bird in the bush?"

Phillips is not overly concerned about being assimilated into the entertainment industry. "After 'Hartman,' the Haileys helped me get an episode to write on a new series called

'Another Day.' It was wonderful of them. Friends helping friends. Elite club and all that. But the point is, that the show *was* right for me: affectionate humor, a relatively feminist premise. And the episode they guided me through was, though conventionally told, both complex and satisfying. When it's right for me to be here, everything works out. When I try to pretend I'm what I'm not, it doesn't work out. So it will be a story of overlap—of the middle way—not compromise, but coincidence of interest between me, my talent, my politics, my aesthetics, the business, and the audience, the times, and fate. To understand the nature of an historical moment—and to be true to the best of oneself in it—that's what I try to do. Sometimes I'm not fast enough on my feet. But I like the motion. Some people like to surf. I like to hang ten on contradictions."

SOUTH END PRESS TITLES

ABOUT SOUTH END PRESS

South End Press is committed to publishing books which can aid people's day-to-day struggles to control their own lives.

Our primary emphasis is on the United States—its political and economic systems, its history and its culture—and on strategies for its transformation.

We aim to reach a broad audience through a balanced offering of books of all kinds—fiction and non-fiction, theoretical and cultural, for all ages and in all styles and formats.

South End Press, Box 68, Astor Station, Boston, MA 02123